THE NADARS OF TAMILNAD

HISTORIES / ANTHROPOLOGIES

General Editors
SAURABH DUBE
CRISPIN BATES

Vol. I: *The Nadars of Tamilnad: The Political Culture of a Community in Change* by Robert L. Hardgrave, Jr.

HISTORIES / ANTHROPOLOGIES

THE NADARS OF TAMILNAD

The Political Culture of a Community in Change

ROBERT L. HARDGRAVE, JR.

Foreword by
DENNIS TEMPLEMAN

MANOHAR
2006

First published in 1969 by the University of California.
This edition with new Foreword and Preface published by Manohar 2006.

© Author, 2006

ISBN 81-7304-700-6 (Series)
ISBN 81-7304-701-4 (Vol. I)

Published by
Ajay Kumar Jain for
Manohar Publishers & Distributors
4753/23 Ansari Road, Daryaganj
New Delhi 110 002

Printed at
Lordson Publishers Pvt Ltd
Delhi 110 007

Distributed in South Asia by
�&OUNDATION
B☺☺KS
4381/4, Ansari Road
Daryaganj, New Delhi 110 002
and its branches at Mumbai, Hyderabad,
Bangalore, Chennai, Kolkata

A NOTE ON TRANSLITERATION

With regard to the transliteration of Tamil names, the only consistency is that of ordinary usage in the case of each word. Each Tamil word is spelled as it normally appears in English text in Tamilnad. Ordinary usage has also determined the spelling of place names. Where the English form has been more widely used than the Tamil, as in *Tinnevelly* rather than *Tirunelveli*, the English form has been retained for consistency.

FOREWORD

I was very pleased when Professor Hardgrave asked me to write a short foreword for the reissue of his classic study of caste politics, *The Nadars of Tamilnad* (1969), especially because his work has been a major influence on my own. Several years ago, David G. Mandelbaurn (of the University of California at Berkeley) suggested that it might be an interesting, valuable, and complementary exercise if I were to study as an anthropologist the same general group of people that Hardgrave had studied as a political scientist. Hardgrave and Lloyd and Susanne Rudolph, in whose *The Modernity of Tradition* (1967) Hardgrave's findings on the Nadars first appeared, were among a growing group of scholars, many of them at the University of Chicago, who were discovering that 'Modernization' was far more distinct from 'Westernization' than the scholarly community – let alone the wider public – had believed through at least the first half of the twentieth century.

Hardgrave focuses on the Nadar caste, a number of related but internally ranked endogamous groups in the far south of the Indian peninsula. He describes this group as poised in a 'social limbo' between the Dalit castes and the Sudra ones. Hardgrave does not assume that the arrival of British rule in the late eighteenth and early nineteenth centuries led to the beginning of the downfall of caste as a 'traditional' unit of Hindu social organization. Rather, he traces the history of the Nadars as entailing a growing sense of social unity. These processes included a strong trend towards the Nadars becoming a single community or caste; their establishment of effective local caste councils; and, after a century of change, the establishment – often in the face of strong and even violent opposition – of the Nadar Mahajana Sangam (NMS), a collective institution intended to serve all Nadars in their efforts toward social uplift.

Early nineteenth century Christian missionaries described the Nadars as so isolated from mainstream Tamil society that they were not considered really to be Hindus. These missionaries found many willing converts among the Nadars. When other Nadars saw the benefits of education received by converts to Christianity, they responded by building English-style and English-language schools yet all the while moving towards mainstream Hinduism. By the late nineteenth century, the Nadars were seeking status uplift through sanskritizing their dress, worship, diet, and other practices. When the high castes still withheld their respect, the Nadars turned to the Non-Brahmin Movement. Further demonstrating their tactical flexibility, once the Temple Entry Act was passed in 1939, they rapidly accepted the rights of all Hindus. In his detailed account of these changes, Hardgrave shows that the Nadars reveal the same remarkable tactical flexibility in religion as they have in caste organization and their political and economic activities.

Hardgrave has a good deal to say about the local Nadar councils – the *uravinmuraikal* – in the various towns and villages in which they settled. At the same time, his most sustained discussion concerns the NMS, its historical development, several activities, internal workings, and diverse interactions with other communities as well as about Nadar participation in city, state, and national politics. With reference to relations with other communities, the leaders of the NMS have been aware that good feelings are essential for a caste with so many commercial interests. Towards this end, the local councils and the NMS have operated a number of educational institutions, from elementary schools through to colleges. These are open to people of all castes and faiths.

Hardgrave found that the Nadars became increasingly differentiated as they entered different occupations, resulting in class divisions among the wider collectivity. Along with these divisions have come different political philosophies, interests, and affiliations. This led a majority of Nadars to support the Non-Brahmin Movement and the Justice Party at one time, the Congress afterwards, and the DMK finally. But what is true of a majority is certainly not true of individual Nadars. Hardgrave includes information on and interviews with Nadars whose political affiliations range from 'left' Communist (as opposed to 'right' Communist) through to the Swatantra Party. Nevertheless, Hardgrave demonstrates that this differentiation has done nothing to counter the Nadars' powerful sense of community solidarity.

Hardgrave found the political culture of Tamil Nadu as changing at different pace in different places. In the most isolated villages, the Nadars of the 1960s were often still severely oppressed. Unsurprisingly, they stayed more aloof from other communities. The NMS had men in the field to find such cases and make the authorities aware of their oppression. At the other extreme, Hardgrave found that Nadars were business associates and friends of people of other castes, joining the same clubs and even eating at the same restaurants. However, the Nadars continued to have very strong feelings for their own community, so that breaking the norm of caste endogamy was very rare indeed.

We know that since Hardgrave's pioneering work, other studies on caste associations have been published. For example, Frank F. Conlon's *Caste in a Changing World: The Saraswat Brahmans, 1700-1935* (1977), demonstrates that a caste association can be as effective in serving the interests of a high caste as it can in promoting the uplift of a once downtrodden group. My own work, *The Northern Nadars of Tamil Nadu* (1996) – based on research conducted during 1968-70; and off and on from 1985 to 1990 – adds discussion of such issues as the growth of Nadar wealth and power, factionalism and conflict resolution within the *uravinmuraikal* and the resultant political changes, and conflicts and attempts at conciliation with other communities, especially during the decades following Hardgrave's research. At the same time, I have found nothing in these years to contradict the overriding impressions that I initially took from Hardgrave's book: the Nadars, like other Indians (but more successfully than some), have reorganized their caste, their town councils, the NMS, and other aspects of their practices and beliefs to meet their goals of caste uplift and to adjust to ever-changing political, economic, and cultural conditions. With some movement back and forth, the great majority remain practicing Hindus. Indeed, the Nadar commitment to their caste – which is actually a British Raj and post-independence phenomenon – is unlikely to simply wither away.

University of Minnesota-Morris   Dennis Templeman

SERIES EDITORS' FOREWORD

Recent decades have witnessed critical crossovers between history and anthropology (and sociology), and between the humanities and the social sciences more broadly. This series entitled *Histories / Anthropologies* seeks to unravel and take forward the terms of dialogue and debate between and across the disciplines. To this end, the series proposes to carry prior, seminal works as well as new, innovative scholarship in history, ethnography, and sociology, including their intersections. Here, each of these disciplinary tendencies is understood in the widest possible way. We invite manuscripts on critical themes, which can range from gender, environment, and ethnicity; to community, state, and civil-society; to nation, politics, and modernity; to art, science, and much else.

It is a pleasure to initiate the series with a work of historical importance and contemporary significance. When it first appeared in 1969, *The Nadars of Tamilnad* was among only a handful of works that explored historically key questions of caste. This had to do with the nature of the development of research in social sciences and history concerning the Indian subcontinent. It was also linked to the fact that caste was something of an embarrassment for the modern Indian nation. In this wider context, the salience of the book was highlighted by Lucien Pye:

> Robert L. Hardgrave has produced a truly remarkable study. His explicit purpose has been to describe the modern folk of a particular Indian community, but his research tells us more about the dynamics of social and political change in India than can be found in more broadly ambitious studies. His title might suggest an obscure, esoteric, if not fictitious subject, rather than one of the soundest recent works on political development ... Professor Hardgrave has in this volume made a great contribution to not only our knowledge of Indian politics, but to our general understanding of the relationships between social and economic change and political life. All students of political development can learn a great deal from this valuable book. (*Political Science Quarterly*, 86, 1971, 511-12)

Unsurprisingly, the work went on to garner critical success, its arguments exerting influence across a range of disciplines.

In the years since the publication of *The Nadars of Tamilnad*, much has changed in the articulations and assertions of caste as well as in the historical, sociological, and political understandings of these processes. Precisely for these reasons, Hardgrave's work should not only be required reading for a new generation of students and scholars, but a study that should be read anew in any case. However, the book has been out of print for a long time now. And so we are delighted to reissue *The Nadars of Tamilnad*, now with a new Preface by the author and a Foreword by Dennis Templeman, a scholar who has also worked on the Nadar community. It is in this way that *Histories/Anthropologies* brings to readers a crucial work in the archival tracks of the social scientific knowledge of the subcontinent, and one that equally speaks to wide-ranging concerns of India today.

November 2005   SAURABH DUBE
                                                       CRISPIN BATES

PREFACE TO THE SECOND EDITION

Over the forty years since I conducted research among the Nadars for my doctoral dissertation and what was to become *The Nadars of Tamilnad: The Political Culture of a Community in Change*, I have returned to India many times on a wide range of projects. No project, however, was so fully consuming or so personally rewarding as the one I pursued as a graduate student in 1964-65 in the southern districts of Tamil Nadu. I experienced what I can only describe as the joy of research, and though it was surely attended by periodic anxiety and occasional frustration, it secured my commitment to an academic life.

I first become interested in India as an undergraduate at the University of Texas in the 1950s. With a 'double major' in government (political science) and anthropology, I took every course on India then offered at the university. My goal was to become a university professor, but before making a career commitment to the study of a country I had never visited, I decided that I needed to go to India before beginning my graduate studies. I had been accepted at the University of Chicago for the doctoral program in Political Science but was able to have my admission deferred for one year so that I might go to India. In 1960-61, as a Rotary International Fellow, I made Madras and Delhi my bases, and the project I undertook was a study of the Dravidian Movement and the rise of Tamil nationalism.

My experience in and of India that year firmly set me on the course of South Asian studies. In graduate study at the University of Chicago, the work I had done on the Dravidian Movement provided the basis for my Master's thesis and my first publication. The structure of the graduate program at Chicago provided sufficient flexibility for me to create, in addition to my core areas in political science, an ad hoc South Asia field focused on social anthropology. For language study, looking to return to Tamil Nadu for my doctoral fieldwork, I chose Tamil. But what then of my dissertation topic? I had become increasingly interested in the relationship of politics and social change in India and was drawn, with particular fascination, to the ways in which caste was being transformed. I decided that I would explore the behavioral dynamics of political change through the analysis of a single caste, one that had risen in status and power over time. I sought to examine the political culture of a community in change.

My selection of the Nadar community could not have been more fortunate. In studying Tamil politics, I had been deeply impressed by the Congress party leader K. Kamaraj. He had been Chief Minister of Madras state when I first came to India in 1960, and, as I was preparing to return to India in 1964, Kamaraj held the presidency of the Indian National Congress. His rise to national leadership was remarkable in almost every respect. He was born to a merchant family of modest means in 1903 in the town of Virudhupatti (now Virudhunagar) in southern Tamil Nadu. He was a Nadar, a caste about which I knew little, save that it had been traditionally associated with toddy-tapping and that it had become prominent as a major trading community in the region. As I considered various castes for my dissertation focus, I kept returning to the Nadars, whose transformation and rise – reflected in some ways by Kamaraj's own ascent to prominence and power – seemed to provide what I was looking for. My judgment was only reinforced by the account of the community by Edgar Thurston, under the entry 'Shanan', in his monumental *Castes and Tribes of Southern India* (1909). In choosing the Nadars as the caste for my research, I struck gold. As I soon discovered in the course of my work in Tamil Nadu, the community had an incredibly rich and well-documented history that dramatically encapsulated social, economic, and political changes experienced by many other castes in India. In the transformation of its political culture, the experience of the Nadars was in many ways unique, but at the same time it mirrored changes in the wider context of Indian society and politics.

As I pursued my research in Tamil Nadu, most Nadars I met

were excited about my project, offering whatever assistance they might provide. Some were uneasy about my digging too deeply into a past they preferred securely buried and forgotten. But, overall, it was the generosity and cooperation of the Nadar community, its leaders and ordinary people, that ensured the success of my project, and I shall be forever grateful.

Successful field research must be guided by a clear project design, but it must also be flexible and responsive to the unexpected – both insurmountable roadblocks (denied access; missing data; archival losses, or deceased prospective informants) and what can only be described as serendipitous discovery (a chance meeting, an unknown manuscript, or whatever it might be). So much depends upon sheer luck. This was the case when in Madurai I boarded a night train for Madras. As I was settling in, I introduced myself to my traveling companion in the compartment. He asked me what I was doing in Tamil Nadu, and I told him that I was working on a history of the Nadar community for my Ph.D. dissertation. He looked puzzled and asked, 'Why would you study those fellows?' I went on to tell him something of what I was doing and why. After some provocative probes, he smiled and identified himself as a Nadar: a doctor in Madras, who I later discovered to be one of India's leading orthopaedic surgeons. It also turned out that members of his family had been among the leaders early in the century in the community's dramatic rise. Through him, I met a number of people, in a widening tree of introductions, who provided documents, letters and diaries, and (most richly) memories of the Nadar past and present.

After a year in India, I went to London to work in the India Office Library, the British Library, and in the archives of missionary societies that had worked among the Nadars in the early nineteenth century. Back in Chicago for the 'write-up', I completed my dissertation in the spring of 1966. Its transformation into a book came with revisions and substantial cuts. In 1969 *The Nadars of Tamilnad* was published by the University of California Press. I was concerned that it be available in India and was able to arrange for Oxford University Press, Bombay, to publish it simultaneously for the Indian market.

The Nadars was widely reviewed, and I was delighted when one reviewer described it as an 'exciting tale, at places as thrilling as any John Masters novel'.[1] Indeed, my account of Nadar conflict with other castes in the late nineteenth century provided, in part, the context for David Davidar's 2002 novel set in South India, *The House of Blue Mangoes*.[2] Another reviewer wrote of *The Nadars* as breaking 'new ground',[3] and it was later described as 'one of the landmarks in South Indian social history'.[4] But of all the reviews, I was perhaps pleased most by that of Lucian Pye, whose work on political culture I had greatly admired. He stated that, 'Professor Hardgrave has in this volume made a great contribution to not only our knowledge of Indian politics, but to our general understanding of the relationships between social and economic change and political life'.[5]

Reaction from the Nadar community varied. I sent copies of the book to a number of the Nadars who had helped me and who spoke English. Most were very pleased, but I was grieved (and alarmed) when I received a letter from the General Secretary of the Nadar Mahajana Sangam, the major association of the caste, saying that I had betrayed the trust of the community by dredging up all sorts of things better left to the past. Not long after this, however, he wrote again to say that he had changed his mind: in fact, he now felt that I had done great service for the Nadar community by chronicling its history, rise, and success.

---

[1] Duncan Forrester in *Pacific Affairs*, 42 (Winter 1969-70), 545.

[2] David Davidar, *The House of Blue Mangoes* (New Delhi: Viking, 2002).

[3] Robert E. Frykenberg in *The American Historical Review*, 75 (April 1970), 1169-71.

[4] G. A. Oddie, 'Recent Writings on the Social and Cultural Aspects of Modern South Indian History', in Robert E. Frykenberg and Pauline Kolenda (eds.), *Studies of South India: An Anthology of Recent Research and Scholarship* (Madras: New Era Publications/New Delhi: American Institute of Indian Studies, 1985), 171.

[5] Lucian Pye in *Political Science Quarterly*, 86 (September 1971), 511-12.

In 1977, 1 received a letter from a Nadar industrialist, director of the Tuticorin Spinning Mills, who expressed the desire to have my book translated into Tamil. In cooperation with the Nadar Mahajana Sangam and the Nadar Mahamai, Tuticorin, the project went forward, and the complete translation was published in 1979 as *Tamilaka Naadar Varalaru* (History of the Nadars of Tamil Nadu).[6] The royalties went toward a scholarship fund for Nadar students of Kamaraj College in Tuticorin.

Some years later, the new General Secretary of the caste association wrote to me that 'The Nadar Mahajana Sangam expresses once again its deepest gratitude for your meritorious work', but he lamented that *The Nadars of Tamilnad* was out of print and urged its reissue. With the advent of email, I found myself the periodic recipient of inquiries from Nadars (and others) in India and the United States as to how they might get copies of the book. Some of these inquiries led to continued correspondence, friendship and (on my most recent visit to Tamil Nadu) meetings with young Nadars anxious to know more about their community heritage. But, alas, there were no more copies of *The Nadars*. With its reissue in the Manohar Histories/Anthropologies series, the volume is again available.

Austin, Texas   Robert L. Hardgrave, Jr.
August 2005

---

[6] Robert L. Hardgrave, Jr., *Tamilaka Naadar Varalaru* (Tuticorin: Murugan Press, 1979).

PREFACE

In this study of the relationship between political sentiment and behavior, on the one hand, and the structure of society, on the other, the unit of analysis will be a single caste, a community in motion over time, in the social space between the village and the state. Although a microcosm, the analytical unit provides a link between social and economic change and political life, between structural change in society and political sentiment and behavior. Through the analysis of a caste in time, it is possible to explore its internal changes as it interacts with society. It offers both the possibility of analysis in a dynamic sense over time and the comparative analysis at the synchronic level of variant situations. The study will be both diachronic and synchronic, focused upon the process through which the caste enters the political system and upon its role in political life.

Among the communities of South India, the Nadars have perhaps most clearly evidenced the effects of change in the past 150 years. Considered by the high caste Hindus in the early nineteenth century to be among the most defiling and degraded of all castes, the Nadars, as toddy-tappers, climbers of the palmyra palm, suffered severe social disabilities and were one of the most economically depressed communities in the Tamil country. In their response to the social and economic changes of the last century the Nadars have today become one of the most economically and politically successful communities in the South. From among their numbers have come leading merchants, physicians, and educators; in politics, Kamaraj, their most illustrious son, has brought fame to the caste as chief minister of Madras and as president of the All-India Congress party.

The analysis of the Nadar community over time required the construction of a social and political history of the community: an examination of the traditional condition of the community before substantial change had occurred; then a focus on the process of change itself, on the transformation of the community over time. For the caste's history, data were drawn both from documentary sources and from personal interviews.

The initial two months' work in Madras was devoted to library research—to the examination of caste histories, anthropological surveys, missionary memoirs, government documents, and court records relating to the Nadars and to the region of the southern districts in which the community was originally concentrated. In addition to materials available in public libraries and archives, such as the Madras Records Office, I was provided with a substantial number of books, pamphlets, diaries, and manuscripts from the personal libraries of Nadar families throughout Tamilnad.

The documents and files of the central association of the community, the Nadar Mahajana Sangam in Madurai, were most important sources. The Sangam gave me complete access to its records, from the founding of the association in 1910 to the present day. More than any other factor, the generosity and cooperation of the Nadar Mahajana Sangam ensured my success in securing materials and in meeting those I wished to see. Soon after my arrival in Madurai, the association's newspaper, *Mahajanam*, carried an article about my research, which proved a most useful introduction in my subsequent travels in the Nadar country of the southern districts. The Sangam provided me with letters of introduction to individuals and, on occasion, as in the town of Kamudi, to the Nadar *uravinmurai*, the community's governing body of elders. This cooperation and interest, reflecting community pride, eliminated almost all of the suspicion normally attendant in social science research.

In addition to the documentary sources, I drew heavily upon personal interviews in reconstructing the history and activities of the community. I tried to keep complete field notes of casual conversations, and I conducted approximately one hundred formal interviews with Nadars about specialized knowledge they had of their community's history, customs, tradition, organization, and political activities. These included Nadars of prominence and power, those who had themselves played an important part in the history of their community. The greater number of those interviewed, however, were distinguished only by a rich and vivid memory of the Nadar past. In visiting a village or town, I usually sought out the oldest people of the community and, almost without exception, was rewarded. For example, the oldest man in Kamudi, aged eighty-eight, described with great gesticulation and excitement his participation in the temple entry of 1897. An eighty-five-year-old widow of Sivakasi told me of the riot of 1899 she had witnessed as a girl and sang a song from memory, long forgotten by others in the town, of this event.

In these interviews, I ordinarily took as complete notes as possible, and on occasion, my research assistant would transcribe the conversation. The elderly Nadars seemed anxious that I not miss a word. During other interviews—those with politicians or in areas of sensitivity—no notes were made. I discovered quickly that, with paper and pen out of sight, a politician is likely to be more frank than he might otherwise be. I made notes of the conversation immediately after the meeting and, with practice, lost little detail in the process.

In these interviews, as in the records relating to the history of the Nadar community, the vital role of the Anglican missionaries was clearly evident. The first available descriptions of the caste are from missionary reports, and the missionaries themselves were deeply involved in the initial stages of change among the Nadars. A degree of caution is probably well advised in working with missionary sources. In their fervor to save the heathen, many were undoubtedly influenced in their view of the native condition by their bias against the indigenous worship. It is remarkable that the missionaries so often remained largely free of this bias, for their perceptions—particularly those of scholars like Robert Caldwell—were often highly sophisticated and sensitive to cultural differences.

The missionaries, in their labor among the Nadars, wrote frequently to their London superiors of conditions in South India and of the changes they were witnessing. They regularly filed reports, and a number of missionaries kept detailed journals of their activities and impressions. These letters and manuscripts have been preserved in the archives of London missionary societies, and there, for the better part of six months, I sorted through what were some of the richest documentary materials of my research.

For the purposes of synchronic analysis, my initial examination of the Nadar community enabled me to select four sufficiently diverse situations for comparison. To explore the range and variety of political sentiment and behavior among the Nadars, I wanted to take several "readings" along the continuum from tradition to modernity at the contemporary level. No community today, even the most isolated, can be taken to represent "tradition" unaffected by innovation and change. Mass communications, for example, have opened the village in exposing it to a broader world. Though not impervious to change, the relatively isolated village may be taken as approximating to some degree the conditions of the past. Structural and behavioral differences between variant situations at the synchronic level cannot be taken as congruent with the spectrum of "stages" in a time sequence. The village–city polarity does not represent a strict parallel to the tradition–modernity continuum. For our purposes, however, it is useful to accept a rough congruence between the diachronic and synchronic models. Thus, as we move from the more isolated village to the industrial city, we would expect to find conditions approximating those in the process of change over time.

The four communities selected for intensive analysis represent structurally different situations and correspond in some ways to periods in the history of the Nadar community, as they reflect the economic change and geographical expansion of the caste. The first is a village in the palmyra forests of southeastern Tiruchendur, the heart of the Nadars' homeland. Its political culture today is essentially parochial. The second community for analysis is the town of Kamudi in Ramnad District, to which Nadar traders migrated in the early nineteenth century. The Nadars of this town, which figured so prominently in the community's struggle for social uplift, are a small, integrated mercantile minority, surrounded by the hostile Maravar community. The city of Madurai, the third community, is a major Nadar center and reveals the initial stages of a differentiated political culture. This differentiation is even more evident in the fourth, Madras City, the economic and political capital of Tamilnad.

In each of these structurally variant situations, I made a general analysis of the position of the Nadar community, its relationship with other castes, and its political involvement. In addition, twelve individuals were selected, three from each situation. They were not taken as a representative sample of the Nadar community; selected informally, they represent distinct types and, together, suggest the range and variation within the community. Each was interviewed intensively following an interview schedule patterned after that used by Robert Lane in his study of political ideology in New Haven (see the Bibliography). The schedule was supplemented, in an effort to explore political sentiment at a more subjective level, by a modified thematic apperception test. These interviews, I hoped, might give a personal reality to the changes which the Nadar community had experienced in the previous 150 years.

This experience of dramatic change may be analyzed in terms of three structural types—the parochial, the integrated, and the differentiated—along the continuum from the more "traditional" to the more "modern."

The first, or parochial, stage may be seen in Tiruchendur in the early nineteenth century before substantial change affected the community. Here the caste was so dominant in numbers that elaboration of caste ranking was minimal in interactional terms. At the same time, the caste was differentiated by subcaste, and, more significantly, by the division between the climbers and the Nadan landowners. Politics took place *within* the Nadar community, between factional client groups.

The second, or integrated, stage is best seen in Ramnad, from the middle of the last century, where the Nadars were confronted by a high elaboration of caste ranking, as a minority community. The distinction between Nadan and climber was no longer present among the traders, and the division of subcastes disappeared as each was integrated into a single community. Tightly organized in defense of caste interest, politics was primarily on a basis of caste, since the Nadars acted as a cohesive unit.

The third stage, differentiation, emerges with urbanization. The very success of the Nadars in their rise led to the increasing differentiation of the community, and in the urban areas of Madurai and Madras City to which they immigrated, they were but one of many communities, each highly differentiated. The elaboration of caste ranking declined as differentiation increased. The caste became politically heterogeneous, reflecting a multiplicity of cross-cutting ties.

The Nadars have had a turbulent and colorful history. Their efforts to rise above their depressed condition assumed dramatic form in the series of escalating confrontations between the caste and its antagonists. From the breast-cloth controversy through the sack of Sivakasi to the Nadar Mahajana Sangam, the Nadars' rise, encapsulating the processes of social mobility in Indian society, has given rich texture to the analysis of a community in change.

ACKNOWLEDGMENTS

This study, based on field work in India and London in 1964 and 1965, grew out of a general concern for the theoretical problems in the relationship between social change and political sentiments and behavior. Lloyd Rudolph first suggested the study of a single caste, and in the course of my research, he provided me with thoughtful guidance. Leonard Binder and Duncan MacRae gave me their insight into the theoretical and methodological problems involved in the analysis. To each of these men in the University of Chicago's Department of Political Science, I owe my greatest appreciation for their encouragement, suggestions, and searching criticism. Ewart Lewis, of Oberlin, provided me with incisive editorial advice on form and discourse for the preparation of the final, revised manuscript. For their assistance, I should also like to thank Carolyn Elliott, Frank Hutchins, and Eugene Irschick. I must express my indebtedness to James R. Roach, who introduced me as an undergraduate at the University of Texas to the study of India and Tamilnad. Special thanks go also to A. K. Ramanujan, who patiently endured my struggles in Tamil, and to Milton Singer, who gave me support and encouragement from the beginning of my graduate studies at the University of Chicago.

The research was made possible through a Foreign Area Fellowship granted me by The Ford Foundation. All views and conclusions are wholly my own and are not necessarily those of the Fellowship Program.

The library facilities used in the course of my research included the Madras Records Office, the Connemara Library, Madras, and the libraries of the University of Madras, the Census Office, the High Court of Madras, and the American College, Madurai. The Nadar Mahajana Sangam, Madurai, and the Dakshina Mara Nadar Sangam, Tinnevelly, provided me with access to their libraries and files of correspondence. In London, the resources of the India Office Library and the British Museum were invaluable. The greatest sources of documents, however, were the archives of the

missionary societies which worked among the Nadars in the nineteenth century. I wish to express my appreciation to the Church
Missionary Society, the London Missionary Society, and particularly to the Society for the Propagation of the Gospel for opening
their archives and libraries to my use.

In the field, many people provided me with their assistance and
cooperation. To Paul Mohan and Thomas Mathew, who served as
my research assistants at various times in the southern districts, I
owe special thanks. So many members of the Nadar community
received me with hospitality and cooperation that it would be impossible to begin even to name them. I must, however, express my
particular gratitude to V. S. K. Doraisami Nadar, S. B. and S. T.
Adityan, K. T. Kosalram, and P. Jagadisan, who sought to make
my work as rewarding and as successful as possible. I owe, more-
over, my greatest appreciation to the community association, the
Nadar Mahajana Sangam. The General Secretaries, P. R.
Muthusami and Gangaram Durairaj, and the Sangam management
endeavored to meet each of my requirements. Without their assistance, this study would have been impossible.

I wish, most of all, to express my thanks to the Nadar community itself. Inevitably, some members of the community may take
offense at my discussion—but even among themselves, the Nadars
are not in agreement about their origins, history, and future. If, in
opening the past, I have inflicted pain, I beg forgiveness, for the
Nadars, as a community, have earned my greatest admiration and
respect. As an "honorary Nadar," I have come to feel a close identity with the community, to share in its pride and sense of achievement.

Robert L. Hardgrave, Jr.

CONTENTS

Introduction: Caste in India   1

I.   The Nadars: Their Condition and Traditional Status   12

II.   Christianity and Change   43

III.   Mythology and Aspiration of a Changing Caste   71

IV.   The Six Town Nadars: Sanskritization and Confrontation   95

V.   Association for Uplift: The Nadar Mahajana Sangam   130

VI.   Politics and the Sangam   173

VII.   Structural Change and Political Behavior   202

VIII.   Political Sentiment: Five Nadars   239

IX.   The Nadars: An Overview   262

Appendixes

    I.   Population of the Southern Districts   269

    II.   The Myth of Nadar Origin   273

    III.   Chronology of Nadar Caste Histories   275

Glossary   279

Bibliography   281

Index   295

INTRODUCTION: CASTE IN INDIA

The specter of caste has increasingly come to haunt both Indian politics and Indian political analysis. "Caste is so tacitly and so completely accepted by all, including those most vocal in condemning it," writes M. N. Srinivas, "that it is everywhere the unit of social action." [1] Srinivas argues that the development of modern communications, the spread of education and literacy, and rising prosperity have contributed, not to the disintegration of caste, but to its strengthening. As caste solidarity has increased, he contends, caste has been politicized and drawn into the political system as a major actor. The role of caste in modern Indian politics has been decried, on the one hand, as a fissiparous threat to national unity,[2] and lauded, on the other, as a channel of communication, representation, and leadership which links the mass electorate to "the new democratic political processes and makes them comprehensible in traditional terms to a population still largely politically illiterate." [3]

The complexity and problems in the relationship of caste to Indian political life have generated an extensive literature in recent years. Social scientists and historians have made impressive contributions both to our descriptive knowledge and to our theoretical understanding of the interaction between society and the political system. In the analysis of caste and politics, however, these studies have tended to focus either on a single village or else, more impres-

[1] M. N. Srinivas, *Caste in Modern India and Other Essays* (Bombay, 1962), p. 41. The essay originally appeared in the *Journal of Asian Studies*, XVI (August, 1957).

[2] See Selig Harrison, *India, the Most Dangerous Decades* (Princeton, 1960).

[3] Lloyd I. and Susanne H. Rudolph, "The Political Role of India's Caste Associations," *Pacific Affairs*, XXXIII (March, 1960), 21–22. Also see Lloyd I. Rudolph, "The Modernity of Tradition: The Democratic Incarnation of Caste in India," *American Political Science Review*, LIX (December, 1965), 975–989; Lloyd I. and Susanne H. Rudolph, *The Modernity of Tradition: Political Development in India* (Chicago, 1967), pp. 17–153.

sionistically, on the society as a whole. This study seeks to fill the
gap in the social and political space between the village and the
state through an intensive analysis of a single caste community in
change over time.

There are in India more than three thousand castes, each a cul-
turally distinct, endogamous community sharing traditionally a
common occupation and a particular position in the localized hierarchy of caste ranking. Each caste shares a culture such that it may
be distinguished from other castes in the village or locality by its
manner of behavior and speech, the style of dress and ornamenta-
tion, the food eaten, and the general pattern of life. The members
of a caste marry only among themselves, and their endogamy may
be narrowly circumscribed geographically to include a limited
range of villages.

Though we speak of the endogamy of a caste, traditionally each
caste, or jati, has been a category embracing a number of endogamous subcastes.[4] In a particular village a caste will normally be
represented by one subcaste alone, although more than one may be
present. Within the caste, the distinctions of subcaste are basic, for
each may be ranked hierarchically just as the caste is ranked within
the larger system. Each individual is traditionally a member of both
a caste and a subcaste. From the outside, however, the caste is
viewed as an undifferentiated group. Exceptions might occur only
if there are radically different forms of behavior between subcastes.
"On the whole," Adrian Mayer writes, "caste membership is significant for relations with other castes, and subcaste membership
for activities within the caste." [5] "For the most part, behaviour is
uniform towards all subcastes of a caste. And even when this is not
so, differential rules are seldom applied because there is rarely more
than one subcaste in a village." [6]

---

[4] The word *jati* itself is variously used to describe different levels of segmentation, subcaste, caste, and even varna. This variance in the degree of inclusiveness is
explained by André Béteille in terms of caste as a segmentary system. See "A
Note on the Referents of Caste," *Archives Européennes de Sociologie*, V (1964),
130–134.

[5] Adrian C. Mayer, *Caste and Kinship in Central India* (London, 1960), p. 5.

[6] *Ibid.*, p. 159.

Ordinarily each caste is relatively small and is confined to a localized region. It is only within the small territorial unit, as McKim Marriott points out, that the intricacy of the traditional caste system, with its usages of avoidance and pollution in the relation of castes, is possible.[7] Traditionally the castes of a localized community, numbering from a handful to as many as twenty or more, are hierarchically ranked and functionally integrated. Each caste occupies a position in a hierarchy of ritual purity which governs its relations with the other castes of the village. The Brahmin is normally the highest; the untouchable, the lowest. The ranking is consensual, representing the body of collective opinion concerning the place of the caste as a corporate whole higher or lower than another in precedence or esteem. The ranking may be either more or less elaborate.[8] The criteria for the ranking of castes are both attributional and interactional, but the legitimation of a caste's position in the hierarchy is determined through interactional recognition. Thus, although a caste may adopt the attributes of a higher caste in seeking to raise itself, it will secure recognition only through interactional acceptance.[9]

Each caste is characterized by a number of attributes significant to its position in ritual ranking. The traditional occupation of each caste is marked by degrees of purity and pollution. Occupations such as leather-working, barbering, and toddy-tapping—the extraction of juice from palms for liquor—are considered to be de-

[7] McKim Marriott, "Little Communities in an Indigenous Civilization," in *Village India* (Chicago, 1955), p. 191.

[8] McKim Marriott, *Caste Ranking and Community Structure in Five Regions of India and Pakistan* (Poona, 1960), p. 2. Marriott suggests four structural conditions for the maximal elaboration of caste ranking: "(1) The concrete structural units of a community—in this case its hereditary, generally endogamous groups—must themselves be numerous. (2) Secondly, their members as corporate groups must interact with members of other groups in a clearly stratified order. (3) Furthermore, so that members of such castes in a community may agree with each other on an elaborate ranking of castes, their interactions as individuals must not deviate widely from the stratified order of interaction among their respective castes taken as wholes. (4) Finally, the totality of such a community structure must be separated from any possible confusion which it may suffer by connection with inconsistent structures outside" (p. 4).

[9] See McKim Marriott, "Interactional and Attributional Theories of Caste Ranking," *Man in India*, XXX (April–June, 1959); Milton Singer, "The Social Organization of Indian Civilization," *Diogenes*, XLV (Spring, 1964), 99–108.

filing and as such low in rank. The consumption of certain foods carries defilement. While the consumption of meat is a mark of lower status than is vegetarianism, there are degrees of vegetarianism, such as between those who take eggs and those who do not. The style of dress, the forms of jewelry worn, the manner of address—all are attributional distinctions denoting a caste's position in the ritual hierarchy.

The attributes of caste status are meaningful only insofar as they are symbolic of interactional recognition. A caste does not gain high status merely by deciding to stop eating beef or by forbidding its members to consume liquor. It must gain the recognition of its status through daily interaction with the members of other caste groups in the village and locality. The pretensions of a caste to higher status through the adoption of "superior" attributes may bring a movement of reprisal on the part of the higher castes. The adoption of the attributes of a higher status will lead to interactional recognition only if the caste commands the economic and political power to demand the deference of the traditionally higher castes. The attributes of high status may, however, be significant in themselves beyond the locality of traditional interaction. In urban centers, or in regions where the caste is unknown, the attributes may determine interaction insofar as no other criteria are available.

The interactional relationship between castes is governed by a prescribed pattern of behavior. Since castes are ranked hierarchically in terms of purity and pollution, the form of each interaction between the members of different castes serves to denote the superiority of one and the inferiority of the other. Pollution may be incurred through food or drink, for example, and an elaborate set of rules govern commensality, prescribing for each caste the groups with which it is permitted to interdine, the castes from whom food may be accepted, and the types of food involved in such exchange. To accept cooked food from a person of another caste is to acknowledge inferiority to that caste; to refuse food is to assert superiority. The interactional restrictions of Hindu caste society go far beyond commensality to embrace almost every aspect of an individual's life. Each caste is thus restricted in its behavior and life-style. Deviation may bring action from the caste itself through a panchayat, or committee, of caste elders. It may also incur the wrath of the higher castes and bring punitive measures against the aberrant individual or the caste group as a whole.

Although conflict between castes certainly occurred, castes must not be regarded as conflict groups. Indeed, the caste *system* presupposes ideally the interdependent relationship of occupational castes functioning according to prescribed patterns of behavior, providing at once economic security and a defined status and role. The caste system is what Alan Beals calls "being together separately." "To survive," he says, "one requires the cooperation of only a few jati; to enjoy life and do things in the proper manner requires the cooperation of many." [10] Kathleen Gough has characterized the traditional system in which each economic function is fulfilled by a particular caste as "relationships of servitude." [11] It was, in fact, a system of reciprocity and redistribution—but not one of equality.[12]

The traditional economic system of caste has been likened to a "super-guild" system, with each caste performing its specific tasks in society by hereditary prescription and divine sanction. Each caste shares a common traditional occupation, and whether or not an individual is actually employed in that profession, he will be known by the caste's traditional calling. Thus a man of the potter caste who becomes an agricultural laborer continues to be known as a potter. A man is born into a caste, and regardless of his personal fortunes, he remains in that caste; he cannot escape it. Although the caste system was once viewed as static, with each caste frozen in its position of rank, the system has offered, in fact, a relatively high degree of flexibility. Within the middle ranges of the caste hierarchy, a degree of group mobility has always been possible.

In the range of castes between the Brahmin and the untouchable, there has been a high correlation between economic position and

[10] Alan R. Beals, *Gopalur: a South Indian Village* (New York, 1963), p. 41.
[11] Kathleen Gough, "Criteria of Caste Ranking in South India," *Man in India*, XXXIX, No. 2 (1959), 15–17.
[12] Walter C. Neale, "Reciprocity and Redistribution in the Indian Village: Sequel to some Notable Discussions," in Karl Polanyi (ed.), *Trade and Market in the Early Empires* (Glencoe, 1957), pp. 222–223.

ritual rank. In the elasticity of the system, when modifications and changes occurred in the relative position of the castes economically, a commensurate readjustment of the ritual ranking usually followed. Thus, the equilibrium between economic status and ritual rank was maintained. As a caste rose in wealth and political power, it tended to rise in the ranking of the hierarchy of ritual purity. Thus, following F. G. Bailey, "the ranking system of caste-groups was validated by differential control over the productive resources of the village." The correlation, however, is not perfect, for "at each end of the scale there is a peculiar rigidity in the system of caste" which has held the untouchable in a position of ritual degradation and has guaranteed the Brahmin his ritual rank against the vagaries of economic change.[13]

In mobility within the middle range of the caste system, it has been generally axiomatic that an individual alone can never rise, that he must bring his entire caste up with him. Bailey argues that a major factor preventing individual mobility is the solidarity of higher caste groups in closing their ranks against the rich men of lower caste. Social mobility arising from new economic opportunities belongs to the caste group and not to the individual. "The forces of change are thus canalized into the idiom of caste, and, given certain conditions, the structure of the caste-group is unimpaired, although the ranking of units within this structure may be modified in accordance with their changed economic rank."[14]

Marriott's study of a village in Uttar Pradesh suggests that this may not be wholly the case. "There has long been an approximate correspondence between the ranking of blocs of castes in Kishan Garhi and the local distribution of power and wealth," he writes, but "whatever the temporary shifts of wealth and power as between the castes, the ritual forms that are significant for caste rank shift but slowly." Marriott contends that "much more responsive to economic and political changes are the position of single persons in the heirarchy of individual prestige. . . . In Kishan Garhi, a man's caste rank counts for little more than seven annas in the sum

[13] F. G. Bailey, *Caste and the Economic Frontier* (Manchester, 1957), pp. 266–267.

[14] *Ibid.*, pp. 270–271.

of his prestige; wealth and political affiliation together count for nine annas." [15]

One of the techniques which castes have employed in seeking to assert a higher status within the hierarchy of ritual purity is "Sanskritization," described by M. N. Srinivas as the process through which "a low caste was able, in a generation or two, to rise to a higher position in the hierarchy by adopting vegetarianism and teetotalism, and by Sanskritizing its ritual and pantheon." [16] The process, according to Srinivas, provided a bridge between secular and ritual rank, for "when a caste or section of a caste achieved secular power it usually also tried to acquire the traditional symbols of high status, namely, the customs, ritual, ideas, beliefs, and life styles of the locally highest castes." [17] The Brahminical model was generally esteemed as the highest, and the aspirant caste, in seeking interactional recognition of higher status, tended to adopt the highly Sanskritized attributes of the Brahmin.

In the aspiration for higher status, the adoption of a more Sanskritized style of life was normally accompanied by the assertion of a claim to higher varna, to Vaisya, Kshatriya, or even Brahmin status. Classically, castes have been divided into five divisions: the four varnas and those beyond the pale of caste. The varnas represented the classes of Aryan society. Ranked hierarchically, the first three varnas—the "twice-born" (*dwija*), who wore the sacred thread—were the Brahmins, who acted as the priests, the Kshatriyas, who were the rulers and warriors, and the Vaisyas, who were the mercantile classes. The Sudras, the lowest varna, were the common people, the agriculturalists and craftsmen. Beyond the embrace of Hindu varna were the outcastes or untouchables, who, because of the defiled and polluted life as scavengers and sweepers, were relegated to the lowest rungs of society. The varnas represent categories in which the numerous jatis may be

---

[15] McKim Marriott, "Social Structure and Change in a U. P. Village," in M. N. Srinivas (ed.), *India's Villages* (Calcutta, 1955), pp. 102–103.

[16] M. N. Srinivas, *Religion and Society among the Coorgs of South India* (Oxford, 1952), p. 30.

[17] M. N. Srinivas, *Social Change in Modern India* (Berkeley, 1966), p. 28. Also see M. N. Srinivas, "A Note on Sanskritization and Westernization" in *Caste in Modern Indian and Other Essays*, pp. 42–62. A bibliography on Sanskritization may be found in Singer, *op. cit.* (n. 9 above), pp. 116–118.

grouped, but the system bears little resemblance to the reality of caste in Indian society. In South India, for example, there are Brahmins, non-Brahmins, and untouchables. The non-Brahmins are Sudras, many of whom, such as the Sivite Vellalas of Tinnevelly in Madras, are highly Sanskritized in life and custom. There are no genuine Kshatriyas or Vaisyas in peninsular India, and the use of these cagetories in this area refers only to local castes which have successfully claimed Vaisya or Kshatriya status.[18] Varna thus has provided a model for the upwardly mobile caste, and it has been the Kshatriya status, more than any other, to which the rising castes have aspired.

Hindu society has been far more dynamic than European scholars of the past have believed. Particularly in the past fifteen years, as anthropologists have brought the tools of modern social science to bear on caste in their studies of the Indian village, an increasingly dynamic view of the nature and operation of caste in Indian society has emerged. Caste may be analyzed in terms of the vertical and the horizontal, the intercaste and the intracaste. The vertical reflects the social, economic, and ritual relationships between castes; the horizontal, the relationships within a single caste community.

Traditionally in India, the low level of communications development precluded the horizontal extension of caste ties and solidarity over a wide geographic area. Political divisions, geographic barriers, and the lack of roads severely limited the range of association the members of a caste group of a particular village might have with their fellow caste members of other villages. Contact with members of their own caste beyond their village was limited often to periodic festivals and the exchange of brides, and rarely did such contact, except for the higher castes, extend beyond the immediately adjacent villages. There was in traditional India no overarching association embracing all members of a particular caste, no sense of community. Caste was localized and parochial—its social

[18] See M. N. Srinivas, "Varna and Caste," in *Caste in Modern India and Other Essays*. The varna model is discussed in Srinivas, *Social Change in Modern India*, pp. 2–6.

existence defined fundamentally by the vertical, intercaste, relationships of village life.

The British anthropologist Eric J. Miller has characterized the system as one of territorial segmentation, which "emphasized the solidarity of the territorial unit as a whole and inhibited the growth of individual caste solidarity over a wider area." [19] In describing the traditional society of Malabar before the advent of British rule, Miller writes that "the only unifying features of a caste over a wide area were the common name and the overlapping zones of kinship and internal administration; and even these often ended abruptly at political boundaries. . . . Territorial segmentation thus overrode the uniformity and unity of castes over a wide area." [20] "Territorial segmentation," he continued, "stressed the interdependence of all the castes at the village level and inhibited the development of internal caste solidarity over wide areas. Cleavages were between political units, never between castes." [21]

The interdependence of the castes at the village level bound each caste to the other in vertically integrated structures. The position of each caste in the ritual hierarchy, as we have said, was associated with its economic status and determined its relationship with the castes both above and below it in the scale of ranking. The lands of a village were normally held by members of one or two "dominant" castes, and it was to these landowners that the economically dependent lower castes owed allegiance. The major landowners, as patrons, commanded the loyalty of all those dependent upon them, thus creating in each village client groups which could be mobilized for factional opposition. "In the traditional system," writes Bailey, "the castes were not ranged in opposition to one another: rather the dependent castes are divided among themselves by their loyalties to masters of higher caste. Political cleavages ran not between castes, but between villages, or between factions within villages." [22] Thus, caste in traditional India was divided not only by

[19] Eric J. Miller, "Caste and Territory in Malabar," *American Anthropologist*, LVI (June, 1954), 419.
[20] *Ibid.*, p. 416.
[21] *Ibid.*, p. 417.
[22] F. G. Bailey, *Tribe, Caste, and Nation* (Manchester, 1960), p. 131.

subcaste and geography, but within the village itself by opposing client groups.

"It was the establishment of Pax Britannica," writes Srinivas, "which set the castes free from the territorial limitations inherent in the pre-British political system." British rule brought important economic changes, such as the opening of plantation estates, which undermined the relations of economic interdependence between castes in the village. Now economic opportunities offered to the lower castes the possibility of release from the traditional economic system by which they were bound to their high caste patrons as dependents. With geographic mobility, as the vertical relations of the traditional village client group weakened, the horizontal extension of caste ties was widened, and caste found a new solidarity, a new self-awareness. The development of transport and communications facilities was central to this process. Roads and railways enabled members of the same caste over a wide area to come together when necessary. Cheap paper and printing facilitated the founding of caste journals to promote the interests of the community, record its grievances, and give permanent form to its aspirations.[23]

British rule, in ending the almost constant warfare between the petty states and chiefdoms, brought a new administrative unity to India in the establishment of a centralized bureaucratic government. The old boundaries, in the words of Eric Miller, "now became porous, ceasing to mark the limits of social relations within individual castes." As the internal bonds of solidarity were extended over wider areas, regional associations were established by aspirant castes with the avowed purpose of elevating the status and prestige of the community as a whole by standardizing and "purifying" customs in a process of Sanskritization. These associations sought to organize and unite all members of the caste so that their claims might be advanced more effectively against other castes. The destruction of the old territorial cleavages with British conquest was, Miller argues, "fundamental to the transition from a system in which castes were interdependent within small areas to a system in which they are becoming widely ramifying classes in

[23] Srinivas, *Caste in Modern India and Other Essays*, p. 16.

opposition to one another." [24] F. G. Bailey describes these changes in saying that "territorial cleavages are being replaced by cleavages between 'castes." [25] The new polarization of caste against caste soon projected itself from the village to the wider social and political arena.

[24] Miller, *op. cit.*, p. 418.
[25] Bailey, *Tribe, Caste, and Nation*, p. 190.

Chapter I

THE NADARS: THEIR CONDITION AND
TRADITIONAL STATUS

HISTORICAL AND GEOGRAPHIC SETTING
OF THE SOUTHERN DISTRICTS

Madras, situated in the southeastern corner of the Indian subcontinent, is the cultural heart of Dravidian South India. Lying within the embrace of the great tradition of Indian civilization, the Tamil country has a culture of its own, often in deep contrast to that of the North. The Dravidian languages, of which Tamil, the language of Madras, is the principal tongue, are wholly unrelated to those of the North and constitute a distinct language family. The two cultural regions are divided, as well, by the food eaten, the style of dress, and the general pattern of life.

Madras State, or Tamilnad, is roughly the size of the state of New York and has a population of more than thirty-three million. Administratively, the state is divided into twelve districts, each of which is subdivided into taluqs. It is within the southern districts of the Tamil country that the more than one and one-half million Nadars are most heavily concentrated.[1]

Corresponding to the modern administrative divisions of Madurai, Ramanathapuram, Tirunelveli, and Kanyakumari, these districts were ruled for nearly two thousand years, beginning in the sixth century B.C., by the kings of the Chera, Chola, and Pandyan dynasties, the Pandyans commanding in these regions the position of preeminence. According to Tamil legends, Cheran, Cholan, and Pandyan were three brothers who lived and ruled in common at their capital of Korkai, near the mouth of the Tambraparni River in the present district of Tirunelveli. Eventually their common lands were divided, as Cheran and Cholan

---

[1] For statistics on the population of the principal castes of the southern districts, see Appendix I, "Population of the Southern Districts."

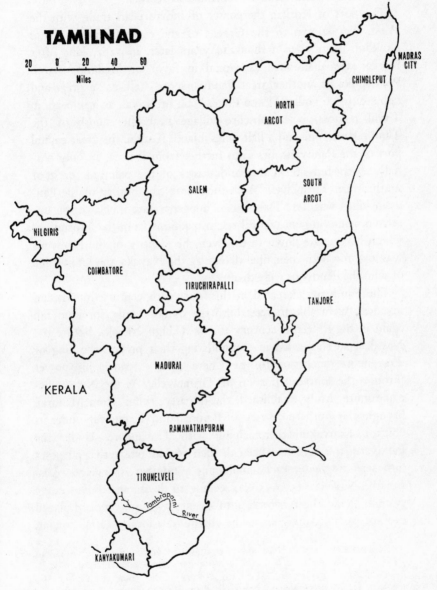

TAMILNAD

20 0 20 40 60
Miles

MADRAS CITY

CHINGLEPUT

NORTH ARCOT

SOUTH ARCOT

SALEM

NILGIRIS

COIMBATORE

TIRUCHIRAPALLI

TANJORE

MADURAI

KERALA

RAMANATHAPURAM

TIRUNELVELI

Tambraparni River

KANYAKUMARI

MAP 1. Madras State, or Tamilnad

13

established separate kingdoms in the west and north respectively. Pandyan, the eldest brother, remained in Korkai.[2]

The port of Korkai, the center of India's pearl trade with the West, was known to the Greeks of the early Christian era as Kolkhoi. More than a thousand years later, in 1292, long after Korkai was abandoned as capital in favor of Madurai, Marco Polo spoke of another great Pandyan port, Cail, as "a great and noble city."[3] Today Marco Polo's Cail, or Kayal, as it appears in Tamil records, is an obscure village near the mouth of the Tambraparni, one and a half miles inland. Korkai, the great capital port of the Pandyans, lies even further from the sea, an only partially excavated site in the sand wastes of the palmyra forest of southeastern Tirunelveli. With these cities the history of the Pandyan kings was lost. These rulers appear today only as often unrelated names in genealogical reconstructions from the inscriptions which have come down to us. Even the identity of the Pandyans was lost, for with their final defeat by the Nayaks, the knowledge of who the Pandyans were disappears.

The Pandyans, defeated in the fourteenth century by Muslim invaders, were able to reestablish the dynasty only for it to fall again in the sixteenth century to the Telugu Nayaks. Before the Nayaks had succeeded in consolidating their power, the king of Travancore, successor to the Chera rule, extended his power through the southern portion of Tirunelveli.[4] As the Nayaks became more firmly established, the dynasty, ruling from Madurai, brought the southern districts of Ramnad and Tirunelveli under its control, Kanyakumari remaining with Travancore. Under the Pandyans, the land had been divided for administrative purposes into separate *nadu*, each embracing a number of villages. Visvanatha Nayaka (1529–1564), seeking to devise an administrative system, divided his territories into seventy-two *palayam* and placed each of the new divisions in the charge of a local chieftain owing

[2] Robert Caldwell, *A Political and General History of Tinnevelly* . . . (Madras, 1881), p. 12. Also see K. A. N. Sastri, *A History of South India* (Oxford, 1958).

[3] Quoted in F. J. Western, "The Early History of the Tinnevelly Church" [c. 1950], p. 12. (Mimeographed.) See H. R. Pate, *Madras District Gazetters: Tinnevelly* (Madras, 1917), I, 56.

[4] Caldwell, *A Political and General History of Tinnevelly*, p. 68.

fealty to the Nayak. These *palayakars*, or *poligars*, as they were called, were to maintain troops for the defense of the land, to manage the civil administration of the *palayam*, and to pay one-third of the land revenue collected to Madurai as tribute.[5] The *palayam* was in turn divided into *nadu*, each, as in the Pandyan system, containing a number of villages.[6]

Many of the poligars, literally "holders of camps," were drawn from the ranks of the Telugu Nayak military leadership. Others were of the Maravar community, traditional warriors of the Tamil kings. In the period of Pandyan decline, the Maravars had sought to establish their position against the central authority in Madurai. With the defeat of the Pandyans, the Maravar lords were confirmed in their power by the Nayaks, who sought their alliance and loyalty. Each poligar gradually asserted his power, so that by the middle of the eighteenth century, shortly after the overlordship of the southern districts had passed into the hands of the Nawab of the Carnatic, the poligars had entrenched themselves with fortifications and large bodies of armed retainers. Most of the land south of Tiruchirapalli and north of the Tambraparni River lay in their control, and a continual state of war among them had thrown the country into "a state of anarchy and misery." "The constant endeavours of each was to encroach on the domains of his neighbours, and especially to swallow up any villages, revenues, or rights that still remained in the possession of the central government."[7]

Under the poligars, the *kaval* ("village watch") system developed, in which Maravar watchmen were paid by villagers to protect their lives and property. Landowners paid according to the extent of their lands; the landless gave a few annas or a measure of grain. In return, the watchmen were expected to make good any losses which the villagers might suffer. If the culprits were unapprehended, the watchmen would ordinarily make compensation to the villagers by thefts of their own in other areas. Often the "insurance" became a form of "protection," as the Maravars were

[5] B. S. Baliga, *Madras District Gazetteers: Madural* (Madras, 1960), p. 48.
[6] Baliga, p. 63.
[7] Caldwell, *A Political and General History of Tinnevelly*, pp. 102–103.

paid by the villagers *not* to plunder and steal their goods. While villagers often welcomed the security of the *kaval*, they also suffered under its abuses.[8]

The Nawab, his rule enfeebled, called upon the British to help him restore the districts to his control. In 1751, the East India Company sent an expedition against the poligars, and shortly thereafter established a permanent garrison at Palamcottah, across the river from Tinnevelly Town. In the years following 1751, the British led a series of "wars" against the poligars. The last of the major Poligar Wars, in 1783 and 1799, were both against the Kattaboma Nayaka, poligar of Panjalamkurichi in eastern Tirunelveli. During the period of these wars, the Nawab gave over the administration of the Carnatic, including Tirunelveli and Madurai, to the East India Company in payment for a portion of the revenue. The arrangement lapsed in 1785, and in 1790, the company by unilateral action "assumed the management of the Nawab's country." With the defeat of the Kattaboma Nayaka in 1801, the whole of the Carnatic territory was formally ceded to the company.[9] A number of the more pliant poligars were invested by the British as zamindars, and their turbulent followers were dispersed.[10] The *kaval* continued very much as before, but Pax Britannica had come to the southern districts.

At the time Tirunelveli—or Tinnevelly, as it was called by the British—was assumed by the East India Company, it included the major portions of the present district of Ramanathapuram (or Ramnad) and parts of Madurai. When the first collector took charge in 1801, he had jurisdiction over the *palayams* (later the zamindaris) of Sivagunga and Ramnad, but in 1803, these were combined in a separate "zilla of Ramnad." In 1808, the separate district was abolished, and the two *palayams* were placed under the administration of the collector of Madurai. The present district of Ramnad was formed only in 1910, placing the seven taluqs of the

[8] J. A. Stuart, *A Manual of the Tinnevelly District* (Madras, 1879), pp. 17–18; see also Pate, pp. 134–135.

[9] Western, "Early History," p. 13.

[10] See Stuart, pp. 17–18; Edgar Thurston, *Castes and Tribes of Southern India* (Madaras, 1909), V, 22–48; Louis Dumont, *Une Sous-Caste de l'Inde du Sud: Organisation Sociale et Religion des Pramalai Kallar* (Paris, 1957).

two zamindari tracts with the taluqs of Srivilliputtur and Sattur, which had formed part of Tinnevelly District. Tinnevelly itself was reorganized several times, and with the creation of Ramnad, it was divided into eight taluqs. In 1956, with States Reorganization,

MAP 2. The Southern Districts of Madras State

Shenkottah was added to the district from Travancore. At the same time, the four Tamil taluqs of southern Travancore were brought together as Kanyakumari District of Madras State.

The southern districts of Tamilnad are bordered on the west by the Western Ghats, rising in height from three thousand to five thousand feet and dividing Madras from Kerala. From the foot of the Ghats, the country then slopes gently toward the sea and is punctuated by detached and scattered hills. To the south of Madurai and in Ramnad and northern Tinnevelly, there is poor soil, precarious rainfall, and an absence of perennial rivers. Well water is often so high in alkaline content as to be opaque. The black soils of these areas yield cotton and groundnut, but the lack of irrigation has left vast tracts as virtual waste, capable of growing little beyond the natural growth of the brambled *udai* scrub and the palmyra palm. Farther to the south, the Tambraparni River cuts across the center of Tinnevelly District from the Ghats to the sea at Punnakayal, between Tuticorin and Tiruchendur. Winding through the district, each side of the river is bordered with a ribbon of green, irrigated paddy fields, the wealth of Tinnevelly. The district takes its name from the central town of Tinnevelly— Tirunelveli in Tamil, meaning "sacred paddy hedge." To the southeast, the rich soils of the Tambraparni give way to the *teris,* the vast sandy tract of the palmyra forest. Farther to the south, crossing the border of Tinnevelly into Kanyakumari, the country becomes more luxuriant, as the palmyras mix with coconut, and the vibrant green of the paddy fields returns. With the exception of Kanyakumari, which shares the tropical vegetation of Kerala, the southern districts of Tamilnad east of the Ghats offer what Robert Caldwell described as only "varieties of flatness and barrenness. The only point open to dispute is whether the black, blistered cotton-soil plain, or the parched, unenclosed, and almost uninhabited plains of the granitic districts, or the fiery-red sandy plains of the palmyra forests are the least fertile and inviting." [11]

The southeastern portion of Tinnevelly District, including Tiruchendur and the greater portions of Srivaikuntam and Nanguneri taluqs, is one of the most desolate areas in South India. The *teris,* ranges of deep, loose, red sands, are peculiar to the region and are often destitute of vegetation. In the *teris,* two of which cover an area of some forty square miles each, the sands

---

[11] Robert Caldwell, *The Tinnevelly Shanars: a Sketch of Their Religion, and Their Moral Condition and Characteristics, as a Caste* ("Missions to the Heathen," No. 23; London, 1850), p. 7. The geography of the southern districts must have changed greatly during the period of British rule. Early travelers described thick jungles where today there are cultivated plains.

constantly shift with every blast of wind, forming ridged dunes.
Despite the substratum of stiff red clay, the loose surface sands
driven by the southwesterly winds, moved the sands toward the
east at a slow but calculable rate. Caldwell recorded that the *teris*
"gradually overwhelmed trees, fields, and even villages in its
course." The *teris* originated, according to local tradition, in
showers of earth which in ancient times covered certain guilty
cities.[12] Beneath the *teris*, many Nadars claim, lay the ruins of the
once great cities of a Nadar kingdom.

ORIGINS OF THE NADAR COMMUNITY

It was within the land of the *teris* that the Nadars traditionally
made their home, drawing life from the palmyra palm as toddy-
tappers. The regions inhabited by the Nadars (or the Shanars, as
they were once most widely known) are "little better than a desert
—sandy, burnt up, barren, and uninviting," but, wrote Caldwell in
1850, "these barren lands literally teem with a Shanar population." [13] It is here that the origins of the community are to be
found.

The traditional account of the origin of the Nadars is little
known today among the community. While most Nadars have
some notion as to parts of the myth, only a few know the story of
the miraculous birth of the Nadars—mostly villagers among whom
the oral traditions of the community have remained alive. Although the account varies slightly in every version, its central core
tells of seven celestial virgins who, while bathing in a stream,
caught the eye of the god Indra. Collecting their saris, Indra sat
down behind a bush to watch and wait for the virgins to emerge
from the waters. As they did so, Indra caught and consorted with
each. The seven virgins each gave birth to a male child, and returning to their celestial world, they abandoned their sons. The goddess
Bhadrakali took pity upon them and brought them up as her own
sons. One day, the tale goes on, the River Vaigai near Madurai

12 Caldwell, *Tinnevelly Shanars*, pp. 7-9.
13 *Ibid.*, p. 9; see also "Remarks on the Province of Tinnevelly," *Missionary Herald* (Boston), XXI (1825), 144.

breached, and as the city was threatened with flooding, the
Pandyan king ordered all males to carry earth in baskets upon their
heads to rebuild the bund. The seven sons refused to obey the king,
although they were not rich. "We were meant to carry crowns
upon our heads, not baskets," the young men cried. The king was
furious and ordered that one of the boys be buried in the sand up
to his neck and that his head be kicked off by an elephant. The
order was obeyed, and the head, as it was cast into the flood waters,
cried, "I will not touch the basket." In a rage, the king ordered that
a second be treated likewise, and as the head floated away, it cried,
"Shall this head prove false to the other?" The king was greatly
frightened by these strange things and freed the remaining five
sons, from whom the Nadar race came forth. To this day, the
Nadars say, they will not touch the basket.[14]

A number of areas are mentioned as the place of the Nadars'
origin: the Cauvery region of the Chola country, Madurai, and
southern Travancore. Robert Caldwell tried to establish the
Nadars as "emigrants from the northern coast of Ceylon." He
found there a caste bearing a grammatical form of the same name,
Shandrar, of which, he said, *Shanar* is etymologically a corruption.
He felt certain, as well, that the Ezhavas and Tiyars, cultivators of
the coconut palm in Travancore, were descendants of Shandrar
colonists from Ceylon. "There are traces of a common origin
amongst them all," he asserted, pointing out that, for instance,
Shanar was used as a title of honor among the Ezhavas. The Tinnevelly Shanars, Caldwell argued, originally came from the neighborhood of Jaffna in Ceylon. One group, those known as Nadans,
entered Tinnevelly by way of Ramnad, bringing with them the
seednuts of the Jaffna palmyra, regarded as "the best in the east."
The Pandyan rulers gave them title over the sandy wastelands of
Manadu in the southeastern portion of the district, the region most
suitable for the cultivation of the palmyra. The other group of
emigrants, "esteemed a lower division of the caste," came by sea
from Ceylon to the south of Travancore, whence, according to
Caldwell, they gradually spread into Tinnevelly on invitation from

[14] See Appendix II, "The Myth of Nadar Origin."

the Nadans to serve as climbers in the immense palmyra forests.[15]
If Caldwell is correct, which seems unlikely, the Nadars would
simply have engaged in circular migration, for he admits that "the
inhabitants of the northern coast of Ceylon [are] themselves
Tamulians—the descendants, either of early Tamil colonists, or of
the marauding bands of Cholas who are said repeatedly to have
made irruptions into Ceylon both before and after the Christian
era."[16] Although the Nadars may have participated in the Chola
invasions of Ceylon—a number of traditions link them with the
island—Manadu, the desolate land of the *teris* seems more probable
as their place of origin as well as the region of their greatest concentration. Here among the palmyras with which the community
has been traditionally associated are the family temples, sites of the
ancestral villages of the Nadars. Even as Nadars have left their
homeland in migration into southern Travancore or into northern
Tinnevelly and Ramnad, however tenuous their links with the land
of their origin may have become, the family deity has bound them
ultimately to the ancestral lands of southeastern Tinnevelly.

TRADITIONAL STATUS

Ancient Tamil literature makes no reference to the inhabitants
of this region. At the beginning of the nineteenth century, as revealed in the first missionary descriptions of the community, the
Nadars appear to have occupied a social limbo somewhere between
the Sudras and the outcaste untouchables. Caldwell described the
Nadars "as belonging to the highest division of the lowest classes or
the lowest of the middle classes; poor, but not paupers; rude and
unlettered, but by many degrees removed from a savage state."[17]

---

[15] Robert Caldwell, *The Tinnevelly Shanars*, 1st ed. (Madras, 1849), pp. 4–5.
There are slight variations, additions, and deletions in the 1849 and 1850 editions.
All references to material appearing in both editions will be cited according to the
pagination of the first edition (1849).

[16] *Ibid.*, p. 5.

[17] *Ibid.*, p. 4. The "in-between" position of the Nadars was noted also in the
Ramnad Manual, where they are described as "inferior to Sudras and superior to
Parayas" (Raja Rama Rao, *Ramnad Manual* [Madras, 1889], p. 36); see also, Madras,
Manual of the Administration of Madras Presidency (Madras, 1885), I, 35.

In some respects the position of the Shanars in the scale of castes is peculiar. Their abstinence from spirituous liquors and from beef, and the circumstance that their widows are not allowed to marry again, connect them with the Sudra group of classes. On the other hand, they are not allowed as all Sudras are, to enter the temples; and where old native usages still prevail, they are not allowed even to enter the courts of justice, but are obliged to offer their prayers to the gods and their complaints to the magistrates outside, and their women, like those of the castes still lower, are obliged to go uncovered from the waist upwards. These circumstances connect them with the group of castes inferior to the Sudras; but if they must be classed with that group, they are undoubtedly to be regarded as forming the highest division of it.[18]

The Nadars were defiled by their ritually impure calling as toddy-tappers. They were forbidden entry into Hindu temples, and their use of public wells was strictly prohibited. Although the Nadars, unlike the Pallan and Paraiyan untouchables, had access to the streets of the Brahmin quarter, the *agraharam*,[19] they did share with them the prohibitions of spatial distance. As a "half-polluting" caste, in villages where they numbered only a small minority the Nadars lived in separate habitations just outside the main village, though not in so remote a site as the untouchables' *cheri*.[20] As their middling position was spatially represented in the location of their house sites, so the Nadars were, by tradition, forbidden to approach nearer than a specified number of paces to a man of higher caste, though they might come closer than the Paraiyan or Pallan.[21]

In the ranking of castes in the southern districts, as throughout India, the Brahmins, by tradition and sanction of the gods, occupied the supreme position in the hierarchy of ritual purity. The Brahmins in these regions were relatively few,[22] however, and the position of preeminence was largely taken by the Saiva Vellala community, which, although a Sudra caste, occupied a position in

[18] Robert Caldwell, *Lectures on the Tinnevelly Mission* (London, 1857), pp. 44–45.

[19] *Rajah M. Bhaskara Sethupathi v. Irulappan Nadan.* Judgment.

[20] Pate, *Madras District Gazetteers: Tinnevelly*, p. 101.

[21] Samuel Mateer, *The Land of Charity . . .* (New York [1870]), p. 32; J. N. Bhattacharya, *Hindu Castes and Sects* (Calcutta, 1896), p. 255.

[22] For caste statistics, see Appendix I, "Population of the Southern Districts."

social prestige and ritual rank second only to the Brahmins. "More Brahmin than the Brahmin," the Vellalas (known by the title Pillai) held themselves aloof from the castes below them and maintained strict vegetarianism and a highly Sanskritized ritual life.[23] Below the Vellalas ranged the clean castes of the Telugu Naickers and Reddiars, and the Maravars, warriors of the Tamil kingdoms and scourge of the Nadar community.

The line between the "clean" and the "unclean" was by no means clearly demarcated, but at its border, among the "polluting" castes, lay the traditional position of the Nadars. Not quite untouchable, they were, nevertheless, regarded by caste Hindus as defiling, just as were the Ambattan (barber) and Vannan (washerman) communities, which ranked just below them. The lowest of the principal castes of the southern districts were the Pallan and Paraiyan communities, both suffering the degraded status of outcaste untouchables, or, as Gandhi later called them, Harijans, "the children of God." [24]

As these castes were ranked in a linear structure, so were they also divided traditionally into the castes of the Right Hand and the Left Hand, a distinction apparently limited to South India. Among the Left Hand castes were the Maravars and the Pallars. Among those of the Right, claiming their privileges to have been bestowed by the goddess Kali, were the Vellalas, Nadars, Ambattans, Vannans, and Paraiyans.[25]

The Nadars shared a common position in the hierarchy of ritual rank, but within the community itself, there were variations of status that were significant. With the Nadars, as with all castes, noted Rhenius in 1827, "there are rich and poor, high and low, intelligent (as far as Heathen intelligence goes) and ignorant; there are masters and servants among them; proprietors of lands, trees, and villages; and labourers. . . . Their employment is chiefly the

[23] For a discussion of the Vellalas, see Thurston, VII, 361–389.

[24] For a discussion of the Pallan caste, see Thurston, V, 472–486; for the Paraiyan caste, VI, 77–119.

[25] J. H. Hutton, *Caste in India* (Cambridge, 1946), pp. 59–61, 143–145; S. C. Chitty, *The Ceylon Gazetteer* (Ceylon, 1834), pp. 231–234; Samuel Mateer, "The Pariah Caste in Travancore," *Journal of the Royal Asiatic Society*, New Series, XVI (1884), 181.

cultivation of the palmira tree, which abounds here; many also live by agriculture; others by merchandize; and the poorer sort by carrying burdens, etc." [26] The vast majority, however, were climbers.

THE CLIMBERS

The cultivation of the palmyra, toddy-tapping, wrote Ringel-taube, is the "whole employment and means of subsistence" of the Nadar community.[27] Beyond the palmyra forest where the palms and the Nadars abounded together, in the areas of northern Tinne-velly and Ramnad districts, and throughout Tamilnad wherever the palmyra was to be found, the Nadars climbed the trees. To the north of the Tambraparni River the palmyras were few, often growing only along the edges of the fields. With an insufficient number of trees for the production of jaggery sugar, the few palmyras did at least provide the juice for fermented toddy, and the scattered minorities of the Nadar community in these northern districts largely depended on this trade.[28] Toddy-tapping could provide a family with income from only a few trees, but jaggery production demanded a larger operation for the industry to be remunerative. The costs of firewood used in boiling the sap into the coarse sugar would alone preclude production in small quantity. In these areas of the north where the Nadars numbered usually no more than a few families in a single village, they suffered all of their community's social disabilities. Forced to reside outside the village itself in a separate hamlet, the Nadars were denied the use of the public well and were refused even the service of the barbers and washermen used by the caste Hindus of the village. Landless and economically dependent on the owners of the trees, the Nadars climbed the palymras during the six-month tapping season, from

[26] Letter from Messrs. Rhenius and Schmid regarding criticism of the Tin-nevelly Mission appearing in the Calcutta press, August 7, 1827, in *Proceedings of the Church Missionary Society, 1827–28* (London: 1828), p. 162.

[27] *Proceedings of the Church Missionary Society, 1823–24* (London, 1824), p. 227

[28] T. Venkataswami, *A Manual of the Tanjore District* (Madras, 1883), p. 201; W. Francis, *Madras District Gazetteers: South Arcot* (Madras, 1906), p. 240.

March to September,[29] and worked as agricultural laborers during the rest of the year.

To the south of the Tambraparni, down along the coast to the tip of India at Cape Comorin, the Nadars constituted the vast majority of the population, as high as 80 or 90 percent in the palmyra forests of the Tiruchendur *teris*.[30] In these sandy stretches, where often the only vegetation is the brambled *udai*, used for firewood, and the palmyra, the Nadars secured a meager living from the fabled eight hundred and one uses of the trees.

The "Palm poem," *Tala Villasam*, by the Tamil poet Arunachalam of Kumbakonam, extols to Lakshmi, the goddess of prosperity, the supernatural origin of the palmyra and its eight hundred and one uses. In a remote age, man, as he grew discontent with creation as it came from the hands of Brahma, supplicated Siva to supply one thing which would at once feed the hungry, heal the sick, and enrich the people, who, for want of it, were "trembling like water on the leaf of the lotus." Siva responded to man's entreaty and directed Brahma to create the palmyra. The tree was dedicated to Ganesa, the elephant-headed son of Lord Siva. It was praised as the Kalpa tree, the Hindu Tree of Life, and it was enthroned as one of the five trees of the Hindu paradise. "The palmyra lives a thousand years," eulogized a Tamil proverb, "and lasts another thousand years when it dies." [31]

The palmyra is perhaps the least elegant of all palms. It thrives alone where others would die in arid sands, sinking roots as deep as forty feet to draw water far beneath the surface.[32] Almost as straight as the mast of a ship, the palmyra reaches a height of from sixty to ninety feet, with an erect plume of fan-shaped leaves at its top. The leaves are stiff, with none of the grace of the coconut's

[29] In Kanyakumari, the palmyra season is from August to February.

[30] In the palmyra forest, the trees reach a density of more than eight thousand to the square mile. Pate, *Madras District Gazetteers: Tinnevelly*, p. 496.

[31] William Ferguson, *The Palmyra Palm* (Colombo, 1850), Appendix, pp. 1-5; W. A. Symonds, "Monograph on the Palmyra and Its Uses," in *Selections from the Records . . . on Palmyra Plantations*, pp. 142-143; V. Nagam Aiya, *Travancore State Manual* (Trivandrum, 1906), III, 68-69.

There is a story that the Pandava kings regained their lost kingdom because they ate the palmyra fruit when in the wilderness. The Pandyan kings are said to have worn garlands of palmyra blossoms. Ferguson, Appendix, p. 5.

[32] Western, *op. cit.* (n. 3 above), pp. 11-12.

long drooping leaves, and they are of manifold use: in the thatching of houses among the lower classes, in the manufacture of mats, baskets, and vessels of almost every description; and the slips of the young leaf form the traditional stationery of southern India. The palmyra is the only palm whose wood is of value, supplying the finest rafters. The greater praise for the palmyra, however, is for the value of its products as food. The young root is edible, as is the ripe fruit, but the unripe fruit is greatly preferable "inasmuch as it contains the purest, most wholesome, and most refreshing jelly in existence." [33]

The most highly valued product of the palmyra is the saccharine sap or juice of the tree. The unfermented juice, called "sweet toddy," is used without cooking or preparation and is a staple in the diet of the Nadar tappers, who take it early in the morning before they begin their labor. When the juice of the palmyra is allowed to ferment, a process which takes but a few hours, a sweet liquor or toddy is produced. [34] Both the sweet and the hard toddy were sold locally for cash by the tappers, but in the regions of the palmyra forest, where the industry was the foundation of economic life, most of the palmyra juice was boiled into a hard, coarse sugar called jaggery, or into palmgur candies. This was the work of the Nadar women, who collected firewood and boiled the juice over a slow fire in large earthen pots. When the juice thickened, it was poured either into coconut shells or into pits dug in the ground for the purpose. The hard, black jaggery cakes were often eaten as the midday meal of the tappers, but most of it was sold, either for low-grade sugar or for the distillation of arrack, the native "gin." [35]

The work of the *panaiyeri*, or climber, begins before daybreak, and in the course of the day, working until noon and then again from late afternoon until night, he will ascend thirty to fifty trees, climbing each twice—sometimes three times—to extract the juice.

[33] Caldwell, *Lectures on the Tinnevelly Mission*, p. 31–32.

[34] *Ibid.*, p. 33; on the uses of the palmyra, also see Pate, pp. 220–222; Mateer, *Land of Charity*, pp. 119–123; *Manual of the Administration of the Madras Presidency*, III, 648–649, 906.

[35] Mateer, *Land of Charity*, p. 126; Pate, pp. 124–125; Samuel Mateer, *Native Life in Travancore* (London, 1883), pp. 279–280.

During the season in which the sap flows, from March through the hottest months of the year until September, the tapper can never leave the trees unattended, even for a day. As a dairy cow must not be left unmilked, so the palmyra—proverbially "the Shanars' cow" —will cease to yield its juice if untapped.[36] The sap of the palmyra is drawn from the flower stalk at the top of the tree, which when bruised or sliced yields, drop by drop, about one pint of juice each day. The flow is received in small earthen pots attached to each stalk. The sap is then collected two or three times during the day by the climber, who with each climb trims the stalk to allow free flow of the juice.

Climbing the palmyra is both dangerous and arduous. Each year, many of the climbers, no matter how skillful, fall from the trees to die or to remain crippled for life. In ascending the tree, the climber clasps the trunk with joined hands, supporting his weight with the soles of his feet, which, held together by a short span of rope, bend inward like grasping hands. Then in a series of springs, in which both hands and feet move together, the climber ascends the tree as rapidly as a man could walk a distance of equal length.[37] In years of climbing, the body of the tapper becomes twisted, his powerful chest scarred, and his hands and feet like the enormous paws of some animal.

The season in which the sap of the palmyra flows is only six months in length, and the yield varies with the rainfall. The climber owned neither the land nor the trees which he tapped— only the sharp, tappers' knife, a few earthen pots, and meager clothing. His home was a palmyra-thatched hut, and if the palmyra

---

[36] James Russell, letter to the London Missionary Society, dated Nagercoil, January 24, 1856, in *Missionary Magazine and Chronicle*, XX (August, 1856), 168.

[37] Caldwell, *Lectures on the Tinnevelly Mission*, pp. 34-35. "Woodpeckers are called Shanara kurivi by birdwatchers, because they climb trees like Shanars" (Thurston, *Castes and Tribes*, VI, 374).

The instruments used by the tapper are described in Aiya, II, 393-394; for a description of the tapping process see Mateer, *Land of Charity*, pp. 123-125; Pate, pp. 222-225; Francis Buchanan, *A Journey from Madras through the Countries of Mysore, Canara, and Malabar* (London, 1807), II, 193-195; *Census of India, 1961*, Vol. IX: *Madras*, Pt. VI: Village Survey Monographs, No. 10, *Pudukulam*, pp. 61-63.

tope, or grove, was situated far from his own village, he would
leave to take seasonal residence with his family among the trees.
The tapper received no money for his labor, but a share system
gave the produce of alternative days to the climber and to the
owner. Whether in the districts to the north of the Tambraparni,
where the owners of the lands were Maravars, Naickers, Vellalas,
or others of high caste, or in the barren palmyra forests of
Tiruchendur, where the Nadans held the land, the climber was
bound to the trees by tradition and an accumulation of debts. The
profits of climbing were small and usually exhausted by the
panaiyeri two or three months after the end of the season, and,
even with the cottage industries from the by-products of the palmyra, such as mat- or basket-making by the women, the climber
had little recourse other than to seek the enfettering advances from
the owners.[38] Even in the best of yields, the climber led a marginal
existence, his poverty "as deep as that of the Pariar and Puller
slaves in the rice-growing districts." [39]

Although most climbers were landless, a few had acquired ownership of the trees (but rarely the lands on which they stood). By
the mid-nineteenth century an increasing number were acquiring
ownership of tiny plots as well, but economically they were little
better off than before.[40] The peculiar double hold which separated
the ownership of land and of trees came about as many landowners
gave the climber title to a percentage of palmyras that he worked
on the condition that he care for the entire tope or that he cultivate
the ground beneath the trees as an agricultural laborer. More commonly the ownership of both land and trees was retained by
Nadan landlords, since trees were transferred by mortgage and sale
apart from and irrespective of the land on which they stood.[41]
Under the Nawab and in the early years of British authority, the

[38] Arthur Margöschis, "Tinnevelly: Being an Account of the District, the
People, and the Missions," *Mission Field*, XLII (October, 1897), 393.

[39] Caldwell, *Tinnevelly Shanars*, 1st ed., p. 48.

[40] *Ibid.*, p. 50.

[41] Letter from the collector of Tinnevelly to the secretary of the Board of
Revenue, dated September 11, 1868, in *Selections from the Records . . . on Palmyra Plantations*, p. 84; letter from the collector of Tinnevelly to the Revenue
Department, August 23, 1872, in *ibid.*, p. 102; S. Sundaraja Iyengar, *Land Tenures
in the Madras Presidency* (Madras, 1922), p. 178.

trees were assessed separately from the land, and in these southern districts alone, the palmyras were taxed.[42]

THE NADANS

A small portion of the community, the Nadans, possessed vast tracts of land in the regions south of the Tambraparni River. Invested as tax gatherers by the Nayaks, and probably by the Pandyans before them, these Nadans, or "lords of the land," held their position either directly under the Nayak, as in the region of Tiruchendur, or as petty lords under the poligars. One account speaks of the appointment by the Pandyans of seven collectors from the Nadar community in the *teri* regions.[43] Another records the appointment in 1639 of eleven Nadans authorized to collect taxes from the people.[44] As hereditary tax collectors, the Nadans held civil authority over the lands in their control.

With great wealth and power, the Nadans commanded the deference of those beneath them. The climbers, totally dependent on the Nadans, came before them only with their arms folded across the chest in respect and with their dhotis tied above the knees, as a mark of their inferiority. In these regions, the few non-Nadars—the Vellala accountant or the Brahmin priest—would alike show deference to the position of the Nadan lords.[45] The Nadans would "buy Pariars and Pallars, to work in their houses as slaves, so as to retain their usual proud customs."[46] They rode horses, and their women rode in covered palanquins. The Nadan women observed strict *gosha*, revealing themselves only to the men

[42] Pate, pp. 306–310.

[43] B. J. M. Kulasekhara-Raj, *A Brief Account of the Nadar Race* (Palamcottah, 1918), pp. 25–28.

[44] L. S. Tangasami, Tinnevelly, "The Nadars." Manuscript. Pate notes (pp. 338–339) that among the most successful *kavals* were those few held by Nadans. The headman of the Nadar village of Chindambarapuram, in Nanguneri taluq, possesses a copper plate, bearing the date *Saka* 1422 (A.D. 1500–1501). According to the inscription, the right was originally granted to the Shanans of the place by Tirumeni Malandan, who may have been the representative of the Travancore ruler at the time he was in possession of a portion of the Tinnevelly district.

[45] Tangasami, "Nadars."

[46] Letter to the Bishop from Rev. D. Gnanapragsam, July 15, 1867, in *Inquiries Made by the Bishop of Madras . . .* (Madras, 1868), p. 77.

of their own household. The Nadans built temples and met the costs of ceremonies and festival expenses. The oldest and highest Nadan family was that of the Adityans of Kayamori, near Tiruchendur. They claimed descent from Surya, the sun god, and held special rights at the Siva temple in Tiruchendur. The family constructed one of the pavilions of the temple and met the costs of various ceremonies. They donated the huge wooden car to the temple, and in return were given the privilege to be the first to touch the rope which would pull the car through the streets at the time of the festival. Despite the privileges of their position the Adityans—like the Nadans of Kuttam and the other villages of southeastern Tinnevelly—were denied entrance into the temples they patronized. Their wealth, power, and prestige came to naught as their small number was submerged in the greater class of Nadars, who by their degraded profession brought ritual defilement to the caste as a whole. The Nadans shared the pollution of the lowest climber.[47]

Among the Nadans, in dispute and litigation over the lands, there was a constant conflict of factions, with each Nadan commanding a client group of dependents. Dispute over the land most often arose over the question of division after the death of the proprietor. Since there was no primogeniture, in most Nadan families, according to Caldwell's analysis, the sons agreed to preserve the original estate undivided and to share the produce from the lands. Everyone was on the alert to secure his own share, hence there arose encroachments and retaliations, feuds and jealousies. Eventually, perhaps in the second or third generation, the parties would determine to effect a division of the estate among the claimants to the land, but it was always more easily determined than effected.[48]

The dispute might be taken for arbitration by a panchayat, or council of elders, and a compromise effected whereby land and trees might be divided equally, or the land go to one, the trees to another. Inevitably, the weaker party complained that he had not

[47] T. Masillamani Nadar, *Pandiya Desa Aditta Vamsa Sarittiram* (History of the Adityan Family of the Pandya Country) (Madurai, 1931); Thurston, *Castes and Tribes*, VI, 366; Tangasami, "Nadars"; interviews.
[48] Caldwell, *Tinnevelly Shanars*, 1st ed., pp. 50–51.

received justice. Seeking the support of friends and a greater number of dependents—and the resources to command them—he
would then reject the decision and attempt to forcibly seize control
of the land.[49] As brother upon brother, so powerful Nadans, as
they succeeded in acquiring greater numbers of men, would encroach upon the lands of their neighbors or challenge their legal
right to the estate through litigation. "A village is divided into two
or more parties," wrote the missionary G. U. Pope in 1850. "Every
occurrence, every feast, every devil-offering, every harvest, every
collection of revenue, becomes the occasion of a grand quarrel." [50]
The palmyra trees, as the most valued property, were particularly
subject to "perpetual litigation . . . , never ending, still beginning." [51] The Nadar community was thus divided into opposing
groups, with each climber owing allegiance to the Nadan upon
whom he was economically dependent as a servant and as a debtor.
Since the control of the land might pass back and forth among the
Nadans, however, the climbers remained always with their trees.
Title to the trees brought control over the climbers.[52]

SUBCASTE, SEPT, AND RELIGION

The distinction between the climbers and the owners of the trees
was the most basic division in the Nadar community. Divided by
prestige, power, and wealth, the two groups were separated as well
by the endogamy of each. Though considered by themselves, as
well as by other castes, to be of the same community as the climbers, the Nadans held themselves socially aloof from the climbers,
and while they would accept food from their hands, they would
not exchange brides, restricting the ties of marriage to certain
Nadan families of a limited range of villages.[53] Communications
within the Nadar community rarely extended beyond the con-

---

49 *Ibid.*, pp. 51–54.
50 "Missions of the Church in Tinnevelly," Pt. IV, *The Colonial Church Chronicle* (London), III (June, 1850), 445–446.
51 *Ibid.*, p. 448.
52 For comparable structure within a traditional community, see Fredrik Barth,
The Political Leadership of the Swat Pathans (London, 1959).
53 T. Masillamani (p. 49) lists the villages, for example, with which the Adityan
family traditionally had marriage relations.

stricted geographic area in which brides were exchanged. The extensions of the village were limited, and even within the region of the *teris*, homeland of the Nadars, the extent of ties beyond the distance of a few miles was minimal. Political divisions before British rule, together with geographic distance and an almost total lack of transport facilities, precluded the development of a wider range of contact within the caste itself. As the community was divided geographically, it was divided also within the smaller regions of interaction into subcastes.

That the Nadans traditionally formed an endogamous group within the larger Nadar community is accepted today with little dispute, but the whole question of subcastes generally is one of the most confused aspects of the traditional culture of the Nadar community. During the nineteenth century, as the subcastes among the Nadars were breaking down, no two descriptions of the community agreed on the number of divisions, much less their names, rank, or occupation. Today most Nadars express only the vaguest knowledge of subdivisions within the caste and are unable to name even the one to which by tradition they would belong. Of those who expressed knowledge of the subcastes, none agree on their names or number.

The legends of the origin of the Nadars tell of the birth of seven sons; with the death of two, the remaining five father the separate divisions of the community. Five is the most generally accepted enumeration of subcastes, as in Pate's *Tinnevelly Gazetteer* and Thurston's *Castes and Tribes of Southern India*. Thurston lists Karukku-pattayar, Mel-natar, Nattatti, Kodikkal, and Kalla.

Karukku-pattayar. Pate, who suggests that the divisions are of territorial origin, gives *Manattan* as another name for the subcaste, which is, according to Thurston, superior to the rest. This class is supposed to have originally inhabited the country around Manadu, "the Great Province," four miles from Tiruchendur. Their alternative title, following Pate, *Karukkumattaiyan* (*karukku*, "sharp edge"; *mattai*, "the leaf stalk of the palmyra") is suggestive of their association with tree-climbing. Because of its derogatory connotation and unpopularity, it was changed to the form generally given, *Karukkupattaiyan* (*pattaiyam*, "sword"), meaning "those of the sharp sword." [54] One of the later caste historians referred to the subdivision as *Mara Nadars* and claimed for them descent from the Pandyans.[55] The subcaste is the largest of the five and, according to some sources, embraces at least 80 percent of the entire community, including the families of the Nadans—called Nellaimaikkarars—as well as the climbers beneath them.[56]

Mel-natar. The *Mel-natars* (*Menattans* in Pate) derive their name from *melnadu*, "the western country," and live traditionally in southern Travancore and western Tinnevelly district.[57] It is claimed that after the fall of the Chera dynasty, the descendants of the Chera kings, the Mel-natars, or the Kuda Nadars as they were called, came into the Pandya country and settled along the Western Ghats. Today their numbers, estimated at 25,000, are concentrated in Ambasamudram taluq, with a few in Tenkasi, Sankarankovil, Srivaikuntam, and Nanguneri.[58]

Nattatti. Concentrated around the village of Nattatti, near Sawyerpuram in Tinnevelly District, the Nattatti Nadars number only a few thousand at the most and were traditionally occupied in cultivation, trade, and money-lending, rather than as climbers. Legendary accounts claim Nattatti descent from union of the Pandyas and the Cholas. Today the community is predominately Christian and, alone of the subdivisions of the Nadars, remains a distinct endogamous unit. While they regard themselves as occupying a high status among Nadars, they are considered by most of the community to be of a lower position. One of their number, the overlord of Nattatti, was a retainer of the Kattaboma Nayaka. Later the family was invested with zamindari rights under the British. The last of the Nattatti zamindars, Tiruvarudi Vaihunda Nadan, died in 1892. The properties, subject to extended legal dispute, were eventually divided among a number of claimants.[59]

---

[54] Thurston, VI, 376–377; Pate, pp. 129–130.

[55] Kulasekhara-Raj, *Brief Account of the Nadar Race*, p. 46.

[56] Interview. Today Nadars speak of the "A" and "B" groups. The "A" group is that of the Karukkupattayar, the Nadars proper, including the elite of this group, the Nellaimaikkarar. The "B" group embraces the other four lower subcastes.

[57] Pate, pp. 129–130.

[58] Tangasami, "Nadars"; Kulasekhara-Raj, pp. 52–53.

[59] Kulasekhara-Raj, pp. 51–52; Tangasami, "Nadars"; and interview.

Kodikkal. Pate identified the Kodikkal subcaste with the Nattattis. All other sources, however, distinguish between the two
groups. The name sometimes associates them with the cultivation
of betel-nut, sometimes with the standard-bearers of the fighting
men. Concentrated in Ambasamudram and Tenkasi taluqs, they are
occupationally climbers by tradition. They are supposed to have
migrated to the Pandya country from the banks of the Cauvery
River in Tanjore, coming under the patronage of the Pandyan
kings as their flag bearers.[60]

Kalla. The Kalla Shanars, also called Pulukka ("cow dung"),
form the lowest division of the Nadar community. Their identity
with the larger community, which would not accept food from
their hands, was marginal, and the name *kalla* denotes "spurious"
or "false." Originally believed to have been slaves and palanquin
bearers of the Pandyan kings, their traditional position in the
Nadar community was as climbers, as menial servants, or as slaves
of the Nadan families. They are believed to be the descendants of
illegal unions within the Nadar community. The name by which
the Kalla Shanars are most commonly known is Servai. Servai,
however, also seems to be an honored title, implying "chieftain,"
but as it is ordinarily used, the term is synonymous with the low
Kalla Shanars.[61]

Whether the Nadar barbers are to be classed with the Servais is a
matter of dispute. They seem, like the Nadars themselves, to occupy some sort of limbo. It is not clearly known whether the
barbers who exclusively serve the Nadars (for ordinary barbers do
not serve the caste, presumably because of their low status) are
actually members of the Nadar community or whether they form
a subcaste among barbers. The latter is more likely, but they do
not exchange brides with the families of barbers serving the higher
classes, and are looked upon as being very low. The Nadar barber
serves, in addition to his duties as barber for the community, as the
village crier and messenger and officiates at Nadar funerals. Some

[60] Pate, pp. 129–130; Kulasekhara-Raj, pp. 55–56; Tangasami.
[61] Pate, pp. 129–130; Kulasekhara-Raj, pp. 55–56; Thurston, VI, 376–377;
Robert Caldwell, "Report of Edeiyengoody District for the year ending 30 June
1845." Manuscript (Society for the Propagation of the Gospel, noted hereafter
as S.P.G.), reprinted in *Mission of Edyenkoody: Report 1845;* and interview.

Nadars today take the fact that the barbers serve them exclusively to indicate that their status is high rather than low, that the Nadars as ancestors of the Pandyans, took their barbers with them into exile when their kingdom fell to the Nayaks.[62]

Ringeltaube, in 1824, described a group of persons within the Nadar community "who may be called learned . . . , Pandarams . . . who know how to read and write, and to sing some stories of their gods. . . ."[63] Although the Pandarams serving the Nadar temples are drawn from the caste of non-Brahmin priests, there appears to have been at one time at least a subdivision of Nadars performing priestly services. Known as Gurukkal, they also took the title Aiyar.[64]

In the reports, gazetteers, and commentaries referring to the Nadar community, an innumerable number of subdivisions appear. The *Salem Gazetteer* speaks of two divisions among the Shanars, the Konga-Shanars and the Kalyana-Shanars.[65] The *Tanjore Manual* divides the community into three groups distinguished by the kind of tree from which they draw toddy: Tennan Shanar (coconut), Panan Shanar (palmyra), and Eetchan Shanar (wild date).[66] The *Ceylon Gazetteer*, published in 1834, lists seven distinct classes of Nadars,[67] and the Government of India Census Report for 1891 lists no less than 324 subdivisions, including among the largest Konga and Madurai.[68] This list, a confused conglomeration of names from a variety of categories, is unrecognizable to Nadars. The enumeration appears to include, in addition

[62] Interview.

[63] "Missionary View of Madras Presidency," *Proceedings of the Church Missionary Society, 1823–24*, pp. 231–232.

[64] Kulasekhara-Raj, pp. 53–56.

[65] F. J. Richards, *Madras District Gazetteers: Salem* (Madras, 1918), I, Pt. I, 183–184.

[66] Venkataswami, *Manual of Tanjore District*, p. 201.

[67] (1) Velan chanar, or husbandman; (2) Katpura chanar, or dealers in small wares; (3) Kalla chanar, or porters; (4) Eeku chanar, or bullock drivers; (5) Tennamatte chanar, or toddy drawers from cocoanut trees; (6) Pannematte chanar, or toddy drawers from palmyra trees; and (7) Pallavaraye chanar, or palanquin bearers. Chitty, *Ceylon Gazetteer*, p. 233.

[68] *Census of India, 1891*, Vol. XV: *Madras*, Caste Index, Appendix, pp. 90–91; see also Vol. XIII, p. 297; the Travancore census of that same year lists eleven Nadar subdivisions. *Report of the Census of Travancore, 1891* (Madras, 1894), p. 979.

to actual subcastes, the names of localities and territorial divisions, occupations, and, most of all, the names of Nadar "houses" or exogamous septs into which the community is divided.

The confusion with regard to subcastes among the Nadars is apparent. If we take the more usually accepted five territorial divisions, all but one are relatively small, and the largest, Karukku-pattayar, embraces both the Nadans and the climbers, which is the most meaningful social and economic distinction within the Nadar community. Although classified in the same subcaste, the two groups were endogamous, forming "sub-subcastes," each marrying only among themselves.

As the Nadars are divided traditionally into endogamous subcastes, they are, within each subcaste, divided into exogamous septs or clans, which they call *kuttams*. There are more than one hundred such divisions,[69] and each village or town may have as many as twelve or more. Each Nadar is a member of a *kuttam* through patrilineal descent, and since all members of the same *kuttam* are believed to be related through a common ancestor, a man is forbidden to take his bride from his own *kuttam*. He is not prohibited, as in some castes, however, from marrying into the *kuttam* of his mother, and indeed, the preferred choice in marriage is the cross-cousin, that is, the daughter of the mother's brother.[70] The people of the same *kuttam* share a family deity, usually the distant ancestor who founded the family and who is worshipped at the *kuttam* temple in the ancestral village. Christian converts among the Nadars continue to recognize the *kuttam* for purposes of marriage, but they do not maintain ties with the family temple. Most of the temples are among the barren *teris* of Tiruchendur, and often the family temples found in the towns of Ramnad to the north are linked to an earlier temple in Tiruchendur. In migrations, families would often take soil from the temple and enshrine it in the

[69] A Nadar from Sivakasi was able to prepare a list of 112 *kuttams* known to him.

[70] For a discussion of marriage customs among the Nadars, see Aiya, *Travancore State Manual*, II, 394-395; J.F. Kearns, *Kalyan'a Shat'anku or the Marriage Ceremonies of the Hindus of South India* (Madras, 1868), pp. 36-41; *Census of India, 1961*, Vol. IX: *Madras*, Pt. VI: Village Survey Monographs, No. 19, *Kuttuthal Azhamkulam*, pp. 7-8, and No. 8, *Kootumangulam*, pp. 9-11.

place of their new home. Traditionally, all the members of a *kuttam* would assemble once a year at the family temple for a festival. A child's name would be entered at birth into the temple's register. With the birth of the first male child, the family traditionally went to the *kuttam* temple, where the hair of the child was shaved and offered to the deity. At the time of marriage, the first invitation is presented to the family deity.[71] The names of the *kuttams* may be derived from the name of the ancestor, from the ancestral village, or from a characteristic or an anecdote peculiar to the family tradition.

The Nadars are almost entirely Saivite, but one *kuttam* is Vaishnavite. Of the deities, Subramania, or Murugan, the second son of Siva, has been widely popular among the community. "But in those extensive tracts of country where the Shanars form the bulk of the population, and the cultivation of the palmyra is the ordinary employment of the people," wrote Caldwell in a description of the Nadars' religion as he first encountered the community, "the Brahmanical deities rarely receive any notice; and the appearance on the foreheads of a few of the more devout, or of the wealthier class, of a streak of holy ashes, the distinctive mark of Sivism, is the only trace or sign of the influence of legitimate Brahmanism which one can see. Demonism in one shape or another may be said to rule the Shanars with undisputed authority." [72] A number of the early missionaries contended that the demonolatry of the Nadars was so far removed from orthodoxy that the community could not, in fact, be counted as Hindu.[73]

[71] Interviews. Some Nadars have sought to identify the *kuttam* with the exogamous division of the Vaisyas, Kshatriyas, and Brahmins, the *gotra*.

[72] Caldwell, *Tinnevelly Shanars*, 1st ed., pp. 12-13; for accounts of devilworship, see pp. 8-29. See also George Pettitt, *The Tinnevelly Mission of the Church Missionary Society* (London, 1851), pp. 482-505; Pate, pp. 113-120; *Manual of the Administration of Madras Presidency*, I, 80-81.

A summary of missionary descriptions of Nadar demonolatry has been made by C. F. Pascoe (drawing largely from Caldwell's reports): *Two Hundred Years of the S.P.G.: an Historical Account of the Society for the Propagation of the Gospel in Foreign Parts*, 1701-1900 (London, 1901), p. 532.

[73] Joseph Mullens, *A Brief Review of Ten Years' Missionary Labour . . .* (London, 1863), pp. 96-98. Caldwell opposed this view, however, in "Ten Years in Tinnevelly: a Missionary's Review," *Mission Field*, XVII (October, 1872), 304.

The anti-Brahminical character of the Nadar religion was illustrated, according to Caldwell, in the interpretation of Lord Rama as a demon. The first day of the solar month Adi is celebrated by the Nadars as a festival commemorating the abduction of Sita, wife of the Hindu god-hero Rama, by Ravana, king of Ceylon. The Nadars believe Ravana's prime minister, Mahodara, to have been of their own caste, and "to this day the Shanars glory in the historical position gained for once by a member of their caste, and rejoice over Rama's grief and in Ravana's joy." [74]

Bhadrakali is the tutelary deity of the Nadar community. Known variously as Mariamman, Kaliamman, or Bhadrakali, the goddess represents the malignant aspect of the wife of Siva and is believed to inflict epidemics of smallpox and cholera. While the Nadars are "the sons of Bhadrakali," all non-Brahmin classes seek to divert the wrath of the deity through supplication.[75] The *ammankovil*, or goddess temple, is central to every Nadar settlement.

THE NADARS AS THE MISSIONARIES FOUND THEM

Although the demons of Tinnevelly were not easily exorcised, the Nadars provided a rich field for missionary labor. The missionaries who came to work among the Nadars brought varying degrees of sophistication, but they agree, in large part, on what they viewed as the lamentable condition of Nadar character.

One of the first missionaries of the London Missionary Society, the Reverend William T. Ringeltaube, recorded his initial impression of the Nadar community in his journal, June 19, 1806: "The Shanans are a set of people more robust than other Indians, very dark in complexion, their features completely European, their ears protracted to the shoulders by mighty ornaments of lead. They divide themselves into five families, one of which exclusively ascends the trees, from which practice their hands and feet acquire a peculiarly clumsy shape. Their religion is not Brahminical, but consists in the worship of one Madan, formerly a washerman.

[74] Caldwell, *Tinnevelly Shanars*, 1st ed., p. 28.
[75] R. R. Meadows, "Our Home in the Wilderness: Recollections of North Tinnevelly," *Church Missionary Gleaner* (London), VI (April, 1879), 40; Aiya, *Travancore State Manual*, 392n, 395; and interview.

Their habits are extremely simple. They are quarrelsome, avaricious, and deceitful." [76]

Another early missionary described the Nadars as "usually very dirty, ignorant and of wild appearance. . . . They can hardly be said to have character. They live almost like the brute creation and every vice is common among them. They are not without abilities; but still seem to be a degree at least behind the Sudras. The reason doubtless, is the abject state of slavery in which they have been held for ages by the superior castes. Their wants are very few, and their desires do not extend beyond the support of their bodies. Of course their ideas and conversations reach no further than the employment in which they are engaged." [77]

All was not lost, however, for the Nadars. "Though the Shanars rank as a caste with the lower classes" and as a community occupy a depressed economic position, Caldwell wrote, describing the condition of the Nadars in the mid-nineteenth century, "pauperism is almost unknown amongst them." The great majority "are equally removed from the temptations of poverty and riches, equally removed from the superficial polish and subtle rationalism of the higher castes, and from the filthy habits and almost hopeless degradation of the agricultural slaves." [78] "They are industrious, simpleminded people, rude, unskillful, and somewhat coarse in person and habits," reported a Tinnevelly missionary in 1851, "yet they are neither destitute of shrewdness nor insensible to kindness. They seem to have been the sponge squeezed out on all occasions of emergency by the native chiefs of former times; and long oppression has rendered them suspicious and covetous." [79] In the eyes of the missionaries who came to work among them, abstinence was surely a saving feature of the caste. "It is worthy of remark, that the Shanars who extract the palmyra juice, which when allowed to ferment is the ordinary intoxicating drink of the Hindu drunkard,

[76] Quoted in William Robinson (ed.), *Ringeltaube, the Rishi* . . . (Sheffield, 1902), p. 69; see also C. M. Agur, *Church History of Travancore* (Madras, 1901), p. 490; Robert Caldwell, *Records of the Early History of the Tinnevelly Mission* (Madras, 1881), p. 141.
[77] Extract from the journal of Charles Rhenius, dated 1822. *Memoir of the Rev. C. T. E. Rhenius* . . . (London, 1841), p. 241.
[78] Caldwell, *Lectures on the Tinnevelly Mission*, p. 45.
[79] George Pettitt, *Tinnevelly Mission* . . . (London, 1851), p. 481.

avoid the use of it in its fermented state as carefully as the most punctilious Brahmins." [80]

In the eyes of the missionaries, the Nadars were nevertheless a degraded community, long-suffering, and in darkness. "The Shanars are, as a class," wrote one missionary, "timid, deceitful, and ignorant." [81] Another reported to the Society for the Propagation of the Gospel in 1854 that "the character of the Tinnevelly Shanars . . . is among the worst types of the human family. A people more abandoned to lying, more practiced adepts in perjury, deception, and the worst features of vice, it would not be easy to find." [82] Caldwell had "no hesitation in asserting that if there be any vice or crime which is not habitually practiced by the Shanars, their abstinence from it is either from want of predilection for that particular crime or vice, through their intellectual dullness, or their cowardice, or from prudential regard to the authority of human laws." [83] Writing in 1849, Caldwell described the most prominent feature in the character of the Nadars as "downright indolence." "They cannot bear to make experiments, or calculate possibilities of advantage; they cannot bear the trouble of thinking," wrote Caldwell. "It is *their custom* to idle away half their time; to do their work in a clumsy, wasteful manner; to be contented with the trade and position of life with which their forefathers were content; to be always in debt and to live from hand to mouth." [84]

Admitting he was not familiar with "the wild hill-people," Caldwell said that, of all the castes he had met with, "down to the very lowest in the social scale . . . , none can be compared with the Shanars for dullness of apprehension and confusion of ideas." [85] The Shanars are as a class "the least intellectual to be found in India." They are "not only unable to read, but unwilling to learn or to allow their children to learn. The only persons who know one letter from another belong to the class of Nadan land-

[80] Caldwell, *Tinnevelly Shanars*, 1st ed., p. 38.

[81] Mateer, *Land of Charity*, pp. 41–42.

[82] J. F. Kearns, "Moodaloor Mission Report, 1824." Manuscript (Society for the Propagation of the Gospel).

[83] Caldwell, *Tinnevelly Shanars*, 1st ed., p. 38.

[84] *Ibid.*, pp. 56–57.

[85] *Ibid.*, pp. 62–63.

owners—men of property and substance, whose pecuniary interests would suffer if at least one of the family were not able to sign his name and keep notes of his accounts. Even amongst persons of this class," Caldwell noted, "not more than one in ten is found to have acquired this ability. . . ." Most commonly, these Nadans joined together to employ a man of high caste, usually a Vellala, as an accountant. Among the other classes of Nadars, Caldwell had "not met with or heard of any individual remaining in heathenism who had learned to read." [86]

In his *Reminiscences*, Caldwell recalled the conditions of the Nadar community when he first arrived in Edeyengoody in 1841. "I found the people of the place in a very low state of civilization. . . . They were all accustomed to work with their hands, not with the heads—most of them with both their hands and feet in climbing the palmyra—and had neither the leisure nor inclination for intellectual culture." The cultural level of the people he worked with was no lower than those of the surrounding villages, some of which were inhabited by the Nadans who considered themselves superior in social standing. "There was a village a few miles off called Kuttam, inhabited then as now by people of the highest division of the Shanars, but the only difference between them and the people of Edeyengoody was in regard to wealth. There was no difference in regard to culture or policy. . . ." [87]

If, in the early nineteenth century, there was little variation in cultural achievement among the groups within the Nadar community, there were significant differences in position and status. The Nadars were divided among themselves by geography, by subcaste, and by the major class division which separated the climbers from the Nadans. The general lack of adequate transport and communications facilities, together with the dangers of banditry and almost constant war among the poligars in the period before the British, had precluded the development of extensive horizontal ties over a wide area among members of the community. Even within the region of their greatest concentration, the *teris* of Tiruchendur, the

[86] *Ibid.*, p. 61.
[87] J.L. Wyatt (ed.), *Reminiscences of Bishop Caldwell* (Madras, 1894), p. 84.

Nadars were isolated one village from another by the difficulty of traversing the shifting sands. The boundaries of the *nadu* were, for most, the end of their social, economic, and political world.

In these circumscribed regions of Nadar dominance, the community's contact with other castes was minimal. The salient divisions of social and economic life were not between castes but within the Nadar community. Within the area of the *nadu*, the position of the Nadan landowners was unchallenged by the dependent and subservient climbers. Every form of social interaction between the two groups served symbolically to emphasize the distance which separated them. The very relationships of inequality which served to create barriers within the community, however, acted to bind the classes together. The symbiotic, if unequal, relationship between the climber and the Nadan served to link each level of Nadar society into solidary vertical structures. These structures of dependence divided the community vertically, as each Nadan sought to consolidate his client group in opposition to others for control of the land. Political life was factional, with Nadar against Nadar. Thus, within the localized region, the community was divided by factions which served, at once, to link and to unite disparate economic classes and to divide each class within itself.

The Nadars recognized themselves vaguely as "the sons of Bhadrakali," but the distinctions made within the caste were far more significant interactionally than the broader distinction between the Nadar community and other castes. Fragmented as they were, the Nadars of this parochial political culture lacked self-conscious awareness of themselves as a community. This consciousness began to emerge, however, in the early nineteenth century with the community's struggle to uplift itself and to secure advantage of the new economic and educational opportunities of British India. An instrumental role in the Nadars' initial struggle to rise was played by the European missionary.

Chapter II

CHRISTIANITY AND CHANGE

THE MISSIONARY INFLUENCE

Of the early European missionaries in India, the Jesuits working among the pearl fishers of the Tuticorin coast were the first to encounter the Nadars. In 1680, the first congregation of Nadars was started at Vadakkankulam, in what is now Nanguneri taluq, with the conversion of a Nadar woman; a church was built in 1685; and a permanent mission was established in 1701. By 1713, there were more than four thousand Christians in the Vadakkankulam parish, nearly all of whom were Nadars.[1] "By its number and its wealth," wrote the resident missionary of the parish, "the Shanar caste is in comparison with all other castes admirably adapted to Christianity. In fact the Shanans easily observe the Christian practices. The nature of their life, the necessity of climbing palmyras, preserves them from laziness, the fountain of all disorders. Besides, they are gifted with an excellent disposition, most inclined to religious matters."[2]

The history of the Anglican missionary efforts in Tinnevelly begins in 1771, as an offshoot of the Society for the Promotion of Christian Knowledge "English Mission" at Tanjore and Trichinopoly. It was not until 1791, however, that the resident missionary was sent to take charge of the district. Before the arrival of the European missionaries, the pastoral and evangelic work of the district was entirely in the charge of catechists, of whom Satyanathan was the most prominent. Missionaries made only an occasional visit; native pastors, such as Rayappan, came with greater frequency.[3]

It was Rayappan, in 1784, who made the first converts to the

[1] F. J. Western, "Early History of the Tinnevelly Church" [c. 1950], p. 31. (Mimeographed.)

[2] Father Calini, 1716, quoted in H. R. Pate, *Madras District Gazetteers: Tinnevelly* (Madras, 1917), p. 495.

[3] Western, p. 55; Pate, pp. 93–95.

Protestant religion among the Nadars, baptizing two families at a village near Tiruchendur. In 1789, six Nadars were among those baptized at Tuticorin, and in 1794, another Nadar was baptized at Palamcottah. It was not until the arrival of a young Nadar cate- chist that the efforts of the missionaries made any real impression upon the Nadar community. Sundaram, who later as "David" be- came the first Nadar catechist, was born in a small village near Sattankulam in the heart of the palmyra country of southeastern Tinnevelly. As a youth, he left his village, wandering as far as Tanjore. There he encountered Christianity and was instructed in the faith and baptized. In 1796, in response to Satyanathan's appli- cation for an assistant, the head of the English mission in Tanjore sent David to Palamcottah as a catechist, and shortly thereafter he was sent to a village near his own birthplace. In March, 1797, a few Nadars of the village had placed themselves under Christian in- struction. Persecuted, the converts left the village to occupy a piece of land purchased for them by David in 1799 in the name of the European missionary. The first Christian settlement in Tinne- velly, it was called Mudalur, "first town." The population was twenty-eight.[4]

Other Christian settlements soon followed, such as Bethlehem and Nazareth, and by 1803, more than five thousand Nadars in southeastern Tinnevelly had been converted to Christianity.[5] The converts were persecuted by the Nadans, who used their economic grip over the climbers to oppose the missionary efforts. Disre- garding the advice of his superiors, the Nadar catechist David, with the support of a sympathetic European merchant named Sawyer, organized a group called "club-men," and "went about from place to place redressing the wrongs to the native Christians by force." Soon thereafter, David died in Bethlehem, allegedly of poison administered to him "through the instigation of some Nadans of Kuttam, who wished to be revenged upon him."[6] After his death,

[4] Western, pp. 89–94; Robert Caldwell, *A Political and General History of Tinnevelly* (Madras, 1881), pp. 246–247; Caldwell, *Records of the Early History of the Tinnevelly Mission* (Madras, 1881), pp. 55–63.

[5] Pate, pp. 93–94.

[6] Caldwell, *Records of the Early History*, p. 100.

the number of conversions among the Nadars began to decline. About this same time, four years after he took over the Tinnevelly Mission, William Ringeltaube left for southern Travancore under charge of the London Missionary Society.[7] In the year of his departure, 1810, heavy rains and severe flooding in Tinnevelly and Ramnad districts brought a malarial epidemic, followed by famine. The Society for the Promotion of Christian Knowledge, (S.P.C.K.) responsible for the Tinnevelly Mission, was unable to resume its activities. By 1816, when the Church Missionary Society (C.M.S.) appointed a chaplain at Palamcottah, half of the converts had given up Christianity.[8]

The Church Missionary Society started schools and immediately began to revive missionary efforts among the Nadars. "The inhabitants of this wild country are Shanars," the chaplain wrote to the C.M.S., and are "more inclined to embrace the Christian Faith than any caste of natives which I have hitherto seen." [9] In 1830, the "Dharma Sangam," or Philosophical Society, was established for the purchase of lands and houses for converts. Some of the sites were donated by people belonging to the mission. Others were purchased directly with mission funds. The merchant, Sawyer, who had befriended the young catechist David, died in 1816, leaving lands to the mission which became the village of Sawyerpuram.[10] On the new mission lands, the missionaries tried to build model Christian villages, with straight streets, parallel to each other and intersecting at right angles. Trees were planted, wells dug, and gardens cultivated. In many of the villages, the houses, well ventilated and with sanitary facilities, were built around the mission compound. Some of the Christian settlements, such as Megnanapuram, were separate villages; others, such as Christianagram by Udankudi, were but distinct sections of a larger village. All the

[7] F. Baylis, "The South Travancore Tamil Missions," in *Proceedings of the South India Mission Conference,* 1858 (Madras, 1858), p. 6.

[8] Western, pp. 135–136; Pate, p. 94.

[9] James Hough, quoted in *Proceedings of the Church Missionary Society, 1820–21* (London, 1821), p. 154.

[10] Paul Appasamy, *Centenary History of the C.M.S. in Tinnevelly* (Palamcottah, 1923), pp. 22–23.

new Christian villages in the southeast were overwhelmingly Nadar.[11]

In 1824, the S.P.C.K. transferred the responsibilities of its mission in Tinnevelly to the Society for the Propagation of the Gospel in Foreign Parts (S.P.G.). Only in 1836, however, did the S.P.G. send its first English missionary to the district, and from that date, a regular succession of missionaries followed, from both the S.P.G. and the C.M.S. The two societies, after initial friction as the native pastors of each attempted to "appropriate" the others' congregations and property, divided their respective mission fields. Although the C.M.S. obtained the greater area, the S.P.G. received the regions of greatest Nadar concentration in the southeastern taluqs of Tiruchendur, Nanguneri, and Srivaikuntam.[12]

In 1841, a young Scottish missionary, Robert Caldwell (1814–1891), was sent to Tinnevelly by the Society for the Propagation of the Gospel. Until his death, Caldwell, who was consecrated as the first bishop of Tinnevelly in 1877, lived and worked among the Nadars, with enormous influence on the community's history. In his *Reminiscences*, Caldwell described his first encounter with the Nadars, at Madurai in 1841. "I could not but be struck first by their long ears," he wrote, "long pendant earrings, long hair tied in a knot behind the head like the women. The presents of sugar candy, and their graceful salaam with folded hands. I was struck also by their mild, subdued expression, so different from the rough forwardness I had been accustomed to further north." [13] The village where he was to establish his mission was Idaiyangudi (or Edeyengoody), south of Sattankulam. The village name meant "shepherds' abode," though it was almost entirely Nadar in population.[14]

At about the time of Caldwell's arrival in Tinnevelly, a "mass movement" began among the Nadars as they converted to Christianity, not as single individuals or families, but as entire villages.

[11] Mary Devapackiam, "The History of the Early Christian Settlements in Tinnevelly District" (unpublished Master's dissertation, Department of Tamil, University of Madras, 1963), pp. 122–123.

[12] Pate, pp. 94–95.

[13] J. L. Wyatt, *Reminiscences of Bishop Caldwell* (Madras, 1894), p. 77.

[14] Wyatt, pp. 79–80; Devapackiam, pp. 73–76.

"Without priests; without a written religious code; without sacred traditions; without historic recollections; without aversion to Christianity as a foreign religion which other classes evince," Caldwell wrote, "[t]hey have always been found more willing to be guided, controlled, and moulded by its principles, than any other class; and the number of this one caste that have placed themselves under Christian instruction is greater than that of all the other converts in India, in connexion with all Protestant Missions." By 1849, "nearly 40,000 souls in Tinnevelly alone, in connexion with the Church Missionary Society and the Society for the Propagation of the Gospel, and about 20,000 souls in south Travancore, in connexion with the London Missionary Society, have abandoned the demonolatry received by tradition from their fathers." [15] The "mass movement" of the 1840's was followed by another period of great missionary activity, after the famine of 1877. In the next six years, the S.P.G. mission in Tinnevelly doubled its numbers—from 22,000 to 44,000—almost all of whom were drawn from the Nadar community.[16] By the end of the century, Tinnevelly had the greatest number of Christians in Madras Presidency, divided about equally between the Roman Catholics and the Protestants. Among the Protestants, as many as 95 percent were Nadars, and of the 92 ordained native clergymen, 75 were Nadars. "This tends to create a dangerous monopoly," wrote Arthur Margöschis, as "people actually now speak of 'the Shanar Church.' " [17] "The sandy districts in the south-east teem with human life," wrote Caldwell, "and it is . . . amongst the inhabitants of these districts that Christianity has made greatest progress. Hitherto, from a variety of causes, Christianity and the palmyra have appeared to flourish to-

[15] Robert Caldwell, *The Tinnevelly Shanars*, 1st ed. (Madras, 1849), pp. 71–72. Caldwell's figures include all those under instruction and not baptized Christians alone.

[16] M. A. Sherring, *The History of Protestant Missions in India* . . . (London, 1884), p. 334; J. A. Sharrock, *South Indian Missions* (London, 1910), p. 49.

[17] "Tinnevelly: Being an Account of the District, the People, and the Missions," *Mission Field*, XLII (October, 1897), 390–391; also see Robert Caldwell, "Fifth Annual Letter to the Bishop of Madras, dated 1882," in *Indian Churchman* (Calcutta), New Series, III (February 3, 1883), 75. Here he speaks of such "excessive preponderance" of Nadars that the mission has become known as the "Shanar Mission"; J. S. Ponniah *et al.*, *The Christian Community of Madura, Ramnad and Tinnevelly* (Madurai, 1938), pp. 28–33.

gether. Where the palmyra abounds, there Christian congregations and schools abound also; and where the palmyra disappears, there the signs of Christian progress are rarely seen." [18]

As most of the Christian converts in Tinnevelly were Nadars, and either owners or climbers of the palmyra, Caldwell assembled his congregation at the commencement of the climbing season for a special service, "including prayers that the tree might yield its fruit, and that the climber's 'foot might not slide' . . ." [19] During the service a set of implements used in the occupation of climbing was brought to the altar. It was felt "that a religious service of the kind was particularly acceptable, and particularly appropriate to our people." [20]

The missionaries made little headway among the lowest orders of the Nadar community. In speaking of the Kalla Shanars, Caldwell said that, with a few honorable exceptions, they had made little progress toward Christianity. "I have always found them peculiarly slow in learning, careless of order and decency, and difficult to manage." [21] The "mass movement" among the Nadars came out of the middle range of the community, primarily from among the climbers, who though living at a near subsistence level, were neither destitute nor, like the Kallas, enslaved to the Nadans.[22]

A number of factors can account for the great response of the Nadars to the missionary efforts. In southeastern Tinnevelly, the Nadar community was overwhelmingly dominant in numbers, hence had little contact with other castes. Although the Nadars were degraded in the eyes of the higher castes, they occupied a middle position and, in the areas of their geographic concentration, maintained a high degree of autonomy. As a community, they were thus more able to respond freely to the missionaries. Further, as they converted in large numbers, often by villages, they risked

[18] Robert Caldwell, *Lectures on the Tinnevelly Mission* (London, 1857), p. 31.
[19] *Ibid.*, p. 37.
[20] Arthur Margöschis, quoted in Edgar Thurston, *Castes and Tribes of Southern India* (Madras, 1909), VI, 375.
[21] Robert Caldwell, "Report of the Edeiyengoody District for the year ending 30 June 1845." Manuscript (S.P.G.), reprinted in *Mission of Edyenkoody*.
[22] Interview, Bishop Jebaraj of Tinnevelly, Palamcottah.

none of the sufferings of being outcast by their own community. They could take Christianity and keep caste too.[23]

The Nadars, Caldwell wrote, "are peculiarly docile and tractable, peculiarly fitted to appreciate the advantages of sympathy, guidance, and protection, and are peculiarly accessible to Christian influences."[24] The advantages of Christianity became rapidly apparent to the Nadar climbers, as the material conditions of their Christian neighbors began to improve. "The establishment of British rule in India was a real boon to this people," wrote a Tinnevelly missionary, "the value of which, however, they but imperfectly understood, till Christian knowledge and education opened their eyes and raised their character; and till, in cases of oppression arising among our earlier converts, it was demonstrated that even the Shanan with the advice of his Christian teacher, could obtain justice and enjoy protection."[25] Another missionary at about the same time described the vast improvements among those who embraced Christianity, saying that above all Christianity had "taught them to feel they are superior to what they originally considered themselves to be."[26] "Though the missionaries in Tinnevelly did not directly aim at gaining converts from heathenism by promoting the welfare of their people in the things pertaining to this life, the temporal advantages of a Christian profession could not but make an impression on the minds of the neighbouring heathen." These temporal advantages included, in the European view:

the expectation of receiving from the missionary of their district advice on difficulties, sympathy in adversity, and help in sickness, and of being at all times friendly inquired after and kindly spoken to; the desire of being connected with a rising, united body, guided by European intelligence, and governed by principles of Christian justice; the expectation of being protected in some measure from the oppressions of their wealthy neighbours; the fact that Native Christians appear after a few years to acquire a higher standing and

23 Joseph Mullens, *A Brief Review of Ten Years' Missionary Labour in India between 1852 and 1861* (London, 1863), pp. 110-111.
24 Caldwell, *Lectures on the Tinnevelly Mission*, pp. 45-46.
25 George Pettitt, *Tinnevelly Mission of the Church Missionary Society* (London, 1851), pp. 481-482.
26 J. F. Kearns, "Moodaloor Mission: Report, 1854." Manuscript (S.P.G.).

to enjoy more peace and prosperity than they had as heathens; the desire of advancement on the part of the lower castes, who find that they are considered by the missionaries as capable of advancement and taught to feel that they are men. . . .[27]

While a few Nadans placed themselves under Christian instruction, and some led their entire villages to embrace Christianity, the Nadans as a class opposed the missionaries. The Reverend J. L. Wyatt, son-in-law of Caldwell, wrote in the *Mission Field* that the Nadans "will not stoop to embrace a religion which is offered to their dependents and slaves as well as to themselves; while many of these dependents and slaves are afraid to adopt a creed which their lords do not patronize." [28] Caldwell noted that "the majority of the wealthier sort of Shanars—those who call themselves by a name signifying 'lord of the soil'—are not Christians, show no intention, generally speaking, of becoming Christians, and are in some instances as much opposed to the idea of actually joining the Christian Church as any class of people in the country." [29]

Regarding the Christian converts "as the adherents of a political party or local faction," the Nadans were fearful of the missions, and with their wealth and influence, often sought to deter poorer members of the caste from joining the movement.[30] Some of the Nadans gave their support to the Vibuthi Sangam, the Sacred Ash Society, which was founded in Tiruchendur during the "mass movement" of the 1840's to put an end to the wholesale conversions. Each person received into the society, composed predominantly of Brahmins and Vellalas, took an oath of allegiance to the gods to oppose the spread of Christianity.[31] As disturbances broke out and charges were leveled from all sides against the Tinnevelly

[27] George Pettitt, "The Tinnevelly Mission," *Madras Quarterly Missionary Journal*, New Series, II (October, 1851), 163–164. For a discussion of the new religious sect as a means for breaking with subordinate status, see H. Richard Niehbur, *The Social Sources of Denominationalism* (New York, 1929).

[28] *Mission Field*, XV (August, 1870), 231.

[29] Robert Caldwell, "Ten Years in Tinnevelly: a Missionary's Review," *Mission Field*, XVII (October, 1872), 303.

[30] Caldwell, quoted in Joseph Mullens, *A Brief Review* . . . , p. 183.

[31] Appasamy, *op. cit.* (n. 10 above), p. 86. While the Vibuthi Sangam was confined to Tinnevelly, a larger group, the Society for Diffusing the Philosophy of the Four Vedas (or the "Salen Street Society") was organized in Madras to combat Christianity. See Pettitt, *The Tinnevelly Mission* . . . , pp. 253–271.

missionaries, from among the Nadars there arose in 1844 a short nativistic reaction to Christianity, as a soothsayer, Alagappa Nadan, proclaimed himself a "champion of heathenism." [32]

By the 1860's the opposition of the Nadans to Christianity began to wane. They found that the benefits of the faith improved the lot of the climbers, and some of the poorer among the Nadans began to respond favorably to the missionaries. "A considerable proportion of those who have joined us during the year," wrote Caldwell in 1860, "consists of young men belonging to the higher division of the Shanars. . . ." [33] A few years later, a native pastor reported the change in Kuttam, a village of wealthy Nadans which had long given the mission great difficulty. "It appears to me . . . ," he wrote, "that a great improvement is going on among the heathen Nadans. Those Nadans who disliked to converse with Christians are now very willing to admit them into their houses. . . ." [34] Nadan women of Kuttam even arranged for their daughters to be received into the mission schools. [35] Although few of the Nadans actually converted to Christianity, their opposition declined as the responsibility and standing of the Christian community rose.

EDUCATION AND ECONOMIC CHANGE
AMONG NADAR CHRISTIANS

By the mid-nineteenth century, rapid strides had been made in education, and of the boys enrolled in the mission schools, nearly one-third were non-Christian. [36] In the years following 1820, when twelve Nadar youths were entered for teacher training, "as the inhabitants of the palmyra forest preferred Shanar Christians to teach them," [37] the number of Nadar teachers and native pastors

[32] Appasamy, *op. cit.*, p. 90.

[33] Robert Caldwell, "Native Education in Tinnevelly," *Mission Field*, V (September, 1860), 194–195.

[34] Report by G. Paranjothy, Taruvel, in *Report of the Madras Diocesan Committee of the S.P.G., 1877–78* (Madras, 1878).

[35] Letter from Mrs. Robert Caldwell, *ibid.*, p. 23.

[36] Among the Christians, almost as many girls as boys were registered, but the idea of female education among the Hindus had made little headway. Caldwell, *Tinnevelly Shanars*, 2d ed., Appendix, p. 2.

[37] Ponniah, *Christian Community of Madura, Ramnad and Tinnevelly*, p. 38.

grew rapidly to a substantial majority of the profession in the district.

Although the Nadars remained poor, wrote Caldwell in 1869, Christianity "promoted their education and enlightenment . . . their position has been greatly improved, and many spheres of uesful, remunerative, and honorable labour which were formerly closed against them are now almost as open to them as to any other class in the community."[38] The opening of sugar refineries at Cuddalore and elsewhere brought an increased price for jaggery, and the opening of the coffee estates in Ceylon brought new money into Tinnevelly as the poorer Nadars responded to the opportunities for profitable labor.[39] The Ceylon plantations opened up in the 1830's, and by 1839, there was systematic recruitment in Madras for laborers. The response was initially slow, but it soon accelerated. Between 1843 and 1867, nearly one and one-half million emigrated from Madras to Ceylon, and of these more than half returned to purchase lands or shops in Madras.[40] Systematic migration to Malaya and the Straits Settlements for plantation work began in 1833,[41] with many going as indentured servants. In 1844, a number of coffee estates were laid out in the Nanguneri hills, and as they developed, they drew large numbers of laborers from the surrounding country.[42]

A substantial number of the emigrants to Ceylon and to Malaya were Tinnevelly Nadars. It is from the unproductive regions of Nanguneri, Tiruchendur, and Srivaikuntam, Pate wrote in the *Tinnevelly Gazetteer*, "that members of the labouring classes migrate in thousands every year to the tea and rubber estates of Ceylon."[43] Of the Nadar migrants, the greatest number were drawn from the Christian community.[44] During the period of

[38] Robert Caldwell, *Tinnevelly and the Tinnevelly Mission* (Madras, 1869), p. 9.
[39] Caldwell, *Tinnevelly Shanars*, 1st ed., p. 55.
[40] Dharma Kumar, *Land and Caste in South India: Agricultural Labour in Madras Presidency in the Nineteenth Century* (Cambridge, 1965), pp. 128–129.
[41] *Ibid.*, p. 131.
[42] Pate, *Madras District Gazetteers: Tinnevelly*, p. 5.
[43] Pp. 193–194; also see Gilbert Slater, *Some South Indian Villages* (Madras, 1918), pp. 15–16.
[44] Ponniah, *Christian Community* . . . , p. 40.

their labor abroad or in the plantations of the Western Ghats, they made remittances to their families in Tinneveily, if not every month, at least several times a year. As soon as they were economically able, the Nadars would abandon climbing and hire someone to climb the trees for them, or seek a more respectable occupation as a petty shopkeeper or as a cultivator. By 1871, a British settlement officer wrote to the collector of Tinnevelly that "in these days . . . many Shanars have nothing to do with climbing" and that "through the increased wealth and comfort of the Shanars as a class, owing to the spread of education among them, and remunerative means of subsistence, it has become every year more difficult for owners of palmyrahs to get people to climb trees." [45] Migrant climbers from southern Travancore were already being brought in for the Tinnevelly season, but lack of climbers left an increasing number of trees untapped.[46]

From the middle of the nineteenth century on, there was an enormous increase in the number of land titles held by Nadars. Where once the landowners among them were limited to the aristocratic Nadan families, there were now thousands of small landowners.[47] The plots were often minute, but they were intensely cultivated for garden crops, such as chillies, onion, and betel-vine. These garden plots in the middle of the desolate *teri* country were watered from deep wells. "If water exists under the ground," wrote Pate, "a Shanan will find it, and will quickly convert into a luxuriant garden a patch of poor soil, which, in the time

---

[45] Letter to the collector from W. A. Symonds, March 25, 1871, quoted in *Selections from the Records . . . on Palmyra Plantations*, p. 94.

The decline of tapping among the Christian Nadars was revealed in a survey of the community in the southern districts taken in 1941. The survey reported that "about 40 per cent of the Nadars of the Tinnevelly District are estimated to be engaged in tapping, but among Christian Nadars, tappers would form only about 20 per cent since, as a result of education and development of trade with Ceylon, several families have given up this vocation." Ponniah, *Christian Community*, pp. 96-97.

[46] Southern Travancore was affected, as well, by the abandonment of climbing. Thurston, in his *Castes and Tribes* (VI, 376), quotes an article in the *Madras Mail* of 1901, saying that the Nadar Christians of that region had, in many cases, "given up tapping the palmyra palm for jaggery and toddy as a profession beneath them; and the example is spreading so that a real economic *impasse* is manifesting itself."

[47] Pate, *Tinnevelly Gazetteer*, pp. 128-129.

of its previous owner, had been a dreary waste." [48] In the *teris*, there were also scattered lakes which collected water from the northeast monsoon. Around the edges of these lakes, the Nadar cultivators quickly planted their gardens, and as the lake evaporated during the dry season, water was bailed for the crops of plantains, vegetables, and even paddy, forming "a fringe of luxuriant green around the lake." [49]

Some of the Tinnevelly Nadars engaged in trade, and Caldwell indicated that "a few of the more wealthy, perhaps twenty persons in various localities, are said to be worth about £1000. . . ." But, he added, "the Nadans and wealthy traders form but a small proportion of the caste; and the poverty of the mass is great and unquestionable. They are rarely in danger of starvation, but are never raised more than a few degrees above it." [50] The Christian Nadars, like the vast majority of their Hindu kinsmen, remained near the subsistence level as climbers or as marginal agriculturalists. Of the two groups, however, the Christians enjoyed a substantially improved position. Through education and migration, they enjoyed a slightly higher economic position, and through their unity in the mission organization they had been able to improve their general standard of living. Where the Hindu Nadars were divided, often without a single village authority, into client groups dominated by influential and powerful Nadans, each in constant dispute and litigation with the other, the Christians, under the direction of the missionaries, sought to achieve unity among themselves for the discipline and well-being of all.

The missionary of Mudalur described the village authority with regard to "worldly matters" as "self-supporting and self-controlled." A council of elders met once a week to "examine into all the complaints and troubles of the people." A smaller body of five village leaders constituted "a court of appeal" and exercised supervision over the local police. In the missionary's view, these two bodies saved him "from entering needlessly into the worldly affairs

[48] Pate, *Ibid.*, pp. 128–129, 157.
[49] *Ibid.*, pp. 496–497.
[50] *Tinnevelly Shanars*, 1st ed., p. 48.

of the people." [51] The ultimate appeal in all disputes, however, inevitably came before the missionaries, and in many villages, the local catechist or resident missionary took a daily hand in the local affairs. Bishop Cotton of Calcutta described the organization of the Tinnevelly missions: "When a village becomes Christian, it forms itself at once into a Christian municipality, in which Church and State are united together. . . . The catechist is received as the counsellor and director of the headman; and the missionary, resident at the central station of the district, is recognized as the superintendent of all the communities scattered through it." [52]

The Bishop illustrated "the complete acquiescence of the people" to the missionary's rule by a story of a government inspector's visit to a Christian school. Inquiring into the political knowledge of the children, the inspector asked, "Who has the chief authority in this country?" "The Queen," the children dutifully replied, as they had been taught in the catechism. "But she is 10,000 miles away," said the inspector. "Who carries on the government in the country itself?" "The Queen sends her orders to the missionaries," came the reply. "To the missionaries!" exclaimed the horrified inspector. "Is there not a great man who lives at Madras and rules over this part of India?" "Yes, sir," the children responded happily, "the Bishop." [53]

THE BREAST-CLOTH CONTROVERSY

The European missionaries working among the Nadars offered them not only the gospel of a new religion, but also the possibility of secular salvation in release from the fetters of the tradition which had for centuries burdened them with social disabilities and economic dependence. The earliest movement for social uplift among the Nadar community came in their response to the efforts of the London Missionary Society in southern Travancore. Here

[51] T. H. Suter, "Annual Report of the Muthaloor Mission, 1856," dated March 22, 1857. Manuscript (S.P.G.).

[52] Bishop G. E. L. Cotton, *The Tinnevelly Mission* (1884) (reprinted from *The Calcutta Review*), pp. 14–15.

[53] *Ibid.*

the mission field was so predominantly Nadar that in 1820, the
year following the founding of the Nagercoil church, nearly all of
the three thousand people who had placed themselves under instruction were Nadars.[54]

The Nadars of southern Travancore, like their brothers in Tinnevelly, were largely palmyra-climbers. A significant number,
however, were subtenants to the Nair landlords and, in the regions
to the east, bordering Tinnevelly District, to the Vellala landlords.
In this eastern region, particularly Agestheswaram, nearly a score
of Nadan families held control over the lands, claiming special
titles.[55] Charles Mead, "the father of the South Travancore Mission," described the principal man of one village as a Nadan who
possessed "a great abundance of 'the good things of life,' and [was]
much respected for his peaceable behavior by all classes." His
wealth consisted of lands and cattle, and his holding was considered
"very extensive for a person of his caste." [56]

In the traditions of these families the lands were bestowed by the
kings of Travancore in return for the Nadans' services.[57] Many
Nadan families claimed that they had come at the invitation of the
king and considered themselves socially superior to the larger community, which had surely migrated into the southern taluqs of
Travancore in economic need. The migration undoubtedly occurred quite early, perhaps during the sixteenth century when the
Travancore king held control of the southern region of Tinnevelly, including the sandy wastes of Manadu. In the more luxuriant
lands of Travancore, these Nadars continued as palmyra-climbers,
laboring on the lands of aristocratic Nadans or Vellalas in the
eastern portion of Kanyakumari and, toward the west, on the lands
of the powerful Nair community. Although Travancore offered a
more hospitable country geographically, the Nadars fared little
better than in Tinnevelly. The vast majority were severely depressed economically and suffered the social degradation of a low
caste in the rigid hierarchy of ritual purity.

[54] G. T. Mackenzie, *Christianity in Travancore* (Trivandrum, 1901), p. 51.
[55] V. Nagam Aiya, *Travancore State Manual* (Trivandrum, 1906), II, 393.
[56] Letter to the London Missionary Society, dated Neyoor, August 22, 1831.
Manuscript (London Missionary Society, hereafter cited as L.M.S.).
[57] Manuscript prepared by Raj Kumar Swamidoss, New Delhi, September, 1964.

Persons of low caste in Travancore were not permitted to approach those of higher status, and fixed distances were prescribed for each caste. A Nadar must remain thirty-six paces from a Nambudiri Brahmin, and must come no closer than twelve to a Nair.[58] As members of a degraded caste, Nadars were prohibited from carrying an umbrella, and from wearing shoes or golden ornaments. Their houses could not be higher than one story. They were not allowed to milk cows; Nadar women were not permitted to carry pots of water on their hips, as was the custom among the higher castes; nor were they permitted to cover the upper portions of their bodies.[59] They were subjected to heavy taxation, and while they were not enslaved, as were the Paraiyans, the Nadars were forced to perform corvée labor in service to the state. The economic dependence of the Nadar climber or cultivator on his landlord bound him to the lowest levels of society, but to the climber the alternate palmyra seasons of Travancore and Tinnevelly offered seasonal migration to Tinnevelly for employment.

The migrant climbers' contact with more socially advanced regions of British India only made the yoke of Nair domination in Travancore weigh more heavily, opening the community to the missionary efforts. Writing to the London Missionary Society, a missionary in Nagercoil proclaimed that "the whole Shanar community, amounting together to about 150,000, is open to us. . . ." With regard to the progress of the mission among the "long-degraded and despised body," he wrote that if the Shanars "continue to grow in mind, intelligence, and character, they must gain influence, and that influence must be felt, and felt for good. . . . Already other Castes are beginning to be jealous of the advantages the Shanars are gaining from their connexion with us." [60]

The Nadars did indeed advance under the protection of the missionaries, but the progress was not always viewed so favorably.

58 Samuel Mateer, *The Land of Charity* . . . (New York, 1870), p. 32; the distances of approach are subject to disagreement. J. Wilson, in his *Indian Caste* (1877), indicated a separation of 24 rather than 36 paces. Cited in J. H. Hutton, *Caste in India* (Cambridge, 1946), p. 70.

59 Mateer, *Land of Charity*, p. 41.

60 W. H. Drew, letter dated Nagercoil, April 6, 1846, in *The Missionary Magazine and Chronicle* (London), X (July, 1846), 100.

Charles Mead wrote, in 1851, "We have raised them in a civil point of view—delivered them from unjust taxes and oppressive customs and a grievous poll tribute, the cause of much cruelty in its collection—but as to mind they are generally as debased as ever. The best instructed have often turned out the worst characters. . . ." [61] Another missionary, writing of his twenty-two years' experience in southern Travancore, shared Mead's doubts:

> The Shanars, . . . although in an oppressed and degraded condition, had many proud references to a noble ancestry and were not only capable of mental improvement, but also exceedingly ambitious to hold positions of importance, and take a part in the government of the country. The more wealthy members of this class would assert that they were originally the ruling powers of the kingdom; and, in consequence of this opinion, would rule over the lower castes with an authority and an assumption of superiority which would be tamely submitted to by those whom they oppressed; in their turn, the Shanars, however rich or influential in their sphere, would submit to the Nairs, addressing them by the same terms of abject servility by which they themselves were accustomed to be called by the degraded pariahs. The Shanars, however, as a class, were not satisfied with their position, and how far this circumstance may have induced them so readily to give in their adherence in large numbers to a profession of Christianity in the early days of our mission, I am not prepared to say . . . the Shanar is very exclusive in his feelings, looking with contempt on those below him, and with jealousy on those who are his social superiors. [62]

With the aid of the missionaries, the Nadars extracted themselves from many of the burdensome taxes and from the corvée labor demanded by the government. But, more important, they began to advance economically. Some of the Nadars turned to trade and secured sufficient wealth to purchase their own lands. [63] Others purchased land with financial assistance from the mission. In the years following the establishment of the mission in South Travancore, the Nadar converts benefited by education and the general

[61] Letter to the London Missionary Society, dated Neyoor, October 8, 1851. Manuscript (L.M.S.).

[62] John Abbs, *Twenty-Two Years' Missionary Experience in Travancore* (London, 1870), pp. 151-152.

[63] James Russell, letter to the London Missionary Society, dated Nagercoil, January 24, 1856. Manuscript (L.M.S.), reprinted in *The Missionary Magazine and Chronicle*, XX (August, 1856), 166.

protection of the mission. Their release from the obligations of
servility and their concomitant rise in economic status aroused
antagonism and jealousy among the higher castes; even where their
economic position was not greatly improved, education and Christianity had given the Nadars hope of an escape from their sufferings under the dominance of the Nair landlords. No longer isolated
in their economic subservience, the Nadars now found a new unity
through the organization of the Church. Supported by the European missionaries, the Nadars sought to use that strength for the
uplift of the community.

The movement for social uplift was symbolized in the Nadars'
attempt to vest themselves with the attributes of higher status, and
their efforts, beginning in the early nineteenth century, soon gave
rise to the "breast-cloth controversy." By tradition in Travancore,
the breast was bared as a symbol of respect to those of higher
status. In the elaborate hierarchy of caste ranking, the Nairs, for
example, bared their breasts before the Nambudiri Brahmins, and
the Brahmins did so only before the deity.[64] The Nadars, like all
of the lower castes, were categorically forbidden to cover their
breasts at any time. The manner of dress prescribed for the Nadars
consisted of a single cloth of coarse texture, to be worn by males
and females alike no lower than the knee nor higher than the
waist.[65] "This style of dress," a missionary wrote some years later,
"was of course incompatible with the modesty and decorum of
Christian women, many of whom had received a good education
and were taught to appear decent in public. Some of the Christian
women were so far advanced," he wrote, "that they won prizes in
the 'Great Exhibition of 1851' for the 'pillow lace.' "[66]

. As early as 1812, Colonel Munro, then resident of Travancore,
issued an order that permission be granted to "the women converted to Christianity to cover their bosoms as obtains among
Christians in other countries. . . ."[67] The government of

---

[64] Samüel Mateer, *Native Life in Travancore* (London, 1883), p. 230.
[65] Petition to His Highness the Rajah of Travancore from missionaries of the
L.M.S., February 7, 1859 (signed Rev. James Russell *et al.*), in *Brief Statement of
Gross Outrages* . . . (London, 1859), pp. 13–14.
[66] C. M. Agur, *Church History of Travancore* (Madras, 1901), p. 935.
[67] *Ibid.*, Appendix, p. 1.

Travancore issued a circular order in May, 1814, permitting the
female converts of the lower classes to cover their bodies with a
short bodice or jacket, as was worn by the women of the Syrian
Christian and Muslim Mopla communities.[68] They were not permitted to wear the upper cloth in the manner of the higher castes:
no Shanar women "were ever to be allowed to wear clothes on
their bosoms as the Nair women. . . ."[69]

The missionary wives had devised a loose jacket for the women
of the mission, which perhaps satisfied the modesty of the European ladies, but it did not meet the social aspirations of the Christian Nadar women. The Nadars of Tinnevelly wore the breast
cloth freely, and the women of Travancore would have nothing
less. Thus, in addition to the prescribed jacket, or often in lieu of it,
the Nadar women increasingly adopted the use of the upper cloth,
which was worn by the women of the higher classes. In May, 1822,
the Nairs reacted against the Nadar pretensions. "The Christian
women thus appearing in decent dress displeased their neghbours,
especially the Sudras who began to mock, abuse and ill-treat them
in various ways in markets and way sides."[70] At Pulpanabapuram,
in 1823, "a complaint was lodged against some Christians under
their heathen names as Shanars, for not paying the arrears of their
toddy-rent and for their women wearing upper cloth. . . ." The
court inquired of the missionary Charles Mead as to whether Christians were required by their religion to wear an upper cloth, and
receiving an affirmative reply, the court decided in favor of the
accused on that point.[71]

Mead, while gaining a great point in the decree, remained cau-
tious in initiating radical changes. The missionaries advised the
converts to wear the jackets alone rather than the upper cloth, but
their advice met with little success. The feelings against the Nadars
were rapidly rising, and in October, 1828, the Nairs in southern

[68] Aiya, *Travancore State Manual*, I, 525.
[69] Quoted in a letter from the government of Madras to Lord Stanley, secretary
of state for India, dated March 26, 1859, in Great Britain, *Parliamentary Papers*,
1859, Session II, XXV, No. 158, 353. East India (Travancore), *Copies of the
Official Papers* . . . , p. 3.
[70] Agur, *Church History of Travancore*, pp. 780–782.
[71] *Ibid.*

Travancore, under the leadership of a local revenue inspector, began to terrorize the Christian converts.[72] "At first threatening language was used by the heathen to deter the people from attending Christian worship," wrote Mead in his report of the situation to the London Missionary Society. Men were seized on the Sabbath for public works, schools were occasionally interrupted, the books were thrown into the streets or torn to pieces, and the women were beaten in the public bazaar for wearing the upper cloth over their bosoms, and the cloths were stripped from their bodies.[73]

The missionaries of the South Travancore Mission petitioned the British resident of Travancore to intervene, as the government had taken no action to prevent further persecution or to punish those who had started the trouble in October. "The Shanars are esteemed a low caste," the missionaries wrote, "and before their acquaintance with Christianity were in general depraved in their morals and filthy in their habits. Christianity has affected a considerable alteration in both these respects." The progress of the Shanars had an unsettling effect upon the higher castes, however. "The Soodras appear to be jealous at seeing the improvement which the Christians present in their outward appearance and habits. They are vexed likewise at the Shanars because they refuse to labour for them without pay, as they had been obliged to do while heathen."[74] Believing that the Nadars used Christianity to evade taxation and corvée labor, as well as to raise their social status, the Nairs lashed out at the mission. As rioting spread, chapels and schools were burned, and when an attempt was made on Mead's life, troops were sent into the area.[75]

The government of Travancore issued a royal proclamation on February 3, 1829, which began:

> Whereas some disturbances have taken place . . . between the Shanars and Nairs originating in a pretension of the women of the Shanars to wear the upper cloth contrary to orders and ancient customs, and in a refusal of that caste to perform the Sirkar ooliam

[72] *Ibid.*, p. 826.
[73] C. Mead, "A Report of the Neyoor Mission, July 1829," dated June 30, 1829. Manuscript (L.M.S.).
[74] Quoted in *ibid.*
[75] Agur, *Church History of Travancore*, pp. 826-844.

work required of them in common with other individuals, I deem it proper to publish the following Proclamation:

First, as it is not reasonable on the part of the Shanar women to wear cloths over their breasts, such custom being prohibited, they are required to abstain in future from covering the upper part of their body.

The proclamation confirmed the circular of 1814, and ordered that it be republished, in contravention of the court decree which was taken by the Nadars as establishing their legal right to wear the breast cloth; required that Christians perform *ooliam* service, that is, corvée labor for the government, like other sections of the population, although they might be exempted from such service on Sundays; warned the Christians that they should act toward the higher castes according to the usages before conversion; prohibited the construction of places of worship "without regular permission" of the Travancore government. The last section of the proclamation was directed against the practice of "certain Shanar converts to Christianity" seeking redress through the local missionaries. The Nadars were notified that the government authorities were the only recognized tribunals of the country, and that all complaints were to be referred only to them.[76]

The proclamation eased the situation, but it in no way deterred the Nadar Christian women from dressing in the manner of the Nairs, as had become their custom. Increasingly the women of the Hindu Nadar community in southern Travancore adopted the upper cloth as well. The women of the superior Nadan families had always worn the upper garment without opposition from the Nairs, but now, for the first time, the lower Hindu classes began to cover their breasts. One of the Nadan families in Agestheswaram which enjoyed special benefits under the Rajah earned the future contempt of the Nadar community by announcing during the controversy that they alone, as Nadans, had the right to wear the breast cloth. The lower classes, being only Shanans, had no such right.[77]

General Cullen, resident of Travancore, began to receive petitions from Hindu Shanars concerning the use of the breast cloth,

[76] Agur, *Ibid.*, pp. 843–844.
[77] Interview, Kunjam Nadar, M.L.A., Kanyakumari.

but the British government declined to intervene, as the matter was one of local caste usage.[78] Cullen suspected the missionaries of attempting to unsettle, if not altogether subvert, the existing political arrangement in the princely state of Travancore. The missionaries believed Cullen the enemy of the Church in Travancore and the opponent of the native Christians' aspiration to higher status. Cullen contended that the Nadar Christians were behind the adoption of the breast cloth by the Hindus. The missionaries denied any connection with the changes in heathen apparel, and asserted that the adoption of the upper cloth among the Hindu Nadars was the consequence of their seasonal migrations into Tinnevelly, where all women, "without molestation," wore the garment. In the regions of Travancore bordering on Tinnevelly, it had become "the rule and not the exception" to wear the breast cloth.[79]

In the eyes of the Nairs, the missionaries were surely responsible for the increased use of the upper cloth, which had become the symbol of change in southern Travancore. The Nairs' antagonism against the Nadars' social innovations and prosperity was heightened with the abolition of slavery in Travancore in 1855. Christianity threatened the tradition of Travancore, and each Christian posed a seditious threat to its government. Many of the missionaries worked actively against the Maharaja. John Cox petitioned the government of Madras in regard to the outrages of slavery, torture, and Christian persecution in Travancore, and appealed for the governor's direct intervention and the supercession of princely authority. The publication of Cox's correspondence with the Madras government revealed a delicate situation between the Church and the government of Travancore, for not only did the publication of the political pamphlet violate the rules under which the mission functioned, but the pamphlet was printed at the mission press at Nagercoil.[80]

---

[78] Letter from the resident of Travancore and Cochin, General W. Cullen, to the chief secretary to the government, Madras (T. Pycroft), dated January 13, 1859, in *Copies of the Official Papers* . . . , p. 5.

[79] Petition to His Highness, February 7, 1859, in *Brief Statement of the Gross Outrages* . . . , pp. 14–15.

[80] John Cox, *Travancore: Its Present Ruin Shown and the Remedy Sought* (Nagercoil, 1857).

The economic and political frustrations of the Nair landowners were directed against the pretensions of the Nadars and their assumption of the breast cloth. "The agitation has been recently revived," General Cullen wrote the chief secretary to the government, Madras, in January, 1859, "the Soodras asserting that the Shanar women are constantly assuming the privilege of covering the upper part of the person, and thereby preventing a recognition of the caste. . . ." [81] Rioting had broken out in October, 1858, as Sudras attacked Nadar women in the bazaars, stripping them of their upper garments. Feelings were aggravated in November, with the Queen's proclamation on the assumption of rule by the British Crown. "Firmly relying ourselves on the truth of Christianity, and acknowledging with gratitude the solace of religion, we disclaim alike the right and desire to impose our convictions on any of our subjects. We declare it to be our royal will and pleasure that none be in any wise favored, none molested or disquieted, by reason of their religious faith or observance, but that all shall alike enjoy the equal and impartial protection of the law; and we do strictly charge and enjoin all those who may be in authority under us that they abstain from all interference with the religious belief or worship of any of our subjects on pain of our highest displeasure." [82] The Nadars imagined that the proclamation granted them all that they had sought, while the Sudras regarded it "as sanctioning their taking the law into their own hands to repress what they took as an aggression into their caste domains." [83] Robert Caldwell wrote that the proclamation was "almost universally interpreted by the natives as a declaration in favour of custom and caste against proselytism in every shape. The purpose of it is supposed to be—Christianity for the Queen and English alone, Hindooism for the Hindoos." [84]

[81] See n. 78 above.
[82] Quoted in Donald E. Smith, *India as a Secular State* (Princeton, 1963), pp. 71–72.
[83] "A Native Statesman," in *The Calcutta Review* (October, 1872), quoted in Aiya, *Travancore State Manual*, I, 526.
[84] Letter to Rev. Whitehouse, late of Nagercoil, dated February 5, 1859, Edeyengoody. Manuscript (L.M.S.).

In a letter to General Cullen, one of the Travancore missionaries said that "ever since the reading of Her Majesty Queen Victoria's Proclamation, the Soodras have taken it into their heads that they are at liberty to do whatever they like with the lower classes. . . . They have begun to close the bazaars, and will only sell to such persons as they please." [85] Certain officials used the misinterpretation of the proclamation to intimidate the Nadars. In a petition to His Highness the Rajah of Travancore, the missionaries of the South Travancore Mission stated that the Sudras in their lawless proceedings were not only encouraged and abetted by some of the lower grades of government officials, "but that these officials themselves are the chief instigators and perpetrators" of the outrages committed against the Nadar community. "They plead authority from Your Highness for what they are thus doing, and either misunderstand or wilfully misinterpret the Proclamation of Her Majesty the Queen, as though for the future all protection were withdrawn from European missionaries and their converts, and such missionaries prohibited from carrying on their works. . . . Their object in all this . . . is to destroy the Christian cause in Travancore, and to restore society to that state in which it existed previous to the year 1809." [86]

In a village market, a petty official, declaring that he had been empowered by the government to do so, stripped Nadar women of their breast cloths. The incident sparked twenty days of rioting in the district, during which time three chapels were destroyed by fire. Rioting soon followed in other districts, but it was in Nagercoil that the rage of the Sudras burst forth with the greatest violence. On January 4, 1859, some two hundred Sudras, armed with clubs and knives, attacked the Christian Nadars of a village near Nagercoil, beating them and stripping the upper cloths from the women. Similar attacks soon followed throughout the district.[87] Houses were burned and looted, and on the tenth of January, the thatched bungalow reserved for the resident when he was in

[85] James Russell, quoted in *Annual Report of the Travancore District Committee (L.M.S.) for the Year 1859* (Nagercoil, 1860), p. 2.
[86] In *Brief Statement of Gross Outrages . . .* , p. 13.
[87] Mateer, *Land of Charity*, pp. 298–305.

Nagercoil was destroyed by fire.[88] During the months of rioting between October, 1858, and February, 1859, nine chapels and three schools were burned.[89] There was no loss of life.

The violence during this period was not wholly one-sided. General Cullen reported that excesses had been committed on both sides, citing the reported attack by a large body of Nadars on a village, where they plundered shops and committed violence.[90]

The military was ordered out on December 27, 1858, soon after the rioting began, and the Dewan issued a public warning that "it is clearly wrong to violate ancient *usage* without authority" and that "whoever does so in future shall be *severely* punished. Shanars are to hear this, and act accordingly. . . . Sudras and people of the higher caste are not to do anything themselves against the Shanars, or to break the peace. If they do so, it will become necessary *to enquire into* their conduct." [91] Later, presenting his position to the missionaries, who took the warning as proof of his "gross and unconcealed partiality" to the high caste Hindus, the Dewan wrote, "It is obvious that as long as the Proclamation of 1829 is in force, the Shanars, both Hindu and Christian, are bound to conform to its provisions; that no section of the subjects can be permitted to infringe a law affecting the great majority of the people, on the ground, that in their opinion, the law ought to be changed; that the only legitimate course open to them is to continue to submit to it and formally to apply to the Sirkar for a change with such facts and arguments as they may have to urge in their favour." [92]

In an order dated January 27, 1859, General Cullen was instructed to be "careful to give no countenance to the idea that the British Government of which he is the representative, recognizes any exclusive distinctions, or the right of any set of men to prevent others from following, in all matters of social or domestic life, such course as they may see fit, provided it be not repugnant to public

[88] Letter from the resident of Travancore and Cochin to the chief secretary to the government, Madras, dated January 19, 1859, in *Copies of the Official Papers . . .*, p. 6.

[89] Agur, *Church History of Travancore*, p. 933.

[90] Letter to the South Travancore Mission, in *Annual Report of the Travancore District Committee (L.M.S.) for the Year 1859*, pp. 3-4.

[91] Quoted in Mateer, *Land of Charity*, pp. 298-305.

[92] Quoted in Aiya, I, 527.

decency and morals." Cullen was reminded that it was his duty to
impress these views on the Rajah and to point out that, in the view
of the British government, the prohibitions on the use of the breast
cloth were "unsuited to the present age, and unworthy of an en-
lightened prince. . . ." [93]

In early February, the missionaries of the South Travancore
Mission, finding no response to their petition to the Rajah, submitted their petition to the new governor of Madras, Sir Charles
Trevelyan. About this same time, the Governor received the report
on the events of the previous months. In consideration of the
events in Travancore, the Governor prepared a minute on his personal observations. The controversy was complicated by the fact
that "the differences on religious principles and caste habits are
mixed up with social and pecuniary interests." "The Shanars" the
Governor observed, "on becoming Christians, claim privileges
which partly, if not entirely, free them from many of the duties
which their state of serfdom, if not slavery, previously entailed
upon them; and on these advantages accruing to the Christian converts, the heathen Shanars evidently aspire to the enjoyment of the
same changes, though without conversion." On the other side, the
Sudras "look with great jealousy on these changes, not only on
account of their placing those whom they consider a degraded race
in a better social position, but also because they themselves become
losers by the emancipation, to some extent, of their serfs or slaves
from some of their duties." [94]

The Governor's feelings on the issue were voiced in a letter to
the resident, May 6, 1859.

I have seldom met with a case, in which not only truth and
justice, but every feeling of our common humanity are so entirely
on one side. The whole civilized world would cry shame upon us, if
we do not make a firm stand on such an occasion. If any thing could
make this line of conduct more incumbent on us, it would be the
extraordinary fact that persecution of a singularly personal and deli-

[93] Government Order, No. 75, January 27, 1859, to the resident from T. Pycroft,
chief secretary to the government, Madras, in *Copies of the Official Papers* . . . ,
pp. 6-7.
[94] Minute by the governor, dated February 28, 1859, in *Copies of the Official
Papers* . . . , pp. 10-11.

cate kind is attempted to be justified by a Royal Proclamation, the special object of which was to assure to Her Majesty's Indian subjects liberty of thought and action, so long as they did not interfere with the just rights of others. I should fail in respect to Her Majesty, if I attempted to describe the feelings with which she must regard the use made against her own sex, of the promises of protection so graciously accorded by her.[95]

The official response to the Dewan's report by the Madras government was recorded in the Minutes of Consultation, observing it to be "a temperate and a fair statement," but "the degree of interference which for many years past has been exercised by the representative of the British Government in the Affairs of Travancore is so large, and his intervention so general, that the credit or discredit of the administration greatly rests with the British Government and it has thereby become their duty to insist upon the observance of a system of toleration, in a more decided manner, than they would be at liberty to adopt, if they had merely to bring their influence to bear on an independent State." [96]

Having consulted the Maharaja, the Dewan now wrote the British resident that "His Highness now proposes to abolish all rules prohibiting the covering of the upper parts of the persons of Shanar women and to grant them perfect liberty to meet the requirements of decency any way they may deem proper, with the simple restriction that they do not imitate the same mode of dress that appertains to the higher castes." [97] With this restriction, the proposed modification may have satisfied the demands of "decency" but hardly of social aspiration. "His Highness would not have made even this small reservation," the Dewan noted, "were it not for the fear, that the sudden and total abolition of all distinctions of dress, which have from time immemorial distinguished one caste from another, may produce most undesirable impressions on the minds of the larger portion of his subjects and cause their

[95] In *Copies of the Official Papers* . . . , pp. 43–44; also in Aiya, I, 530.

[96] Order, No. 161, dated March 12, 1859, signed T. Pycroft, chief secretary to the government, Madras, in *Copies of the Official Papers* . . . , p. 36; also in Aiya, I, 530.

[97] Letter dated May 17, 1859, in Aiya, I, 530–531.

serious discontent." [98] The British accepted the concession,[99] and
a royal proclamation was issued accordingly by the state of Travancore on July 26, 1859.[100] "We hereby proclaim that there is no
objection to Shanar women either putting on a jacket, like the
Christian Shanar women, or to Shanar women of all creeds dressing
in coarse cloth, and tying themselves round with it as the Muk-
kavattigal [low caste fisherwomen] do, or to their covering their
bosoms in any manner whatever; but not like women of high
caste." [101]

The proclamation did very little to change the situation. The
missionaries of the South Travancore Mission submitted a petition
in July, 1859, to the governor of Madras denouncing the reser-
vations of the proclamation. A copy was forwarded to the secretary of state for India in London. The petition begged the intervention of the governor in the affairs of Travancore in order to
secure the position of the missionaries and the converts. Describing
the barbaric laws and customs to which the European missionaries
were subjected, they demanded "the exemption of all Europeans
from liability to native law, and the rendering them subject to
authorities appointed by the British government." The petition
further protested the continued presence of General Cullen in
Travancore as resident, since, in their view, he had supported the
Rajah and the Dewan in their opposition to the missionaries' en-
deavors.[102]

The mission had provided an organizational base for unity
among the Nadar community which extended beyond the Christian fold. The Christians themselves had been brought within the
protective embrace of the European missionary, and within each
village, a unified structure of authority was established. Each vil-

[98] *Ibid.*
[99] Order, June 6, 1859, No. 347, in *Copies of the Official Papers . . .* , p. 46.
[100] Aiya, I, 531.
[101] Mateer, *Land of Charity*, p. 305.
[102] Petition to the Honorable Sir C. E. Trevelyan, Governor of Madras, from
the missionaries of S. Travancore (signed James Russell *et al.*), dated July 18, 1859.
Manuscript (L.M.S.).

lage parish was then linked to the other through the hierarchy of the church organization. Through the structure of the mission in the southern districts, the Nadars, for the first time, were brought into association with each other over a wide area. The continued intimacy between Christian and Hindu within the Nadar community served increasingly to draw the Hindu Nadars within the sphere of mission influence, and many Hindu children attended the mission schools. The Hindu Nadar shared with his Christian brother an awakening consciousness of caste. The breast-cloth controversy served as the initial catalyst of increasing community self-consciousness. As the first movement for social uplift, it brought to the Nadars the awareness and solidarity of an emerging integrated culture.

Chapter III

MYTHOLOGY AND ASPIRATION OF A CHANGING CASTE

THE TINNEVELLY SCHISM

As the Christian Nadars of Kanyakumari were beginning to create a community consciousness among the Nadars in the movement for the adoption of the breast cloth, the Christians of Tinnevelly began to work for the uplift of the Nadars in that district to a position of higher status. Their first organized attempt to gain recognition to the claims came in 1856, in response to the use of what they deemed a "term of reproach" by a catechist of the Pallan caste at the Sawyerpuram Mission. In a petition to the resident missionary, H. C. Huxtable, the Nadar congregation expressed its great distress at having heard that the native pastor, A. David, had "called the Shanars an Ilappajathi." In defense, David presented his case to the missionary in a letter. He had intended no reproach by the use of the term, but had intended it, following Turnbull in his survey of Tinnevelly in the 1820's, to be descriptive of the middle position occupied by the Shanar community.

David addressed a formal apology to the congregation. They refused to accept, declaring, "If the Reverend Mr. David or any of his relatives instructs us, we refuse to listen. . . . We refuse in future to have catechists of any caste not equal or higher than our own." David replied, "The Brahmins have a rule, by which no Shanars or those of an inferior caste are at liberty to enter the precincts of their temples, on the plea that if they do so, pollution would ensue. Accordingly Heathen Shanars and others being prohibited from entering, worship standing outside the temple." He then went on to describe the general structure of the caste hierarchy. "Those said to be of the inferior (Ilappa) caste are those counted as occupying the middle position between high and low

castes, both in their occupations and customs. Such as Shanars,
. . . and others." [1]

David's clarification only compounded the indignity, and the
militant of the congregation withdrew from the church. The
events had caused uneasiness among the wealthy Nadans, the
Sawyerpuram missionary recorded in his journal, and "rumours
were rife that they were preparing to offer a vigorous and persevering opposition to the further spread of Christianity." [2] Speaking
later of the schism, another missionary said, "Of all Hindoos the
Shanars are the most sensitive about caste, to an extent indeed that
is perfectly ludicrous, seeing that they possess the smallest possible
claim to such distinction." [3]

A much more serious schism in the Tinnevelly church occurred
one year later in Nazareth, resulting in the formation of a separate
church and a nativistic reaction against the European missionaries.
While the origins of the trouble are by no means clear, the central
figure in the schism was a young employee of the Nazareth Mission, Arumanayagum. Born October 24, 1823, of Christian parents,
the boy received his education at the mission and went on to the
seminary in Sawyerpuram. The most brilliant student at the mission, he gained proficiency in English and studied Sanskrit,
Hebrew, Latin, and Greek as well. In 1850, he returned to Nazareth, where he was engaged as the mission school monitor, or
Sattampillai. Previously, A. F. Caemmerer, Society for the Propagation of the Gospel (S.P.G.) missionary at Nazareth, had employed a Pallan as the schoolmaster. According to J. A. Sharrock,
describing the situation some years later, Arumanayagum, or Sattampillai, as he was most frequently called, to get rid of the objectionable schoolmaster attempted to implicate the man in a woman's
suicide which had occurred shortly before. Outraged, Caemmerer
dismissed Sattampillai from mission employment. When Sat-

[1] The above communications are to be found in the manuscript collections,
Society for the Propagation of the Gospel, London (cited as S.P.G.).
[2] H. C. Huxtable, "The Mission of Sawyerpuram," *Mission Field*, I (September,
1856), 195–196.
[3] A. R. Symonds, "Sawyerpuram Mission of Tinnevelly," 1860. Manuscript
(S.P.G.).

tampillai refused to retract his accusations,. Caemmerer excommunicated him and refused to permit him to marry a young lady of the congregation to whom he had been engaged.[4] Arthur Margöschis, a later missionary of Nazareth, challenged Sharrock on this point. "It was not uncommon for the missionary . . . to arrange the domestic affairs of his flock. . . . The missionary of Nazareth arranged a marriage for Sattampillai, who being far and away the most educated and intelligent man in the whole mission, had ideas of his own, and . . . refused to marry the girl chosen by the missionary, who thereupon, dismissed him from service." [5]

Another version of the dismissal was that Sattampillai "was pious and learned in Greek and Latin, but when he went against the will of the Reverend Caemmerer in regard to marrying a Nadar girl of an impious family, he was thrown out of the church." [6] The evidence of the missionaries' letters at this time, while leaving the matter unsettled, at least gives support to Sharrock's argument. In any case, Sattampillai left the Nazareth Mission in 1850, and going through a form of marriage service himself, married the girl in question.[7]

Sattampillai then went for a time to Madras, where he was perhaps the first of his community to read a pamphlet by Caldwell on the Tinnevelly Shanars. Published in 1849 by the Christian Knowledge Society Press at Madras, the pamphlet was entitled *The Tinnevelly Shanars: A Sketch of Their Religion and Their Moral Condition and Characteristics, as a Caste.* Caldwell expressed his concern for the general lack of knowledge "respecting the characteristics and condition of the inhabitants in their heathen state." [8]

The following year, 1850, Caldwell sent a slightly revised version of the paper to the Society for the Propagation of the Gospel

[4] J. A. Sharrock, "Caste and Christianity," *Indian Church Quarterly Review,* VII (January, 1894), 9.

[5] Arthur Margöschis, "Christianity and Caste," *Indian Church Quarterly Review,* VI (October, 1893), 539–540.

[6] J. S. Ponniah *et al.,* "Notes and Reports for the Survey Volume" [*The Christian Community of Madura, Ramnad and Tinnevelly*]. Manuscript (American College Library, Madurai).

[7] Sharrock, "Caste and Christianity," *loc. cit.,* VII, 9.

[8] Robert Caldwell, *The Tinnevelly Shanars,* 1st ed. (Madras, 1849), p. 3.

for publication in England.[9] In an accompanying letter, Caldwell wrote that the pamphlet's original publication in India "was but a secondary idea," as it was written expressly for an English audience.

Sattampillai was greatly disturbed by Caldwell's description of the low and degraded position of the Nadar caste, of heathenish practices of devil-worship, of their predilection to vice, and of their intellectual dullness.[10] When he returned to Nazareth, Sattampillai found a number of malcontents within the mission and took up the caste question as the instrument by which "he could best detach large numbers of Christians from the Church to join his own party."[11] His efforts were derided by Caemmerer as "inane attempts to raise, what he calls the Shanar caste. . . ."[12]

Sattampillai's opportunity came in 1857, with fresh discontent within the Nazareth Mission. In January, Swamiadian, a catechist of Mukupury of twenty years standing in the mission, was suspended when Caemmerer learned that the catechist had poured molten lead down the throat of a pig to obtain some folk medicine. Discontent simmered until August, when Swamiadian led his congregation in a walkout. Sattampillai immediately gave his support to the dissident, as did Visuvasam, also a dismissed catechist of Nazareth, and Maduranayagum, associated with the Church Missionary Society (C.M.S.) and a headman of Peragasapuram village. These four soon came to the attention of Caemmerer when they were accused "of forcibly raising money from the people who frequented [a local] market, for the ostensible purpose of publishing a book, said to be prepared by Arumanayagum to refute certain allegations of Dr. Caldwell and Mr. Kearns derogatory to their vaunted caste. . . ." It seems that the dissidents had sought to ex-

[9] Caldwell, *The Tinnevelly Shanars*, 2d ed.

[10] Sattampillai, according to his son, translated the Caldwell pamphlet into Tamil and sent it throughout the country, Ceylon and Burma to eminent Nadars to "make them to understand about the misrepresentation of the Nadar community in that book." A. C. Asiratanadar and T. T. Thomas Nadar, *Shandrar Ethnography* (Madras, 1912), quoted in B. J. M. Kulasekhara-Raj, *Nadar Kula Varalaru, A Brief Account of the Nadar Race* (Palamcottah, 1918), pp. 94–95.

[11] Sharrock, "Caste and Christianity," *loc. cit.*, VII, 9.

[12] A. F. Caemmerer, "Report," dated Nazareth, September 25, 1857. Manuscript (S.P.G.).

tract a four-anna contribution from every Nadar "as a matter of conscience and obligatory on all who wished to save their caste from aspersions." [13]

In response, Caemmerer addressed a letter to the sub-collector of Tinnevelly District: "A young man named Arumanayagum has been lately maliciously reporting in my district and elsewhere that the Reverend Messrs. Caldwell and Kearns have woefully maligned and misrepresented the Shanar cast. This mischievious fellow collects people about him at fairs, convenes meetings, excites and ferments agitation on the subject of caste, tries to disappoint the minds of the Shanars against the missionaries in general, and aided by three other individuals equally wicked as himself . . . is daily extorting money by *intimidation* and under *false pretences* from the people at Mukupury." [14] Warrants were issued for the arrest of Sattampillai and his three confederates, and each was subsequently fined.

In that same month, two petitions were sent to the bishop, one complaining in particular that Caemmerer had not permitted a "certain female in the Nazareth congregation to marry Arumanayagum," and the other that Caemmerer was "afflicting" the congregation at Mukupury. Another petition soon followed wherein Caemmerer, along with Caldwell and Kearns, was represented as "degrading the Shanar caste." "I am thoroughly disappointed in the Shanar character," wrote the Nazareth missionary. "After 19 years' labour among these people I must confess I had hoped to see other fruits." [15]

Caemmerer's disappointment turned to personal tragedy as Sattampillai and his followers led several congregations in a breakaway from the mission to establish a separate church at Prakasapuram, one mile distant from Nazareth. Held "in some measure responsible" for the schism,[16] Caemmerer, after twenty years' missionary labor in Nazareth, was transferred in 1858 by the S.P.G. to the Tanjore Mission. In his report of the situation in Nazareth to London, a visiting missionary described caste feelings as "very

---

[13] *Ibid.*

[14] Nazareth, August 8, 1857. Manuscript (S.P.G.).

[15] Caemmerer, "Report."

[16] A. R. Symonds, "Report of the Nazareth Mission, 1860." Manuscript (S.P.G.).

strong" among the Nadars, and "they are somewhat explosive on the point. There is a great deal of zeal no doubt among them, but it savours too much of the zeal of party. There is considerable proficiency of learning, but it is too much the knowledge that puffeth up." [17]

The missionary at Mudalur, but a few miles from Nazareth, reported more favorably that "my people have no sympathy whatever with this foolish and Quixotic movement of raising what is called the Shanar caste." "The poor Shanars," he said, "have no caste to raise," and they are conscious that were it not for the protection of the missionaries and of Christianity, their condition would be deplorable. He warned, however, that the agitation was widespread among the missions of both the S.P.G. and the C.M.S., and that "the feelings of discontent and lawless insubordination are rife. . . ." [18] With the Indian Mutiny in mind, Henry Pope, who had formerly been a catechist at the Nazareth mission and returned in 1858 as the resident missionary, took an uneasy view. "There is an innate antipathy in the Native Christian mind to the European minister. The present state of native morality obliges the latter to be *reserved*, even with his confidential helpers. . . . As far as I can judge, the people here long for independence—'White men use the Bible to rule us' is their general complaint. Scores of catechists and others eat the white man's salt, but that brings about no oneness of sentiment. Something galls somewhere." [19]

The new church, under Sattampillai, called itself the Hindu Church of Lord Jesus and its faith the Hindu Christian Religion, although it was known variously as Jehovah Messianism, Sattampillai Vedam, and simply Nattar, or national party. The faithful "in their zeal for caste and Hindu nationality . . . rejected from their system everything which appeared to them to savour of a European origin." They "cut themselves off as completely from all European help in money and influence as if there were no

[17] Symonds, *Ibid*.

[18] T. H. Suter, letter to the Society for the Propagation of the Gospel, London, dated Muthaloor, 1857. Manuscript (S.P.G.).

[19] Henry Pope, "Report of the Nazareth Mission," dated December 31, 1858. Manuscript (S.P.G.).

longer any Europeans in the country. . . ." [20] Seeking to divest Christianity of what were considered European trappings, they sought to go back to the Jewish origins of the religion. Sattampillai took the title of Rabbi, and the church at Prakasapuram was built in the fashion of a Jewish temple. The schismatics observed the Judaic traditions of Passover, and the seventh day was taken as their day of worship. They were called to worship by the blowing of trumpets, and they washed their feet and legs before entering the church. They abandoned infant baptism and an ordained ministry. Days were reckoned from evening to evening. Frankincense was offered in worship, and several animal sacrifices were reported. Hindu rites not inconsistent with the tenets of their dogma were accepted, and the Hindu Law with regard to marriage and inheritance was binding.[21]

Toward the end of his life, Sattampillai saw his congregations decline from more than six thousand adherents to but a few families. In the years before his death in 1918, at the age of ninety-five, Sattampillai was comforted by his two daughters, who had remained virgins "for religion's sake," and by his sons, Rabbi P. V. Pandion and B. J. M. Kulasekhara-Raj, who had taken the leadership of the church.[22] After the death of Sattampillai, his congregations, spread out in five villages within a two-mile radius of Nazareth, divided into two hostile factions. The Rabbi's library, once famous throughout the southern districts, disappeared as volumes were given away or sold for a pittance, and the original church at Prakasapuram remained only as a bare site.[23]

[20] Caldwell, quoted in Joseph Mullens, *A Brief Review of Ten Years' Missionary Labour in India between 1852 and 1861* (London, 1863), pp. 51–52.

[21] *Ibid.*; Ponniah, *The Christian Community of Madura, Rammad and Tinnevelly;* Paul Appasamy, *Centenary History of the C.M.S. in Tinnevelly* (Palamcottah, 1923), p. 129; Somerset Playne, *Southern India: Its History, People, Commerce, and Industrial Resources* (London, 1914–1915), p. 484; A. N. Sattampillai, alias S. A. Nayaga Nadan, *A Brief Sketch of the Hindu Christian Dogma* (Palamcottah, 1890).

[22] Playne, *Southern India,* p. 484.

[23] Hilda Raj, "Persistence of Caste in South India—An Analytical Study of the Hindu and Christian Nadars" (unpublished Ph.D. dissertation, Department of Sociology, American University, 1958), p. 134. A more successful and widespread nativistic Christian movement is described in Bengt G. M. Sundkler, *Bantu Prophets in South Africa* (London, 1948).

The Hindu Church of Jesus Christ never gained a wide following, but the schism in the Tinnevelly church had a strong influence
on the emergence of the Nadar caste as a self-conscious community. Although in 1857 Sattampillai did not secure the funds to
publish his pamphlet against Caldwell and Kearns, his manuscript
appears to have been the first attempt by a Nadar to establish the
claims of the community to higher status through the mythological
reconstruction of a kingly past.

THE NEW MYTHOLOGY OF A CASTE IN CHANGE

In the seventy-five years following 1857, the date of Sattampillai's unpublished treatise on the Nadar caste, some forty books,
pamphlets, and periodicals were published extolling the high status
and greatness of the Nadars. Education had given the Christian the
aspiration to higher status, and the Hindu traders sought a social
position commensurate with their rising economic power. "As the
lower castes, in these days, frequently send out into the world men
who accumulate wealth," wrote W. R. Cornish in the Census
Report of Madras Presidency, 1871, ". . . the surplus funds of
such men are often employed in the feeding of pundits to prove the
ancient glories of their particular caste." The process was not
greatly different in Europe, where the rich parvenu purchased his
"pedigree" from some unconscientious heraldic agent. In India,
however, "it is the exaltation of the *caste*, rather than of the individual, that is desired, and for this reason, that no man can rise,
socially, above his caste level." [24]

"The uneasiness of the lower castes in regard to the social position assigned to them by Brahmanical authority," Cornish contended, "is simply an indication that, under British rule, they have
increased in wealth and intelligence, and naturally desire to prove
that the yoke imposed upon them by the caste system was tyran-
nical and unjust." They did this, not by attacking the system itself
as unjust, but by claiming a higher, more ritually pure position in
the caste hierarchy. They sought to retain the system and, through

[24] India, Census Commissioner. *Report on the Census of Madras Presidency,
1871* (Madras, 1874), I, 118–119.

the new mythology of the caste histories, to place themselves at the top. "A whole literature of ponderous tomes is springing up in Southern India with no other object than the exaltation of caste." Caste distinction had not declined. Indeed, "there probably was never a time when the great bulk of the people of Southern India were so pertinacious in the assertion of the respectability and dignity of their castes" as they have been since the development of this species of literature. Cornish urged the caste historians to inquire honestly into and compile the traditions of their caste and to curtail "the natural tendency of the Hindu imagination to run riot." [25] The census commissioner cited the observations of a missionary: "The *Shanars* of Tinnevelly have just now had their heads turned by an absurd tract written to prove that the Shanars are the descendants of the great warrior caste. They do not merely mean that they were the original kings of the soil, but that they are descended from the Aryan Kshatriyas." [26]

The Bishop of Calcutta, on his visit to Tinnevelly in 1865, commented on a "strange notion" propagated, he believed, by the Nazareth schismatics, that the Nadars were "a princely race like the Rajpoots, and that their progenitors were palmyra-climbing kings." The Bishop referred, in his discussion, to the "Shanar cash," Venetian sequins frequently dug up in Tinnevelly, relics of the time when Tuticorin was a great trading port. These coins, like others of the Republic of Venice, bore the name of the Doge and were stamped with a bishop's mitre and pastoral staff. "Some of the Shanars believe these emblems to represent the tool-bag and climbing stick used in mounting their beloved trees, to which they undoubtedly bear a considerable resemblance. Hence they conclude the sequins to be the coinage, not of the ancient spouse of the Adriatic, but of their own royal ancestors, cultivators of the palmyra like themselves." [27]

[25] *Ibid.* (See "Chronology of Nadar Caste Histories," Appendix III.)
[26] Quoted *Ibid.*, p. 118.
[27] G. E. L. Cotton, *The Tinnevelly Mission* (1864), p. 27. This portion of the article was reprinted in the *Church Missionary Intelligencer*, New Series, I (May, 1865), 144. Thurston quotes Rev. Fawcett on the "Shanar cash" (*Madras Museum Bulletin*, III [1901]). The coin is known as an "Amada," since one day, according to legend, Amada, consort of Bhagavati, appeared before a Shanar and demanded food. The Shanar said he was poor and had nothing to offer but toddy. Amada

The first of the published histories of the Nadar community, to which reference is available, was *Shandror Marapu* [*Shandror Antiquity*], published at Madras in 1871, by the Reverend H. Martyn Winfred, son of the first Indian pastor of the American Madura Mission. His father, S. Winfred, published another treatise three years later entitled, *Shandror Kula Marapu Kattala* [*To Safeguard the Customs of the Shandrors*]. The lengthy volume sought to establish the Nadars as the descendants of the Pandyan kings, and, having established their noble status, exhorted all Nadars to assume the customs of the Kshatriya. "Ladies of Shandrors must not go outside," Winfred states, "and if they leave to go out, they can do so in a covered vehicle so that nobody can see them." [28] At the Madras Church Conference in 1876, a European missionary referrred to Winfred's study as "imprudent" in its "endeavor to prove that they are of the Kshatriya caste . . . and that therefore they are superior to the *Vellalar* Sudras." He derided, as well, a pamphlet written by a Tinnevelly Christian to prove that the Nadars were the descendants of the Lost Tribe of Israel.[29] Another early tract reportedly claimed Jesus Christ himself as a Nadar.

Basing his arguments on Winfred's work, in 1880, Samuel Sargunar, B.A. (1850–1919), a Christian Nadar employed as a sub-registrar for Chingleput District, published a small pamphlet, *Dravida Kshatriyas*, in which he sought to reconstruct the glory of the Nadar past on the basis of an etymological analysis of the word *Shanar*.[30] Denying the low status of the community, Sargunar stated that the word *Shanar*, used contemptuously to refer to the caste, was in fact a corruption of *Shandrar*, the Tamil word meaning "the learned" or "the noble man." The claims soon created a

drank the toddy from a cup fashioned from a palmyra leaf, and performing a mantram (consecrated formula) over the leaf, turned it into gold coins, which on one side bore the pictures of Amada, the Shanar, and the palmyra tree between them. Cited in Edgar Thurston, *Castes and Tribes of Southern India* (Madras, 1909), VI, 366–367.

[28] S. Winfred, *Shandror Kula Marapu Kattala* (Madras, 1874), p. 213. Also see John Chandler, *Seventy-five Years in the Madura Mission* (Madras, 1909), pp. 23–25.

[29] *Report of the Madras Church Conference, February 24, 1876*, pp. 14–15.

[30] "Shanar Characteristics," letter from a "non-Shanar," *Madras Mail*, July 12, 1899.

linguistic imbroglio which remained unsettled even with the compilation of the *Tamil Lexicon* in 1900. The word *Shanar*, which appears neither in Tamil literature nor in inscriptions, is ordinarily derived from *saru*, meaning toddy.[31] The census superintendent in 1891 notes that a learned missionary derived the word "from *san* (a span) and *nar* (fibre or string), that is the noose, one span in length, used by the Shanars in climbing palm-trees."[32] For Sargunar, however, and the Nadar caste historians to follow him, *Shandrar* was the key word, and taking it to refer to his particular community, he reconstructed the history of the Nadars through the references in Tamil literature using the word. Since Shandrar, "the noble man," was used frequently to refer to the kings of Tamilnad, the Nadars were taken to be the ancestors of these rulers and therefore Kshatriyas.

Caldwell accepted *Shanar* as a corruption of *Shandrar*, but he did not equate reference to the specific class with the term of distinction as it was more broadly used.[33] Sargunar took every use of *Shandrar* to refer specifically to the Shanar community. The three nouns, *Shandror*, *Shandrar*, and *Shandravor*, are all, he said, derived from the root *sal*, meaning great or abundant. "The persons denoted by the word [*Shandrar*] are the Shanars or Kshatri-

---

[31] Letter from "W," *Madras Mail*, June 30, 1899. Reply from "a Shanar" dismisses the derivation from *saru* as "childish." *Madras Mail*, July 4, 1899.

[32] *Census of India*, 1891, Vol. XIII p. 297. In an interview, a young Nadar Christian gave the same derivation, indicating the meaning as "you need one span of fiber for your living."

Another derivation is from the Sanskrit *Saundigar* used as an equivalent for Ezhava. *Census of India, 1901*, Vol. XV: *Madras*, Pt. I: *Report*, p. 178.

In the Kamudi case (see chap. 4), the plaintiff argued that the Nadars were Saundigars (or Soundikans), which were declared by the *Smritis* to be "persons born of a man of inferior caste on a women of superior caste and . . . therefore interdicted from entering Hindu temples." The judge ruled that there was no basis for the derivation "excepting opinion." He likewise rejected the derivation from *saru*. He ruled also that the defendants had not established their claims for derivation from Shandrar. *Rajah Bhaskara Sethupathi* v. *Irulappan Nadan*, p. 96.

[33] Caldwell, *The Tinnevelly Shanars*, 1st ed., p. 4; *Shandrar* was also used, according to K. V. Soundra Rajan, superintendent of the Archeological Survey of India, Madras, in regard to a group of cobblers who were "hardly kings." This class, commonly called "Shanars," had a secondary occupation of toddy-tapping. The term, he suggests, may have been applied to the caste of exclusive tappers. Interview.

yas, learning having been their speciality as much as palm wine." [34]
One of the most learned of the Shandrars, according to Sargunar,
was Enadinatha Nayanar, one of the sixty-three apostles of Siva.[35]

In 1883, Samuel Sargunar published another pamphlet, *Bishop
Caldwell and the Tinnevelly Shanars.* Presenting the Nadars as
learned Kshatriyas, Sargunar attacked Caldwell for having drawn a
"dark picture" of the condition and status of the community in
The Tinnevelly Shanars, published thirty-four years previously.
Sargunar reiterated the *Shandrar* argument, then asked, "If the
Shanars are really Kshatriyas, how came they to occupy a position
which appears to be somewhat lower than that of the Sudras?" and
replied that, having been conquered, the Shandrar Kshatriyas were
reduced to servitude. "The disappearance of the Kshatriyas from
their rightful position in society, the coming into power of successive governments which ignored the time-honored landmarks of
caste, and that mysterious yet perceptibly working principle in the
relation between masters and servants, which prompts the servants
not only to imitate their masters but to assert that they are their
'masters' caste,' or are of equal rank with them, are among the chief
causes that have contributed to the apparent elevation of the
Sudras." [36] Not content to claim past glory for the community,
Sargunar went on to say that toddy-tapping was not in fact a low
occupation. "In truth, palm juice was esteemed a luxury fit to be
consumed by the Kshatriyas and the Brahmins. It was regarded as
the earthly counterpart of the celestial nectar of the gods." [37]

Until the publication of *Bishop Caldwell and the Tinnevelly
Shanars,* Caldwell's early pamphlet had receded from attention
after the row it had stirred in the schism of 1857. Sargunar's tract,
presenting Caldwell as reviling the Nadar caste, opened the issue
again. Caldwell was in Scotland at the time of the pamphlet's publication. Several petitions against his return to Tinnevelly were

[34] Samuel Sargunar, *Bishop Caldwell and the Tinnevelly Shanars* (Palamcottah,
1883), p. 12; also see "The Shanars: Who Are They?" *Madras Mail,* June 19,
1899.

[35] Sargunar, p. 16; see also V. Nagam Aiya, *Travancore State Manual*
(Trivandrum, 1906), II, 392n.; *Rajah Bhaskara Sethupathi v. Irulappan Nadan,* pp.
35, 88–89.

[36] Sargunar, pp. 17–18.

[37] *Ibid.,* pp. 13–14.

circulated among the Nadar Christians and submitted to the Society for the Propagation of the Gospel and to the Archbishop of Canterbury.[38] Among the most active petitioners was Y. Gnanamuthoo Nadar, "Graduate, S.G.C., L. Clerk, District Court, Tinnevelly, Antiquarian and Representative of the Shanar Race." In a letter to the secretary of the S.P.G., London, Gnanamuthoo blamed Bishop Caldwell's writings for the Tinnevelly schism of 1857 and for the resuscitation of caste feeling among Nadar Christians.[39] He wrote also to the Archbishop and to Prime Minister Gladstone himself.

Soon after Sargunar's pamphlet was published, a rejoinder was made by S. Chenthinatha Iyer of Jaffna, Ceylon. Styling himself a "Saivite Preacher," the Brahmin attacked Sargunar in a pamphlet under the English title, *Shanars Not Kshatriyas* (the text was in Tamil and the Tamil title translates as *The Shanar-Kshatriya Storm*). Iyer asked why the Nadars waited so long to issue their attack on Caldwell and only when he left Tinnevelly. It is because, he said, they "fattened" themselves while he was there. "The Nadars were so low they didn't even know how to tie a dhoti around their waist." [40] Iyer attacked Sargunar personally and said that the Nadars had been "bought" by the church. Caldwell's book was a warning to Europeans about the ways of the Nadars, and also, Iyer continued, an attempt to show to other castes that Christianity was not the "Shanar religion" merely because large numbers had embraced it.[41]

The Saivite Preacher's pamphlet was later described by a "non-Shanar" as "full of reasoning and witty pleasantry," [42] but it was not so received by the Nadar community. One Sunday morning, copies of a small, anonymously published pamphlet were distributed among the Christians as they left the Palamcottah church.

[38] "Shanar Characteristics," letter from a "non-Shanar," *Madras Mail*, July 12, 1899.

[39] Y. Gnanamuthoo Nadar, letter dated May 19, 1883, in *Shanars are Kshatriyas* . . . (Madras, 1889), pp. 128–129.

[40] S. Chenthinatha Iyer, *Shan Kshatriya Pirasanda Marutam* (Shanar-Kshatriya Storm), *Shanars Not Kshatriyas* (Palamcottah, 1883), pp. 2–6.

[41] *Ibid.*, pp. 37–38.

[42] "Shanar Characteristics," letter from a "non-Shanar," *Madras Mail*, July 12, 1899.

Entitled *Chenthinathanukku Cheruppadi,* "a shoe-beating to Chenthinatha," the pamphlet abused the Brahmin in violent language. Iyer filed a complaint before the deputy magistrate, charging the distributors of the pamphlet and Samuel Sargunar with defamation. They were convicted and sentenced to a fine and imprisonment.[43] Sargunar became a martyr of Nadar caste pride, and to his defense came Gnanamuthoo Nadar. In *Shanars are Kshatriyas, being a Reply to the Objectionable Statements Made by Chenthinatha Iyer Regarding the Shanars,* Gnanamuthoo presented the Kshatriya argument with a new attack on Caldwell. His formula was simple: "The *Shandore Caste* is the *Kshatriya Caste;* the *Shanar Caste* is the *Shandore Caste:* therefore the *Shanar Caste* is the *Kshatriya Caste.*"[44]

Despite the attempts of the early Nadar caste historians to associate the community with the Kshatriyas through the word *Shandrar,* the caste name of *Shanar* continued to carry a derogatory connotation,[45] and members of the community increasingly sought to abandon its use altogether in favor of the title *Nadar,* which had long been used by the landed aristocracy in the Tiruchendur region. The word was taken to mean lord of the land, or *nad,* but the caste historians then took all references to "lords of the land" to refer to their own community. In his voluminous study, *Research on the Word Nadar,* T. V. Doraisamy Gramani equates *Nadar* with *Kshatriya,* the former being the Tamil equivalent of the Sanskrit word. "Kshatriya comes from *kshetra,* meaning country. Nadar comes from *nadu,* meaning country. Both are the same.[46] Having "established" the caste as Kshatriyas, Doraisamy

---

[43] "Shanar Characteristics," *Ibid.* E. S. Sargunar, nephew of Samuel Sargunar, says that his uncle's arrest and conviction was because, as a government servant, he did not secure permission to publish the book. Interview.

[44] Gnanamuthoo, *op. cit.,* pp. xii–xiii.

[45] One Nadar writing years later claimed that the word *Shanar* "was first coined and used by the Rev. J. P. Rottler in a Dictionary compiled by him in 1834." J. S. Ponniah, "Human Geography of the Ramnad District," *The Journal of the Madras Geographical Association,* VII (1932–33), 272 n.

[46] T. Vijaya Doraisamy Gramani, *Research on the Word Nadar: A Manual Relating to the Kingly Community* (Madras, 1927), pp. 67–68.
  The word *Nadar,* while generally accepted as meaning "lord of the land," has been given various meanings. The plaintiff in the Kamudi case (see chap. 4) claimed that it was based on the negative form of a verb and meant "don't approach or come near" (*Rajah Bhaskara Sethupathi v. Irulappan Nadan,* p. 87); a

then drew a genealogical chart, tracing the descent of the Nadar community through the Chera and the Pandyan kings. The Gramanis, a caste of toddy-tappers in the northern Tamil districts of Madras, he contended, were an allied community of the Nadars, both being of equally high and kingly status: the Nadars are of the moon dynasty, descendants of Chandra; the Gramanis of the sun dynasty, descendants of Surya.[47] For the propagation of the Kshatriya argument, Doraisamy founded a monthly, *Kshatriya Mitran,* published at Madras, and from its presses turned out a series of books on the divine origins of the Nadar community and its kingly tradition.[48]

The claims advanced for the divine origins of the Nadars confronted the Christian Nadars with certain theological difficulties. Cornelius Nadar, a clerk of the collector's office at Salem, attacked the problem with Panglossian diligence. He related the Nadars not only to the rulers of the Tamil kingdoms, but to the gods as well. As a Christian, herein lay his problem: while proving that the Nadars are a high—indeed, the highest—community in the traditional realm of Hinduism and the children of the gods, he must at the same time cast off the tradition. His solution is to link the Nadars to the kings and to the gods of the pantheon, but to deny the true divinity of the deities. All the gods and avatars—Siva, Vishnu, Rama, and the whole pantheon—were Shandrars, that is, Shanars, who in their great power as rulers deified themselves for the lowly to worship. For this great sin of pride, God, in his wisdom, punished their community with inferior status. In their fallen state as the climbers of the palmyra, Cornelius does not wholly abandon his community, for he seeks elsewhere to establish that the palmyra itself is, as sacred to Siva, the Hindu Tree of Life.[49]

The Nadar caste historians, claiming a grandiose mythology and

Nadar today derives the word from the verb "to submit," giving the meaning as "one who will not submit" (interview).

[47] Gramani, pp. 67–68.

[48] See the Bibliography: Tamil Sources. In addition to Doraisamy's *Kshatriya Mitran,* another monthly, *Nadar Kula Mitran,* edited by S. A. Muthu Nadar, was published by the Aruppukottai Nadar Education Association. The first issue was September, 1919. Newspapers published at various times for the uplift of the Nadars were *Vijaiya Vihadan, Dakshina Dipam, Pandiya Kula Dipam, Dravida Abimani, Gnanodhayam, Sachithanandam, Kodar Kulam,* and *Nadar Nanban.*

[49] J. S. Cornelius Nadar, *Amarar Puranam, Being the Antiquities of the Gods of India* . . . (Salem, 1901), p. 233.

such titles as Valamkai Uyarkonda Iravikula Kshatriya ("Kshatriyas of the Solar Race belonging to the Right-hand faction"),[50] explained the fallen state of the community as a product of the Kaliyuga, the present age of decline in which the purity of caste observances have been subverted.[51] In the good old days, went one story, the palmyra juice flowed as ambrosial nectar from the gods, and, with the utterance of a mantra, a sacred formula, the trees would bend their heads to the ground and the sap would pour freely into the awaiting pots. "But alas, a wicked Kshatriya offended the gods, who cursed the manthras, and ever since then the trees have had to be climbed and they remain obstinately perpendicular." [52]

As the number of the caste histories grew, a fairly consistent pattern began to emerge. Some, like *Traditions of the Solar and Lunar Races, and the Claims of the Shanar Caste to Kshatriya Origins on These Grounds,*[53] remained essentially mythological. Others, however, at least made allusion to historical reality. The Nadars' Kshatriya argument faced criticism that the Tamil kings were themselves not Kshatriyas, "but simply Dravidian chieftains . . . whom their Brahminical preceptors and spiritual directors dignified with Aryan titles. . . ." [54] In an attempt to meet these critics and to retain the claims to high status, a "correspondent" wrote to the *Madras Mail* that the Brahmins who came to the South styled the Tamil rulers "as Sanrors, raised them to the position of Kshatriyas, and prepared a fictitious genealogy to gratify the vanity of the rulers." It would, therefore, be quite patent that the claims of the Nadars to the Kshatriya title of the Aryan are absurd, but, he went on, "that they were Dravidian rulers of the South of the Peninsula and Ceylon seems very probable." [55]

A few days later, "an Indian Lady" reiterated these views. "The

[50] *Census of Travancore, 1931,* Pt. I: *Report,* p. 384; for a discussion of titles see Aiya, *Travancore State Manual,* II, 393.

[51] *Rajah Bhaskara Sethupathi* v. *Irulappan Nadan,* p. 75.

[52] Arthur Margöschis, "Tinnevelly: Being an Account of the District, the People, and the Missions," *Mission Field,* XLII (October, 1893), 392.

[53] K. Shanmuga Gramani, *Shandrarakiya Surya Chandra Vamsa Paramparai Saritaram* (Madras, 1889).

[54] *Rajah Bhaskara Sethupathi* v. *Irulappan Nadan,* pp. 82–83.

[55] "The Shanars: Who Are They?" *Madras Mail,* June 19, 1899.

'Sanrors' don't claim themselves to be the 'Aryan Kshatriyas,' but their claim is only for the title of 'Dravidian Kshatriyas,' i.e., they claim themselves to be those Dravidians whom the Brahmins have raised to the dignity of Kshatriyas." With the fall of the Pandyans before the Nayaks, the Nadars "were oppressed and bitterly persecuted . . . to prevent their rising again to assert their lost power." After three centuries of oppression, the Nadars "like the Israelites under Pharoah, found a Moses in the person of the Englishman who destroyed the power of the Poligar. . . ." [56]

The Nadar claims were not without some weight, for traditions among the Nadans and the existence of the ruins beneath the *teris* suggest that they might well be heir to some early Pandyan dynasty. The idea that the Nadars had originally been the possessors of the southern districts and the kings of Tamilnad gradually became almost an official dogma of the Nadar community. After a continuous reign of about four thousand years, so the stories go, the Pandyans—ancestors of the Nadars—were defeated at the hand of the Telugu Nayaks in the sixteenth century. With their defeat, the traditional system of moral duty, on which social position rested, was completely overthrown. The Pandyans were stripped of their privileges and rights, their titles, and their properties. They were branded as untouchables, and their use of public places was prohibited. Forced from the city of Madurai and divested of their rich lands, the Pandyans were scattered across the southern districts to become homeless wanderers. Degraded by the new rulers who usurped power and status, the Pandyans were forced to pursue the most arduous of occupations, the cultivation and climbing of the palmyra, in the uninhabited wastes of Tiruchendur.[57] So that they

[56] Letter from "An Indian Lady," *Madras Mail*, June 24, 1899. A Christian Nadar schoolmaster in Madurai said in an interview, "God sent the British to save the Nadars because he held them in special favor. If the British had not come, the Nadars would have been destroyed."

[57] E. M. Jayaraj, deputy collector, "The Nadars," manuscript prepared at the request of the Dakshina Mara Nadar Sangam for submission to the Special Tahsildar for the District Gazetteer, Tinnevelly, March 16, 1964. See also S. A. Siralinga Nadar, "Our People," *Kshatriya Mitran*, VI (1925–1926), 85; Ramalinga Kurukkal and V. A. Kumaraiya Nadar, *Nadar Mannarum Nayakka Mannarum* (The Nadar Kings and the Nayak Kings) (Virudhunagar, 1937); interview, Gangaram Dorairaj, reprinted in *Mahajanam* (Madurai), December 29, 1964.

might never rise again, the Nayaks sought to erase the glory and tradition of the Pandyans from history. Besides suffering great persecution, wrote a Nadar caste historian, P. V. Pandion, son of Sattampillai, "during the last three hundred years, in order to stifle our antiquity and vitiate our tribal honour these opponents have greatly spoiled the Tamil literature in various ways, by fabricating numerous records, and by mutilating and misinterpreting almost all old *Sassnas* and Cadjan books that were within their reach." [58]

The Pandyans and their Nadar ancestors were denied entrance into the temples, and as a symbol of their final defeat, according to the tradition of the community, the western gates of the temples were permanently closed. The Nadars claim today that it was through the western gate that the Pandyan kings entered the temples to worship. With the victory of the Nayaks, the western gates were sealed, and to this day, the western gates of all the temples in the southern districts are closed.[59] Some Nadars assert that the community was never denied entrance into the temples, but when the western gate was closed, they refused to enter through another gate, as it was beneath their dignity.[60]

[58] P. V. Pandion, *A Memorial, on Behalf of the Nadar Community to J. C. Molony, Esq., I.C.S., Superintendent of Census Operations, Madras, 1911* (Trichinopoly, 1910), pp. 3-5.

[59] Many Nadars who are unfamiliar with the claims to Pandyan ancestry or Kshatriya status have some notion of the connection between the western gate and the prohibition on Nadars' temple entry. The western gates in these regions are closed and temple authorities seem unable to give any consistent explanation. K. V. Soundra Rajan, superintendent of the Archeological Survey, Madras, says that many temples have only two or three gates open and that only the largest will keep all four open. He expresses no knowledge of the legend regarding the closing of the western gate. Interview.

Chandler says the Nadars' were excluded from the temples, according to their claims, not because they were low, but because they were of high rank. "The story was that King Tirumala [Nayaka] when building the great pillared hall opposite the Eastern pagoda, had called upon each section of the community to provide the materials furnished by its own occupation; that the Shanars, as tree-climbers, were ordered to furnish the coarse palm sugar to mix with the mortar; and that they had refused because they were traders and not tree-climbers and had no sugar to give; and that Tirumala thereupon forbade their entering into the temple" (John Chandler, *Seventy-Five Years in the Madura Mission*, p. 24).

[60] One Nadar of Sivakasi related in an interview that "The Nadars would not show their back to the deity, for this was a symbol of defeat, so they would enter through the east—to which the god faced—and would exit by the western gate.

The schismatics of Nazareth, the first of the Nadar propagandists, mixed Hindu and Christian notions of creation to claim divine status for the Nadars, or, as they preferred, the Dravida Kshatriyas. They were, for Nabhi P. V. Pandion, son of Sattampillai, cousins of the northern Rajputs. "Most certainly they were born, not with the Darwinian savageness, but with all Noaic intelligence and morality. . . ." [61] In 1901, Edgar Thurston, superintendent of the Ethnographic Survey of Madras, visited Nazareth and was presented with a petition by Pandion, then known as S. V. Nayaka Natar. Entitled, *A Short Account of the Cantras of Tamil Xatras, the Original but Down-Trodden Royal Race of Southern India*, the petition claimed descent from "the Pandya or Dravida Xatra [Kshatriya] race, who, shortly after the universal deluge of Noah, first disafforested and colonized this land of South India. . . . One of [Noah's] grandsons . . . was Atri, whose son Chandra was the ancestor of the noblest class of the Xatras ranked above the Brahmans, and the first illustrious monarch of the post-diluvian world." [62]

Thurston received Pandion's work "as partly printed and partly in manuscripts, together with 265 petitions bearing 29,100 signatures of the Nadars." Thurston then toured the district, according to Pandion, "in order to verify the statements made in the book. . . ." The Nazareth Nadars volunteered their assistance, and in the course of a day's tour of the village, Mr. Thurston, according to Pandion, "bore a public testimony to the value of the book. . . . But he failed to publish his ordinary bulletin on the result of his personal investigations about our caste . . . , and when he had to go away on long furloughs, he unfortunately left his Ethnography work in the hands of his Brahmin assistant who had accompanied him to Nazareth but had returned therefrom with prejudice against us caused by some malevolent persons in the neighborhood. With the very assistance of such a Brahmin (as openly acknowledged by himself) Mr. Thurston recently brought out his *Castes*

When the western gate was closed, Nadars refused to enter. Gradually, by custom, it grew up that they were denied entrance."

[61] Thurston, *Castes and Tribes of Southern India*, VI, 367.

[62] Pandion, *A Memorial*, pp. 3-5.

and Tribes of Southern India in seven volumes, in which he simply vilified the Cantra caste, only satiating the anti-Cantras." [63]

"It must not be supposed that the 'Sanror' theory has by any means spread a general infection over the whole community," wrote Pate in the *Tinnevelly Gazetteer* in 1917. "In villages near the source of its origin it finds often vehement supporters; but one need not go far, for preference to a village where hard work is the order of things, to find the story either treated with mild derision or even not known. Possibly it may die of inanition." [64] Despite the ridicule to which the story was subjected, by scholars such as Thurston and Pate and by the higher-caste communities, the new myth of Kshatriya status became increasingly a reality for the Nadar community. As they advanced claims to Kshatriya status, they began to adopt Sanskritic customs in imitation of the Brahmins, pointing to them as proof of their high status. The new mythology of the caste histories was their authority; Sanskritized custom was their proof; and wealth and education were the catalysts to higher status.

CASTE AND CHRISTIANITY

In the mass conversion of the Nadars in southeastern Tinnevelly, the solidarity of the caste was retained, since the new Christian ran no risk of being outcasted. As entire villages came into the Christian fold, the manner of life continued very much as it had before. Their ties with the Hindu community were retained. Among the higher castes, such as the Vellalas, the convert to Christianity was refused entrance into the home of his Hindu relatives. The Vellala lost status by conversion, but the Nadar gained status, rising above his former position. "Hence it does not follow," wrote Sharrock, "that, because a man has changed his faith, he has also given up his caste. His title remains, his customs are unaltered, and to his neighbors he is in this respect what he always was." [65]

[63] Pandion, *Ibid.*, pp. 7–8; also see A. N. Sattampillai-Aiya, *The Chantro-Memorial* (Madras, 1911), pp. 1–2.
[64] P. 129.
[65] J. A. Sharrock, "Caste and Christianity—II," *Indian Church Quarterly Review*, VIII (April, 1894), 142.

Numerous Christian families maintained marriage alliances with the Hindu families with which they had traditionally exchanged brides. The Christian Nadar would give his daughter in marriage to a Hindu Nadar—but never to a Christian of another caste. He would dine with his heathen brethren, but not with a man of his own faith who was beneath him in the social scale. In Tinnevelly, among the Hindu Nadars, Christianity was accepted as a new sect which had brought benefits of education and higher status to the entire Nadar community. "Caste," a native pastor observed, "sticks to the people as closely as their skins." [66] The blood of caste was thicker than the spirit of religion.[67]

The persistence of caste in the Christian Church had been recognized by the Roman Catholics, and in 1599, a decree was issued whereby Christians were permitted "to refrain from touching persons of inferior caste, when in the company of heathen of superior caste. . . ." [68] The early Jesuit missionary Robert de Nobili recognized the rights and privileges of the caste hierarchy, and within the church, the traditional usages of caste prohibition were accepted. Churches were even divided into two sections. While sharing a common altar, the high caste Christians were separated from those of low caste by a wall from the church door to the altar. The wall was hollow, so that the priest could enter at the door and emerge at the altar without siding with either the high caste or the low.[69]

[66] Quoted in J. A. Sharrock, *Indian Problems: Caste,* paper read at the Missionary Conference, London, May 30, 1894 (Ramnad, 1894), p. 3.

[67] "It is commonly said here that among Nadars one brother will do puja to God Shiva in one of the rooms of the family house and the other brother will pray to God Jesus Christ in another room of the same house" (Dakshina Mara Nadar Sangam, "Special Features of the Nadar Community," manuscript).

For a discussion of the close relationship between the Hindu and Christian Nadars, see *Census of India, 1961,* Vol. IX: *Madras,* Pt. VI: Village Survey Monographs, No. 8, *Kootumangulam,* p. 79; No. 19, *Kuttuthal Azhankulam,* p. 125.

[68] James Hough, *History of Christianity in India from the Commencement of the Christian Era,* II (London, 1839), 114.

[69] H. Bower, *Essay on Hindu Caste* (Calcutta, 1851), p. 57; J. C. Molony, *A Book of South India* (London, 1926), p. 133.

The use of the dividing wall continued into the twentieth century. In the village of Vadakkankulam, the Catholic congregation was predominantly Nadar, with a substantial minority of Vellalas. A wall had traditionally separated the two

The Protestants were no less tenacious in the adherence to caste than the Roman Catholics, and while the Vellalas looked down on the Nadars and discriminated against them, the Nadars were equally overbearing in the treatment of the Pallans and Paraiyans. The Nadars particularly were "very sensitive and touchy with respect to the honours due to their caste," [70] as they sought recognition of higher status. The Protestant missionaries were immediately confronted with the barrier of caste in the initial attempts to make conversions among the Nadars. In 1821, before the Nadar movement into the Church, Charles Rhenius endeavored to establish a seminary in Palamcottah. The first students were all Vellalas or other high caste Sudras. On the arrival of eight Nadar boys "from the country," the Sudras refused to eat with them, even after Rhenius agreed that they would be permitted "to hide themselves from view, as much as they please, by mats." They refused to accept even this, and the seminary was disbanded.[71] In the predominantly Nadar villages, the burden of social disabilities fell upon the untouchables. In a letter to the Bishop of Madras, a Tinnevelly missionary wrote that "on first coming to this district, when traveling among our Shanar congregations, the people would not allow our horsekeepers or other servants, being Pariahs, to draw water at the village well. . . . Pariahs and Pallars in passing through a Shanar village would not be allowed to do so with shoes on their feet." [72] In the village of Sawyerpuram, where the congregation had refused to be instructed by a low-caste catechist on threat of secession, the Nadars occupied the front pews of the church, while the Pallars sat in the back.[73] Sharrock reported that

communities within the church. When the new priest, a Paraiyan, knocked the wall down, the Vellala Christians sued for a "mandatory injunction to erect certain walls for separating" the high and low congregations, but retaining the common altar. The court ruled that such a suit could not be brought, as the Christian faith and the Canon Law did not recognize the theory of pollution and defilement by touch. *Kattalai Michael Pillai v. J. M. Barthe,* All India Reports 1917 Madras 431.

[70] Robert Caldwell, *Lectures on the Tinnevelly Mission,* p. 46.

[71] C. T. E. Rhenius, *Memoir* (London, 1841), pp. 208–209.

[72] From Edward Sargent, dated Palamcottah, July 2, 1867, in *Inquiries Made by the Bishop of Madras* . . . (Madras, 1868), p. 105.

[73] Letter to the Bishop from Rev. D. Vethamuttu, dated Sawyerpuram, July 12, 1867, in *ibid.,* pp. 86–87.

in one congregation, the Paraiyan pastor "never presumed to sit down in the houses of his Shanar flock because of his recognized inferiority of caste," and when, in another village, a Paraiyan pastor did violate the proprieties of status, he was beaten by his congregation with slippers.[74]

As the Christian converts advanced in education and improved their economic situation, caste feeling grew in intensity. "The folly of men is great," wrote Rhenius, describing the poor member of a village congregation who had been employed to clean the chapel. "Some time ago he got back four Palmyra trees, which some evil-minded Nadan had taken from him. Immediately he became lifted up with pride; the business of chapel-keeper was too mean for him; and he told the people to call him Nadan. . . ."[75] The title *Nadan*, previously limited to the few aristocratic families who held control of the land, was increasingly adopted by the aspirant Christian community. Before 1875, the church registers of the Tinnevelly Mission, in a measure of changing consciousness, show only a limited use of the title, but, according to Sharrock, "from 1875 to the present time [1894] there has been a regular increase in its frequency, till the use may now be described as universal." Nadar Christians, he noted, go so far as to threaten with legal proceedings anyone who does not give them their title.[76]

In an attempt to exorcise caste from the native church, Sharrock, in February, 1892, published banns—notices of marriage—in the church at Tuticorin, omitting the title *Nadar*, and in opposition to the wishes of the congregation, issued orders to the native pastors of the districts of Sawyerpuram, Pudukottai, and Tuticorin to omit the title from all future banns. The Nadar Christians of the district submitted a petition to the Bishop of Madras, protesting the action as a violation of "immemorial custom."[77] The following year, Sharrock and a few of those who sympathized with his opposition

---

[74] Sharrock, "Caste and Christianity," *loc. cit.*, VI, 53.

[75] Extracts from the journal of C. T. E. Rhenius, *Church Missionary Record*, V (April, 1834), 60.

[76] Sharrock, "Caste and Christianity—II," *loc. cit.*, VII, 150; see also "Caste and Christianity," a letter from "a Tinnevelly Pastor," *Indian Churchman* (Calcutta), XIV (July 15, 1893), 199; S. Paul, *Caste in the Tinnevelly Church* (Madras, 1893).

[77] Margöschis, "Christianity and Caste," *loc. cit.* (n. 5 above), p. 559.

to the persistence of caste met to form the Voluntary Society for the Suppression of Caste. The objectives of the society were (1) to abandon all titles and markings denoting caste; (2) to cease using these titles when addressing any other Christians; (3) to visit and to dine in the houses of any other Christians irrespective of caste; (4) to encourage mixed marriages; and (5) to publish and distribute tracts and handbills showing the evils of caste.[78] In July, 1895, in the midst of the controversy over the use of the title, the Bishop of Madras issued a pastoral letter on caste: "I hereby authorize and direct all the Clergy in this Diocese, whether they have been in the habit of doing so or not, to abstain, when publishing Banns of Marriage, from adding to the name of the parties, or of their parents, any social or religious title." [79]

Sharrock's anticaste society carried little weight among even the missionaries, and by 1898 only three had joined.[80] The use of the caste title *Nadan* was defended by many of the missionaries, notably Margöschis, who considered it only "a mark of respect used among the Shanar people. . . ." [81] Despite the bishop's letter, the continued use of the title in banns persisted and, if anything, became increasingly widespread. The Christians, as the more literate of the Nadar community, initiated and sustained the caste literature of the new mythology, claimed traditional Kshatriya status, and took the title *Nadan*. It was within the Hindu Nadar community, however, that the aspiration of the caste manifested itself in the movement for a Sanskritized life and customs and for entry into the temples. This drama of change was acted out in northern Tinnevelly and Ramnad, where the community had found wealth and power as a rising merchant class.

[78] S. Paranjoti, Caldwell College, Tuticorin, in *Madras Diocesan Record*, VI (July, 1893), 92.

[79] *Madras Diocesan Record*, VIII (July, 1894).

[80] C. F. Pascoe, *Two Hundred Years of the S.P.G.* (London, 1901), p. 504b.

[81] Margöschis, "Christianity and Caste," *loc. cit.*, p. 547.

Chapter IV

THE SIX TOWN NADARS: SANSKRITIZATION AND CONFRONTATION

MIGRATION TO THE NORTH

At the beginning of the nineteenth century, the Nadars of south-eastern Tinnevelly lived almost wholly from the products of the palmyra, and the vast majority of the community was engaged in climbing. The trade of the region was handled by Nadars who, with load bullocks,[1] would wander among the palmyra topes, collecting the products of the tree, particularly the jaggery cakes which were the primary medium of exchange. The use of this fluid and common medium of value and exchange gave the Nadar traders an economic independence and mobility which enabled them to respond positively and effectively to the economic changes that were to come. These traders would travel with their wares among the weekly markets, dealing in jaggery, dried fish, salt, and the products of small garden plots.

The area of their trade was restricted in this early period, for north of the Tambraparni the difficulties of transportation and the dangers of incessant wars and dacoity precluded the development of commerce.[2] Roads were virtually nonexistent before the British. At the time the southern districts were acquired by the East India Company, "there was not one complete road throughout the whole Presidency on which it would have been possible to employ

---

[1] Cart traffic was never possible in the deep sands of the *teris*. Here pack-bullocks were used for transport, with lighter loads being carried by coolies on their heads or in baskets suspended from the ends of a pliant stick slung across their shoulders—the patterns of transport throughout the southern districts and in Madras Presidency as a whole. H. R. Pate, *Madras District Gazetteers: Tinnevelly* (Madras, 1917), pp. 240–241.

[2] Robert Caldwell, in his *Political and General History of Tinnevelly* (Madras, 1881), described the peril to merchants as so great that even within their restricted area of trade, they "did not dare to appear to grow rich" (p. 63).

wheeled carriages. . . ."[3] Internal trade was further restricted by
duties levied by the poligars on goods passing through their estates.
In some areas, a stretch of road might have customhouses as close
together as every eight miles.[4] Land traffic was thus so expensive
and hazardous that it was restricted to articles of small bulk and
high value.[5]

British rule brought peace to the southern districts and the abolition of internal customs, opening the way for the expansion and
development of trade. Pax Britannica brought a cessation to the
wars which had disrupted trade, and it also established effective
police against the dacoities of hereditary highwaymen.[6] With
peace and relative security of travel, Nadar traders now loaded the
side packs of their bullocks and pushed northward into the
Maravar country with jaggery, dried fish, and salt. In these regions
to the north of the Tambraparni River, there had long been Nadar
tappers scattered over the area, a few families in a village. In addition, along the Western Ghats in Ambasamudram and Tenkasi
there were pockets of the community, from immigrations at some
earlier time. For the first time, however, large numbers of Nadars
began to move into the region.

To secure effective control over the area, the British began to
construct roads and bridges. The gradual improvement in transportation facilities enabled traders, for the first time, to transport
large stocks of wares by cart without danger to life or property.[7]
Many Nadars acquired carts for more extensive trade, and in their
return journeys brought back to Tiruchendur the cloth of Muslim

[3] Report of the Public Works Commission in 1852 on early conditions, quoted in
S. Srinivasa Raghavaiyangar, *Memorandum on the Progress of the Madras Presidency* (Madras, 1893), pp. 33–34.

[4] Raghavaiyangar, p. 22.

[5] *Ibid.*, p. 67.

[6] Writing to the collector of Tinnevelly in 1802, C. W. Gericke tried to relate
the feeling of the people on the introduction of British rule. "Where before we
could not travel without fear in the day we may now pass with great security in
the night. Since the time the English got the better of the Poligars, there is not a
thief in the thickest jungles." Quoted in Robert Caldwell, *Records of the Early
History of the Tinnevelly Mission* (Madras, 1881), p. 99.

[7] In the whole of Madras Presidency in 1850 there numbered only 50,000 carts.
By 1877, there were 284,000, and by 1893, 436,000. The increased use of the cart was
an important part of the modern development of trade and communications. See
Raghavaiyangar, pp. 61–62.

weavers, cotton seed, sheep, bullocks, and tobacco. Travel in the Maravar country, as the regions to the north were then known, was by no means wholly safe, and along their trade routes, the Nadars established *pettais*, fortified enclosures in which they could safely keep their carts and bullocks and in which they might market their goods.[8] Around the *pettai*, small shops were established, and increasing numbers of Nadar traders migrated with their families to build their houses and businesses around the new trade centers.

Their movement, determined from the distribution of the *pettais*, seems to have been west from the region of Tiruchendur and up along the Western Ghats through Tenkasi and into what is now Ramnad District. The Nadars settled in six primary centers— Sivakasi, Virudhunagar (first called Virudhupatti), Tirumangulam, Sattankudi, Palayampatti, and Aruppukottai—the "Six Towns of Ramnad." In addition to these "mother villages," Nadar merchants settled in a number of smaller, subsidiary towns, such as Kamudi, to the south of Aruppukottai.

NADAR ORGANIZATION IN RAMNAD

The Nadar merchants and traders of the Six Towns of Ramnad rapidly established themselves as an enterprising community in the early years of the nineteenth century. As middlemen and moneylenders, they soon began to acquire wealth. The first of the towns to be settled, Sivakasi, had by 1821 become a predominantly Nadar town.[9] Thomas Turnbull, a surveyor, described Sivakasi in that year as "a considerable merchant town . . . , chiefly inhabited by Shanars who from their reputation and commercial character are styled Naddikals." These Shanars, he continued, "carry on an extensive commerce especially in tobacco and cotton; they employ

---

[8] T. Brotherton, "Sketch of a Mission in Tinnevelly," *Mission Field*, XIII (June, 1868), 161–162; J.S. Ponniah, "Human Geography of the Ramnad District," *Journal of the Madras Geographical Association*, VII (1932–1933), 272; *Gnanadoraisami Nadan et al.* v. *S.P. Sivasumbramania Nadar et al.* In the Court of the Subordinate Judge, Tinnevelly, Original Suit No. 13 of 1942; and interviews.

[9] In interviews with elders of Sivakasi, I was told that their ancestors had come to Sivakasi six or eight generations ago.

upwards of 2,000 bullocks for the purpose of exporting their tobacco to Travancore. The petty dealers among the tribe barter in giving their cotton for earthen pots and chatties, also for bamboo mats and baskets. Here is a weekly market on every Tuesday . . . cotton yarn, paddy and all sorts of grain, jaggery, salt-fish, mats, seines, baskets, ghee, fruits and vegetables in abundance."

In addition to the *pettai*, a commercial warehouse had been constructed for the East India Company's cotton, and long rows of bazaars were "plentifully stored with grain and every other article which affords comfort and convenience to a dense population as well as to the inhabitants of the neighbouring villages." The Nadars had constructed their own temples, and a wealthy merchant had built a hostel for the accommodation of travelers.[10]

In Turnbull's survey of the region of Ramnad, 1814, he described Aruppukottai as a town principally inhabited by weavers "and a few opulent Shaunars."[11] Palayampatti, three miles' distance from Aruppukottai, was noted as "a place where a few opulent tradesmen reside."[12] Turnbull described Kamudi as a town of narrow and crooked streets and low thatched houses built of earth. A few of the houses were tiled, and almost in the center of the town, the residences were dominated by "a grand terraced house . . . belonging to a Shaunan; its elegance and situation affords an agreeable prospect." He spoke of the Nadars as cotton traders and as "very opulent men."[13]

Although the Nadar merchants of the Six Towns commanded increasing wealth, their numbers were few and limited to scattered towns. The surrounding countryside was dominated by the more numerous Maravars, Reddiars, and Naickers. As middlemen and moneylenders, the Nadars hardly endeared themselves to the vil-

[10] Thomas Turnbull, *Geographical and Statistical Memoir of Tinnevelly District,* surveyed in 1821 and published under order of the collector, R. K. Puckle, Palamcottah, 1877, quoted in *Disturbances in Madura and Tinnevelly* (Madras, 1899), p. 8.

[11] Thomas Turnbull, "Statistical and Geographical Memoir, Maravar or Ramnad, the Isle of Ramiseram and Tondiman's Country, survey in 1814," Fort St. George, Surveyor General's Office, 1817. Manuscript, India Office Library, pp. 127–128.

[12] *Ibid.,* p. 128.

[13] *Ibid.,* p. 109.

lagers, and the rising economic power of the Nadar merchant community in Ramnad increasingly bred animosity. In southeastern Tinnevelly, homeland of the Nadars, the community was numerically dominant and, with no external threat, was divided among opposing client groups. The Christian villages found unity through the mission, but among Hindu Nadars there was virtually no village organization. The village accountant was often the only all-village officer, and ordinarily he was of another community. Confronted by a great majority of non-Nadars, as they migrated from the south in the early years of the nineteenth century, the traders of the Six Towns of Ramnad sought a tight and cohesive organization for the protection of the community. In order to maximize unity within the community, the caste organization was to be the final authority, and all contact with government officials would be through the organization of the community as a whole. In relations with other castes, the Nadars would present a common face. The fundamental institutions of the new unity of the Ramnad Nadars were *mahimai* and the *uravinmurai*.

The *pettais*, around which the Nadar towns grew, were originally built and maintained through a tax levied on all goods bought and sold. Each trader using the facilities of the *pettai* was required to contribute a portion of his income as "common good funds," or *mahimai* (literally, "to glorify oneself"). As the towns grew, resident merchants and businessmen were required to contribute *mahimai*, the amount of the levy to be determined by common decision of all the Nadar family elders. In Sivakasi, the Nadars required non-Nadar merchants to contribute *mahimai* to the Nadar coffers and extracted a levy on all carts passing through the town. From these funds, the Sivakasi Nadars constructed *pettais* for the use of their traders in ninety-six towns and villages in Tamilnad and Travancore.[14]

The Nadar council controlling the *mahimai* funds was composed of the head of each household in the community and came to be known as the *uravinmurai*. The *uravinmurai* was the corporate

---

[14] Interview. Hereafter in this chapter an asterisk will indicate that the information has been obtained in interviews, with the principal or with other participants or observers.

power of the community; its power was absolute. While the organization of the *uravinmurai* varied among the towns of northern
Tinnevelly and Ramnad, the structure and operation of the
Palayampatti *uravinmurai* was typical and remained essentially the
same from the early nineteenth century well into the twentieth.
Toward the latter part of the nineteenth century there were some
two hundred Nadar families in the town. Participation in the
uravinmurai was limited to the married head of each household.
Widowers and unmarried men were excluded, but as soon as a boy
married, his name was entered in the list of members. In Palayampatti, there was a hereditary headman, the *ambalakaran*. There also
was a hereditary secretary of the *uravinmurai*. The substance of
power, however, lay in the hands of a committee, each member
being known as *muraikarar*—literally "one who holds the turn."
The number of *muraikarars* varied with each town; in Palayampatti there were four, each holding the position of president for
one week in a four-week cycle. At the end of the week, the
muraikarar then handed over the accounts and cash to the next.
Since the Nadar tradesmen generally were unlettered, the *uravinmurai* frequently employed an accountant of another caste, normally a Vellala. Each evening the accountant, having made daily
mahimai collections, brought the cash to the *muraikarar*. As
mahimai was the foundation of the *uravinmurai*, payment was
watched closely, and if any doubt was raised as to proper payments, the *uravinmurai* would exercise its right to examine the
man's accounts. A failure to pay *mahimai* would double the tax.
The burden of time demanded by the position of *muraikarar* meant
that ordinarily the most prominent and wealthy members of the
community did not serve, the posts being held rather by respectable merchants and shopkeepers of medium-income status.

While the temple was the seat of the *uravinmurai* in many villages, Palayampatti had a meeting place specifically for the *uravinmurai*. Meetings were held in both ordinary and extraordinary
sessions. Although there was no stipulated date, ordinary meetings
were usually held at least once a month. In the evening, a few
hours before the appointed time for the meeting (normally about
9:00 P.M.), the barber in his role as town crier would go through

the streets calling the *uravinmurai* members. Each was bound to attend or be subject to fine. The order of business began with the reading of the accounts followed by an open session for the introduction of complaints.

The *uravinmurai* sought to keep all disputes within the community, and in cases involving morality or minor criminal offenses, the *uravinmurai* would accept jurisdiction if it were possible to avoid police intervention. If a charge—of defamation or adultery, for example—was brought against someone within the community, notice was given to the accused to appear at the next meeting to defend himself. In Palayampatti, the "court" sessions of the *uravinmurai* were held in the open streets in the heart of the Nadar quarter, and no outsider was permitted within range. In an adultery case, the woman would be brought in. The accused was brought before the *uravinmurai* and, by standing on three lines drawn in saffron, was obliged to tell the truth. Any man of the *uravinmurai* could ask questions of the accused and the witnesses. In important cases, special invitations might be issued to widowers to attend and occasionally even to an "expert witness," a Nadar from outside the town.

The "court" was opened by the headman, who requested permission to read the complaint. If a compromise could not be reached between the parties, the assembly was opened for discussion. The discussion and questions ended when all the relevant points in the case had been made. The decision was by a sense of the meeting, rather than by formal vote. In some cases, a few individuals would be selected to make the decision as a jury, although selection could be challenged by the accused. The views expressed by prominent persons of the community were a decisive factor. When a decision had been reached, the headman was informed, and the verdict and sentence were announced by him to the *uravinmurai*.

In the case of sexual molestation or adultery—viewed as most serious offenses—the sentence was a public beating before the *uravinmurai*. The barber executed the sentence, beating the accused with sandals. For a grave crime, such as theft, the sentence might demand that the accused run a certain distance, some hundred feet or so, and return. On both sides the young men of the village would stand to give him a blow as he went by. Minor crimes were normally punished by admonition and fine. Fines were initially set at a staggering figure. The accused would then prostrate himself before the assembly. If the elders considered him sufficiently repentant, the figure would gradually be lowered with successive prostrations. The final figure must be paid immediately. If the accused was unable to pay and no one would offer security, a limited time might be given to pay. Installments were also occasionally permitted. If payment was not made, the whole case would be reopened and a more severe verdict reached. In such rare cases the *uravinmurai* would itself go to the house of the accused and remove the door and all movables.

The most severe punishment was used only when the *uravinmurai* was defied. A man may have thought himself sufficiently powerful to refuse to comply with the orders of the *uravinmurai*. If he refused to prostrate himself before the body, he would be ostracized from the community. No Nadar would be permitted to talk with him, to give him fire, water, or food. He would be denied the right to participate in community life, including the services of the temple. Shops would be closed to him, and the barber and washerman would refuse him their services. The accountant would prepare a resolution of outcaste, and copies would be sent to the *uravinmurai* of Aruppukottai, Virudhunagar, Sattankudi, Tirumangulam, and Sivakasi. The outcasting of a person imposed difficulties upon the entire community, and many people would continue to associate with him, bearing fines to do so. The pressures for a reconciliation were great, and it was normally effected after some time. Otherwise, the ostracized family was forced to move away.

An extraordinary meeting of the *uravinmurai* was convened when the community was threatened, as in a dispute between castes. All shops were closed during the continuous deliberations, and no man dared leave the assembly. If there was a dispute between two *uravinmurai*, or between certain Nadars of two villages, a joint session might be held—either a meeting of the two whole assemblies or of deputized elders of each. In certain cases, the dispute was taken for settlement to a body of the Six Town Nadars at Sattankudi, the town traditionally recognized as preeminent among the merchant communities of Ramnad.

In civil disputes within the community, the *uravinmurai* would seek to refer the case to a committee of mediators, prominent persons especially selected and acceptable to both parties. All attempts would be made to effect a compromise in order to keep the dispute out of the courts. In major cases, prominent Nadars from Sattankudi or another of the Six Towns would arbitrate as an *ad hoc* panchayat committee. Decisions were binding on all parties. The Nadar *uravinmurai* was frequently called upon to settle disputes among or between other communities as well.[15]

In Kamudi, the organization of the *uravinmurai* was fundamentally the same. It consisted of the head of each of the five hundred Nadar families and was led formally by the hereditary headman. In Kamudi, there were twelve trustees, or *muraikarars*, each holding the presidency of the *uravinmurai* for a period of one month in a twelve-month cycle. The *muraikarars* were selected by the ten *kuttams* residing in Kamudi. Every five years, each *kuttam* would select one of its number as a trustee. Once an individual was selected, he normally continued 'as long as he desired or until he lost the confidence of the community. The ten *muraikarars* selected in this way elected two additional trustees, bringing the total number to twelve.

The *muraikarars* met together on the third day of each Tamil month. The *uravinmurai* met ordinarily about once a month. Meetings were held in the Bhadrakali temple, and in the "court" sessions the accused stood on seven saffron lines (rather than three, as in Palayampatti) and swore "by the Seven Sons of Bhadrakaliamman" to tell the truth. Punishments were often severe. In the case of sexual molestation, the accused would be beaten and his head shaved and covered with cow dung, and in this condition he would have to walk around the village six times, suffering the insults of the townspeople. The Kamudi *uravinmurai* maintained its own jail,

[15] The description of the traditional operation of the Palayampatti *uravinmurai* is based on extended interviews with Judge S. Ganesan, a Nadar originally from Palayampatti and now residing in Madras.

and petty crimes might bring short sentences. Repeated violations might lengthen the sentence or lead to social ostracism and out-casting.[16]

The Sivakasi *uravinmurai* was organized on the basis of twenty-four street associations. The head of each family was automatically a member of the street association. The head of these associations served for life and was ex officio a member of the *uravinmurai*. Of the twenty-four members of the *uravinmurai*, a committee of four (later increased to six) provided the leadership. Each member of the *uravinmurai* was treated with great respect, but to the leaders a special deference was made. In their presence, a man would remove his upper cloth and tie it around his waist, as when entering the temple. The organizational structure of the Sivakasi *uravinmurai* was a product of the town's size. In Virudhunagar, increasing population in the latter part of the nineteenth century led to the formation of six separate *uravinmurai*, each based on a major field of trade. There was, for example, one *uravinmurai* for cotton merchants, another for grocery tradesmen. For matters affecting the entire community, such as the management of the Mariamman temple, there was a body of representatives drawn from the different *uravinmurai* on a basis proportional to their membership.*

Madurai, which became an important Nadar trading center, was not one of the original Six Towns, and as a "colony" never had its own *uravinmurai*. Traders from the "mother towns" of Ramnad established *pettais* there for the protection of their bullocks and goods. The Nadars of Virudhunagar, Aruppukottai, and Palayampatti purchased land in Madurai on East Masi Street in 1813.[17] Sivakasi set up its own separate *pettai* some blocks away. Even as late as 1890, however, relatively few Nadars had made their residence in Madurai. In the last decade of the nineteenth century and the first few years after the turn of the century, a heavy migration of Nadar tradesmen into Madurai occurred. The impetus came with the construction of the railroad south from

[16] Based on discussions with elders of the Kamudi *uravinmurai* and on an interview with a leading businessman and political figure of Kamudi.

[17] *S. A. Muthu Nadar et al. v. K. Hussain Rowther et al.*

Madurai to Virudhunagar and then to Tinnevelly and Tuticorin. The concentration of trade at the rail center at Virudhunagar adversely affected the other trading towns of Ramnad, and the Nadar merchants, seeking to take advantage of the new opportunities for expanded trade, left for Madurai. Palayampatti, which had had between two hundred and two hundred and fifty Nadar families, was left with hardly twenty-five. Sivakasi was severely affected, as much of its trade was lost to Virudhunagar. From the 1880's to 1928, when Sivakasi was linked by rail with Virudhunagar and Madurai, a steady flow of merchants and traders left the town. While some went to Madurai, the larger portion of Sivakasi migrant traders went south to Tinnevelly Town and Tuticorin, where they established branches of the Sivakasi businesses. The Nadar migrants to Madurai and Tuticorin maintained their ties with the "mother village" and continued to be members of the *uravinmurai* of their home town and to pay *mahimai* there. In Madurai, each of the Six Towns and many of the smaller Ramnad towns had their own *uravinmurai* organizations. In Madurai, among the Nadars, there were thirty-two *uravinmurai*, each affiliated with its "mother village," but there was not an overall association for the Nadar residents of the town. The largest and most important *uravinmurai* in Madurai were those of Sivakasi, Aruppukottai, and Virudhunagar.*

ASPIRATION AND CHANGE

As the wealth of the Nadar merchant communities grew during the nineteenth century, the common funds of *mahimai* were used for the welfare of the community as a whole. The poor among the caste were fed and clothed, and jobs were secured for those of able body. Business failures were prevented with the considered use of *mahimai* funds. Wells and public buildings for the community were constructed, and in each of the towns, a Mariamman temple was constructed to the community deity. Perhaps the most important use of *mahimai* funds was in the establishment of schools by the Nadar *uravinmurai*. The first of the Nadar schools, the

Kshatriya Vidyasala High School, was established by the Virudhunagar *uravinmurai* in 1885, and it was one of the first free schools in Tamilnad open to the children of all caste communities.[18] The school in Kamudi was opened by the *uravinmurai* there in 1889,[19] and the Kshatriya High School at Aruppukottai was established in 1895.[20]

The incongruity between the economic position of the Six Town Nadars and their low social status led these Nadars increasingly to attempt to disassociate themselves from the community's traditional occupation. Even by the mid-nineteenth century, the palmyra was seen as a curse by the Ramnad Nadars, to whom it was an unwelcome reminder of their defiled ritual status. Having abandoned the cultivation and climbing of the despised palm, these Nadars held themselves superior to their caste fellows in Tinnevelly. Intermarriage was prohibited and interdining discouraged. It was the gravest insult to suggest that a Nadar trader might in any way be connected with the palmyra or that a not-too-distant ancestor might have sold dried fish.* The Ramnad traders almost universally adopted the title *Nadar*, rejecting the appellation *Shanar* as degrading, and some went so far as to suggest that there was no connection between the two groups. "The Shanans have a great objection to being called either Shanan or Marameri (tree-climber), and much prefer Nadan," noted Thurston.[21] In deeds and documents, the community began to describe itself as Kshatriyas, seeking recognition to its claims by the signature of men of high caste.[22] Some styled themselves Pandyans, and in Coimbatore, Salem, and Trichinopoly districts, many Nadar businessmen called themselves Chetties. A few even took the Vellala

---

[18] A letter to the *Madras Mail*, June 24, 1899, says that the school "is a charitable institution where instruction is given free of cost to pupils of all castes and religions. There are now about 300 boys in the school, of whom not less than half the number are non-Shanar boys, including, Brahmins, Vellalas, Naidus, and Maravars." Also see Edgar Thurston, *Castes and Tribes of Southern India* (Madras, 1909), VI, 378.

[19] Discussion with elders of the Kamudi *uravinmurai*.

[20] Discussion with elders of the Aruppukottai *uravinmurai*.

[21] Thurston, VI, 376.

[22] *Rajah Bhaskara Sethupathi v. Irulappan Nadar*, p. 70.

title *Pillai*. In Coimbatore, the title *Muppan*, or headman, was also used.[23]

As the increasing wealth of the Nadar merchant community widened the gap between their economic status and their traditional position in the hierarchy of ritual purity, the Nadars sought to bring their social status to a level commensurate with their economic power through imitation of the Brahminical customs of the higher castes. Claiming high Kshatriya status, the Nadars, from about the 1860's, began slowly to Sanskritize their manner of life. Men began to tie their dhoti in the manner of the Brahmins, to crop their hair in the fashion of the Brahmin tuft,[24] and to abandon the heavy jewelry and ear-pieces which had been common among them. The women adapted their jewelry and dress to the new style. It had been the custom for women to wear a conglomerate ear-piece composed of a large bunch of studs and rings. These were once of lead, but with wealth, gold was used. Under the heavy weight of the jewelry, the lobes were extended, often hanging to the shoulders—the length of the lobe indicating material prosperity. The custom, however, was limited to the lower range of castes, and as hardly fitting to Kshatriya status, the practice was opposed by Nadar leaders. Widows were permitted to wear only white saris, like the Brahmins, and remarriage of widows was forbidden.[25] Nadar leaders decreed that women would cease to carry water on their heads and, like the higher castes, would carry the water pots against their hips. To enforce the order, men were stationed at the gates of the gardens where the wells were located.[26]

[23] J. A. Sharrock, "Caste and Christianity," *Indian Church Quarterly Review*, VI (January, 1893), 60; Thurston, VI, 377; and interviews.

[24] Robert Caldwell, "Observations on the Kudumi," *Indian Antiquary*, IV (1875), 168–169.

[25] There is some dispute over whether the ban on remarriage of widows was introduced in the process of Sanskritization or whether the custom was indigenous to the community. As early as 1867, a native pastor in Tinnevelly wrote that "remarriages of widows are deemed by the majority of the Shanars in my District a great insult and disgrace" (letter to the Bishop from Rev. Jesudosen John, dated Kadatchapuram, July 20, 1867, in *Inquiries Made by the Bishop of Madras*, p. 120).

[26] John Chandler, *Seventy-five Years in the Madura Mission* (Madras, 1909), pp. 23–24.

Where once burial had been the custom among the Nadars, the community increasingly chose cremation as symbolic of higher status.[27] In marriages, while the traditional bride-price continued as a part of the ceremony, its importance came to be replaced by the more Sanskritized custom of dowry.[28] Palanquins, though long used by the Nadan aristocracy of Tiruchendur, were generally considered an attribute of the higher castes. In the latter part of the nineteenth century, the use of palanquins in marriage processions became widespread among the Nadars of Ramnad. In order to emphasize their position of wealth and power, the Nadars hired Maravars as their palanquin bearers.[29]

Vegetarianism came into vogue among some Nadars, and fathers named their children after the Sanskritic gods which had come into favor among the community. They constructed temples to Siva and made rich gifts to established temples, to which they were denied entrance. They met the costs of festival days, paying puja (worship) expenses and feeding Brahmins. Brahmin priests were found who were quite willing to provide their services to the wealthy Nadar temples and to officiate in the ceremonies of the caste.[30] Perhaps the most important symbol of status adopted by the Nadars was the sacred thread of the "twice-born." Investiture of the venerated thread is limited to the Brahmins, the Kshatriyas, and the Vaisyas—the Dwijas, or twice-born castes. The Brahmin priests, or purohits, were paid to conduct the Upanayanam, the sacrament of investiture, for the Nadars, thus endowing them with the symbolic attribute of Kshatriyahood.[31]

[27] Pupathi Chinnalakshmana Raja, Shanar Kshatriya? (Salem, 1924), p. 110. For a description of the traditional funeral ceremony, see V. Nagam Aiya, Travancore State Manual (Trivandrum, 1906), II, 396–397.

[28] Census of India, 1961, Vol. IX: Madras, Pt. VI: Village Survey Monographs, No. 19, Kuttuthal Azhankulam, p. 7.

[29] Evidence introduced by the Nadars in the Kamudi case showed that Maravars carried palanquins for the Six Town Nadars. Rajah Bhaskara Sethupathi v. Irulappan Nadan, pp. 68–69.

[30] In the Kamudi case, witnesses for the plaintiff testified that such purohits as serve the Nadars "will go wherever they are invited or paid" and have "a reputation for avarice." The Judge concluded that the use of Brahmin purohits did not mark the Nadars as a superior caste. Ibid., pp. 65–66.

[31] A Panchangam Brahmin testified in the Kamudi case that he officiated for the Nadars' domestic sacraments. On perusal of his deposition, the Judge said that "he exhibits gross ignorance of the Upanayanam ritual as prescribed for the

In 1891, some 24,000 Nadars returned themselves as
"Kshatriyas" in the census,[32] and in the years between 1891 and
1911, in the districts of Tinnevelly, Ramnad, and Madurai, there
was an increase of 63 percent in the number of "Kshatriyas" returned. "Not content to pollute without eating beef," wrote the
census superintendent, Molony, in the report for 1911, "they claim
to be Kshatriyas." [33]

THE SACK OF SIVAKASI: THE TINNEVELLY RIOTS OF 1899

The economic rise of the Nadar community and their attempts
to achieve a social status commensurate with their new economic
position inevitably brought the community into conflict with the
higher castes. As the Ramnad Nadars sought the recognition of
high status, the Maravars, the dominant caste of the region, inter-
posed their strength against the aspirant community, beginning in
1860 at Aruppukottai and Palayampatti, with a series of confrontations.

The pretension of the Nadar community to higher status
through the adoption of the symbolic paraphernalia of those above
them was soon compounded in their attempt to gain entry into the
temples. With the attributes of the higher castes, the Nadars now
sought interactional recognition to their claims through their admission into the temples which had denied them entrance. In 1872,
a case was brought by the Brahmins and the Vellalas of
Tiruchendur against seven Nadars for entering the temple.* The
Nadars of Madurai, in 1874, attempted to assert their right to
temple entry through a criminal complaint lodged against the servants of the Meenakshi temple. In the suit against the temple servants, Mookka Nadan claimed that "criminal force" had been used
in expelling him from the temple. According to the prosecution,
Mooka Nadan entered the temple and went to the Parrot's altar,
where he worshipped the goddess Meenakshi. Temple servants

Kshattriyas according to the Dharma Shastras. . . . He is one of those men who
pander to the craving of the lower castes for sake of lucre" (*ibid.*, p. 76).

[32] *Census of India*, 1891, Vol. XIII: *Madras Report*, p. 297.

[33] *Census of India*, 1911, Vol. XII: Madras, Pt. I: *Report*, p. 160; also see Pate,
Madras District Gazetteers: Tinnevelly, p. 125.

recognized him as a Nadar and asked why he had come. Mookka replied that he had come to worship God. The temple servant said that he should not have entered, and Mookka was struck on the nape of the neck and, by the neck, was then led to the cloth bazaar, just outside the temple. The judge, aware that the case had been brought to establish a legal recognition of the right of entry, refused to rule on the entry at all.[34] A similar case was brought two years later, in 1876, at Tiruthangal, in Srivilliputtur taluq. This too was unsuccessful.[35]

The Srivilliputtur District *munsif* in 1878 passed an order forbidding Nadars of Tiruthangal from entering the temple and from offering the deity coconuts. The order did, however, permit the Nadars to take their own procession around the village streets. The right of procession was not always uncontested. In 1885, the Nadars of a village in Sattur taluq petitioned for the privilege to conduct a procession through the streets of the village. The local zamindar and the people of higher caste in the village opposed the petition, and it was ruled that the procession could go only through the streets of the Nadar quarter of the village. Rioting ensued.[36]

The feeling of hostility between the Nadars and the Maravars in the area of northern Tinnevelly and Ramnad District culminated, according to the *Administrative Report of the Police* for 1887, in the murder of four Maravars by a band of Nadars. A number of Nadars were arrested and brought before the Sessions Court at Tinnevelly on what appeared to be substantial evidence. The Nadars were acquitted, and the Maravars retaliated with the murder of three of the Nadars involved.

A year later, in 1888, the superintendent of police reported an "unstable equilibrium" in Tinnevelly. "Everywhere the lower castes are asserting themselves, while still denying the caste below them the right which they themselves newly claim." The Shanars, "waxing in wrath," were seeking the privileges of Kshatriya status, and the Maravars and Vellalas were determined that they should

[34] Judgment in Calendar Case No. 799 of 1874, on the file of the 2d Class Magistrate of Madura Town.
[35] Pate, p. 126.
[36] *Disturbances in Madura and Tinnevelly*, p. 6.

not have them. The question of processions, the superintendent warned, was "a burning question and fruitful of grave riots . . . if not watched carefully. The processions which require care are those which are attempts at self-assertion and glorification." [37]

The warning was well taken, for in 1895, the zamindar of Ettaiyapuram, as trustee of the local temple, obtained an injunction restraining the Nadars of Kalugumalai village from conducting processions in the "car streets" of the town. The Nadars, in response, countered by converting to Roman Catholicism as a body. The mission, to provide a place of worship for its new converts, purchased a shop on one of the car streets. At the time of the temple festival, it was the custom that a car bearing the deity be pulled through the car streets around the temple by the devotees. Just before the day arrived on which the Hindus would drag the car through the streets, a pandal, a framed canopy, was constructed across the road in front of the new Nadar chapel. As the car reached the site, it was obvious that the procession could not pass unless the pandal was removed. Seventy Nadars, determined that the pandal would not come down, began to throw stones at the crowd collecting before the chapel. The Brahmin manager of the Ettaiyapuram estate was stabbed to death. In the rioting that followed, seven Nadars and two of the manager's followers were killed. The thatched roof of the chapel was burned, and the crowds looted the Nadar quarter. Additional police were stationed at Kalugumalai until March, 1899, when they were withdrawn— just one month before more serious rioting broke out in Sivakasi and throughout the district.[38]

In 1899, Sivakasi was the site of major rioting between the Nadars and other communities, particularly the Maravars. It was the apogee of the Nadars' conflict with the Maravars, and for the older generation of Sivakasi, even today, the riot is the event by which time is reckoned.

At the time of the 1891 census, the population of Sivakasi was just over 12,000. Of this number, probably some 1,500 were Muslims and another 150, Christians. Of the Hindus, over 80 percent

[37] Quoted in *ibid.*
[38] Pate, p. 126.

were Nadars. The Maravars, who lived in a separate quarter of the
town, numbered about 500. They disappeared after the riots.
Sivakasi, though a Nadar trading center, was not originally a
Nadar town. The town was built around a central Siva temple, to
which the Nadars were denied entrance. The Nadars, of course,
had their own temples, constructed and maintained by *mahimai*
funds. In addition to a number of family temples, there was on the
north side of town a Bhadrakali temple and, on the east, a
Mariamman temple. The main Nadar temple and the meeting place
of the *uravinmurai* was the Ammankoil, located in the center of the
city. Here the festival deities were kept for procession in the car
streets around the temple. These Nadar temples were served both
by Nadars and by Pandarams, non-Brahmin priests. Turnbull
noted in 1821 that "the votaries consist of their own class who
make offerings of coconut and fruit, which are heaped up before
its shrine." [39]

Beginning about 1890, the process of Sanskritization in Sivakasi
was accelerated, antagonizing the Vellalas and Maravars. "The real
trouble-makers were Vellalas," recalls an elderly widow of social
prominence in Sivakasi, who was a young woman at the time of the
riots in 1899, "and it was they who instigated the Maravars. The
Vellalas took objection to the Nadars even wearing footwear." [40]
Some of the Nadars began to tie their dhotis in the fashion of the
Brahmin, to wear the tuft, and a few became vegetarians. P. Shenbagakutti (humorously called "Pannaiyeri"), leader of the Sivakasi
Nadars, appealed to the community in 1898 to adopt the use of the
sacred thread, but it came into daily use only just after the rioting. [41] One of the elders of Sivakasi recalls that "As the Nadars had
become depressed, the leaders insisted that the people should bring
themselves up to the level of the Brahmins. In about 1892, a
nandavanam, bathing place with garden, was built near the
Bhadrakalikoil, and the Nadars were asked to bathe every day and

[39] In *Disturbances in Madura and Tinnevelly*, p. 8.
[40] Interview, Chellammal Nadar (mother of N. P. A. S. Perianna Nadar,
former vice president of the Sivakasi municipality), widow, aged 85.
[41] Interview with a group of Sivakasi elders, July, 1965. There is question over
the tuft. Chellammal Nadar says that the tuft was not an innovation, but was
traditional with the Nadars.

to wash their own clothes, in the manner of the Brahmins." * In 1897, the Nadar priest of the Amman temple was replaced by a Brahmin *purohit,* brought from a temple near Trichinopoly to serve the Nadars of Sivakasi.[42]

While the elder of Sivakasi believes "the ill-feelings between the Nadars and Maravars arose when the Nadars began to change their customs," these changes were but symbols of more fundamental changes in economic relationships as the Nadars rose to economic dominance as traders and moneylenders. The dependence of the higher caste people on the Nadars, whom they despised as a ritually unclean caste, fostered a jealousy only exacerbated by the Nadars' pretensions to higher status and by their adoption of Sanskritic attributes. "These pretensions of the Shanars excited the Maravars," wrote an old Indian Civil Service officer, long attached to Madras, "and broken heads were the consequence whenever an opportunity occurred. The broken heads invariably were those of Shanars." [43] As antagonism grew, a missionary of the area warned that the Nadars "appear to be intoxicated with their silly claims to be Kshatriyas" and that "mischief" was at hand.[44]

Toward the close of 1895, one of the trustees of Viswanadhaswamy temple, the local Siva temple, resigned. The Nadars of Sivakasi, seeking at once to force temple entry and to get a footing in the management of the temple, submitted a petition to the president of the Devastanam (Temple) committee in Tinnevelly, praying that a Nadar might be appointed to fill the vacancy. A counterpetition was then filed, protesting against the recognition of the Nadars' pretensions. The counterpetition threatened that compliance with the Nadars' request for trusteeship "would be the occasion of causing a most tremendous occurrence" and that the "Kalugumalai occurrence will be repeated." [45] After the committee declined to appoint a Nadar as temple trustee, rumor circulated

[42] Today there are two Brahmin priests in attendance at the temple. The head priest is the grandson of the priest who came in 1897.
[43] Colonel H. W. W. Cox, I.C.S., quoted in the *Madras Mail,* July 17, 1899.
[44] Quoted in *Disturbances in Madura and Tinnevelly,* p. 3.
[45] Additional Sessions Court, Tinnevelly, C. C. No. 39 of 1899 (F. D. P. Oldfield, presiding). The citation is incomplete, as the first page of the case record is missing; p. 14.

that the subsequent death of the two Nadar candidates for the appointment was a divine retribution against the Nadars.[46]

In the next four years in Sivakasi, a series of confrontations brought the Nadars against an alignment of almost all the other communities of Sivakasi. Each community found itself either financially indebted to, economically dependent on, or in competition with, the Nadars. The Maravars, traditionally a warrior community and numerically the dominant caste of the surrounding region, found the Nadars rising above them in wealth and power. The Vellalas found their position of leadership and superiority threatened, and their embitterment was deepened by the Sanskritized arrogance of the Nadars and their claims to higher Kshatriya status. The Muslims also found their position as traders jeopardized by growing Nadar economic power. The Pallans, dependent on and allied to the Maravars, sided with the anti-Nadar faction.

As the situation worsened, the doors of the Siva temple were closed to prevent the Nadars from attempting to enter. After reports were circulated among the non-Nadars that the door had been broken in and the temple had been clandestinely entered during the night, several Nadar houses were burned. Charges of various outrages, attacks, and attempted temple-entries were hurled back and forth between the communities.[47] As the cases came to court, the judge—later accused of "timidity and vacillation"—dismissed each as "false." The police report said that "the Deputy Magistrate entirely misapprehended the situation; he underrated the pitch of excitement to which feeling on both sides had risen; and he apparently hoped that by taking no distinct line things would right themselves and that he at all events would not be blamed for having done anything wrong in the matter." [48]

During the early months of 1899, there were scattered cases of arson on the part of both Nadars and Maravars, and the Nadars of Sivakasi, afraid of trouble, called off their major festivals of Mariamman and Bhadrakali. On April 26, serious rioting broke out

[46] *Disturbances in Madura and Tinnevelly*, p. 7.
[47] *Ibid.*, pp. 8-15.
[48] *Ibid.*, pp. 12-13; see also the *Hindu* (Madras), June 27, 1899.

and was brought under control only when police fired into the air above the crowd. The Maravar quarter of the town was almost completely destroyed, and the Maravars fled from the town.[49] The determination of the Maravars to take revenge on the Nadars began to take form. Rumors in the town said the Maravars were collecting in large numbers in the outlying villages and intended to attack Sivakasi at the first favorable opportunity. Various petitions were sent to the collector warning that anti-Nadars were organizing the plunder of Sivakasi. Scott, the Tinnevelly collector and district magistrate, wrote in his diary, "I think too much has been made of this whole matter." [50]

While European officials of the district were being assured by local village heads (who were all against the Nadars) that no mischief was at hand in Tinnevelly, the attack was organized. Supported by the Brahmins, Vellalas, and the Maravar zamindars, roving bands of Maravars, Kallars, and Pallans, drawn from the regions of western Ramnad, northern Tinnevelly, and southern Madurai districts, soon began to attack and pillage Nadar villages in the area of Sivakasi. The plunder began on May 23, at a village five miles from Srivilliputtur, where the Nadars were looted and driven from the village.[51] As the marauders moved closer to Sivakasi itself, the Vellalas and people of other communities, with their properties and goods, evacuated the town, throwing the Nadars into a panic.

Unable to secure the protection of local authorities, who were believed to be either in league with the attackers or intimidated by them, the Sivakasi Nadars pleaded with the government to protect them from forthcoming doom. Scott remained unresponsive. With no hope of government support, the Nadars wrote to Vellaiya Thevan, leader of the mobs, which had come to number some 4,000, saying that if he were a true Maravar he would fix a day for the attack and meet the Nadars in daylight, but that if he were a Kuravan, an untouchable, he would raid by night in surprise.

[49] *Disturbances in Madura and Tinnevelly*, pp. 2, 16–17.
[50] Quoted in *Ibid.*, p. 18.
[51] M. S. Shanmuga Nadar, *The Sack of Sivakasi and Other Atrocities in Tinnevelly District* (Madras, 1899), pp. 1–3.

Vellaiya declared himself true to his caste and posted a public notice on the wheel of the temple car in Sivakasi. Above his signature, the attack was set for June 6, and notice was given that the leaders E. Ayya Nadar and P. Shenbagakutti Nadar would be hanged and that the entire Nadar community of Sivakasi would be exterminated.[52] Sivakasi would become Siva-thusi—the dust of Siva.[53] On the afternoon of June 5, Scott and his police superintendent rode into Sivakasi on horseback. The Nadars begged him to stay. Satisfied with the assurances of the local police that these fears were without justification, Scott went on to Srivilliputtur.*

On the morning of June 6, 1899, as the Maravars closed in around the town of Sivakasi, the Nadars prepared to meet them. During the preceding days, the Nadars had smuggled in guns wrapped in bedding. During the night before the attack, the Nadars felled trees onto the roads leading to the town and constructed barricades, leaving a few places open to draw the attackers together. The rich buried iron safes filled with money and jewelry. The poorer people, who lived in thatched huts on the outlying sections of the town, were brought into the center, where the *pucca* houses, two or three stories high, offered substantial protection. Here barricades were put up in the narrow streets, and planks connected the terraced roofs of the houses. In the week before the attack, many of the women and children had been sent out of the town for protection, some as far as Madras City. Many of the refugees, however, were sent back to Sivakasi by the Maravars. In the south car street, a fortification was built for the safety of the women and children who remained, and there they pounded chili powder, which together with stones and boiling oil, would be poured from the roofs onto the Maravars below. If the men were defeated, the women were to immolate themselves rather than be captured. Monday night, the Nadars brought their weapons to the temple, laid them before Karuran, the god of war, and consecrated them and their lives to his service. With early morning, boys were stationed on roofs to watch for the approaching Maravars, and on

[52] Smt. Sangammal, daughter of the late E. Ayya Nadar, aged eighty-two, prepared statement; and interviews.

[53] G. S. Price, letter to the *Pioneer* (Allahabad), June 26, 1899, reprinted in the *Hindu*, June 27, 1899.

top of the temple car—still richly decorated for festivals that were never held—a lookout was posted with a telescope.[54]

The attack lasted less than two hours. The Maravars were sent into retreat, carrying their dead in the dozen carts brought to haul away the loot.[55] Eight hundred and eighty-six Nadar houses had been destroyed, and twenty-one people were known dead.[56] After the last of the Maravars had fled, Scott arrived. Overcome by the situation, he telegraphed for fifty sepoys to be sent from Trichinopoly to Virudhunagar, where the Nadars were in a state of alarm, fearing that they would be attacked next. Leaving the superintendent to hold inquests and to tend the wounded, Scott set out for Tinnevelly. There he handed over his charge to a subordinate European officer and left from the port of Tuticorin for Australia.[57]

With threats that they would return to finish Sivakasi, the Maravars, in roving bands, began to attack Nadars of scattered villages. Moving south along the ghats into Tenkasi and into Shencottah taluq of Travancore, they looted and burned indiscriminately as each attack became more brutal.

In the attack on Sivakasi and in the early phase of the rioting, Christian converts had been spared, for the Maravars' quarrel lay only with the Hindu Nadars.[58] During the attack on Sivakasi, homes marked "Christian" were left untouched,[59] but as rioting spread, the exemption was no longer recognized. Many Nadars sought protection within the Muslim fold. From the Tenkasi-Shencottah region, the special correspondent of the *Madras Mail* covering the riots wrote that "hundreds of Shanars are being converted to Islamism. . . ."[60]

As the military finally brought the riots under control in mid-

[54] L. S. Tangasami, "The Nadars," (manuscript); statement by Smt. Sangammal (n. 52 above); Additional Sessions Court, p. 13; and interviews. Smt. Sangammal recalled that in the smoke and confusion of the riot, many Maravars mistook the lookout on the temple car for the goddess Kali herself and fled in terror of divine intervention.

[55] Additional Sessions Court, p. 13; *Madras Mail*, June 17, 1899.

[56] *Disturbances in Madura and Tinnevelly*, p. 26.

[57] *Disturbances in Madura and Tinnevelly*, p. 25.

[58] Price, *op. cit.*

[59] *Madras Mail*, July 14, 1899.

[60] *Ibid.*, July 21, 1899.

July, nearly 150 villages had been attacked, and the reported figures of the number of houses destroyed varied from 1,600 to 4,000.[61] Nadar memorialists of Tinnevelly expressed their gratitude to the governor of Madras for the steps taken to quell the riots and requested that "the military forces be left in the several troubled centers of the district till absolute quiet is restored and the perpetrators are brought to justice." [62] During the six weeks of rioting in northern Tinnevelly, nearly two thousand people were arrested, and in the trials, which required the appointment of special magistrates and three additional sessions judges, more than five hundred were convicted, seven being sentenced to death. None of the convicted were Nadars.[63]

The inspector-general of police, M. Hammick, was appointed by the governor as special commissioner to investigate the riots. Hammick recommended that the special police force sanctioned for the maintenance of order during the period of rioting should be maintained in the district for at least five years, and that the costs of maintaining the police should be borne by all classes, without exception, through the levy of a punitive tax.[64] After some days of inquiry, Hammick saw that "as long as the temple at Sivakasi remained shut, the feeling of discontent and unrest would continue." He brought a restraining order against the Nadars, denying them permission to enter the temple if opened. The trust then "reopened the temple and worship was recommenced." [65]

During this time, rumor implicated a number of local Maravar zamindars as having backed the rioters with money and guns. In an article appearing in the *Hindu*, a correspondent suggested that the Raja of Ramnad, who had instituted a suit against the Nadars for temple entry at Kamudi, some thirty miles east of Sivakasi, may have inspired the Sivakasi riot in order to bring pressure on the court for a decision in his favor. The Raja, in reply, disclaimed any

[61] *Madras Mail*, July 19, 1899; *Census of India, 1901*, Vol. XV: *Madras*, Pt. I: *Report*, p. 178. A relief fund was established and contributions were received from Nadars throughout Tamilnad.

[62] *Madras Mail*, July 1, 1899.

[63] Pate, *Madras District Gazetteers: Tinnevelly*, p. 127: Thurston, *Castes and Tribes of Southern India*, VI, 363-364.

[64] *Disturbances in Madura and Tinnevelly*, p. 38.

[65] *Ibid*.

involvement or interest in the Sivakasi disturbances. "I possess friends among [the] Nadar community," he said, and "I am no bigot but a practical sympathizer of lower castes and foreign religions. . . ." [66]

Whether the Nadars had earned the sympathy of the Raja of Ramnad is doubtful, but the tragedy of Sivakasi had brought the case of the Nadars' aspiration to the front pages of newspapers throughout India. In Great Britain, *India*, a review of news from the subcontinent, in speaking of their aspirations, wrote that surely in all their years of struggle, "some gradual accommodation should have been established." [67] In Madras Presidency, the *Madras Mail*, a European newspaper, sympathized with the position of the Nadars and opened its pages to a discussion of the caste and its ambitions. The *Hindu*, the premier paper of the South, Brahmin-owned and staid in character, took a more critical view of the events. In a review of the situation, the *Hindu* discussed the spread of lawlessness and the siege of Sivakasi, in which the anti-Nadar party had included all other communities, "the Brahmins excepted." The paper placed the blame for the riot on local officials, especially the collector. "The fact is apparent that there were people who apprehended trouble, and that these gave notice of it to the authorities so that they might be able to prevent the catastrophe that has now befallen the people in several villages." The ultimate blame for the disturbances, however, was attributed to the Nadars' defiance of custom and tradition. [68]

The economic changes in the nineteenth century to which the Nadars had responded gave them a new economic power and the aspiration to close the widening gap between their new position and their traditional status. As traders and moneylenders, the Sivakasi Nadars and those of other trading centers of northern Tinnevelly and Ramnad had incurred the hatred and jealousy of the traditionally higher communities—particularly the Maravars, who now found the Nadars rising above them. In Sivakasi, the

[66] The *Hindu*, June 28, 1899.
[67] *India*, XII (July 14, 1899), 15.
[68] The *Hindu*, June 10, 1899 (editorial).

pretensions of the Nadars to Sanskritized customs and their attempt to gain entry into the temple engendered the violence which spread over the district as wandering Maravars attacked Nadar villages. At this time the conflict between the Nadars and the other communities was brought to the courts, as the Raja of Ramnad sought an injunction to bar Nadars from entry into the Kamudi temple. In the case, which lasted nine years and went as high as the Privy Council in London, the Nadars' claims and aspirations to higher status were brought to trial.

THE KAMUDI CASE

Kamudi, situated in the Ramnad zamindari and surrounded on all sides by Maravar villages, was a trading town of less than 7,000 people in the late nineteenth century, of whom the greatest number were Nadar and Muslim merchants and traders. The Nadars of Kamudi shared the rising prosperity of their caste in the towns of Ramnad, and, with them, sought the recognition of higher social status. Here also the Nadars began to tie their dhotis in the manner of Brahmins, to wear the tuft, and to wear the sacred thread of the twice-born.

In November, 1885, the Nadars of Kamudi petitioned the Meenakshi Sundareswara temple of the town, a temple under the trusteeship of the Raja of Ramnad, for permission to conduct a ritual feast as a part of the festival being celebrated. As the request involved the addition of a day to the festival, it was referred to the *devastanam* superintendent, and his approval was given, providing that the feast "be conducted so as not to contravene the custom that Nadars not enter into the temple." In such cases, the practice was to honor the deity by proxy. The Nadars asserted that the superintendent's qualification violated the "highly valued and ancient privilege" of the Nadars to worship in the temple, and that an anti-Nadar combination had been formed by Vellasami Thevar to prevent the Nadars from exercising their rights.[69]

Vellasami Thevar, like his father, Muthuramalinga, before him, was the hereditary ruler of a vast estate under the Raja of Ramnad.

[69] *Raja M. Bhaskara Sethupathi v. Irulappan Nadan*, pp. 20–27.

From his village of Pasumbom, only two miles from Kamudi, he commanded the loyalty of the Maravar community over a wide area, and demanded the deference of all classes. Before him the people removed their upper cloths and offered him betel. The Nadars, however, with a tightening economic hold over the area, refused to humble themselves before him. To bring the Nadars into line, Vellasami ordered the washermen to deny their services to the Nadars,[70] and under his leadership, the Maravars of the surrounding villages and the caste Hindus of Kamudi "entered into a combination against the Shanars and covenanted themselves not to buy things from or sell things to them." [71] The boycott of the Nadars was extended to the Nadar quarter, as even the route of the processions of the deity was changed to avoid the Nadar street.[72] Maravars waylaid the Nadars, cutting the sacred thread from their bodies, and with the thread, tied their thumbs and toes together in the manner of the dead.* The boycott of the Nadars lasted for one and one-half years.[73] The combination ended only with the arrest and five-year imprisonment of Vellasami Thevar.[74]

On May 14, 1897, a group of fifteen Nadars entered the Hindu temple of Meenakshi Sundareswara in Kamudi. As the facts of the case were established in the Subordinate Court at Madurai, these Nadars, carrying torches, and accompanied by drums, forcibly entered the temple in spite of remonstrance by the temple servants. Entering into the inner shrine, they garlanded the idol, offering it coconuts and swinging a lighted censer before it. They went then into the *sanctum sanctorum* of the principal deity, relighted their extinguished torches from a lamp burning near the festival idol, and touched the sacred image.[75]

The *gurukkal,* or officiating priest of the temple, asserted that

---

[70] Interview with seventy-six-year-old Nadar at Kamudi. Vellasami Thevar is the grandfather of the late Muthuramalinga Thevar, leader of the Maravar-dominated Forward Bloc.

[71] Judgment in C. C. No. 65 of 1887, on the file of the 2d Class Magistrate of Tiruchuli, in *Rajah M. Bhaskara Sethupathi* v. *Irulappan Nadan*, pp. 20–27.

[72] *Rajah M. Bhaskara Sethupathi* v. *Irulappan Nadan*, p. 24.

[73] *Record of Proceedings, Rajah M. Bhaskara Sethupathi* v. *Irulappan Nadan*, in the Subordinate Judge's Court of Madura (East), February 6, 1899, p. 449.

[74] *Rajah M. Bhaskara Septhupathi* v. *Irulappan Nadan*, p. 3.

[75] *Ibid.,* p. 2.

the Saiva Agamas, the doctrines governing the ritual life of the Meenakshi Sundareswara temple, prohibited the entrance of Nadars. According to the Agamas, entry into the temple where the ritual was prescribed by these shastras was forbidden "to all those whose profession is the manufacture of intoxicating liquors and the climbing of palmyra and coconut trees." [76] It was the custom, the *gurukkal* stated, that the Nadars stand outside the tower gate of the temple and tender their offerings to the deity only through an intermediary temple servant or through some other person of high caste.[77] Even the higher castes were prohibited from entering into the innermost shrine, entry being permitted for the *gurukkal* alone. Brahmin *pujaris* might enter into the antechamber, following the prescription of the Agama Shastras, but the worshippers of clean caste, the Kshatriyas, the Vaisyas, and the Sudras, could go no further than the Mahamandapa, the great hall. All other castes were required to offer their prayers to the deity from outside the temple walls.[78] Thus, by their acts, the Nadars "violated the religious tenets, rules and customs, committed sacrilege, desecrated, defiled and polluted the temple and caused annoyance, disgrace and obstruction to the lawful worshippers." [79]

Alleging that the temple had been defiled and that the Nadars, being of low caste, were denied by tradition the right of entry, the zamindar of Ramnad, Raja M. Bhaskara Sethupathi, as hereditary trustee of the temple of Kamudi, filed a suit against the Nadars. The suit sought a permanent injunction restraining the Nadars from entering the temple, together with payment of 2,500 rupees for the costs of the temple's ritual purification.[80] The Raja had originally sought to bring suit against the Nadars as a class. The judge ruled, however, that the contentions raised in the suit were to be confined to the Nadars of Kamudi and to the Meenakshi Sundareswara temple alone.[81] However limited the decision might

[76] *Rajah M. Bhaskara Sethupathi v. Irulappan Nadan*, p. 105.
[77] *Rajah M. Bhaskara Sethupathi v. Irulappan Nadan*, p. 5.
[78] *Ibid.*, p. 104.
[79] *Ibid.*, p. 2.
[80] *Ibid.*, p. 1. The original judgment runs to a length of 121 printed foolscap pages. *The Record of Proceedings* totals 650 pages.
[81] *Ibid.*, pp. 4–5.

be by legal definition, the Nadars as a community were, nevertheless, on trial.

As the case opened, the Nadars submitted a written statement asserting their right as a high caste to enter the temple and "to participate in the worship therein performed in the same manner and to the same extent as any other class (Brahmins excepted). . . ." These rights were "immemorial and permitted by the Shastras as well as custom," the Nadars contended. The Nadars were not of low station, but were "in fact superior to the Maravar caste" to which the Raja of Ramnad belonged.[82]

After much difficulty in securing legal representation, the Nadars finally succeeded in hiring a Brahmin advocate to present their case. Rabbi Sattampillai, the Nazareth schismatic, assumed the responsibility for gathering and preparing documentary evidence attesting to the high status of the Nadar community: a vast array of "puranic" caste histories, eulogistic poems, and selected quotations from European missionaries, officials, and scholars. Sattampillai also set out to raise funds with which to contest the case.* The Nadars assembled seventy-five witnesses from all communities to testify in their behalf. The reliability of almost all the witnesses —for plaintiff as well as defendants—was open to question because of widespread bribery, perjury, and intimidation. "The defendants," the judge noted, "have called a considerable number of witnesses to contradict the plaintiff's evidence as to custom, and there are some Brahmins among them, but it may be generally said that the defendants' witnesses are men of much lower standing and respectability, and are to a large extent in the pay or under the control of the Nadars, or are under pecuniary obligation to them, or are servants in the temples under their control."[83]

In an effort to counter the evidence of the plaintiff's witnesses to the effect that throughout the southern districts the Nadars were

[82] *Ibid.*, p. 2. This superiority was claimed, first, because of the Brahminical character of Nadar customs "as compared with those of the Maravars which constitute a wide departure from the universal practice of caste Hindus. . . ." It was further contended that the Maravars were the customary palanquin bearers of the Nadars and necessarily, therefore, inferior. *Ibid.*, p. 68.

[83] *Sankaralinga Nadan and others* v. *Rajeswara Dorai and others.* On appeal from the High Court of Judicature at Madras. Privy Council. Indian Law Reports 31 Madras 236 (1908).

prohibited both by custom and the Shastras from entering Siva
temples, the Nadars sought to establish the custom of their entry in
the temples of districts to the north. Witnesses, including a priest
from the Chidambaram temple in South Arcot District, testified
that the Nadars were not barred from entrance and were given the
full privileges of caste Hindus in the temples of Tanjore and Coimbatore districts, and at Chidambaram, Trichinopoly, and Palani in
Madurai District.[84] Of substantial wealth as traders and merchants,
the few Nadars of these districts commanded a position of social
respectability. Ponnusami Nadar of Porayar, Tanjore District, who
held the *akbari* distillery contract for the greater portion of Madras
Presidency and Travancore-Cochin, had served since 1889 as a
member of the Devastanam Committee controlling the temple at
Kumbakonam. The Porayar family had customarily worshipped in
the temple, according to witnesses for the defense, and in 1889,
under orders of the district judge of Tanjore, Ponnusami had been
appointed to the temple committee.[85]

One of the witnesses from Porayar spoke of a class of palmyra
climbers, *panaiyeris*, in Tanjore known as Shanars. These were, he
said, distinct from and inferior to the Nadars, a respectable trading
community.[86] In the course of testimony, several witnesses alluded
to the distinction between the two groups. "There is no foundation
whatsoever," the judge ruled, "for the contention that the Nadars
who are also called Shanars form a separate section apart from the
Shanar caste whose calling is the manufacture of the palm juice."
The judge was not unaware, however, of the efforts of the Nadar
traders in Ramnad and northern Tinnevelly to disassociate themselves from their tree-climbing kinsmen.

On July 20, 1899, as the rioting in northern Tinnevilly was
beginning to ebb, the judge delivered his decision against the

[84] *Sankaralinga Nadan and others* v. *Rajesward Dorai and others*, p. 55.

[85] *Ibid.*, p. 53. The appointment came after Ponnusami secured a clear majority
over opposing candidates for the position. Objection was taken to his appointment
on the grounds that he belonged to the Shanar caste, which, it was alleged, "was
not a recognized caste among Hindus." The objection was disallowed as imma-
terial for the purposes of the Religious Endowments Regulations, but the objection indicates that even in Tanjore District, where the Nadars enjoyed comparatively high social status, their position was by no means uncontested.

[86] *Ibid.*, pp. 53, 71–72.

Nadars. The Nadars had gone beyond their hereditary calling, he said, and "many are engaged in agriculture, trade and in money lending," and in these walks of life "have accumulated wealth and acquired influence." Some, like the Porayar family in Tanjore District, had "obtained social recognition." The Nadars had come to be recognized for their piety and charity, he said, as evidenced in the construction of rest houses, gardens, wells, and in the schools established "in which pupils of all communities are taught." Throughout the southern districts, however, though in the larger towns Nadar houses had become "mixed up with the houses of caste Hindus," "the non-Brahminical classes yet keep aloof from mixing with them." With their advanced wealth, Sanskritized manners, and good works, the social status of the Nadars was still "held in low estimation. . . ." [87]

The substantive question for the court was to determine the recognized local custom with regard to the status of the defendants. The Nadars were found to be in the category of those denied entrance into a Hindu temple, and it was not necessary, the judge ruled, "to go behind that usage and to see whether it can be supported in the light of modern ideas of what is right and proper." [88]

The court ruled that neither the defendants nor any member of their community were entitled to enter into any part of the temple of Meenakshi Sundareswara, and a permanent injunction was issued to that effect. The defendants were ordered to pay the sum of 500 rupees for the necessary purification ceremonies in the temple. Each side was to bear its own costs. [89]

The decision was received publicly with some surprise, as it had been generally believed, even by the Maravars, that the Nadars would win the case. During the rioting of the preceding six weeks, reports linked the attacks on the Nadars with the Kamudi case, suggesting that the Raja of Ramnad had stirred up the Maravars "in order to terrorize the Native Judge." [90] There was no evidence that the judge was in fact intimidated by the disturbances, but the

[87] *Ibid.*, pp. 110–111.
[88] *Ibid.*, p. 111.
[89] *Rajah M. Bhaskara Sethupathi* v. *Irulappan Nadan*, pp. 113–114.
[90] Price. *op. cit.* (n. 53 above).

Madras Mail editorialized, "the importance of the Sub-Judge's find-ings, in relation to the state of general unrest at the present existing in the south can hardly be over-estimated." The decision might have had a quieting effect on the Maravars and others indulging in the "excesses" of the preceding weeks, but "it is bound to have a very disturbing effect on the Shanars. . . ." [91]

With a fund of 42,000 rupees collected from members of the community throughout Tamilnad,[92] the Nadars appealed to the High Court of Judicature at Madras. The ruling went against the Nadars,[93] and they then carried their case to the Privy Council in London. Sitting in 1908, the Privy Council affirmed the decree of the Subordinate Judge of Madurai, citing the decision of the High Court.

"The evidence is, as might be expected, conflicting," the Madras judges had ruled, "but there can be no doubt whatever as to its general result." In review of the evidence, "there is no sort of proof, nothing we can say, that even suggests a probability, that the Shanars are, as the defendants contend, descendants from the Kshatriya or Warrior caste of Hindus, or from the Pandiya, Chola, or Chera race of kings, and the futile attempt of the Shanars to establish the connections has brought well-deserved ridicule on their pretensions." Dismissing the distinction drawn between Nadars and Shanars, the court stated that "all 'Nadars' are Shanars by caste," and that "the Shanars, as a class, have from time im-memorial been devoted to the cultivation of the palmyra palm and to the collection of its juice and the manufacture of liquor from it. . . . There are no grounds whatever for regarding them as of Aryan origin." Their position in general social estimation appeared to be just above that of the Pallars and Pariahs, "who are on all hands regarded as unclean and prohibited from the use of the Hindu temples," and "below that of the Vellalas, Maravars, and other cultivating castes usually classed as Sudras, and admittedly free to worship in the Hindu temples." [94]

[91] *Madras Mail*, July 21, 1899.
[92] "The Anti-Shanar Riots," *Missionary Herald*, XCVIII (1902), 252–253.
[93] *Sankaralinga Nadan et al.* v. *Rajeswara Dorai et al.* In the High Court of Judicature at Madras, February 14, 1902. Appeal No. 11 of 1900, and Appeal No. 77 of 1900.
[94] *Sankaralinga Nadan et al.* v. *Raja Rajeswara Dorai et al.*, Privy Council.

The High Court recognized economic and social differentiation within the Nadar community itself and noted that "in many villages they own much of the land and monopolize the bulk of trade and wealth." "With the increase in wealth they have, not unnaturally, sought for social recognition and . . . a footing of equality in religious matters." No doubt many of the Nadars had abandoned their traditional occupation, the court continued, in phrases suggesting the "separate but equal" doctrine of *Plessy* v. *Ferguson*,[95]

> and have won for themselves, by education, industry, and frugality, respectable positions as traders and merchants and even as vakils and clerks, and it is natural to feel sympathy for their efforts to obtain social recognition and to rise to what is regarded as a higher form of religious worship; but such sympathy will not be increased by unreasonable and unfounded pretensions, and in the effort to rise the Shanars must not invade the established rights of other castes. They have temples of their own, and are numerous enough and strong enough in wealth and education to rise along their own lines and without appropriating the institutions or infringing the rights of others, and in so doing they will have the sympathy of all rightminded men, and, if necessary, the protection of the Courts.[96]

The Nadars were also admonished by the missionary Sharrock. Despite their eagerness to rise in the social scale, he said, "they have still to learn that the progress of a nation, or a caste, does not depend upon the interpretation of words, or the assumption of a title, but on the character of the individuals that compose it. Evolutions are hindered rather than advanced by such unwise pretensions resulting in violence; but evolutions resulting from intellectual and social development are quite irresistible, if any caste will continue to advance by its own efforts in the path of freedom and progress." [97] The efforts of the Nadar community, however, had not been without fruit, as Pate recognized in the *Tinnevelly Gazetteer:* "Though their social aspirations may be deemed ill-judged and though their methods of expressing them have from time to time been deplorable, it must in fairness to the caste be said that, as persevering and resourceful cultivators, as traders both at home

[95] 163 U.S. 537 (1896).
[96] *Sankaralinga Nadan et al.* v. *Raja Rajeswara Dorai et al.* Privy Council.
[97] J. A. Sharrock in the *Madras Mail*, 1901, quoted in Thurston, VI, 372.

and abroad, as unwearied tappers of the palmyra and as capable clerks and officials in the service of Government, the Shanar community by their own merits are steadily earning for themselves a position and reputation infinitely more valuable than any social pre-eminence attainable by violence or pamphleteering." [98]

Although the Nadars had suffered a defeat in court, they had gained widespread sympathy, and—even more important—through the litigations and the concurrent rioting, community consciousness was aroused. While the vast majority of the Nadar community remained miserably depressed economically and continued to suffer severe social disabilities, the increasingly important role of education and the rise of the Nadar business classes had given the community a new self-respect. The development of roads and communications had served to bring the community closer together, and increasing interactions within the caste over a wide geographic area were beginning to erode the endogamous subcastes into which the community had been divided. The Nadars had found a new strength—not in their claims to Pandyan ancestry, whether real or fictional, nor in their aspiration to Kshatriya status, but rather in the industry and unity of the community and in its determination to uplift itself.

As an aspirant community in conflict with other castes, the Nadars of northern Tinnevelly and Ramnad were, by the beginning of the twentieth century, a highly cohesive and solidary community. In their homeland of the *teris* in southeastern Tinnevelly a hundred years before, the Nadars constituted virtually the entire population. Without external threat, they were divided into the conflicting factions of a parochial culture. They lacked organization, unity, and awareness of themselves as a community. In the mercantile situation of the Six Towns, the old divisions of subcaste, of climber and Nadan were no longer relevant, and in these northern regions, the community was overwhelmingly Hindu. Threatened by a hostile social environment, the Nadars in the early years of the nineteenth century had established a tightly knit organiza-

---

[98] Pp. 128–129. In another case during this same period, the High Court ruled that the Nadars belonged to the lower classes, and as such could be punished by confinement in stocks. Thurston, *Castes and Tribes of Southern India*, VI, 373.

tion in the *uravinmurai*. Unified for survival, the Nadars were soon endowed by Christian scholars of the community with an elaborate mythology of a glorious and kingly past. Armed with a vision of greatness and a determination to uplift the community in social status, the Nadars engaged in a series of confrontations which served to reinforce internal unity and to deepen caste consciousness, consolidating a more integrated political culture.

These confrontations served to mobilize the community in assertion of the rights and privileges demanded. Confrontation served also to test the degree and limits to which the other communities were willing to accept the Nadars' claims to higher status. The Nadars, however, despite Sanskritization of ritual and custom, were frustrated in their attempt to win interactional recognition by the allied opposition of the higher castes. With the defeats of the Kamudi case, it became increasingly clear to Nadar leaders that they must strive for more harmonious relations with other castes and that they must address themselves to the problems of the entire Nadar community and not merely to those of the more advanced portions of it. They realized further that the Nadar community must organize to effectively petition the government for recognition of its claims and redress of grievances, and that it must also gain direct representation in access to political power for the protection and advancement of its interests.

With a new community awareness, the Nadars turned from the "sacred" to the "secular." Sanskritization had failed. It now remained for the Nadars to use their resources of wealth and power in a united effort to raise the entire community to a position of political influence in Madras. The instrument of social and political mobilization was the caste association, the Nadar Mahajana Sangam.

Chapter V

ASSOCIATION FOR UPLIFT:
THE NADAR MAHAJANA SANGAM

THE FOUNDING OF THE SANGAM

The movement for temple entry and the dramatic confrontation between the Nadars and the communities which opposed their aspirations gave the Nadar community a new impetus toward unity and social uplift. The Six Town system was no longer sufficient, as the movement of Nadars to Madurai, Madras City, and abroad demanded a more comprehensive association. There was also among the Six Towns a restive opposition to the continued leadership of Sattankudi, a town dwarfed by the rapid growth of Sivakasi, Virudhunagar, Aruppukottai, and Tirumangulam. The Tirumangulam Nadars attempted in the latter part of the nineteenth century to secure leadership for their own *uravinmurai*.[1] At this point, in 1895, a number of prominent Nadar merchants and traders assembled at Madurai, but the Kshatriya Mahajana Sangam, as they named their association, never really took form.[2]

It was not until fifteen years later that Rao Bahadur T. Rattinasami Nadar of Poraiyar, Tanjore District, of a distinguished and wealthy family of *akbari* contractors, sought to revive the association.[3] Rattinasami was motivated in part by his own political

[1] Interviews. Hereafter in this chapter an asterisk will indicate that the information has been obtained in interviews, with the principal or with other participants or observers.

[2] Nadar Mahajana Sangam, *Rules and Regulations of the Nadar Mahajana Sangam, Madura* (Maduari, 1919), p. 3.

[3] Traders of the palmyra country greatly benefited from the increasing demand for jaggery from sugar factories and distilleries in the nineteenth century. The climbers themselves enjoyed little from the growth of the industry, however, for under the government's excise system, manufacture and sale were separated. The tappers were provided with small advances by the toddy-shop owners or by the large contractors. The toddy-shop keeper, ordinarily a Nadar, operated under government contract and his sign was a small earthen pot (used by the tappers) inverted on the end of a stick. The major distillers, of whom T. Rattinasami was the most prominent, collected jaggery at various stations, transporting it to scat-

ambition. He had requested the government to nominate him to
the Legislative Council as a representative of the Nadar community, just as a Nattukottai Chetti had been nominated as a representative of his caste. Rattinasami was reportedly informed by the
government that the Chetti councilman was a representative of a
Chetti association and that there was no comparable organization
among the Nadars. Rattinasami invited a number of leaders within
the Nadar community to Poraiyar for a plenary session in February, 1910. The transportation expenses of the 450 delegates were
borne by the local *uravinmurais,* and Rattinasami met the cost of
lodging and food during the conference.*

Rattinasami's uncle, V. Ponnusami Nadar, was elected president
of the association, the Nadar Mahajana Sangam. Membership was
originally open to any adult male, of "any sub-class, any religion."
Loyal to the British crown, the Sangam resolved that anyone in
opposition to the government would be removed from the association. It also resolved to request the government to select one man
for the council as a representative of the Nadar community. The
purpose of the association was to be the uplift of the Nadar community. "The Nadar class of people have money, but do not have
higher status," it was stated, and therefore the leaders of the community "had come together to improve their lot." [4]

In December of that same year, 1910, the second conference of
the Sangam was held at Madras, with more than 750 delegates
attending.[5] Soon after this the death of the Sangam's founder, T.
Rattinasami, and that of the chairman of the second conference,
dealt the association an almost fatal blow.[6] With the Sangam
greatly weakened, it was not until 1917 that another conference
was convened at Madurai. The conference, like the two earlier

tered distilleries. With the enormous growth of toddy and distilled arrack, the
Nadar middlemen grew to great wealth.

For a discussion of government policies on toddy and distillation, see H. R. Pate,
Madras District Gazetteers, Tinnevelly, (Madras, 1917), pp. 224-225, 323-325,
501-502; W. Francis, *Madras District Gazetteers: Madura* (Madras, 1909), pp.
211-212; *Manual of the Administration of Madras Presidency,* I, 445-446; III,
648-649, 906.

4 Nadar Mahajana Sangam, *Report,* 1st conference, Poraiyar, 1910.
5 Nadar Mahajana Sangam, *Report,* 2nd conference, Madras, 1910.
6 Nadar Mahajana Sangam, *Report,* 3rd conference, Madurai, 1917.

meetings, was overwhelmingly dominated by the northern Nadars of Ramnad and Madurai. Of the thirty-four executive council members, only two were from Tinnevelly, local leaders from Arumuganeri and Nazareth. Of the others, nearly all were merchants and traders, and fifteen were from Madurai, the site of the Sangam's new headquarters.[7]

The objectives of the Nadar Mahajana Sangam were:

(a) To promote the social, material, and general welfare of the Nadars; (b) To protect and promote the interests and rights of the community; (c) To take practical measures for the social, moral, and intellectual advancement of the Nadars; (d) To start schools and colleges for imparting western education to Nadar children and to help poor but deserving pupils belonging to the community with scholarships, books, fees, etc.; (e) To encourage and promote commercial and industrial enterprise among the members of the community; (f) To foster and promote the spirit of union and solidarity among the members of the community; (g) The raising of funds by subscription, donation or other means for the above objects, and the doing of all such other things as are incidental and conducive to the attainment of the above objects or any of them.[8]

In a circular, distributed widely among the Nadars in 1921, the Nadar Mahajana Sangam urged all Nadars to join the association, and each member was encouraged to enlist as many Nadars as possible and to establish branch offices. Youths between the ages of five and fifteen were encouraged to attend school, and educational facilities for girls were advocated.[9] The success of the Nadar Mahajana Sangam encouraged the founding of the Travancore Hindu Nadars Association. In 1918 Nadar merchants and traders in Rangoon established the Hindu Nadar Mahajana Sabha "to feed the poor and to promote the advancement of the welfare of the Nadar community and to serve other public interests."[10] That same year, in Ceylon, the Indhia Kshatriyakula Nadar Mahajana Sangam was founded, and in 1925, Nadars in Malaya established

[7] Nadar Mahajana Sangam, *Rules and Regulations,* pp. 9–10.
[8] *Ibid.,* pp. 12–13.
[9] Nadar Mahajana Sangam, *Circular* No. 8, August 9, 1919.
[10] Hindu Nadar Mahajana Sabha, *Second Annual Report* (Rangoon, 1919).

the Nadar Paripalana Sangam, or the Nadar Protective Association.[11]

THE CENSUS: FROM "SHANAN" TO "NADAR"

One of the first concerns of the Nadar Mahajana Sangam was to disassociate itself from the word Shanar and to seek official recognition of the community's Kshatriya status. The hierarchy of caste status was recorded dutifully in the government census, each caste being listed, with its traditional occupation, in an order which reflected the caste ranking in the Hindu hierarchy of ritual purity. The Shanars, as traditional toddy-drawers, came very near the bottom. According to the 1891 census report, the Nadars "are usually placed only a little above the Pallas and the Paraiyans and are considered to be one of the polluting castes. . . ." They are classed in the census division with "the castes which pollute even without touch but do not eat beef." [12]

In 1910, P. V. Pandion, son of Sattampillai, addressed a petition to J. C. Molony, census superintendent, in the name of the Nadar Mahajana Sangam. He requested that the census register Nadars as Kshatriya–Sandrores.[13] In a letter to the collector of Tinnevelly, Molony stated that it was too late to issue any detailed instructions to census enumerators regarding the entry of Shanars in the census schedule, "but as no one but a Shanar is likely to call himself Kshatriya Sandrore, there is no objection to an enumerator making this entry. Generally speaking, it does not matter what a man chooses to call his caste as long as the new term he employs can be easily identified as a synonym for the more used term." [14]

In January, 1921, the executive council of the Nadar Mahajana Sangam passed a resolution calling upon all Nadars to return their caste as Kshatriya in the forthcoming 1921 census, and circulars were distributed throughout the community urging compliance

[11] *Kshatriya Mitran*, V (1925–1926), 180.
[12] *Census of India, 1891*, Vol XIII: *Madras Report*, p. 297.
[13] P. V. Pandion, *Chantror Sangam* (Madras, 1911), p. 32.
[14] Quoted from a "circular" from the Tinnevelly collector, February 1, 1911, in *ibid.*, p. 33.

with the resolution. In explaining their position in a letter to the chief secretary to the government, Madras, the Sangam stated that

> the term Shanan has acquired an offensive and contemptuous signifi-cance in common parlance. The Nadars, as a rule, resent being called Shanans and no one ordinarily refers to them by the name except when he intends to be discourteous or reproachful. The Nadars are usually described in formal documents such as title deeds, pleadings in court, etc., as Kshatriyas or as Nadars simply. The term Shanan as a caste name has long ago gone out of the use except in Government records where it still lingers.
>
> There is no reason why the Government should continue to re-tain an offensive expression in describing a community which is among the most loyal of His Majesty's subjects.

In deference to the objections of the collector of Madurai and others that Kshatriya was, as a caste name, "too general and too vague," the council of the Sangam agreed that the members of the Nadar community should return their caste as Nadar-Kshatriya rather than as Kshatriya alone.[15] G. T. Boag, superintendent of census operations, Madras, received a delegation from the Sangam and agreed to instruct all census enumerators to accept Nadar-Kshatriya as the community's name if so returned.[16] The Sangam then distributed circulars informing Nadars that the government had agreed to list them as Nadar-Kshatriyas, and that irregularities in census enumeration should be reported to the Sangam immedi-ately.[17]

Seeking legal recognition of Boag's assurances, the Sangam re-iterated its plea in a memorial to the governor of Madras. The Nadars, the Sangam stated, "are the descendants and representa-tives of the ancient Kshatriya race of Pandya and Chola kings,"

---

[15] Letter to the collector of Tinnevelly from the N.M.S., February 4, 1921 (N.M.S. Letterbook, 1920–1921). In *Circular*, No. 5, January 22, 1921, the Sangam requested Nadars to return themselves as "Nadar-Kshatriyas" and to give enumer-ators only their *actual*, not traditional, occupation.

[16] Letter to the N.M.S. from G. T. Boag, Madras, February 2, 1921. Subse-quently, on February 17, Boag issued a circular asking the collectors to instruct the census officers in their districts that "everyone who at the census returns his caste as Nadar-Kshatriya should be so described on the Census Schedule." Nadar Christians, however, were to be returned only under the category "Indian Chris-tian" and not distinguished by caste.

[17] N.M.S. *Circular*, No. 6, February 9, 1921; No. 7, February 22, 1921.

and that census references to them as Shanans and toddy-drawers was "most unfair and essentially misleading." "The Nadar community has thus cause to feel acutely grieved that the name by which they are referred to in the Census Report should carry no suggestion as to the race they represent." Even the title Chantror was unacceptable, "since the term shows a natural tendency to degenerate in use into 'Shanan,' " and the community wanted to leave no room "for mischievous people to foist that term upon it." The Nadar Mahajana Sangam, therefore, humbly prayed that the community "should be known in the Census and other Government records by its proper name of 'Nadar-Kshatriya' " and that the occupations of the community be entered as agriculture and trade according to actual fact.[18]

On April 8, 1921, a government order was issued, informing the petitioners "that the procedure followed at the recent census was to leave everyone to return his caste name as he chose, adapting for use in the report that name which the majority of the caste actually return." The order further indicated the government's decision "to discontinue the tabulation of the traditional occupation of particular castes and to report only the actual occupation by which each person lives." [19]

The Sangam then wrote to Boag, urging that Nadar-Kshatriya be adopted for the census report, regardless of the specific names returned for the caste. Their concern arose from reports that enumerators were not entering the caste name as told, but as Shanar. "We can safely assert," the Sangam wrote, "that a vast majority of Nadars would have returned their caste as Nadar-Kshatriya if the enumerators had allowed them to do so."

In compliance with the government order, Boag, in the Madras Census Report, states: "The 1921 Census records the caste as *Nadar* rather than Shanar as in 1911. . . . In deference to the wishes of the representatives of the Nadar community, the Madras Government have decided on this occasion not to show traditional

[18] *To His Excellency the Governor of Fort St. George in Council. The Humble Memorial Presented by the Nadar Mahajana Sangam, Madura* (Madurai, 1921).
[19] Government of Madras, Law (General) Department, G. O. No. 56, dated April 8, 1921.

occupations in the census tables; the traditional occupation of the Nadars has hitherto been shown as toddy-drawing; but they now claim that they are by tradition and inheritance lords of the soil and that toddy-drawing was the occupation only of comparatively few degenerate members of the caste." [20]

Following the government's order with regard to the census, the Sangam council resolved "to request the Government to adopt the term 'Nadar-Kshatriyas' in place of 'Shanans' for use in all Government records." Accordingly, a letter was written to the chief secretary to the government. While responding to the Sangam's petition, the government chose to recognize the simple term Nadar rather than Nadar-Kshatriya. In July, a government order was issued to that effect.[21]

The Sangam's concern over the continued use of the term Shanar was directed also toward the use of the word in commercial publications. In response to the Sangam's request, for example, Macmillan Publishing Company agreed to "drop the words 'Shanars' altogether" from their *Tinnevelly District Geography* and to "omit all references to the occupations of the caste." [22]

THE CAMPAIGN AGAINST TODDY

During this same period, the Sangam began a campaign against toddy-tapping within the community. The community, the Sangam contended, had "suffered in prestige by the common notion that its traditional occupation is toddy-drawing," when, in fact, only a comparatively small section of the community, "by vicissitudes of fortune," had been driven to the manufacture of hard drink. "In view of the fact that toddy-drawing is held in low estimation by the people, the Council of the Nadar Mahajana Sangam, which stands for the social and moral advancement of the Nadars, resolved . . . to appeal to such members of the community as live by toddy-drawing to abandon the occupation which is certainly not conducive to the health and prosperity, to ethical

[20] *Census of India, 1921*, Vol. XIII: *Madras*, Pt. I: *Report*, pp. 153–154.

[21] Government of Madras, Law (General) Department, G. O. No. 785, dated July 7, 1921.

[22] Letter from Macmillan Publishing Company to the Nadar Mahajana Sangam, October 12, 1921.

or religious excellence, or to the domestic felicity of the people who indulge in drink and to take to the extraction of 'sweet toddy' and the manufacture of jaggery, sugar candy, etc., instead." In a letter to the government, the Sangam urged that the resolution had "nothing whatsoever to do with politics" and was "not to be confounded with the non-cooperation propaganda now so much talked about." [23]

While the greater number of Nadars in Tiruchendur taluq and throughout the palmyra forests of southeastern Tinnevelly District were engaged primarily in the manufacture of jaggery, many Nadars in the other regions of Tinnevelly and to the north were engaged in the tapping, distribution, and sale of hard toddy. The Sangam distributed circulars among the Nadars urging them to abandon toddy-tapping and the operation of toddy shops.[24] Touring agents from the Sangam were dispatched throughout these areas for propaganda against toddy.

In response to the Sangam's campaign, in December, 1921, Nadars in many villages took it upon themselves to enforce the resolution. Holding kangaroo courts, Nadars forcibly brought tappers and toddy-shop owners before tribunals of the community. "Large numbers of toddy tappers," according to a report in the *Madras Mail*, January 7, 1922, "were adverse to giving up a hereditary and obviously profitable industry merely to satisfy the whims and caprices of some of their leaders; and expressed their determination in unambiguous language to carry on the calling of the forefathers. This gave umbrage to the leaders, and finding that peaceful methods of persuasion were unavailing they tried to enforce tenets of their cult by intimidation, extortion and in not a few instances by assault and battery." As the situation got out of hand, the district magistrate of Tinnevelly issued a proclamation restricting the assembly of Nadars "within two furlongs of any place where the sale of fermented toddy is lawfully allowed to be sold or where toddy is lawfully to be drawn. . . ." [25]

[23] Letter to the deputy commissioner, Salt, Akbari, and Customs Department, Tinnevelly, May 23, 1921.

[24] *Circular*, No. 3, 1920, and *Circular*, No. 11, 1921.

[25] Order under Section 144, C. P. C. Proclamation, District Magistrate, Tinnevelly, December 22, 1921.

The Sangam's anti-toddy campaign was effective for only about a year, and some of the Nadars engaged in tapping soon returned to the lucrative profession when the community's enthusiasm had quieted. During the campaign, the Poraiyar family supported the Sangam's efforts and, while continuing to accept *akbari* contracts, the family refused to handle toddy.* Throughout the years following, the Nadar Mahajana Sangam continued to support prohibition, and as the community became more secure in its advancing position, the Sangam began to work for the welfare of the palmyra climbers, who still constituted the major portion of the community population.

PROHIBITION

In seeking to uplift the depressed palmyra climbers among the Nadar community, the Sangam fought in 1933 to abolish the tax levied on palmyra trees in Tinnevelly and Ramnad districts.[26] With the introduction of prohibition, the Sangam, together with the Dakshina Mara Nadar Sangam of Tinnevelly, sought government benefits for the displaced tappers. Prohibition was introduced into four northern districts of Madras Presidency in 1937, soon after C. Rajagopalachari formed the first Congress ministry. The other districts would soon have come under prohibition but for the resignation of the Congress ministry in 1939. The British advisor government suspended the Prohibition Act in all four districts. With Independence, however, prohibition was reintroduced, and by 1948, all districts in the state were dry.[27]

Under the provisions of the act, and the subsequent Sweet Toddy Rules, the stipulations and restrictions on the palmyra industry were so complicated as to endanger both the production of sweet toddy and the manufacture of jaggery. An elaborate licensing procedure confined tapping to the hours of 4 A.M. to 2 P.M., and rules required that sweet toddy be sold only by license holders, in a palmyra garden, and only between the hours of 6 A.M. and

[26] A resolution at the 15th conference, 1933, at Palamcottah, urged the repeal of the tree tax. Letter to the governor of Madras from the N.M.S., 1933.

[27] B. S. Baliga, *Madras District Gazetteers, Madurai* (Madras, 1960), pp. 209–210.

2 P.M.[28] During the first four months of prohibition, only 500 licenses were issued,[29] although the number of tappers numbered near 100,000. The climbers were threatened with being economically displaced altogether. In late 1948, a conference of palmyra owners and climbers was convened at Tuticorin. In pursuance of a resolution, the conference submitted a memorandum to the chief minister and to the minister for prohibition, Daniel Thomas, a Nadar Christian, which emphasized that, while in other districts the extraction of hard toddy was widespread, in Tinnevelly the palmyra juice was used almost solely for the production of sweet toddy and jaggery.

The Nadar Mahajana Sangam in a letter to the minister for prohibition, January 16, 1949, urged an amendment of the act. "In places where palmyras thrive abundantly in the Tirunelveli and Ramnad Districts the soil is quite unsuitable for any cultivation whatsoever. Palmyra is the chief source of income for the ryots and the jaggery-producers forming their main occupation and trade. These restrictions of the Prohibition Act now in force deprive lakhs of people of their main stay in life, throwing out of employment thousands of workers." The Dakshina Mara Nadar Sangam, concerned wholly with the Tinnevelly Nadars, took a bolder stand. "The economy of the district," the Dakshina Mara Nadar Sangam wrote to Nehru, "will be seriously disturbed and a famine is likely to follow in the wake of Prohibition." "We do not concede that prohibition is in the interests of the general public," they submitted, in a memorandum to the President of India in February, 1950. "Even if it is granted for the sake of argument that it is in the interests of the general public the restrictions imposed on the tapping for sweet juice and the manufacture of jaggery . . . are not reasonably necessary for the enforcement of prohibition." [30]

---

[28] *Memorandum Submitted to His Excellency the President, Republic of India, New Delhi, on Behalf of the Palmyrah Sweet Juice Tappers by Dakshina Mara Nadar Sangam, Tirunelveli,* in pursuance of a resolution passed February 18, 1950.

[29] Letter to C. Rajagopalachari, Governor-General of India, from the Dakshina Mara Nadar Sangam, February 9, 1949.

[30] With the easing of the regulations, the D.M.N.S. later moderated its position significantly. In a letter to the deputy superintendent of police, Tinnevelly, the Sangam said that it "enthusiastically supports prohibition" and "agrees with the

The licensing procedures and the requirements governing the tapping of the trees had brought the industry to a virtual standstill in the months immediately following the enactment of the law. Only with the pressure of the two *sangams* and a number of *ad hoc* committees was the enforcement of the regulations eased. In the mid-1950's, cooperative societies were established under government auspices to facilitate licensing and to promote jaggery production.[31] Although the price of jaggery has risen in recent years, it is increasingly difficult for palmyra tree owners to secure tappers. Wages are low, and education and urban employment offer an attractive alternative to the arduous and degraded profession.[32]

THE NADARS AS A BACKWARD CLASS

Although many Nadars, particularly those in the Ramnad and Madurai merchant community, might still shy away from the sight of a palmyra, the community, as it continued to rise and to gain the respect of the traditionally higher castes, became more self-assured. Indeed, Alexander Gnanamuthu, in his presidential address at the 1960 Nadar conference, said, "The palmyra palm is associated with our community. I feel proud of this symbolic association. It is the tree which grows tall, straight and heavenwards."[33]

The Sangam, while still oriented largely to the commercial interests of the Six Town Nadars, had from the late 1920's shown increasing concern for the plight of the palmyra climber. In their anxiety to assert high status the Nadars had once denied the continued backwardness of the larger portion of their caste—the tap-

policy of punishing people who make or drink liquor." It opposed, however, the licensing and regulatory procedures which had resulted in the conviction of innocent tappers who had not secured the license. Letter, dated May 16, 1956.

[31] Interview, V. V. Ramasamy, president of the State Palmgur Co-operative Federation, Virudhunagar, March, 1965; Madras State Palmgur Co-operative Federation, "A Note on Palmgur and Palm Products Industries in Madras State." Manuscript.

[32] In the 1961 census survey of a Nadar village in Kanyakumari, tapping remained the main source of livelihood for the Hindu Nadars, but of the 74 tappers questioned, 53 said that they did not want their sons to continue in the same occupation. *Census of India, 1961*, Vol. IX; *Madras*, Pt. VI: Village Survey Monographs, No. 19, *Kuttuthal Azhankulam*, pp. 72–76.

[33] N.M.S. *Report*, 28th conference, Tuticorin, 1960.

PLATES

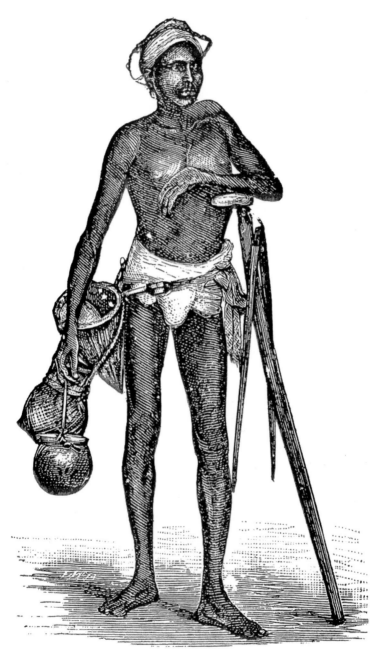

Plate 1. "Palmyra Tree Climber," from Samuel Mateer, *Native Life in Travancore* (London: W. H. Allen & Co., 1883).

Plate 2. "Shanar Climbing a Palmyra Tree," from *Mission Field*, XIII (1868). Courtesy, Trustees of the British Museum, London.

Plate 3. "The Tree-Climbers of Travancore," from *The Missionary Magazine and Chronicle*, XX (August, 1856). Courtesy, Trustees of the British Museum, London.

Plates 4a and 4b. "Toddy Tapper," sculpture by Malvina

Hoffman. Courtesy, Field Museum of Natural History, Chicago.

Plate 5. Nadans of Kayamoli, circa 1900. Courtesy, S. Chellasamy, Madras.

Plate 7. Bishop Robert Caldwell. Courtesy, United Society for the Propagation of the Gospel, London.

Plate 6. Tiruvarudi Vaihunda Nadan, Nattatti Zamindar. Courtesy, Dakshina Mara Nadar Sangam, Tirunelveli.

Plate 8. Samuel Sargunar (center) and family, circa 1915. Courtesy, Miss Dolly Simon, Madras.

Plate 9. Rao Bahadur T. Rattinasami Nadar, founder of the Nadar Mahajana Sangam. Courtesy, Nadar Mahajana Sangam, Madurai.

Plate 10. Kamaraj. Courtesy, Press Photo Bureau, Government of Madras.

pers. In 1917, for example, ten Nadars of Virudhunagar and Madurai submitted a petition to the governor of Madras, praying that the Nadars be removed from the list of depressed classes, as the community held large tracts of land and owned many prospering businesses. In 1918, the executive council of the Sangam had resolved to send a personal representation to the Madras government for removal of the name of the Nadar community from the lists.[34]

Having once sought to remove the caste from such government lists, the Sangam began to urge that the Nadar community be included among the "backward classes." In 1935 and again in 1940, the Nadar Mahajana Sangam requested that the government list the Nadars among the educationally backward communities so that fee concessions might be given to Nadar students.[35] It was not until after Independence, however, with the establishment of the Backward Classes Commission, that the Nadars made a concerted effort to have themselves listed as a depressed class.[36] In December, 1952, at Sivakasi, the twenty-second Nadar conference "resolved to request the Government of India, the Government of Madras and the Government of Travancore-Cochin to include the Nadar Community in the list of Backward Classes in education as, with the exception of a few towns inhabited by Nadars, 90 per cent of the Nadars living in other areas are backward in education, economical conditions and industries."[37]

The Nadars were placed in a peculiar position. Having tried for so long to build the image of an advanced community, they now had to depict its depressed state for the benefit of the commission. The fact was, of course, that while sections of the Hindu Nadar community in Ramnad and Madurai had become one of the most important business communities in Tamilnad, the far greater por-

[34] N.M.S. *Report*, 4th conference, Madurai, 1918.

[35] The government replied to the Nadars' request of August 19, 1935, that it could not consider further additions at that time to the list of backward classes. The Sangam's request of October 1, 1940, was also unsuccessful.

[36] For a discussion of the Backward Classes Commission and the "vested interests in backwardness," see Donald E. Smith, *India as a Secular State* (Princeton, 1963), pp. 316–322.

[37] Quoted in a letter to the secretary, Education Department, government of Madras, from the N.M.S., February 10, 1953.

tion continued to scratch out only the barest existence in the villages—and the Christian Nadars fared little better when taken as a whole, although many had prominent positions as educators, lawyers, physicians, and government servants. In a letter to the Backward Classes Commission in January, 1954, the Nadar Mahajana Sangam said that while "some of those who took to trade and commerce, have become rich and flourishing in some towns from humble beginnings . . . , the lakhs and lakhs of poor and backward people of the community should not be prejudiced by the handful of well-to-do persons, viz., about 10 per cent of the whole community scattered here and there."

Both the Nadar Mahajana Sangam and the Dakshina Mara Nadar Sangam submitted responses to the commission's questionnaire, in which they recounted the historical myth of the Nadars' former glory and of the fallen state. In a letter, August, 1955, to the minister of education, government of India, the Nadar Mahajana Sangam stated succinctly the case it had put before the Backward Classes Commission:

> The Nadar community is treated as an outcaste even today in several villages in the Madras State and they are denied the ordinary rights of citizens such as use of public streets, wells, etc.
> . . . The Nadar community has acquired right to enter public temples in South India only under the Temple Entry Act passed in the Madras State. Further, though the Civil Disabilities Act was passed to get rid of all caste disabilities, yet the status quo before the advent of the Act still continues, due to the fact that the people have to indulge in labourous task of going to the court to fight for their rights resulting in loss of time and wealth which they are unable to afford. It may be that there is no social disability legally speaking but the community is looked upon as outcaste.
> Barring a few individuals who can be counted in numbers, the community is illiterate, economically poor and socially boycotted even today. We respectfully submit in considering the social and economic conditions of the community the status and condition only of those living in the villages and who form nearly 90% of the population . . . to be taken into consideration.[38]

[38] In an earlier letter to the chairman of the Backward Classes Commission, January 12, 1955, the Sangam said that among Hindu Nadars there were only "786 degree-holders, about 11 Gazetted officers and about 26 non-Gazetted officers."

The Backward Classes Commission was confronted with a situation in which vast numbers of the caste surely met the commission's criteria for a depressed class, yet a sizable portion of the community was one of the most advanced communities educationally and economically in Tamilnad. Their solution was to list "Shanars" among the "most backward classes," to receive educational concessions. In the most backward regions of eastern Ramnad and parts of Tiruchendur and Nanguneri, the climbers called themselves Shanars, and in Madras State generally, the term Shanar was still widely used, although always with a derogatory connotation. Although the commission's use of the word Shanar was designed to restrict benefits to those families actually engaged in tree climbing, it soon gave rise to confusion and unhappiness. V. S. K. Doraisami Nadar, originally from Sivakasi and serving in New Delhi on the Income Tax Commission, wrote to the Nadar Mahajana Sangam in March, 1955, "The [Backward Classes] Commission have agreed to include in the list of backward classes 'Gramanies' and 'Shanars' and that the term 'Shanars' will include 'Nadars,' which is but a title of the 'Shanars.'

"From my discussions with the Secretary of the Commission sometime back . . . , it will be impossible to include 'Nadars' since many witnesses have told the Commission that the 'Nadars' are not at all backward. So we, should not agitate for inclusion of the term 'Nadars.' After all what is there in a name, especially in these days?" There was, of course, a very great deal in a name.

In January, 1957, the Madras government placed the "Shanar" community among the "most backward classes" for educational concessions.[39] These concessions were available only to Hindu Nadar families with an annual income of less than 1,500 rupees. Scholarships extended to those in the "most backward classes" category were awarded to those students with marks above 45 percent.[40] The denial of educational concessions to the poor Christian Nadars simply because of their religious affiliation was a clear inequity of the government order, and in 1958 concessions were

[39] G. O. Ms. No. 353, Department of Industries, Labour and Cooperation, January 31, 1957.
[40] Interview, Director of Harijan Welfare, Madras.

extended to all converts of those communities listed in the "most backward" category.[41] Few of the Nadars referred to themselves as Shanars, and consequently, in the school registers, students were listed as belonging to the Nadar caste. The president of the Dakshina Mara Nadar Sangam, Raja Palavasmuthu, sent a circular in July, 1957, to schools and colleges in the southern districts, requesting that they "change the caste 'Nadar' in the applications as 'Shanan' and give all concessions granted to the Backward Classes." In response to inquiries on this procedure, the education officer at Madurai ruled that such a change was permissible, but only on presentation of a certificate by a Revenue Department officer certifying that the pupil belongs to the "Shanar" community.[42] The government wanted "to make it clear that the concession . . . contemplated for the Shanan community is only admissible to persons whose traditional occupation is toddy-tapping." [43] This only compounded the difficulties, as the *traditional* occupation of all Nadars was toddy-tapping. In 1962, the government clarified its position, saying that the concessions "should be given only to the children of those persons who had been actually toddy-tappers until the introduction of total prohibition in their native districts." [44] In a memorandum to the chief minister, the president of the D.M.N.S. opposed "actual" occupation as the criteria for eligibility to "backward classes" benefits. "This is a patent injustice," he wrote. "In the case of no other community is the actual occupation of the individual parent made the criterion." [45]

In 1963, in supercession of all previous orders on the subjects, the government ordered that the community "Nadar" be treated as synonymous with the communities "Gramani" and "Shanan" and that all three be treated as "other backward classes," to be allowed the concessions awarded to that category. "Gramani" and "Shanan" were to be deleted from the list of "most backward

[41] G. O. Ms. No. 889, Department of Industries, Labour and Cooperation, July 3, 1958.

[42] Letter from the District Education Officer, Madurai, July 23, 1958.

[43] G. O. Ms. No. 833, Education, April 26, 1960.

[44] G. O. Ms. No. 182, Education (Education and Public Welfare Department), January 24, 1962. Also see the earlier order, G. O. Ms. No. 2665, Education, November 14, 1961.

[45] *Indian Express* (Madurai), June 18, 1962.

classes," and students belonging to those communities who had already availed themselves of the more liberal benefits of that category would be entitled to a continuation of those concessions until they had completed the particular stage of education they had undertaken at the time of the grant of concession. Since "Nadar" was to appear in the listing of "other backward classes," Christians within the community were no longer entitled to receive concessions. As before, the income criterion of 1,500 rupees remained.[46]

NADAR SCHOOLS AND COLLEGES

The Nadar community, while seeking the benefits of the concessions awarded by the Backward Classes Commission, did not rely solely upon the government for educational advancement. Perhaps more than any other community in Tamilnad, the Nadars recognized the importance of education for social uplift. Education was stressed by the missionaries among the Nadar converts in Tinnevelly District, and in the nineteenth and early twentieth centuries, the Church Missionary Society established elementary and high schools throughout the southern districts, and several important colleges, such as St. John's in Palamcottah. The Hindus were at first less responsive to education, but in Ramnad, as the Six Town Nadars began to advance in the fields of business, schools were established through *mahimai* funds by the *uravinmurai*. The first of these schools was the Kshatriya Vidhyasala High School at Virudhunagar. Established in 1885, the school provided free education to the children of all communities. The high school, with a complex of lower schools, today serves some 4,000 students with the modern facilities of what is one of the best school systems in South India.

The most important advance in education among the Hindu Nadars came with the founding of the Nadar Mahajana Sangam in 1910. From its inception, education became one of its primary concerns. One of the early objects of the Sangam was to provide financial aid to needy students. In 1921, the first scholarship-loans

[46] G. O. Ms. No. 651, Education and Public Health Department, April 3, 1963.

were awarded, and from that date to 1964, more than three thousand students had received scholarships amounting to more than 400,000 rupees. In the academic year 1964–1965, the Sangam awarded 150 recipients nearly 35,000 rupees in scholarships and books, awards being made by district in proportion to the number of members in the Sangam.[47] The loans were awarded to qualified students of the Nadar community and were to be repaid, without interest, after the completion of their schooling. Some students were given financial assistance not only for higher education, but for education abroad.[48] The Sangam has also assisted villages and towns to establish their own schools, and each year as many as forty or fifty elementary schools receive direct financial assistance from the Sangam. The scholarship and educational expenses represent the largest expenditure of the Nadar Mahajana Sangam, and the fund draws from general Sangam income, from donations, and from the Nadar Bank and cooperative societies, which give 5 percent of their profit to the scholarship fund.

The Sangam also has played an important role in the founding of new colleges. As early as 1928, at the twelfth Nadar conference, held at Aruppukottai under the presidency of P. Sububrayan, chief minister of Madras, it was proposed that a Nadar college be established.[49] Twenty years later that dream was realized. Rao Bahadur M. S. P. Senthikumara Nadar, at the 1947 Nadar conference, announced that he was prepared to contribute two lakhs of rupees toward the founding of a Nadar college. In response to his offer, the leaders of the Nadar community in Virudhunagar agreed to accept the responsibility, and in August of that same year, the Senthikumara Nadar College was inaugurated.[50] A woman's college and a polytechnic at Virudhunagar and the Ayya Nadar Janakiamal College at Sivakasi soon followed. The newest of the Nadar colleges, the S. Vellaisami Nadar College at Madurai, was endowed by the Nadar Mahajana Sangam itself, which accepted

[47] Nadar Mahajana Sangam, *56th Annual Report*, 1965.
[48] Nadar Mahajana Sangam, *55th Annual Report*, 1964.
[49] N.M.S., *Report*, 12th conference.
[50] P. Thangarajan, "History of the College," in *V. V. Ramasami Paaraattu Malar* (Virudhunagar, 1964), p. 289.

the responsibility for management.[51] The college is, in the words of the Sangam's general secretary, P. ĸ. Muthusami Nadar, "a turning point in the history of the Nadar Mahajana Sangam." [52] The college, "open to all students of all castes and creeds," was inaugurated in July, 1965, by K. Kamaraj Nadar, President of the All-India Congress Party. In that same year, the Nadars of Kanyakumari District laid the cornerstone of the Vivekananda College at Kanyakumari.

THE NADARS IN BUSINESS, INDUSTRY, THE PROFESSIONS, AND PUBLIC LIFE

The Nadar Mahajana Sangam had founded libraries, reading rooms, and a cooperative bank in addition to schools and colleges, yet one of its main concerns has been the stimulation of trade and industry among the community. The Nadars have become famous —and infamous—for their business acumen. They are often considered indigenous *banias*, skilled in the arts of usury, false weights, and adulteration. In the field in which the Nadar traders have established a virtual monopoly throughout Madras State, food grains and groceries, the Nadar merchants and shopkeepers are often accused of adulteration. Perhaps jealous of their success, many non-Nadars tell stories of the Nadars' "scientific" adulteration. Small cement coffee beans are allegedly manufactured in Virudhunagar and a certain percentage mixed with coffee. Another firm allegedly devised a machine which chops bamboo into the tiny shape of pulses. The Nadars of Virudhunagar, the most successful of all Nadar traders, receive the burden of such blame, but the Nadars are probably no more guilty of adulteration than any other class. Because they deal in wholesale food products, a major share of accusations have been directed at the Nadars. As Nadar grocery

[51] The Sangam's endowment to the college was a transfer of properties worth 100,000 rupees. The Madurai *uravinmurai* (founded in the early 50's) donated 40 acres of land for the college site from the 60 acres it held as the grounds of the Jayaraj Nadar High School. The college was named for S. Vellaisami of Virudhunagar, who donated 100,000 rupees to the college.

[52] Speech at the N.M.S. Council meeting, Aruppukottai, January 24, 1965.

shops seem to crop up on every corner of Madras and the major cities of Tamilnad, people speak of them as "taking over." A non-Nadar of Madras voiced his own reaction to the Nadars' commercial success. "They are unscrupulous businessmen—everyone admits it—but they attract business. They move easily with the people and give credit. They will sell readily available goods at a reasonable price, taking only a small margin of profit, and for goods not readily available, when other shops will not have it, the Nadar shop can always supply the needed commodity at black-market prices."

The secret of the Nadars' success as businessmen must be traced to their industry and frugality. In their determination to rise, each pice and all the energy of the family are turned back into the business, no matter how small or how large. The firewood merchants of Madras, for example, are almost entirely Nadars. They live in their shops, and day or night, they are prepared for business. The wealth of a Nadar trader is difficult to determine, for a man worth lakhs of rupees may sit cross-legged in his tiny shop—just as he did some forty years before when profits were reckoned in a few annas. Few of the older wealthy Nadar businessmen today were born into wealth. As soon as he had saved enough from his meager salary, the young man would open his own shop and hire his own assistants.

The Nadars are the Horatio Algers of South India. Each businessman can tell of his rise from poverty—or of his father's rise. S. Vellaisami of Virudhunagar, the Nadar philanthropist, rose to wealth from a salary of eight rupees a month. P. R. Muthusami, general secretary of the Nadar Mahajana Sangam for many years, began at ten rupees a month. Jayaraj Nadar began with nothing. A Christian Nadar from Tinnevelly, he went to Kodikanal in 1910 and established a small grocery shop. Forty years later, he was one of Madurai's wealthiest men, with a fleet of buses and wide business interests.* A. V. Thomas, a Tinnevelly Nadar Christian, rose from humble origins to become the wealthiest Christian in the Nadar community. As a distributor for a number of national and international manufacturers and as the holder of vast estates in tea, rubber,

and coffee, the A. V. Thomas business complex today commands a capital of more than 32 million rupees.

Although he began as heir to the Kayamoli estates of the artistocratic Nadan family of Adityan, S. B. Adityan expanded the traditional wealth of his family. His father was the first of the Adityans to be educated, and took his law degree. S. B., born in 1905, received his M.A. from Madras University, and studied law in the United Kingdom, entering the Middle Temple. He practiced as a barrister in Malaya from 1933 until 1942, when he returned to Madras before the Japanese seized Singapore. In Madras, he established the Tamil daily, *Dina Thanthi*, with a circulation today of 250,000—the largest in South India. Still a major landholder in Tiruchendur, Adityan, with his brother, S. T., a former Member of Parliament, decided to utilize the *udai* scrub grown on the land for the manufacture of paper and established the Sun Paper Mills. Adityan's investments cover a wide range of industries, including the new India Cement Corporation just outside Tinnevelly.[53]

The wealthiest man in the Nadar community is surely M. S. P. Rajah, "the Duke of Virudhunagar." M. S. P.'s great-grandfather came to Virudhunagar from Sivakasi in the mid-nineteenth century, but it was his grandfather who began to build the business, expanding from cardamom to coffee. His grandfather, for whom the Virudhunagar college is named, was born in 1880. He studied at the Kshatriya High School established by the *uravinmurai* and was one of the few Virudhunagar Nadars to learn English at that time. In 1910, he was elected as the first chairman of the Virudhunagar municipality. It was at his urging that the town, then known as Virudhupatti, became Virudhunagar, with the suffix denoting larger size and importance. Recognized by the British, he was awarded the title "Rao Bahadur." M. S. P.'s father had become involved in the family business at an early age, and in 1937 he went to Europe to establish contacts for the development of coffee export trade. Like his father, he served as municipal chairman, and upon his death in 1955, M. S. P. Rajah, at the age of twenty-nine, was elected chairman. Although Hindu, M. S. P. was

53 Interview, S. B. Adityan, Madras.

educated in Roman Catholic schools and took his B.A. from Loyola in Madras. He and his brother manage both the affairs of Virudhunagar and their family business, which includes an enormous export trade in coffee and cardamom. The main firm of the family is "Hill and Tiller," a name selected to appeal to those who prefer to buy under an English name. In 1964, the family exported 80 million rupees' worth of coffee—a major portion of India's total coffee export.[54]

M. S. P. married the daughter of Ayya Nadar, Sivakasi's most prominent industrialist. In the past thirty years, Sivakasi has achieved fame all over India as a producer of matches, fireworks, and lithographs. Sivakasi was, in the early nineteenth century, the center of the Nadars' tobacco and cotton trade, but from the 1880's, after Virudhunagar was linked by rail to Madurai, Sivakasi began to decline, as traders migrated elsewhere for business. By the 1920's, trade had all but disappeared and the community was mainly dependent upon agriculture. The land was poor and the times were hard. In 1922, two young friends in Sivakasi, P. Ayya Nadar and A. Shanmuga Nadar, read that the match industry offered good profit, and Ayya's father agreed to finance their trip to Calcutta to learn the process of match manufacture. They stayed in Calcutta six months, returning to Sivakasi with machines imported from Germany. They established a factory together, and found that mechanized production was costly, as only certain quality woods could be used. Owing to the economically depressed condition of the area, however, labor was plentiful and cheap. Influenced by Gandhi's plea for cottage industries, they decided after a year and a half to switch over to hand production. After initial success, the two parted in 1926 to establish separate factories. Ayya became known as "Anil," or squirrel, from the brand of his matches. Shanmuga became "Kaakaa," or crow.

From matches, fireworks production began and grew by leaps and bounds, and it was here that the greatest margin of profit lay. As the match and fireworks industries grew, trademark labels were needed. They were originally purchased from Bombay, but because of the delay, litho printing was introduced into Sivakasi in

[54] Interview, M. S. P. Rajah, Madras.

1930 as a subsidiary industry. There are today about 50 litho printing presses in Sivakasi, employing 1,000 workers, with a gross of 10 million rupees per year, and the Sivakasi lithographs of India's film stars and deities have won fame throughout the subcontinent and are familiar to any traveler. The match industry continues to be the major industry of the town. There are nearly 800 match factories in Sivakasi, which produce 125,000 boxes daily—all by hand. The match production of the Sivakasi area accounts for nearly 50 percent of India's national match consumption.[55]

The Nadars have been primarily associated with trade and have been generally reluctant to invest major blocks of capital in an industry, which may require years for a return. The Nadar Mahajana Sangam has long urged Nadars to go into industry, and the industrial progress of the community has increasingly become a major concern of the Sangam. The Sangam has aided in the establishment of private and cooperative industries and has itself begun to take an active part in stimulating industrial growth by starting a flour mill near Madurai. There has been in Tamilnad, as in all India, heightening criticism of private food-grain and grocery marketing, and the opening speech of the 1964 Nadar conference warned of "the increasing sense of discontent which the common people are coming to have towards the merchants of all classes of our country." Industrialization, not trade, was offered as the new level of achievement to which the Nadar community must aspire.[56] The theme of the 1965 conference, which the writer attended, held at Karaikudi, was the Nadars' role in the industrialization of India. The government will by-pass the middlemen through the establishment of a food corporation, a speaker warned. The tide may be beginning to turn against the Nadar, and if he is to advance with India, he must invest in the future through industry.

The emphasis in the Nadar community of Ramnad and Madurai has always been on trade and commerce, but for a few families, education was seen as the road to advancement. In Palayampatti, the father of S. Ganesan wanted the best education for his children.

[55] Interview, A. Ayya Nadar, Sivakasi.
[56] Nadar Mahajana Sangam, *Report*, 32nd Nadar Conference, Coimbatore, opening speech by Dr. P. H. Daniel, chief medical officer, Karumalai.

From the Kshatriya High School in Aruppukottai Ganesan went on to American College, Madurai, and St. Joseph's at Trichinopoly for his M.A. On a scholarship from the Nadar Mahajana Sangam, he went to the London School of Economics for study under Laski, returning to Madras to take his law degree. In 1956, he joined the judicial service and served various appointments as district judge. One of Madras' most respected judges, he now serves as principal judge, city civil court and sessions judge, Madras.[57]

V. S. K. Doraisami Nadar struggled against the wishes of his father that he go into business in Sivakasi. From Annamalai University, where he was among the first Nadar students, V. S. K. D. entered government service, despite the warnings of friends who said that a Nadar would not be able to rise in the services. He soon became the first Hindu Nadar to achieve gazetted rank and went on to become income tax commissioner of India during the 1950's. Now retired from government service, he serves as a tax consultant and has established a paint factory just outside Madras City. Through both his own and his wife's family, V. S. K. D. continues an active role in Sivakasi business.[58]

It has been the Christian Nadars, rather than the Hindus, who have responded most to the opportunities for advancement through education in government services and in the professions. The background of the mission schools and the emphasis on education in the Christian home gave them an important headstart. In education in Madras State, a great proportion of teachers at all levels are drawn from the Nadar Christian community, and a number of prominent physicians and lawyers are Christian Nadars. In the field of government service, Tamilnad's chief engineer is a Christian Nadar, as is the inspector-general of police, Arul, son-in-law of the businessman A. V. Thomas.

As the Nadars have made their mark in business and in the professions, increasing numbers of the community have entered political life. The most prominent, K. Kamaraj Nadar, is one of the most powerful and dynamic leaders in Indian public life today.

[57] Interview, S. Ganesan, Madras.
[58] Interview, V. S. K. Doraisami Nadar, Madras.

Kamaraj was born in Virudhunagar on July 15, 1903. His father, Kumaraswami, married Sivakami Ammal, the daughter of his mother's brother—the traditionally ideal choice in a bride. The family was not wealthy, but they enjoyed a frugal prosperity, and at his fifth year of age, it was decided that the young Kamaraj would attend school. The event was celebrated in a grand manner, with the child dressed in a silk dhoti and velvet coat and taken in procession to the school, where, with the help of the teacher, he wrote the letter "A" on a palmyra leaf, formally initiating his education. The following year, Kamaraj's father died. The family placed little value on education beyond the requirements of business accounts, and in the middle of his sixth class, Kamaraj was taken from the school and placed in his uncle's cloth shop to learn the business.[59]

Kamaraj took little interest in business, and during the First World War, the young man began to follow politics. To wean him from this inclination, his family sent him off to Trivandrum to work in another uncle's timber shop. Hardly had he arrived than the Congress party staged the Vaikom satyagraha for the admission of Harijans to temples. Kamaraj, at the age of seventeen, was drawn into the movement, and his mercurial political career was launched. Within three years, the young Kamaraj had become a lieutenant of the Tamil Brahmin Congress leader, Satyamurthi. In 1936, Satyamurthi was elected president of the Tamil Nad Congress Committee (T.N.C.C.), and on assuming office, appointed Kamaraj secretary of the committee. In 1937, Kamaraj was elected to the Legislative Council, and in 1940, backed by Satyamurthi, he contested and won the election for the presidency of the T.N.C.C. Having held the key to the party machine for four years as T.N.C.C. secretary, Kamaraj now began to consolidate his position in the Congress. With Independence, as president of the provincial Congress committee, Kamaraj became the "king-maker" of Madras politics. In 1954 he took the reins of power himself as chief min-

---

[59] M. Namasivayam, *Kamaraj Varalaru* (Madurai, 1963), pp. 61–85; L. S. Mani, "A Golden Age," in *Sri K. Kamaraj 6oth Birthday Commemoration Volume* (Madras, 1962); "A Gandhite," *Kamaraj—the Shrewd, 1903–1940* (Madras, 1961), pp. 6–7. For a life of Kamaraj, see V. K. Narasimhan, *Kamaraj: A Study* (Bombay, 1967).

ister and held that position until he resigned in 1963 to become
president of the All-India Congress party.

A man of simple tastes, hailed as "a *sanyasi* in white clothes," and
"a man of the people," Kamaraj is, in the words of Nehru, a man
"with extraordinary capacity, ability, and devotion to his task." [60]
He is a man of great power, and, as the illustrious son of the Nadar
community, Kamaraj has bestowed, through his success, a sense of
prestige and pride upon all Nadars.

The success of Nadars in trade, industry, the professions, and
public life had a decisive effect upon the Nadar community and on
its relationship with other castes. Increasing economic and educational differentiation widened the gap between the cultural levels
within the community. As they advanced in life, individually mobile Nadars of the major urban areas, such as Madras City, were
increasingly accepted by their peers of other communities on a
level of equality and mutual respect. In the heterogeneous city,
caste counted for less, and achievement rather than ascriptive criteria determined social status. But the traditional implications of
caste were not entirely lost. The Nadar community as a whole was
frequently regarded as "pushy," and their low origins were not
completely forgotten. In the villages of the southern districts, caste
jealousies nourished old resentments. In the regions of northern
Tinnevelly and Ramnad, tensions between the Nadars and other
communities carried over from the nineteenth into the twentieth
century.

COMMUNAL CONFLICT

One of the earliest concerns of the Sangam was an improvement
in the relations between the Nadars and other communities. At the
second conference in 1910, it was urged that "while we improve
our lot, we must mingle with other communities." [61] Conflict and

[60] Quoted in the *Hindu*, October 11, 1961. See also V.K. Narasimhan,
"Kamaraj—the Party President," *Forum Service* (London), No. 710 (May 2, 1964);
J. Anthony Lukas, "Political Python of India," *New York Times Magazine*,
February 20, 1966.
[61] Letter from the Aruppukottai Nadars' Educational Association, read at the
conference. N.M.S., *Report*, 2nd conference.

hostility between the Nadars and other communities, particularly the Maravars, had not declined, however, in the years following the decision in the Kamudi case.

The Sanskritized life and customs adopted by the Nadars in the latter part of the nineteenth century had not heightened their position in the eyes of the caste Hindus, but had only subjected the community to ridicule and outraged protest. If the Six Town Nadars had gained a new self-awareness and caste consciousness, the other communities had been united as a force against them. The mutual antagonism had by no means been abated by the Kamudi judgment.

In areas where they lacked the strength of numbers and wealth, the Nadars continued to suffer severe social disabilities. Recourse to the courts offered little salvation. In 1913, for example, seven Nadar residents of Kallorani village in Ramnad brought suit against the caste Hindus for a declaration that the Nadars were entitled to the use of the village tank and well, which alone contained water during the periods of scarcity. The defendants, Brahmins, Vellalas, and Maravars, contended that the wells were reserved exclusively for the "clean" castes. The judge ruled that the Nadars had a right of access to the tank, but that the custom against the use of the well by lower castes was clear and that the court was bound to uphold it. "If a Hindu custom is not too irrational or immoral and has been definitely and clearly established as prevailing for a very long period courts should give effect to it." [62]

In the tension between the Nadars and the other communities, conflict was easily sparked, and in Kamudi, where there was economic unrest and bitterness against the Nadar traders for rising food prices, the situation was particularly sensitive. In August, 1918, a disturbance arose at the weekly market, when Maravar villagers squatted upon a stall site prepared by the Nadars in the market compound. The Maravars were attacked by the Nadars and filed a complaint before the police. A panchayat composed of leading persons on both sides was convened in an effort to quell

[62] *Mariappa Nadan* v. *Vaithilinga Mudaliar*, 1913, Madras Weekly Notes 247. See also, Paul Appasamy, *Centenary History of the C.M.S. in Tinnevelly* (Palamcottah, 1923), p. 153.

emotions. The panchayat decided the Nadars were the aggressors and a fine was levied against them. No action was taken by the police, on the impression that the matter had been thus settled. The Maravars, led by Ukkarapandia Thevar, the son of Vellasami Thevar, wanted more definite action against the Nadars, taking the affray "as an affront on their time-honoured tradition and prestige."[63] The old hostilities had been rekindled, and scattered robberies led the Kamudi Nadars to fear a recurrence of the Sivakasi massacre. Apprehension rose as the rumor circulated that Kamudi would be stormed and sacked on September 17. Telegrams to the authorities brought a detachment of fifteen constables and their commander on September 16.

The police immediately set out to disperse the mobs collecting near Kamudi, but as they approached a palmyra tope near the town, the Maravars advanced. The rioters closed in, pelting with stones and clubbing the police, leaving five officers seriously injured. The head constable wired his superiors, "Big rioting, reserve very weak, people loitering on all sides, expect more rioting, send more men. . . ."[64] The police were equipped with carbines and stationed in the bazaar street just as a mob of some 1,000 Maravars entered the bazaar, "devastating the shops and houses that lay on both sides by ravaging and setting fire to them as they passed." The police then opened fire, killing, it was reported, some fifty rioters. As the riot was brought under control, three constables were found to be severely wounded, stripped of their guns and clothing. The head constable had been killed, along with one of his men. Some forty shops and houses in the Nadar bazaar street had been looted and burned.[65] Property losses were estimated at 50,000 rupees.[66]

In October, 1918, a punitive force of fifty reserve police was quartered at Kamudi "with a view to restore order and to prevent further disturbance." A penalty tax was imposed on both Nadars and Maravars to pay the costs of maintenance. The special force

[63] *Kamudi Looting Case.* Records of the Preliminary Enquiry in Connection with the Kamudi Looting Case . . . , pp. 477–482.
[64] *Ibid.*
[65] *Ibid.*
[66] The *Hindu*, September 23, 1918.

was to be stationed for one year only, but it was continued by subsequent proclamations from year to year. In January, 1922, W. P. A. Soundrapandian Nadar, the first Nadar member of the Legislative Council, introduced a resolution calling for the repeal of the punitive tax. "The continued imposition of the tax for three years had caused much oppression and indescribable misery to the people, both Nadars and Maravars," he said in the council debates. "Many families have been ruined. Several Nadar families have been forced to abandon their homes and migrate to distant parts, being unable to withstand the oppression of the tax gathering officers. . . . There is no longer any hostility between the Nadars and the Maravars. Normal trade relations between the two communities have been resumed long ago." Both the Nadar Mahajana Sangam and the less active Maravar Mahajana Sabha tried to improve relations between the two communities in Kamudi, and "the leaders of both communities have begun to realize the need for cooperation and cultivation' of fraternal feelings." [67] The Raja of Ramnad (son of the plaintiff in the 1897 Kamudi Case) joined his Nadar colleague in assuring the council that "there will no longer be any disturbance on account of the old feud between the Nadars and Maravars." [68] The motion to repeal the tax was carried.[69]

In order to ease the continued hostility between the Nadar and Maravar communities, the Nadar Mahajana Sangam invited the Raja of Ramnad to preside over the eighth Nadar conference, to be held at Sivakasi in 1922. Only twenty-three years before, Sivakasi had been the scene of a major confrontation between the Nadar and Maravar communities.

RESOLUTION OF 'CONFLICT

While it has sought improved relations between communities, the Sangam, from its founding in 1910, has been primarily concerned with community solidarity. Nine traveling agents, kept constantly in the field by the Sangam, visit villages and towns

[67] *Madras Legislative Council Proceedings*, IV (January 21, 1922), 2100.
[68] *Ibid.*, p. 2104.
[69] *Ibid.*, p. 2109.

through the southern districts in an attempt to organize the Nadar community in each place as a *uravinmurai* or as a *sangam*, which in turn is established as an autonomous branch of the Nadar Mahajana Sangam. The *uravinmurai* is then encouraged to collect *mahimai* for the establishment of schools and public buildings for general community welfare.

Disputes over the management of these *mahimai* funds and properties had often posed a threat to the unity of the caste. The fifth conference of the Nadar Mahajana Sangam in 1919 was held at Virudhunagar in order to settle a major *mahimai* dispute there.* At the tenth Nadar conference in 1925, a prominent Nadar leader warned against the "evils caused to our community by factions and feuds among ourselves" and advocated the "formation of Nadar community panchayats in all the leading centers to deal with local troubles and misunderstandings. . . ."[70]

Recognizing the *uravinmurai* as the foundation of the community's strength, the Sangam accordingly established a panchayat system whereby any internal dispute could be placed before a body of uninvolved Nadar leaders for mediation. Upon request to intervene in a dispute, the Sangam would appoint an *ad hoc* panchayat committee under the direction of one of the Sangam officers. An initial investigation of the facts would be made, and all parties to the dispute would be required to sign an agreement to accept as binding any decision made by the panchayat. The agreement was rarely broken, although the number of internal disputes has begun to rise in recent years.

The Nadar Mahajana Sangam receives approximately two hundred complaints each year regarding disputes in villages.[71] Of these, fifty involve disputes among Nadars. The remaining number involve intercaste disputes. In recent years there has been an increase in the number of internal disputes and a concomitant decline in the number of disputes between the Nadars, as a community,

---

[70] Address by V. Balaguruswami Nadar, June 9, 1925, in *Report*, 10th Nadar conference.

[71] The Dakshina Mara Nadar Sangam receives a number of petitions each year as well. In 1964, 112 cases were received by the D.M.N.S. Most were forwarded on to the appropriate police authorities. The D.M.N.S. has no panchayat system, and it does not normally handle disputes within the Nadar community.

and other castes. Each year the Sangam has received fewer complaints from Nadars describing their suffering and ill-treatment at the hands of other community people, although the Nadars are by no means yet free of caste oppression. In many areas where the Sangam has not effectively organized the Nadar community, they remain weak, divided, and at the mercy of the dominant caste. In many villages where the Nadars number only a small minority, as in the rural areas of Ramnad, they continue to suffer various social disabilities, and in scattered villages, they still face harassment when refusing to pay the *kaval* protection to the Maravars. The *kaval* system—whereby the villagers pay the Maravar "watchmen" *not* to pillage their crops and rob their houses—once widespread throughout the southern districts, is rapidly disappearing. The decline of *kaval*, while due in part to the attempts of the Maravars themselves to uplift their own community, is significantly due to the efforts of the Sangam to strengthen the position of the Nadar villagers.

The social disabilities suffered by Nadars today were described in the 1961 census survey of the village in eastern Ramnad. The Nadars continued to live in a separate cluster of houses somewhat removed from the caste Hindus. Even though they were permitted to use the public tank, they were required to draw water from a particular corner, distinct from the place used by the higher castes. The survey concluded that "the ritual rank for the Shanans is generally just above the Adi-Dravidas," that is, the untouchables.[72]

The Sangam's touring agents in these villages attempt to eliminate factional antagonism among the Nadars and to reduce their dependency upon the landowners. In organizing the Nadars of any village, the Nadar Mahajana Sangam backs them with the strength of the larger community.* In any dispute arising between Nadars and the members of other communities, the Nadars may petition for the Sangam to intervene. The Sangam will take action only after an investigation to establish the truth of the situation as described by the "plaintiffs." If a settlement of the dispute is possible

[72] *Census of India, 1961*, Vol. IX: *Madras*, Pt. VI: Village Survey Monographs, No. 14, *Visavanoor*, pp. 16–17.

only through police intervention and subsequent court action, the Sangam will make a full report to the proper authorities, presenting the situation as accurately as it has been able to ascertain. While the Sangam will neither contest the case for the Nadar claimants nor provide financial support for litigation, the Sangam will offer all assistance in securing legal counsel and in seeing that the Nadars' case is properly heard.[73]

Typical complaints, of which the greatest number come from eastern Ramnad, involve denial of social privileges such as the right to ride a bicycle on the public street of the village, to eat in the coffee hotel, to conduct marriage processions, and often even for a presumptuous Nadar boy to attend the village school.[74] In September, 1964, for example, the Sangam received a complaint from a Nadar in a Maravar-dominant village in Paramagudi taluq of eastern Ramnad. The Sangam found that the Nadars were not allowed to take water from the public well, even though it had been constructed by the Panchayat Union, that they were denied entrance into the public hotel, that they were not allowed to walk on certain streets, or even to sit on the verandahs of their own houses in the presence of Thevars. Most important, the Nadars were prevented from cultivating their lands. The implements were damaged, and the services of the carpenter were denied to them. "In short," the Sangam wrote to the deputy superintendent of police at Muthukalatur, "the Thevar community is trying to drive the Nadar community from the village, leaving their property there." An even more serious case involved an Inam village [75] also in Paramagudi taluq. Before land reforms, the Inamdar, or landlord, was a Mudaliar residing in Paramagudi. As the ryots—Nadars, Maravars, and Harijans—secured lands of their own under court order, the Inamdar began to harass the villagers with threats and armed rowdies. The harassment culminated in March, 1964, when the village properties were ravaged by a band of armed men in the

[73] Interview, Arul Thomas, assistant manager of the Nadar Mahajana Sangam.
[74] Random cases from the complaint files of the Sangam.
[75] A village exempt or partially exempt from the payment of revenue. Inams were almost wholly endowments to religious and charitable institutions or grants to esteemed individuals, chiefly Brahmins.

pay of the Inamdar. Crops were destroyed and trees cut down. The Nadar Mahajana Sangam represented the villagers—Maravars and Harijans, as well as Nadars—before the police authorities.[76]

If the dispute does not involve deep caste antagonisms and if police intervention can be avoided, the Sangam will approach the leaders of the other community to discuss the possibilities of a settlement. In many cases, a panchayat will be formed for compulsory arbitration, as in the case of internal disputes. In a village dispute in 1960 in western Ramnad, for example, the Nadars were denied the use of the public road through the dominant Konar section of the village for the purpose of carrying their dead to the cemetery which lay beyond. By tradition, the Nadars carried their dead around the Konar hamlet, but a crisis arose when bad weather forced the Nadars to carry the body of a dead child through the Konar hamlet for burial. Feelings ran high, and the Nadars brought the case to the Sangam. An influential Konar businessman living in Madurai, who had ties with the village, and another Konar, a subregistrar in Madurai, agreed to participate, together with Sangam officials, in a panchayat committee for the mediation of the dispute. The final settlement, agreed to by all, broke the tradition and allowed the Nadars to pass freely along the road.*

Where once the Nadars sought high Kshatriya status in the ritual hierarchy, increasingly the Nadar Mahajana Sangam has sought the relations of equality among all castes. The Sangam, while seeking the unity and uplift of the Nadar community, has sought to create the image of itself as a *community* but not a *communal* organization, and as such, has won the respect of the wider Tamil community. The Sangam has become increasingly conscious of the secular "casteless society." Indeed, the Sangam recently changed the name of the Nadar Bank to the Tamilnad Mercantile Bank, and in the establishment of a new hotel in Madurai, it was by general consensus agreed that the word Nadar should not appear in the name, since the hotel's facilities would be available to all commu-

[76] Petition before the district superintendent of police, Ramnad, at Madurai. Tamil, dated April 10, 1964; letter to the deputy inspector of police, Southern Range, Madurai, from the N.M.S., December 11, 1964.

nities.[77] In reviewing "42 years of service," in 1952, the Sangam wrote that it did not seek to create "caste feeling," but aimed rather at "bringing up the Nadar community and the country along with it." [78] Among the resolutions for the uplift of the Nadar community drafted by the Sangam's annual meeting in 1964 was one expressing the desire "to have cordial relationship with other communities. The Nadar community must allow other communities to use the schools, tanks, temples and wells started or established by Nadars." [79]

ORGANIZATION OF THE NADAR MAHAJANA SANGAM

In its activities for the advancement of the Nadar community, the Nadar Mahajana Sangam has earned the respect of all those familiar with its work. The Raja of Ramnad has urged the Maravars to emulate the Nadars: "Many people are saying that the Nadars have come up because of Kamaraj. This is not true. They have come up through their own efforts. Some people are jealous of them—but why should we be jealous of success. We should try to do the same. The Nadars have come up because they were united." [80]

Although its actual membership is but a fraction of the Nadar population, the Nadar Mahajana Sangam is accepted as the representative of the community by nearly all Nadars and is so viewed by other caste people. The sovereign body of the Sangam is the General Body of members. The General Body meets once a year, as a part of the Nadar conference held annually in different cities and towns of Tamilnad. Most of the conferences have been held in Ramnad and Madurai districts, reflecting the heaviest concentrations of membership. There were only 824 members of the Sangam

[77] The decision was taken at the N.M.S. council meeting at Aruppukottai, January 24, 1965. The profits of the lodge, opened in 1965 as the "Mahajana Mansion," will go to the Sangam Scholarship Fund.

[78] Nadar Mahajana Sangam, *Nadar Mahajana Sangam: 42 Years of Service* (Madurai, 1952).

[79] Nadar Mahajana Sangam, *55th Annual Report*, 1964.

[80] Interview, Raja of Ramnad, Madras.

in 1920–1921. By the tenth conference in 1925, there were just over 4,000, and by 1965, membership totaled 20,620.[81]

The conference itself, attended by from 2,000 to 5,000 people, rallies the community to social uplift and community action and, above all, to unity. At the fifty-fifth annual meeting at Coimbatore in 1964, the Nadar Mahajana Sangam drafted six resolutions for the uplift of the Nadar community:

(1) To have unity among Nadars of all creeds and status, far and wide. (2) To establish and maintain *uravinmurai* and to start collecting *mahimai*. (3) To have cordial relationship with other communities, welcoming those communities that gave all sorts of trouble in the past into the schools and temples which the Nadars have erected and bearing no ill-feeling towards them. (4) Not to utilize others' finance or labor for your own good, but to lift yourself through your own efforts. (5) To help in the uplift of the poor. (6) To strive to rise up independently, to stand on your own legs, and coming up in life serve as an example to others.[82]

The General Body elects the Executive Council of the Sangam, the substantive governing body. The composition of the council, according to the Rules and Regulations, is to be determined in proportion to the membership of the Sangam by district. This weights the council heavily toward Madurai and Ramnad. Nominations are received for the council at the annual conference, but there are never enough nominations to fill the 150 seats, and each nominee has, in fact, been elected. Anyone desiring to participate in the council may do so. Because of the location of the Sangam office in Madurai and the demands of time upon the council members, the largest number of council members have been in Madurai and in the towns within easy access, particularly Virudhunagar. In the year 1964–1965 only 99 nominations were received, 13 seats

[81] The breakdown for that year was as follows: Ramnad 4,856; Madurai 4,587; Tirunelveli 3,413; Coimbatore 1,777; Madras City 1,179; Tanjore 1,137; Kerala 736; Trichinopoly 735; Kanyakumari 690; Salem 535; Bombay 323; N. & S. Arcot 276; Chingleput 138; Mysore 96; Nilgiris 58; Pondicherry and Karaikkal 51; Malaysia 17; Delhi 10; Ceylon 3; Andhra 3. From Nadar Mahajana Sangam, *56th Annual Report*, 1965.

[82] Nadar Mahajana Sangam, *55th Annual Report*, 1964. A similar list of "Six Canons" appeared earlier in *Mahajanam*, March 14, 1960.

going to Madurai town.* The executive council may meet as many as twenty or more times during the year, but the burden of the Sangam's management rests with the two general-secretaries. The offices of president and vice president are honorary. It was resolved, after the death of the founder, T. Rattinasami Nadar, that the Sangam presidency would stay in the family of the Poraiyar Nadars. The president in 1965 was Ganagasabai Nadar of Poraiyar, the fourth Sangam president elected for life and a nephew of the founder.[83]

Although the general-secretaries are responsible for the affairs of the Sangam, the routine of actual day-to-day management rests with the office staff of the association, headed by the Sangam manager, a Christian Nadar from Nagercoil. Indeed, nearly all the office staff are Christian Nadars, reflecting the emphasis on education among the Christians of the community. The office handles a great quantity of mail, sending, for example, more than 20,000 letters in 1963–1964. In addition to the staff in Madurai, the Sangam keeps nine traveling agents in the field. The Sangam, while it does not officially sponsor district or taluq conferences, will provide all aid and assistance to any branch *sangam* desiring to hold an annual conference. In 1964–1965, there were two taluq conferences, Ramnad and Tiruppattur. The Sangam publishes a biweekly newspaper, *Mahajanam*,[84] and the total assets of the association in 1965 were nearly 700,000 rupees![85]

THE DAKSHINA MARA NADAR SANGAM

The Nadar Mahajana Sangam seeks to represent the entire Nadar community, Hindu and Christian, southern and northern. As we have seen, however, the N.M.S. has been essentially an association of Ramnad-Madurai Nadars, and while it has involved prominent Tinnevelly Nadars, both Hindu and Christian, there has been relatively little involvement on the part of the southern, or "Dakshina Mara," Nadars. There is in Tinnevelly a separate Nadar caste asso-

[83] Interview, V. Ganagasabai Nadar, Karaikudi Conference.
[84] Nadar Mahajana Sangam, *55th Annual Report*, 1964.
[85] Nadar Mahajana Sangam, *56th Annual Report*, 1965.

ciation for the Nadars of Tinnevelly and Kanyakumari, the
Dakshina Mara Nadar Sangam. The D.M.N.S., although incor-
porated only in 1942, traces its origins to the community *pettais*
established in the mid-nineteenth century.

Toward the middle of the nineteenth century, forty or fifty
years after the major migrations into northern Tinnevelly and
Ramnad which were the foundations of the Ramnad Nadar community, Tinnevelly Nadar traders began to establish their own
pettais throughout the southern districts. The *pettais*, like those
which were the base of the Six Towns, were established for the
protection and shelter of bullocks and goods and for the conduct
of business. These sites were purchased and maintained through
mahimi collections. Some were only a bare site, others an enclosure of mud walls; a few had a complex of buildings, with shops,
rest houses, and sanitary facilities. The *pettais* were managed locally by those members of the community who frequented that
particular place. Most of the traders, unlike those who preceded
them, did not establish their permanent residences around the
pettai, but chose to remain based in Tinnevelly. The Dakshina
Mara Nadar *pettais* were supposed to be held in trust for the community, but the profits often enriched private pockets, and the
pettais soon became the subject of endless disputes. In 1869 the
management of the Tinnevelly Nadars' *pettai* at Virudhunagar fell
into a dispute which dragged on for nearly thirty years. In order to
secure control over the management of the *pettais* for the benefit
of the community as a whole, a number of Tinnevelly Nadar
leaders met in 1898 to settle upon measures for the proper and
efficient management of the *pettais*. They chose seven from among
their number to act as their representatives in a management trust,
the Dakshina Mara Nadu Nadars Sabha. The trust functioned for
several years, but without a visible improvement in the general
state of affairs. Various attempts were made to prepare a scheme
for management, and in 1904, a general-body meeting was held in
Madurai. Under the constitution framed at the conference, a president and an executive committee of thirty-nine members were
selected. The scheme immediately encountered opposition from
local managers, and in 1925, 1927, and 1928, various meetings were

held, with resolutions to form a new *sangam* for the management of the properties. After protracted negotiations between Nadars connected with different *pettais*, a society was formed in 1932, assuming possession and management of all thirty-eight disputed *pettais*.

Soon after the conference, a locally organized *sangam* in Madurai sought to take control of the Tinnevelly Nadar *pettai* in that city. Other disputes soon followed. The integrity of the society itself was called into question with serious charges of misappropriation of funds. A case was brought against the society in 1942 in order "to ascertain and define the properties and funds of the trust . . . and for a settlement of a proper scheme of management of the trust. . . ." The judge decided against the defendants, and the court laid down a scheme for the management of the *pettais* by an association to be known as the Dakshina Mara Nadar Sangam. In addition to the responsibility for management of the properties—*pettais*, buildings, shops—the court's enumeration of Sangam aims and objectives included a number of welfare activities. From the profits yielded by the properties, the Sangam was to encourage "the advancement of education, industry, trade, agriculture and cooperation among the members of the community." It was to establish schools, hospitals, libraries, orphanages, hostels, poorhouses, and similar institutions; to promote industrial progress through the establishment of a bank; to publish a newspaper and periodicals, and to arrange for propaganda, lectures, and conferences for the unification and welfare of the community. The Sangam was to grant free scholarships and to advance interest-free loans to deserving and poor students of the community.

The ultimate authority in all matters relating to the administration of the Sangam was to be vested in the General Body, to meet once a year. An administrative council, composed of 51 members elected on a regional basis, would meet quarterly, and from among themselves would elect an executive committee of 11 members, including a president, vice president, secretary, and assistant secretary. The secretary would be responsible to the executive committee for the general supervision of Sangam affairs.[86]

---

[86] The description of the origin and establishment of the D.M.N.S. is drawn from the 1942 decision establishing the scheme. *Gnanadoraisami Nadar et al. v. V.*

Under the motto, "Unity is strength," the D.M.N.S. held its first conference in December, 1946. Elected as president was Raja Palavasamuthu, heir to the power of the Nadans of Arumaganeri, a few miles north of Tiruchendur town, and one of the "strongmen" of the Tiruchendur Nadars. A wealthy landowner, he is a man of enormous size and power, commanding respect and fear. Under him, the Sangam's properties have increased and grown in value, but few of the court's aims have been realized. With a yearly income from properties totaling about 150,000 rupees (1959), the D.M.N.S. spends only about 12,000 per year on scholarships, and any welfare benefits beyond that are minimal. There have been virtually no attempts by the D.M.N.S. to organize the Nadars in the villages for social uplift. Among the Tinnevelly Hindu Nadars, particularly in the *teri* regions of the Southeast, there is no more unity today than one hundred and fifty years ago, and many Nadars are helplessly dependent on and indebted to powerful local leaders, such as Raja Palavasamuthu. The only *uravinmurai* in the region of Tinnevelly and Kanyakumari districts have been organized in the larger towns through the efforts of the Nadar Mahajana Sangam, and the membership, like that of the *uravinmurai* of Tuticorin, established only in 1960, is composed primarily of Ramnad Nadars who have migrated there for trading purposes. On the petitions received regarding disputes between the Nadars and other communities, the Dakshina Mara Nadar Sangam rarely takes any action on its own and usually forwards the petition to the appropriate authority. The D.M.N.S. has not held regular conferences, and the management, according to critics of the association, is held by a clique who use the association for personal enrichment and power. Whether there is any foundation or not for the charges, the D.M.N.S. has not utilized its resources for the betterment of the community, and it has not gained the respect of the community generally.[87] The Nadar Mahajana Sangam, on the other hand, is recognized even in Tinnevelly, where its activities

S. P. *Sivasubramania Nadar et al.* In the Court of the Subordinate Judge, Tinnevelly, Original Suit, No. 12 of 1942.

[87] Dakshina Mara Nadar Sangam, *13th Annual Report* (Tinnevelly, 1964); interviews with Raja Palavasamuthu and L. S. Tangasami, Secretary of the D.M.N.S. Criticism of the D.M.N.S. comes from interviews with a number of Nadars in Tinnevelly District.

are not extensive, as the organizational representative of the Nadar community.

The economic changes and the movement to achieve higher social status during the past one hundred years have brought a new self-awareness and a concomitant decline in the divisions of subcaste which had separated the community into endogamous units in the early part of the nineteenth century. Today few Nadars have any idea of their own subcaste, and most express only the vaguest knowledge of such divisions at all. Of the subcastes, only one has today retained its distinct identity, the Nattatti. The Nattattis number only a few thousand, and most have left the village of Nattatti for Madras City, Tuticorin, or other towns of the southern districts. Almost all the Nattattis are literate, and the community is almost equally divided between Christian and Hindu. Intermarriage between Nattattis of the two religions is frequent, but marriages between Nattattis and other Nadars have been rare: less than a dozen during the past fifty years. The reasons for the continued endogamy of the Nattattis are not altogether clear. In some respects the Nattattis occupied a position *within* the Nadar community somewhat analogous to that of the Nadar community as a whole in relation to the larger Tamil society. Its position was "middling," between the clearly degraded position of the Servai Nadar and that of the higher subcastes. While looked down upon by other Nadars as in some ways inferior, although the customs were the same, the Nattattis were relatively prosperous as traders. They were among the first Nadars to migrate to Ceylon and Malaya, and prospering in foreign lands, they began to rise as a *nouveau riche* class of rather "brassy types," often incurring the jealousy of their non-Nattatti fellow Nadars. These factors, together with their historical memory and zamindari tradition, may account for the continued separation of the group from the larger Nadar community. Dr. A. Devasugnayom, a Nattatti physician in Madras, said in an interview that he sees a change coming. "Probably after some time, this community will be merged with the larger community—but it has not come yet."

The Servai Nadars, viewed as an inferior subcaste, were traditionally the menial servants to the Nadans. Although their distinct identity was retained well into the twentieth century, the Servais, as they began to come up in education, increasingly dropped any appellation which might distinguish them from the larger Nadar community. The Nadar Mahajana Sangam in the late 1940's formally recognized the Servais as in no way separate or distinct from the Nadar community, and in 1947, the government received a representation from "Servaikarars" of Nanguneri taluq, requesting that they be called simply Nadars in government records.[88]

Some Nadars say that the Gramani caste is a subcaste of the Nadar community, and it was so treated by the government under the British. Gramanis were listed for the census along with the Nadars under the name Shanan, and even today, for purposes of educational concessions under the Backward Classes Commission, the Gramanis are classified under the title Nadar. In fact, however, the Gramanis constitute a separate caste; though by tradition they are toddy-tappers, they share no historical roots and have never exchanged brides. The Gramani community numbers only a few thousand and is concentrated in the district of Chingleput. They were traditionally tappers of the coconut palm and have been economically dislocated with prohibition. The community remains extremely backward, and educational advancement is low. One of the few men of prominence to emerge from their ranks is M. P. Sivagnanam Gramani, a leader of the Congress party during the Independence movement and founder of the Tamil Arasu party. He founded the Gramani Kula Mahajana Sangam in 1937 and published the periodical *Gramani Kulam*. The Sangam died in 1941, and Sivagnanam has not been involved in caste affairs since that time. He maintains that, although both names mean "lord of the land," the Nadars and Gramanis are distinct castes.[89] The movement for caste unity among the Nadars has thus not been extended to embrace the Gramanis.

The identity between the northern and southern Nadars has, however, been greatly heightened. During the latter part of the

[88] Press communique from the chief secretary to the government, Madras, September 5, 1947. In the files of the Nadar Mahajana Sangam.
[89] Interview, M. P. Sivagnanam Gramani, Madras.

nineteenth century, many Nadars in Ramnad denied any connection between the two groups, but the efforts of the Sangam to draw all Nadars together and the advances in education among the Tinnevelly Nadars, particularly the Christians, have led to increasing contacts. While there are still few marriages between the Tinnevelly and the Ramnad Nadars, the barriers are beginning to break down, particularly in the larger cities, Madurai and Madras. An aged Palayampatti Nadar residing in Madurai explains it on an economic basis. "Money is the great social solvent. I wouldn't give my daughter to a tree-climber," but, he said, and laughed, "we were all up in the trees once." He said that he would have no compunction against giving his daughter in marriage to the son of a Tinnevelly tapper. The important criteria would be money and education—of the son, not of the father.

The relationship between the Christians and the Hindus of the Nadar community, always close in Tinnevelly, has improved greatly in Ramnad and Madurai. In Ramnad, the missionaries encountered hostility to Christianity among the Nadar merchants. In Sivakasi, for example, the Nadars in the latter part of the nineteenth century sought recognition for their claims to higher status through the adoption of Sanskritized customs and life. They adopted the sacred thread, muttering mantras under their breath, and were hardly disposed to embrace a new religion. Although the men would have nothing to do with the missionaries, the mission of Sachiapuram, two miles from Sivakasi, found a response among the Nadar women, beginning with widows, who were not permitted to remarry. The men were determined to remain Hindu, but permitted their wives to enter into Christian instruction, provided that it not be publicly acknowledged. A sizeable portion of the Sivakasi women converted and became known as "secret Christians." Although they are still known by that name, the secrecy has passed. The men of Sivakasi have retained their religious conservatism, but many have donated generously to churches and Christian institutions.* Hindu Nadars today, not only in Sivakasi but throughout Tamilnad, have recognized the vital role which Christianity has played in the community's rise. K. T. Kosalram, a Hindu Nadar from Arumuganeri, near Tiruchendur, and a member of the Legislative

Assembly, said in an interview that "Christianity has been the major factor in the Nadars' rise. The missionaries and their schools provided the means for the community to raise itself." This was certainly true for the Tinnevelly Nadars, for many Hindus were educated in the mission schools and colleges. Even in the schools established by the Hindu Nadars in Ramnad, the principals and staff have been drawn largely from the Tinnevelly Christian Nadar community.

In the course of change, the divisions of subcaste, geography, and religion have given way to horizontal differentiation as economic and occupational differences have increased. The Nadar community increasingly embraced a wide range of occupations and economic positions—from the toddy-tapper to the trader and businessman and the professional. The demands of deference to new economic status in the urban areas of change began to erode the hierarchy of ritual purity. As Nadars received differential treatment and respect from other community people, dependent on their station in life, the ties of solidarity which had bound the highest levels to the lowest began to weaken. The sophisticated and highly educated Nadar barrister or physician had for most purposes far more in common with professionals of other castes than he did with Nadar shopkeepers or palmyra climbers. The prominent Nadar businessman would be far more likely to receive a Chetti industrialist into his home than a toddy-tapper—and though fifty years ago it would never have happened, the Chetti would probably accept and reciprocate the invitation. The Nadars have incurred much jealousy and resentment in their rise, but the wealthy and educated among them can today command respect and deference from traditionally superior communities. The wealthy, however, remain but a small minority among the mass of poor shopkeepers and palmyra climbers.

The increasing differentiation within the Nadar community, and the concomitant decline in the differentiation between the Nadars, as a community, and other communities has affected the organization of the caste. In 1950, a speaker at the Nadar conference said, "The outstanding advancement of our community in social, political and commercial fields has been mainly due to the establishment of the *uravinmurai* . . . and the collection of *mahimai*. But now unfortunately disunity and dissatisfaction seem to have set in. . . . The *uravinmurai* in most towns and villages are not able to command as much respect and confidence as in the past." [90] At the 1965 conference, a speaker warned that "the material factor—of rich and poor—has been an increasing factor in the disruption of the *uravinmurai*, and it has become pronounced in recent years. People will not obey the *uravinmurai* leaders if they are rich, because of jealousies. The discipline is gone."

Most *uravinmurai* since 1947 have registered as societies and have adopted formal constitutions. Speaking of these changes, Judge S. Ganesan said, in an interview:

> The control of the *uravinmurai* over the lives of the people is largely gone today. The old tradition of the barber as crier is gone. The rules and regulations of ordinary societies now govern the *uravinmurai*. Committees have been set up. People are no longer fined for absence at the meetings; the "trials" are gone; punishments have disappeared. All is now voluntary, and only mediation is retained. *Mahimai* continues, but the *uravinmurai* can no longer demand to inspect accounts. The old tight organization was necessary when Nadars were opposed by other communities, but this is gone today. There may be slight prejudice against the Nadars, lasting from the past, but the antipathy between communities has greatly declined. Jealousies may carry on, but today the idea of superiority-inferiority is gone.

The traditional monolith of the Nadar *uravinmurai* is gone, and the Nadar Mahajana Sangam finds that each year there has been a rise in the number of petitions it receives with reference to internal disputes as the number of petitions on intercaste disputes has declined. The Nadars remain one of the most caste-conscious of Tamilnad's communities, and cliqueishness is hardly less notorious today than in years past; but the changes are evident and are reflected in the political history of the Nadar community.

[90] Dr. P. Vadamalayan, presidential address, in *Report*, 20th conference (Madurai, 1950).

Chapter VI

POLITICS AND THE SANGAM

LOYALTY TO THE RAJ

The first conference of the Nadar Mahajana Sangam at Poraiyar in 1910 expressed its "genuine and sincere loyalty and devotion to the throne of his Imperial Majesty King Edward VII, Emperor of India and his august representatives in India, the excellencies the Viceroy of India and the Governor of Madras for the manifold blessings enjoyed by their community under the benign British rule." [1] Loyalty to the British raj was reaffirmed as a resolution in each of the Nadar conferences which followed during the years before Independence, and as set forth in the Rules and Regulations of 1919, support for the government was a condition for membership in the Sangam.

In 1919, the Montagu-Chelmsford reforms brought a limited measure of self-government to India under the system of dyarchy, whereby certain reserved subjects were to remain the responsibility of the governor and certain transferred subjects would be entrusted to the elected Legislative Council. In the year preceding the proclamation of the reforms, Montagu, the secretary of state for India, and Chelmsford, the viceroy, had toured India in an attempt to ascertain the needs of constitutional reform. Before their visit to Madras in October, 1917, some of the leaders of the Nadar Mahajana Sangam met at Madurai under the chairmanship of W. P. A. Ponnusamy Nadar of Pattiveeranpatti. It was resolved to send a deputation to Montagu and Chelmsford, petitioning the government to look into the needs of the Nadar community. The request was rejected "on the ground that no political reason was furnished in the request." The Sangam president, V. Ponnusamy Nadar, however, along with other representatives of the non-Brahmin community, met with Montagu. [2]

[1] Telegrams to the viceroy and the governor of Madras from the Nadar Mahajana Sangam, in *Report*, 1st conference, Poraiyar, 1910.
[2] Nadar Mahajana Sangam, *Report*, 4th conference, Madurai, 1918.

The reactions of the Indian National Congress to the reforms were initially mixed, but in 1920 at a special session in Calcutta, Gandhi led the action to pass the resolution on Non-Cooperation, recommending the boycott of the legislative councils. The objective of the Congress was proclaimed to be *swaraj*, self-rule, and the Montagu-Chelmsford reforms could only be taken to be inadequate, disappointing, and unsatisfactory. The executive council of the Nadar Mahajana Sangam, at the same time that it was seeking government recognition of the name Nadar, resolved in the following year, 1921, to place on record "its emphatic disapproval of the Non-Cooperation Movement which it considers most ill-advised under the new conditions created by the reforms act, and exhorts the members of the community to hold aloof from the movement." In forwarding a copy of the resolution to the chief secretary to the government, Madras, the Sangam sought to assure the government "that our community is loyal to the core and keenly alive to the benefits of British Rule. The Nadars are law-abiding people and have no sympathy whatsoever with any movement which tends to weaken the forces of law and order."

Three factors contributed to the Nadars' support for the government. Among the Nadar converts of Tinnevelly, association with the missionaries favorably disposed most Nadars to European rule. The Europeans were seen as protectors, not only by the Christians, but by Hindu Nadars as well. British rule was seen to vitiate the oppressive tyranny of the high caste communities. Further, the Nadars as a mercantile class found it in their interests to support whatever government might be in power. Thus, from its inception the Nadar Mahajana Sangam pledged its loyalty to the government, and in its early years sought to associate itself with the government by inviting ranking government officers to preside over the yearly Nadar conferences. These early conference presidents were mainly Brahmins, who by their presence endowed the conference not only with the aura of the official but of the sanctified as well. They included such notables as S. Srinivasa Iyengar, Sir P. S. Sivasami Iyer, and Sir C. P. Ramaswami Aiyar. In the 1920's, during the rule of the Justice party, the Sangam's favor shifted to the prominent non-Brahmins of the movement, the Raja of Ramnad, Sir A. P. D. Patro, and Sir R. K. Shanmugam Chettiar, Dewan of Cochin. It was not until 1928 that a Nadar presided over a Sangam conference, and after that year, although the conferences were often addressed by distinguished leaders of other communities, only Nadars served as conference president.

The non-Brahmin movement in Madras arose in reaction against the overwhelming dominance of the Brahmin community in government services and in political life. There was particular alarm among some prominent non-Brahmins that the growing Brahmin agitation for Home Rule could result in the creation of a ruling Brahmin oligarchy. In December, 1916, P. Tyagaraja Chetti, secretary of the newly formed South Indian Peoples' Association, issued the "Non-Brahmin Manifesto." "We are not in favour of any measure, which, in operation, is designed, or tends completely, to undermine the influence and authority of the British Rulers, who alone in the present circumstances of India, are able to hold the scales even between creed and class . . ." the manifesto proclaimed. The association stood firmly against a transfer of power from the British to a Brahmin overlordship. "We are deeply devoted and loyally attached to British Rule." [3] With the proclamation of the Non-Brahmin Manifesto came the announcement of the organization of the South Indian Liberal Federation, which came to be popularly known as the' Justice party. The first elections under the Montagu-Chelmsford reforms were in November, 1920, and the Justice party was returned by a substantial majority. [4]

NADAR REPRESENTATION

Members of the Legislative Council, under the new Reforms Act, would be both elected and nominated. In an article in *Nadar Kula Mitran* (1920), the manager of the Nadar Mahajana Sangam suggested that the Sangam select a Nadar to contest the elections in

[3] P. T. Chetti, "The Non-Brahamin Manifesto," in T. Varadarajulu Naidu (ed.), *The Justice Movement: 1917* (Madras, 1932).

[4] See Eugene F. Irschick, "Politics and Social Conflict in South India: The Non-Brahmin Movement and Tamil Separatism, 1916 to 1929" (unpublished Ph.D. dissertation, Department of History, University of Chicago, 1964); Robert L. Hardgrave, Jr., *The Dravidian Movement* (Bombay, 1965).

the Madurai-Ramnad-Tinnevelly constituency. Three Nadars filed to contest the elections. It had been assumed that there were some 7,000 Nadar votes and that with them all, the Nadar candidates could win. With the publication of the voter lists, however, it was discovered that there were only 2,100 Nadars who met the property qualifications for voting. As there were 46,000 voters, it was understood that no Nadar candidate could expect to win, even if he were able to get all the Nadar votes. One Nadar withdrew his candidacy, and the other two were defeated.

The Sangam then urged the government to consider the nomination of Nadars to the Legislative Council.

> The Nadar Mahajana Sangam, Madura, respectfully prays that in view of the numerical strength, tax paying capacity and loyalty of the Nadar community Your Excellency will be pleased to nominate at least two Nadars to the Madras Legislative Council, as otherwise owing to the peculiar social position which the Community occupies its interests [will] altogether be unrepresented. The Community has numerous grievances, social, economic and political which will not be properly voiced by members of other communities in the Council. . . . Direct representation of the Community is indispensable for the protection of its interests.[5]

A few days later, the governor, on the recommendation of the leader of the Justice party, announced the nomination of W. P. A. Soundrapandian Nadar (1893–1953) to the Legislative Council. Soundrapandian, the twenty-seven-year-old son of a prominent planter family of Pattiveeranpatti estates near Kodikanal, became the first Nadar to enter the Madras legislature. The Pattiveeranpatti family, originally from Virudhunagar, was one of the wealthiest and most influential in the Nadar community. It had been one of that family who had recommended the nomination of Rattinasami Nadar of Poraiyar to the Legislative Council back in 1910.[6] The family gave support to the Justice party during the 1920 elections and worked for the victory of its candidate, P. T. Rajan, in Madurai District. W. P. A. Soundrapandian took an active part in the campaign and caught the eye of the Justice

---

[5] Letter to the Governor of Madras from the Nadar Mahajana Sangam, December 14, 1920 (N.M.S. Letterbook, 1920–1921).
[6] *Nadar Kula Mitran*, II (February, 1921).

leaders. Thus, to reward the Pattiveeranpatti family and at the same time to appeal to the Nadar community by nominating one of their number to the council, the Justice party put W. P. A.'s name forward and won the support of the Ramnad-Madurai Nadars.

THE JUSTICE PARTY AND SELF-RESPECT

W. P. A. Soundrapandian, who served in the Legislative Council from 1920 until 1937, considered himself the representative of the Nadar community and of the Nadar Mahajana Sangam.[7] He served as president of the Ramnad District Board from 1928 to 1930, and as president of the Madurai District Board from 1943 to 1947. Soundrapandian was general secretary of the Nadar Mahajana Sangam for four years and its vice president for seventeen years. His position in the Sangam was so towering that there was even a period of one year, 1929, in which the Sangam headquarters was shifted from Madurai to Pattiveeranpatti.

Soundrapandian exerted a strong influence over both the Nadar community and the Nadar Mahajana Sangam, and came to be known as "the uncrowned king of the Nadar community." W. P. A. Soundrapandian sought to weld the Sangam into an effective representative of the Nadar community as a whole, and in his desire to embrace the whole, he wanted to spur into action the sense of community which had been created in the years of struggle. The Sangam would be both the voice and the arm of the community as it articulated the interests of the caste and formulated its demands. But more than an interest group, the Sangam became under Soundrapandian the agent of community mobilization, the catalyst to a more participant society. Soundrapandian, active in the Justice party, involved the Sangam in the politics of Madras, and as it was drawn more deeply into the political system, the Sangam became the vehicle for the politicization of the Nadar community.

Under the influence of Soundrapandian, the Sangam began

[7] In one of his first speeches in the council, Soundrapandian said "I was instructed as the representative in this House of our Mahajana Sangam. . . ." *Madras Legislative Council Proceedings,* VII (March 22, 1922), 3313.

active work for the social uplift of the community—the
scholarship program, rural development, and welfare. Soundrapandian himself toured villages, urging Nadars to unite in
forming an *uravinmurai*, to collect *mahimai*, and to build schools.
He spoke against the divisions of subcaste that lingered, and in his
efforts for unity between the northern and southern divisions of
the caste, W. P. A. was instrumental in bridging the gap in the
Nadar community and in bringing closer contact between the two
groups. Seeking more than mere "virtual representation" of the
entire community, he worked for increasing Sangam membership,
urging all Nadars to join the Sangam and to participate as active
members. In order to increase the community's political strength in
terms of numbers, Soundrapandian proposed in 1926 that the
Sangam extend its membership to embrace the Gramanis of the
northern Tamil districts and the Ezhavas and Tiyars to Kerala.
The proposal was almost universally opposed by the Nadars, however, for these other communities, while tapper castes, were socially depressed and were regarded as inferior in status and wealth
to the Nadars at that time.[8] Soundrapandian's proposal, nevertheless, indicated a feeling that numbers were politically significant.
Even without democratic rule, there was an underlying popular
principle, for it was assumed that the Sangam, representing a larger
social base, would have a greater bargaining position with the
government.

As Soundrapandian worked for the strength and unity of the
Nadar community through the Nadar Mahajana Sangam, he also
sought an improvement in the relations between the Nadars and
other communities. With his friend and colleague in the Legislative
Council, the Raja of Ramnad, Soundrapandian had succeeded, for
example, in bringing an end to the Kamudi punitive tax.

Soundrapandian felt a great concern for Harijan welfare, and
during his presidency of the Ramnad District Board he threatened
withdrawal of recognition from all schools refusing to admit
Harijan children. Likewise, bus owners were to have their licenses

[8] Interview. Hereafter in this chapter an asterisk will indicate that the information has been obtained in interviews, with the principal or with other participants
or observers.

revoked unless Harijans were served. Soundrapandian fought also to have all Nadar temples and schools opened to the Harijans, and under his influence, many *uravinmurai* agreed to open their facilities to the untouchable communities.[9]

W. P. A. soon fell under the spell of E. V. Ramaswamy Naicker, the non-Brahmin militant and leader of social reform. Seeking to draw in the mass support of the Nadar community for his new Justice-aligned Self-Respect movement, E. V. R. selected Soundrapandian as the president of the first Self-Respect conference, held at Chingleput in February, 1929. Soundrapandian, in his presidential address, affirmed the philosophy of Self-Respect in rejecting the whole system of caste as alien to Tamil society. "From the time when the Aryans came to our land from the north and strengthened and consolidated their position in our land, a great calamity overtook the country. The foundations of our society were shaken."[10] Tamil society had been without caste, he declared, but the Brahmins introduced caste as the instrument by which they could overpower the people and assert their own superiority.

During the latter part of the nineteenth century, the Nadars, in emulating the Brahmins in the process of Sanskritization, had accepted the tyranny of the caste system: they desired, not to overthrow it, but to secure a higher position in its ranks. Soundrapandian, reinforced by E. V. Ramaswamy Naicker, now sought to overthrow the system, to deny the legitimacy of ranking altogether, and to oppose the Sanskritization of Nadar life and custom. He urged Nadars to abandon the pretensions they had adopted without success in the previous generation: discard the sacred thread, cut the tuft, and assert the Dravidian Self-Respect of the Nadar community. He advocated remarriage for widows and campaigned against the use of Brahmin purohits in the ritual of Nadar life. Under his influence, the Self-Respect marriage came into almost universal favor among Nadars. The marriages were performed without the use of Brahmin priests; dispensing with

[9] Interview, S. Ganesan, son-in-law of W.P.A. Soundrapandian.
[10] *Justice Year Book, 1929*, p. 120, cited in Irschick, *op. cit.* (n. 4 above), p. 378.

Hindu ritual, a respected elder of the community, with no sacer-dotal position, presided over the exchange of garlands and the tying of the tali which bound the couple together in marriage. The Self-Respect movement also advocated intercaste dining, and Ramaswamy Naicker selected Nadar cooks (from whom tradition-ally no higher caste Hindu would accept food) to prepare food for each of the Self-Respect conferences.*

Under the leadership of W. P. A. Soundrapandian, the Nadars abandoned the Brahminical pretensions and de-Sanskritized their ways. The Nadars of Ramnad and Madurai, loyal to the British raj and supporters of the Justice party, now extended their over-whelming support to the Self-Respect movement. E. V. R. at-tended two Nadar conferences, and the third Self-Respect con-ference was held in the predominantly Nadar town of Virudhunagar, the place of Soundrapandian's family origin and the bastion of Justice party support among the Nadars.

One of the most active Justice party supporters in Virudhunagar was V. V. Ramasami Nadar, who was born into a wealthy trading family in 1898. While a student at the Madras Christian College he attended a Congress conference in 1914 and was drawn emo-tionally into politics. Two years later, he became a devotee of Annie Besant and joined the Home Rule movement. Although V. V. R.'s application to Presidency College, Calcutta—then a cen-ter of political agitation—was accepted, he had to return to Virudhunagar to take over the family business. Still a Congress supporter, V. V. R. had come increasingly to oppose the over-whelming influence of the Brahmin and Brahminism in Madras public life. In 1919, at his marriage, he refused to allow the *purohit* to perform the ceremony and demanded that the tali and rings be exchanged without a priest. During his youth, he had been close to W. P. A. Soundrapandian, and under W. P. A.'s influence, V. V. Ramasami joined the Justice party, and from 1925 on served on the party's executive council. V. V. R. became Soundrapandian's most trusted colleague, both in the Justice party and in the Nadar Mahajana Sangam.[11]

In the early 1920's, as the reservation of seats for non-Brahmins

[11] Interview, V. V. Ramasami; N. Somasundaram, "V.V.R., a Versatile Genius," in *V. V. Ramasami Paaraattu Malar*, p. 140.

began to open up the government services, the Nadar Mahajana Sangam telegraphed the governor, praying that as the Nadars are "among the most loyal, law-abiding and enterprising communities in South India . . . in the forthcoming selection of candidates for I. C. S. [Indian Civil Service] scholarships and recruitment of District Munsifs the Government may be pleased to give serious consideration to the claims of the Nadar community to representation in the public services." In the Legislative Council, Soundrapandian inquired of the minister for local self-government the number of Nadars in the lower levels of government. The Nadars in 1921, only beginning to become politically active, had three elected members of the district board in Tinnevelly, three in Ramnad, and one in Madurai. For the taluq boards, in Tinnevelly there were four elected Nadars and one nominated; for Ramnad, two elected and four nominated; for Madurai, three elected. On the municipal councils, there was one nominated Nadar in Tinnevelly District; six elected and five nominated in Ramnad; and in Madurai, there were two elected Nadars.[12]

In view of their number in the southern districts, the figures were not impressive. In the council debates, Soundrapandian urged the government to appoint qualified Nadars to available positions as sub-judge and district *munsif*. In the Legislative Council in 1921, W. P. A. also brought up the issue of the census and the prejudicial light in which the Nadars were described. He urged the government to rectify its mistaken listing of the community as Shanans and as traditional toddy-drawers. The decision was administrative, and pressures from the council would not necessarily carry sufficient weight to influence the decision. The government's response to the Nadars' petition on the census, however, was strongly motivated by the position of the Nadar community. Recognition of their demands, which were of little consequence to the government, secured Nadar support for the government, and in the political context, with the stirrings of Non-Cooperation, the British were anxious to aggregate wide support from the non-Brahmin community. The Nadar Mahajana Sangam had, after all, pledged its loyalty to the emperor and to the British raj in India.

The Government of India Act of 1919 had provided for a re-

12 *Madras Legislative Council Proceedings*, I-B (April 1, 1921), 1509.

view of the political situation in India every ten years. In 1927, the governor-general of India, Lord Irwin, announced that a commission to undertake this review had been appointed under the chairmanship of Sir John Simon. The commission's two trips to India were boycotted by the Congress and were generally poorly received in India. The Nadars, however, were most anxious to make their views known, and the Nadar Mahajana Sangam prepared a lengthy memorandum for submission to the Simon Commission.

The Sangam described the community's Pandyan ancestry and submitted that it was "therefore just and proper that in any distribution of larger powers to the people under the Reform, a large share might go to the Nadars who were originally the ancient predecessors of the present British Government." In the past fifty years, the Nadars had come up through trade and education, and "the phenomenal progress and advancement of the Nadar community has raised the jealousies of many other communities who find it easier to envy rather than emulate." The Nadars, according to the Sangam, had found that they could secure election to local bodies in the southern districts, but that they were unable to be returned through general election to the Legislative Council. In these elections, all the other communities united against the Nadar candidate.

> The Nadars however are wholly opposed to representation by communal election. They are convinced that the advantages of having a candidate of their own choice will not compensate for the evils arising from communal representation [as] fissiparous tendencies will soon manifest themselves and the community which hitherto had been united and organized will be thrown into confusion and a series of warring camps. Besides the extension of communal representation is disastrous from a national point of view. It isolates minorities, cramps and cripples their national outlook and tends to promote inter-communal factions and feuds, and stimulates . . . caste and racial prejudices.

The Sangam feared that special reserved constituencies would, in eliminating the need for unity among Nadars in the face of opposition, fragment the solidarity of the community. As an alternative to a system of separate electorates, the Sangam proposed that the Sangam itself be given the right to elect the community's representatives to the provincial council. If this proposal was not acceptable, the Sangam urged that the seats then be reserved for Nadars within a general Hindu electoral district. "This will give representation to the Nadars while at the same time it will not take away the influence they now possess by being included in the general electorate and which makes the non-Nadar candidate solicit the favour of their votes at least during the election time. . . ."

In its memorandum to the Simon Commission, the Sangam expressed its concern over the immediate prospect of responsible government, which while desirable itself, would "at the present moment . . . hand over millions of Indians to the control of their countrymen who to judge by their past history and present tendency are utterly unfit to assume any such control." Responsible government must be opposed, the Sangam asserted, until the political principles of the West are learned. As it was, political leaders, in a most un-English way, "go to District centres and find out which castes or communities are likely to have a predominating part in deciding the election. They there attempt to secure candidates so as to find favour with those communities. . . . The fight in the electorate runs on communal and not on party lines. . . ." [13]

The Sangam was not talking only about other castes, for among the Six Town Nadars the community acted as a unit in political behavior. The Sangam admitted as much when it expressed opposition to separate electorates on the grounds that it would fragment the community, which had been united and organized, into "a series of warring camps." In Ramnad and Madurai districts, the Nadars had come up in life, but opposition to them on the part of other castes had by no means abated. The Maravars of central Ramnad, in the region of Aruppukottai, Kamudi, and Virudhunagar, followed the leadership of Muthuramalinga Thevar, grandson of Vellasami Thevar, the Nadars' Kamudi antagonist in the late nineteenth century. Muthuramalinga was an active Congressman and a follower of Subhas Chandra Bose. The

[13] Nadar Mahajana Sangam, "Memorandum to the Simon Commission." Manuscript.

Maravars of the region owed loyalty to him, not to the Raja of
Ramnad, a leader of the Justice party. The polarity of the Nadar
and Maravar castes in central Ramnad compounded the inclination
of the Nadars to support the government. As businessmen they
found it in their interests to do so. With their traditional enemy,
the Maravars, in the Congress ranks, the Nadars of this region
aligned solidly with the Justice party, and the *uravinmurai* instructed Nadar voters to support the party at the polls. The
Sangam had clearly allied itself with the Justice party, although
officially nonpolitical, and W. P. A. Soundrapandian, the undisputed leader of the community, actively sought the support of
all Nadars for the Justice party and the Self-Respect movement.

POLITICAL FISSURES AMONG THE NADARS

Today, in retrospect on the 1920's and early '30's, many Tamili-
ans will speak of the solid support of the Nadar community for the
government. In fact, however, a major portion of the Nadar community opposed the Justice party and gave its wholehearted support to the Congress and the Non-Cooperation movement. It was
not E. V. Ramaswamy Naicker but Gandhi who captured the
imagination of the Tiruchendur Nadars. The Nadar Mahajana
Sangam, despite Soundrapandian's efforts to extend the association
to include more active members in Tinnevelly District, remained
essentially an organization of the merchant community of Ramnad
and Madurai. The Sangam's support for the Justice party reflected
the solid support of the Six Town Nadars for the non-Brahmin
party. In Tinnevelly, however, the Nadars had never achieved the
unity in organization and purpose which characterized the northern Nadars. There were no *uravinmurai* to enforce caste solidarity,
and in the regions where the Nadars constituted the vast majority
of the population as the dominant caste, there was no desire and no
need for such an organization. As they had been one hundred years
before, the Nadars were divided factionally on the basis of economic dependence, family, kin, and friendship.

The threat of opposition which unified the Ramnad Nadars was
simply not present in Tinnevelly. Many of the Dakshina Mara

Nadars were strongly inclined to support the government. For Hindus, as well as Christians, the effect of missionary work in the district had favorably disposed the Nadars to European rule. The British were seen further as protectors. The situation in Tinnevelly, however, was fundamentally different from that of Ramnad and Madurai. In Tinnevelly, it was the Vellala community which gave its support to the Justice party and nourished the echelons of party leadership with its traditional talents. The Vellalas, the most powerful opposition to the Nadars in Tinnevelly and their traditional oppressors, came to power in the Justice party victory. The Nadars of Tinnevelly and in regions of Ramnad where the political situation was comparable went into opposition. Although still divided among themselves in the regions of their dominance, the Nadars presented a common Congress face to the Justice Vellalas. Their old factions became Congress factions, struggling for leadership among the Nadars in the Congress fold.

During the late 1930's, fissures began to appear in the solidarity of the Ramnad Nadars for the Justice party. As W. P. A. Soundrapandian and the Virudhunagar leadership began to rise, the traditional rivalry between Sivakasi and Virudhunagar began to assert itself. In the years after 1880, Sivakasi had lost most of its trade to Virudhunagar and, before the growth of the match industry, had come to rely heavily on agriculture. The Sivakasi Nadars were unwilling to remain followers of a Virudhunagar clique, and as the Justice party began to take on the color of atheism in the Self-Respect movement, the more conservative Sivakasi Nadars reacted with profound distaste. The Self-Respect movement, because of its association with W. P. A. Soundrapandian, was a particularly bitter pill for Sivakasi. In opposition to Soundrapandian, many of the Sivakasi Nadars withdrew their support from the Justice party and, because of the close relationship between the Virudhunagar group and the Nadar Mahajana Sangam, from the caste association as well.[14]

In Virudhunagar itself, the Justice leadership did not go unchallenged, but opposition was silenced by the overwhelming power of the Justice party group, in both wealth and numbers. The western

[14] Based on a conversation with elders of Sivakasi and on other interviews.

portion of Virudhunagar, "the wrong side of the tracks" at that time, was the section in which many of the poorer Nadars lived, together with Muslims and other castes. Coolie laborers and small shopkeepers, they were a backward community in comparison with their educationally advanced and wealthy neighbors east of the tank. The traditional enmity of this group toward the established power of the town polarized them politically in opposition to the Justice party. There was a strong but rarely voiced sympathy for the Congress.*

Kamaraj Nadar was born and reared on Virudhunagar's west side. During the First World War, the young Kamaraj began to follow politics with interest and to attend political meetings. Drawn toward nationalism, Kamaraj spent his free time in activities for the Congress. The mood in Virudhunagar was strongly against the Congress and the Non-Cooperation movement. His family decided that the responsibilities of marriage would wean Kamaraj from his political interests. Kamaraj refused to marry, and before the wrath of the *uravinmurai* fell upon the family, Kamaraj was sent off to Trivandrum to work in an uncle's timber shop. At the age of 17, Kamaraj took part in the 1920 Vaikom satyagraha against the exclusion of Harijans from the temples. Now totally involved in Congress work, Kamaraj returned to Virudhunagar, where he began to organize public meetings and distribute propaganda for Non-Cooperation.

The Nadars of Virudhunagar were outraged that one of their own caste men would defy the community. Branded as a traitor to his caste, Kamaraj was forced to leave Virudhunagar. In Tirumangulam, however, among the members of other communities, Kamaraj was welcomed as a Congress volunteer. In 1923, Kamaraj became an assistant to the Tamil Brahmin Congress leader, S. Satyamurthi, the man who was to be his political guru. Satyamurthi was a member of the Swarajist wing of the Congress, favoring entry into the Legislative Councils, and in seeking votes in Tamilnad, Kamaraj was most useful in attracting non-Brahmin support to the Congress. Kamaraj, however, commanded no following among his own community. Indeed, when he once tried to speak in Kamudi, he was stoned by the Nadars.

With Satyamurthi, Kamaraj toured Tamilnad extensively, acquiring the knowledge of the political terrain which he was later to use as a master of Congress organization. He learned the peculiar needs of each town and village, who commanded power and influence, and the weaknesses and fallibilities of those leaders. Kamaraj slowly acquired his political skills and gained the respect and confidence of his political master, Satyamurthi. In 1930, Kamaraj joined Gandhi's salt satyagraha and was arrested. His imprisonment was the first of six sentences, totaling nearly eight years. With Gandhi's agreement to abandon the satyagraha, Kamaraj and the others arrested during the campaign were released. In that year, 1931, he was elected to the Tamil Nad Congress Committee (T.N.C.C.). Hardly had he been released, however, than Kamaraj was jailed again, this time for one year for refusal to give security. In 1936, in the elections for president of the T.N.C.C., Satyamurthi succeeded in defeating his factional opponent, C. Rajagopalachari. Satyamurthi appointed his lieutenant, Kamaraj, as secretary of the T.N.C.C.[15]

In 1937, the Congress decided to contest the elections for the new Legislative Council, and Kamaraj was chosen to run in the Sattur constituency, which included the towns of Virudhunagar and Sivakasi. The Nadars in this constituency were an urban minority. The vast rural majority were Maravars, Naickers, Reddiars, and Harijans—nearly all of whom supported the Congress party. When Kamaraj was placed on the ballot, one other name had already been filed, V. V. Ramasami, the Justice leader who had been chairman of the Virudhunagar municipality since 1931. The prospect of defeat for the Justice party, which had been on a steep decline since the late 1920's, was very high. V. V. R. had been defeated only the year before in the elections for the Ramnad District Board. More immediate than simply a Justice defeat at the hands of the Congress, however, was the defeat of the Virudhunagar Nadar leadership by a maverick of their own community. There was silent support for Congress and Kamaraj

[15] L. S. Mani, "A Golden Age," in *Sri K. Kamaraj 6oth Birthday Commemoration Volume* (Madras, 1962); A. K. Navanithakiruttinan, *Muthalamaichar Kamarajar* (Chief Minister Kamaraj) (Tirunelveli, 1957), pp. 49-55.

among many Nadars of the west-side faction, and V. V. R.'s defeat
by Kamaraj might well erode the power of the V. V. Ramasami-
M. S. P. Senthikumara group in Virudhunagar. V. V. Ramasami
withdrew his name, and Kamaraj was elected to the Legislative
Council unopposed.[16] In that election, the Sivakasi Nadars gave
heavy support to Kamaraj, although many Nadars there were unwilling to make the final break with the British raj. While
Kamaraj's election was greeted with resignation in Virudhunagar,
the Sivakasi Nadars made him a hero, claiming their town as his
political birthplace.*

The year 1937 marked the turning point in the politics of the
Nadar community. In the elections of that year, the vast majority
of the Nadars in Ramnad and Madurai had voted for the dying
Justice party and reaffirmed their loyalty to British rule. The break
came, not with the elections, but with their aftermath. In 1937, a
new government came into power. The Congress, under Chief
Minister C. Rajagopalachari, now commanded the bounty of
office, and the days of British rule were clearly numbered. The
dramatic symbol of change for the Nadars came as Rajagopalachari
introduced legislation for the removal of the civil and social disabilities under which the lower castes had suffered. This legislation
included the Temple Entry Authorization and Indemnity Act of
1939, which paved the way for the opening of the temples to the
people of all communities. In that same year, the great Meenakshi
temple at Madurai threw open its gates to the Harijans and to the
Nadars.

In 1921, the Nadar Mahajana Sangam wrote to the president of
the non-Brahmin conference to be held in Tinnevelly, urging that
the conference press for the removal of all disabilities suffered by
non-Brahmins with regard to temple entry. The conference took
no action on the issue, for while opposing the Brahmins, the high
caste leadership of the non-Brahmin movement was, for the most
part, unconcerned with the removal of caste privileges. The
Vellalas, who contributed a major portion of the Tamil leadership
in the Justice party, were a highly conservative community who
would hardly consider opening the temples to the Harijans or the
Nadars. The Congress, on the other hand, under Gandhi's leader-

16 Interview, V. V. Ramasami.

ship, had made temple entry for the Harijans a major issue. It was precisely on this point, however, that the Nadars felt the rub. While desiring temple entry, they were not at all ready to identify their cause with that of the Harijans. Their claims to Kshatriya status would hardly permit them to join the untouchables in opening the temples. The Nadars chose simply to withdraw. The Sangam recommended that Nadars make no effort to enter temples to which they were forbidden. "Don't enter the house where you are not respected." Some Nadars said that they had no desire to enter the temples until the western gates were opened. The Nadars, others said, were coming up, and having no desire to antagonize other castes, preferred to let the matter take care of itself. With the rise of the Self-Respect movement, many Nadars advocated a boycott of Brahminical temples. Why should the Nadars lower themselves, they asked, to accept the priestly authority of the Brahmin? A Nadar might claim that he was indifferent to questions of ritual status and temple entry, but to be *denied* entrance because he was of low caste cut to the quick, and the wounds of Sivakasi and Kamudi had by no means healed.*

The temple-entry act was the divide in the political history of the Nadar community. The tide began to turn away from the moribund Justice party, which had in its years of power done nothing to remove the ban on temple entry. C. Rajagopalachari introduced two major pieces of legislation, the Removal of Civil Disabilities Act (Madras Act XI of 1938) and the Temple Entry Authorization and Indemnity Act (Madras Act XII of 1939). The first removed a number of social disabilities suffered by the low castes: their inability to have access to public streams, rivers, wells, tanks, pathways, sanitary facilities, and means of public transport. The second act indemnified and protected government officers and the trustees of the Meenakshi temple in Madurai, and six other temples, against legal action for having permitted Harijans to enter the temples and to offer worship. At the same time, the act permitted the trustees of other temples to throw open the doors to Harijans provided that the worshippers were not opposed.[17]

17 B. S. Baliga, *Madras District Gazetteers: Madurai* (Madras, 1960), pp. 212–213, where Baliga also discusses later legislation that forbade discrimination against Harijans and gave them certain rights.

Sivakasi, the scene of the 1899 rioting, remained a scar on the historical memory of the Nadar community. After the riots, the government had imposed an injunction against the Nadars' entering the Siva temple in the town, and the order had remained untouched for forty years. With the announcement of the temple-entry legislation, the trustees of the Sivakasi temple extended an invitation to the Nadar *uravinmurai* for Nadars to enter the temple three days before the legally enforced day of opening. The action was taken so as to distinguish the Nadars from the Harijans. On the appointed day, the Nadars assembled at their temple, the Ammankoil, and in a procession led by the trustees of the Siva temple, they entered the temple with full honors.* In 1949, P. Ayya Nadar was appointed as the first trustee of the Siva temple at Sivakasi, and no objection was raised. Today two of the three trustees are Nadars; the third is a Brahmin.* In Tiruchendur, and in many of the temples to which Nadars were formerly excluded, Nadars now occupy respected positions as trustees.

The temple-entry legislation of 1937 brought the Congress into increasing Nadar favor; the image of Gandhi and the momentum of the movement for *swaraj* soon brought growing numbers of Nadars into the Congress fold; but, more than anything else, it was the election of Kamaraj as president of the Tamil Nad Congress Committee in 1940 which attracted Nadars to the Congress party. Although Kamaraj had had little influence within the Nadar community, his ascendancy in the Congress acted as a catalyst to draw the support of the Nadars. He had come up in political life wholly within the ranks of the Congress, in opposition to his own community. He had never been a Nadar leader, but now because of his political position within the Congress leadership, he became, ex officio, a leader of the Nadars. The prestige of his position accrued to the entire community. He had transcended Nadar identification, and for this very reason was able to mobilize the Nadars and to draw them toward the Congress. While Kamaraj, whose own career was a virtual attack on Nadar political identity, sought to extend the identity horizon of the community beyond the bounds of caste, he in some ways sustained and reinforced Nadar identity, in that the community gloried in his political success.

THE NATIONAL NADAR ASSOCIATION

Although the Nadar Mahajana Sangam and its leader W. P. A. Soundrapandian were closely associated with the Justice party and the Self-Respect movement, the Sangam itself had never officially supported any party or candidate. It had, of course, pledged its loyalty to the British raj and had pointedly denounced the Non-Cooperation movement. As the forces of the Congress grew within the Nadar community, however, the leadership of the Sangam remained in the hands of the old Justice party men. The sentiments within the Nadar community were shifting, nevertheless, and by 1940 the Sangam was confronted with political schism. There was within the executive council of the Sangam a group of Congressmen, led by P. R. Muthusami and S. T. Adityan. In response to the temple-entry legislation, the Congress group in a session of the council put forward a resolution calling for an official appreciation to Rajagopalachari. The resolution was defeated by a substantial majority. It was decided then that, without leaving the Sangam, the Congressmen would form a separate association designed to win support for Congress from among the Nadars. The organization, the National (or *Desia*) Nadars' Association, called for immediate independence and stated its opposition to the war effort.[18] The Sangam, on the other hand, reaffirmed its loyalty to the government and pledged its vigorous support to the British war effort.[19]

In the preparations for the seventeenth conference, to be held at Madurai in September, 1941, the Sangam extended an invitation to G. T. Boag, the former census superintendent, to inaugurate the conference. With the resignation of the Congress ministry on orders from Gandhi in October, 1939, the British assumed power in a caretaker government, with Boag as the advisor to the governor in Madras. The invitation to Boag outraged the Nadar nationalists, and a separate National Nadar Conference was announced. In the invitation to the conference, the Nadar Congressmen said, "The world is now making great progress in the political and social

18 Interview, P. R. Muthsami.
19 Telegram to the viceroy from the N.M.S., 1940.

life, and the Nadar community feels that they must join together and must decide what they have to do for the benefit of the community. . . ."

The conference, held at Madurai on September 15, was attended by about one thousand people. The conference opened with a procession led by M. P. Sivagnana Gramani, secretary of the T.N.C.C., and in opening the meeting, the president of the Tamil Nad Harijan Sevak Sang declared that Nadars wielded much influence in the country both economically and socially and that the time had come for them to take their legitimate share in the fight for freedom. "This Conference," it was resolved by the meeting, "strongly condemns the attitude of the British Government which, notwithstanding its declaration that it is fighting for world democracy, has not given freedom to India even after 150 years; . . . and resolves to request members of our community to support all legitimate movements for the attainment of the country's freedom." [20] P. R. Muthusami, in the welcoming speech, accused the Nadar Mahajana Sangam of having become the preserve of a clique who sought to use the association for party purposes. He urged members of the Nadar community to join the Congress in the national struggle for independence. In his address, the conference president declared that the spirit of nationalism in India is growing, and no community can afford to keep aloof from its common cause. Whether the Nadars joined the movement or not, the country would soon attain freedom through the efforts of the Congress. The well-being of the Nadar community, he believed, depended upon the extent to which they associated themselves in the freedom movement. But for some reason the Nadar Mahajana Sangam did not agree; they were not prepared to support the cherished right of temple entry. This conference, the president urged, must turn the Nadar Mahajana Sangam to its view. He appealed to all Nadars to strengthen *mahimai* funds for the advancement of the Nadar community and to join and strengthen the Nadar Mahajana Sangam. The community must be united, but it must also associate itself with other communities in the national struggle.[21] Among

20 *Hindu*, September 17, 1941.
21 Address by A. R. A. S. Duraisami Nadar, *Hindu*, September 16, 1941.

the resolutions of the first National Nadar Conference were expressions of gratefulness to the Maharaja of Travancore and to his Dewan, Sir C. P. Ramaswami Aiyar, for opening the temples, and in Madras, to C. Rajagopalachari for the temple-entry act. It was also resolved that all temples under the control of the Nadar community be thrown open for worship to all Hindus on an equal footing.[22]

A few days after the National Nadar conference, G. T. Boag wrote to the Nadar Mahajana Sangam regarding the political division among the Nadars. "Whether my information be right or wrong, the fact remains that your Sangam has for the moment lost the right to claim to represent all sections of the Nadar community. . . . Until unity has been restored within your ranks I cannot possibly appear upon your platform." Boycotted by Congress Nadars and without Boag, the seventeenth Nadar conference opened under the presidency of V. V. Ramasami. The municipal chairman of Sivakasi inaugurated the conference, and his opening remarks stressed that there should be no party politics in the Nadar conferences. The members of the Sangam may belong to any party or religion, and if they come to the conference they must look only to the welfare of the community.[23] Politics, however, could not be set aside. In his presidential address, V. V. R. identified the Nadar community with the non-Brahmin movement and denied Boag's assertion that the Sangam could no longer claim to be the representative of the entire Nadar community. A resolution was passed criticizing Boag's refusal to attend after having accepted the invitation.[24] On the critical issue of temple entry, V. V. R. recognized the benefit of the Congress legislation, but he said that it had not gone far enough. While Congress activity in the matter of temple entry is to be commended, "it would have been quite welcome and up with the times, had a comprehensive Act, giving all Hindus free access to all temples, to enter the precincts of the deity and worship, been passed with a provision to punish all those who attempt to prevent such entry." [25]

[22] *Hindu*, September 17, 1941.
[23] Nadar Mahajana Sangam, *Report*, 17th conference, Madurai, 1941.
[24] *Hindu*, October 2, 1941.
[25] *Hindu*, September 28, 1941.

As the political agitation for Independence reached its peak in the Quit-India movement of 1942, the Congress Nadars planned their second conference. C. Rajagopalachari was asked to preside. Accepting the invitation, the Congress leader suggested that the association change its name to more clearly identify its national rather than community aspirations. The second conference was held in 1942 under the new name, the Nadars' National Association.* The scales of support within the Nadar community had shifted toward the Congress, and the Nadar Mahajana Sangam decided that if it were to remain viable, it must avoid any conferences which might force an open break in the association. Thus, the annual Nadar conferences were suspended between 1941 and 1947. P. C. Chidambara Nadar, vice president of the Sangam, acting as mediator, succeeded in bringing Muthusami and others back into the executive council. The leadership thus passed to the pro-Congress faction, and the old Justice party supporters withdrew to the background for the sake of the Sangam.* The Nadars' National Association was deactivated, and with its mission accomplished, it disbanded in 1944. In 1945, P. R. Muthusami was elected general-secretary of the Nadar Mahajana Sangam.[26] In 1947, with Muthusami firmly in control, the Sangam held its eighteenth conference at Koilpatti. P. C. Chidambara Nadar presided, and the conference was opened by the Tinnevelly Christian Nadar, Daniel Thomas, the minister for prohibition.

Although P. R. Muthusami was firmly in control of the Sangam, it was agreed that one of the two general-secretaries would be a Self-Respector, and Arumugam Nadar was selected. V. V. Ramasami remained as vice president. In 1950, Arumugam suffered business difficulties and resigned as general-secretary. W. P. A. Soundrapandian then proposed that V. P. R. Gangaram Durairaj be elected to fill the vacancy. Gangaram, elected unanimously, was a Kamudi Nadar residing as a wholesale food-grains merchant in Madurai. Although in background he had been associated with the Self-Respectors, he had by Independence firmly sided with the Congress.*

Congress had brought temple entry. It had brought *swaraj*. For the business classes, it had also brought a new government to which

26 Interview, P. R. Muthusami.

their economic interests owed allegiance. The Nadars' support for
the Congress as the party in power was a continuation of the pattern of their political identification from the early nineteenth century. They had sought, as a minority community, protection and
advancement in association with the ruling power. The Nadars had
responded to the missionary efforts in greater numbers than any
other community. They had pledged their loyalty to the British
king and had given their support to the ruling Justice party. Now a
new government was in power—the Congress. For most Nadars,
the Congress was the party of Kamaraj, their illustrious son who
was to become the chief minister of Madras and later the president
of the All-India Congress party. If Kamaraj brought them no special benefits, he did endow the Nadars with a new sense of pride.
He was the symbol that the community had at last "arrived."

POLITICS AND THE SANGAM SINCE INDEPENDENCE

Although the great majority of the Nadar community, both
southern and northern, enthusiastically supported Kamaraj and the
Congress, a significant portion of the Ramnad Nadars chose to
remain aloof. W. P. A. Soundrapandian, V. V. Ramasami, and
M. S. P. Senthikumara and the close followers of the Self-Respect
movement were never drawn into the Congress. In 1944, although
remaining faithful to the principles of E. V. Ramaswamy Naicker,
W.P.A. and V.V.R. opposed the creation of the monolithic
Dravida Kazhagam out of the old Justice party. At the time,
V. V. R. was chairman of the Virudhunagar municipality and
W. P. A. was the nominated president of the Madurai District
Board. E. V. R., in forming his new party, demanded that all
members resign official posts and renounce British titles. Neither
V. V. R. or W. P. A. were prepared to do this, and both resigned
to form the Self-Respect party as a continuation of the old move-
ment—but without E. V. Ramaswamy Naicker. They took with
them a major portion of the old Self-Respect Nadar following, but
the party never gained wide support, and after one year it died.
Both men then became anti-Congress Independents.[27]

In 1949, C. N. Annadurai left the Dravida Kazhagam to form

[27] Interview, V. V. Ramasami.

the more vital, politically active Dravida Munnetra Kazhagam (D.M.K.). On the foundations of E. V. R.'s advocacy of a separate and independent Dravidasthan, Annadurai sought mass electoral support by appealing to Tamil nationalism, to the glories of the Dravidian past. Denouncing the dominance of North Indian Brahmin-*bania* elements, the D.M.K., tongue in cheek, advocated the secession of Tamilnad from the Indian federation.[28] Although W. P. A. Soundrapandian did not join in the founding of the separatist party, he did extend his support to the D.M.K. Soundrapandian soon withdrew from active political life, and in 1953 he died.* In Virudhunagar, V. V. Ramasami shared power with the M. S. P. family. In turn, M. S. P. Senthikumara, M. S. P. Nadar, and M. S. P. Rajah held the chairmanship of the municipality. It had been a bastion of Justice party support, but after 1947, remaining anti-Congress, Virudhunagar became a pocket of Independents sympathetic with the Dravida Munnetra Kazhagam.

At the twentieth Nadar conference, held in Madurai in 1950, it was resolved that "in the General Elections . . . all Nadars must fight tooth and nail to secure as many seats as possible so that the Nadar community will have representatives in the Parliament." [29] In the Sangam's biweekly, *Mahajanam*, an editorial (May 15, 1951) was addressed to the voters: "Electing the right person is a most important job. If you misuse it, you will be doomed. . . . Don't look at the candidates through their political parties. Count on the candidates' sacrificial attitude and ability. They must be intelligent and interested in the upgrowth of the country." Although the editorial did not specifically urge support for Nadar candidates, it hardly advocated party loyalty. The twenty-first conference in 1951, a few months before India's first General Elections, made the point clear. "Because we want to have Nadar representatives in Parliament, we want as many Nadars as possible to contest in the General Elections and the Nadar commu-

[28] See Hardgrave, *The Dravidian Movement.* Subsequent developments in the D.M.K. are discussed in Robert L. Hardgrave, Jr., "The DMK and the Politics of Tamil Nationalism," *Pacific Affairs,* XXXVII (Winter, 1964–1965), 396–411; Lloyd I. Rudolph, "Urban Life and Populist Radicalism: Dravidian Politics in Madras," *Journal of Asian Studies,* XX (May, 1961).

[29] Quoted in *Mahajanam,* October 1, 1950.

nity must support them only. At the same time there must not be contest between Nadar candidates themselves, and so only one Nadar candidate, who will be prominent and agreeable to the people, will be set up in each constituency." [30]

P. R. Muthusami, general-secretary of the Sangam, as a Congressman to the core vehemently opposed the Sangam's support of any candidate merely because he was a Nadar. Rather than bring the issue to a fight in the conference, Muthusami preferred to wait until the quarterly council meeting, where the conference resolution was overruled.[31] In the 1951–1952 elections, Muthusami campaigned actively for the Congress in the southern districts. In the Virudhunagar constituency for the Legislative Assembly, Muthusami backed the Congress candidate, a Nadar, against the victorious V. V. Ramasami, vice president of the Nadar Mahajana Sangam, who ran as an Independent sympathetic to the D.M.K. In the Madurai parliamentary constituency Muthusami supported the Congress victor, a man of the Saurashtra weaver community, against K. T. K. Tangamani, a prominent Nadar running on the Communist ticket. In that election, 1951–1952, Kamaraj contested the Srivilliputtur parliamentary seat against an Independent, G. T. Naidu. Another Independent, a Nadar, also ran. Kamaraj won, but V. V. Ramasami had given his support to G. T. Naidu.

In 1954, V. V. Ramasami was elected to the upper house of the Madras legislature, the Legislative Council. In the election, V. V. R. ran as an Independent and was actively opposed by P. R. Muthusami. V. V. R., as vice president of the Sangam, felt that Muthusami should have at least remained silent. Although Muthusami's political activity did not involve the Sangam officially, V. V. R., embarrassed by the situation, resigned his office in the association—although he retained his membership and continued to support the Sangam's welfare activities.[32] In 1957, before the Second General Elections, the executive council defeated a motion that the Sangam support Nadar candidates in the election. The way a man votes, the Sangam said, must be a matter of personal

---

[30] Quoted in *Mahajanam*, November 1, 1951.
[31] Interview, P. R. Muthusami.
[32] Interview, V. V. Ramasami.

conscience, and the association must not extend its support to any candidate on the basis of caste or party.

The old Justice party–Self-Respect group in the Nadar Mahajana Sangam is today weak and aging. V. V. Ramasami, although he still supports the association, no longer attends the annual conferences. The Self-Respectors are often critical of the Sangam for the Hindu motif of the conferences and for the involvement of priests in the proceedings. They favor a more thoroughly secular association, one not so closely identified with Hindu Nadars. They too have been restive with regard to the relationship between the Sangam and the Congress party. P. R. Muthusami's personal views, for example, were often taken to be official Sangam pronouncements. The old opposition, however, has chosen to remain silent. The values of unity in the association for the advancement and welfare of the community override any other considerations.

P. R. Muthusami was the architect of Sangam activity between 1945 and 1966. In his last years as general-secretary, he came under criticism for not having made way for youth. Despite the feeling by many that Muthusami should resign, he was re-elected every year without opposition. Even those critical of his political activity or of his lengthy tenure as Sangam general-secretary admitted that he was the pillar of the association's strength. M. S. P. Rajah, who opposed Muthusami politically, said in an interview that it is Muthusami who must be given credit for building the Sangam into the association it is today.

At the thirty-third conference, held at Karaikudi in 1965, a resolution was brought to limit the tenure of office for the general-secretaries and the vice president to a maximum of three years. It was resolved also that there should be a full-time paid secretary to manage the Sangam's day-to-day affairs. The resolution, it was urged, was not meant to be a challenge to Muthusami, but was brought so that the elders might make way for the youth. There should be, it was said, no talk of "after Muthusami, who?" Younger men should be elected to the positions of leadership in the Sangam. The resolution was poorly received, and those speaking out against it were heavily applauded. M. S. Ramasamy, a jaggery

merchant, opposed the resolution, saying that there was no reason
for a constitutional change, as the General Body had the right to
elect anyone else each year. That it had not chosen to do so in the
past was an affirmation of support for Muthusami. The resolution
was then withdrawn.[33] A year later at the meeting of the Nadar
conference, the General Body accepted the resignation of
Muthusami and elected M. S. Ramasamy as the new joint secretary
of the Nadar Mahajana Sangam. His election served to give the
Sangam a new unity, for M. S. Ramasamy, as a devotee of E. V.
Ramaswamy Naicker, was acceptable to both the Self-Respect and
Congress wings of the caste association.

Despite Muthusami's personal involvement in the Congress
party, he had gone a long way to remove the Sangam from partisan
political involvement, for he realized full well that if the Sangam
were to involve itself in politics, the association would split. As the
community has differentiated occupationally and economically,
there has been a concomitant political diffusion, and despite the
fact that a majority of Nadars support the Congress, an increasingly large number of Nadars have extended their support to opposition parties. A portion of the old Justice party men have transferred their support to the Dravida Munnetra Kazhagam, but, far
more significantly, the D.M.K. has made a strong appeal to Nadar
youth. The Communists have also found support among Nadar
factory workers, and a few prominent businessmen and professionals have been drawn to Rajagopalachari's Swatantra party. The
Nadars today are spread over a wide political spectrum, and if the
Sangam were to continue to represent the Nadar community as a
whole—and not merely one pro-Congress section, no matter how
large it might be—the caste association would have to avoid align-
ing itself with any one political party. It would have to be non-
partisan in order to survive.

THE CASTE ASSOCIATION

The caste association represents the adaptive response of caste to
modern social, economic, and political change. Caste itself has his-

[33] From notes taken by the writer during the conference.

torically revealed its resilient qualities, its ability to persist in the midst of change. Frustrated by the persistence of caste, the missionary Robert Caldwell wrote in 1860, "Caste is so deeply rooted in the Hindu mind, that no amount of intellectual enlightenment compels it to quit its hold. . . . Whenever convenience or gain is at stake, it [caste] lays aside its scruples to be resumed again at a more favorable season. It adapts itself to the new stage of things, whatever that new state may be, with wonderful elasticity, forms new alliances instead of those that failed it in the hour of need, shifts its front, changes its mode of warfare, bends to the blast, like the river reed, and as soon as the storm is over raises its head as vauntingly as ever." [34]

Caste has been fundamentally affected by social mobilization and economic change, but it has by no means disappeared, and its modern manifestation, the caste association, reveals often a curious mixture of the traditional and modern. The *uravinmurai* have now adopted formal constitutions, have registered as societies, and function under a system of committees. The caste association itself, the Nadar Mahajana Sangam, operates in the context of the traditional unit of caste, but its idiom is distinctly modern. It advances "secular" demands, upholds the Congress image of the casteless society, and has organized itself in bureaucratic form, with secretaries, manager, and agents who often act as local public relations men.

The Nadar Mahajana Sangam is a voluntary association, drawn from the ascriptive reservoir of caste—what the Rudolphs have called the *natural* association of traditional India.[35] Its actual membership is but a fraction of its potential in full caste recruitment, but the association claims to speak for the community as a whole, asserting virtual representation. If this claim is to be accepted as credible in the light of economic differentiation and the diffusion of political support within the community, the association must withdraw from active political involvement. The caste association has played a vital role, nevertheless, in the political mobilization of

[34] Caldwell, "Native Education in Tinnevelly," *Mission Field*, V. (September, 1960), 204, 206–207.

[35] Lloyd I. Rudolph, "The Modernity of Tradition: The Democratic Incarnation of Caste in India," *American Political Science Review*, LIX (December, 1965), 976.

the Nadar community, serving as the agent of community integration and as the vehicle for its entrance into the political system of modern India.

The Nadar Mahajana Sangam, as the voice of the community interest, has demanded an increase in prestige, influence, and benefits within the system. It has sought to maximize resources within the given political framework, first of the British raj, and then of the Congress party. As it has formulated demands—for representation in the Legislative Council and government services; for the inclusion of the word *Nadar* in place of *Shanar* in government records; for benefits to the displaced toddy-tappers; and for educational benefits as a Backward Class—the caste association has increasingly involved the community in the political process. The modern "incarnation" of caste, the association, "provides the channels of communication and bases of leadership and organization which enable those still submerged in the traditional society and culture to transcend the technical political illiteracy which would otherwise handicap their ability to participate in democratic politics." [36] The Sangam has thus provided the critical link between tradition and modernity.

[36] Lloyd I. and Susanne H. Rudolph, "The Political Role of India's Caste Associations," *Pacific Affairs*, XXXIII (March, 1960), 5–6.

Chapter VII

STRUCTURAL CHANGE AND
POLITICAL BEHAVIOR

STRUCTURAL CHANGE

The degree to which any group may be said to possess a common political culture will be a function of (1) the form and extent of differentiation between it and other groups and (2) differentiation within the group itself. The extent to which a caste may be said to possess a political culture common to the community as a whole will be determined by the relative degrees of (1) elaboration in caste ranking and (2) internal differentiation. Following our hypothesis, we may distinguish three basic structural types in the political culture of a caste: the parochial, the integrated, and the differentiated.

The parochial political culture is essentially that of tradition. At this level, the caste is characterized by its local isolation and by a high degree of differentiation in the elaboration of caste ranking between it and other caste groups. While sharing a common position in the ritual hierarchy, the caste is internally differentiated by subcaste endogamy and territorial segmentation. Within the localized village community, the caste is divided by "the relationships of servitude" which separate its members into potentially opposing client groups. The cleavages of political life are not between castes, but between the vertically integrated structures of village factions. A single-caste village, while lacking the elaboration of caste ranking in terms of ritual usages to be found in the traditional multi-caste village, may be taken as functionally equivalent insofar as the economic groups, often themselves endogamous subcastes, are hierarchically ranked and the structure of the village is characterized by the factionalism of economically dependent client groups.

The second, or integrated, stage emerges only with the development of community consciousness and when, from within the group itself, community leaders with organizational skills arise to weld that consciousness into a force for action. This is the critical stage of mobilization, the catalyst to political participation by the community. The vehicle of solidary participation is the caste association, which acts both as a force for political mobilization within the community and as a representative of the community interests to the outside world. The integrated political culture represents a high degree of cohesion and solidarity within the caste community. It is characterized by a decline in the vertical relations of dependence between castes in favor of the horizontal extension of caste ties over a wide geographic area. In the first stages of the integrated culture, there continues to be a high elaboration in caste ranking, but differentiation within the caste itself is minimal, as the divisions of subcaste, locality, and client group give way to a new caste consciousness, self-awareness, and solidarity. The cleavages of political life are now between castes. With economic change, however, the caste becomes increasingly differentiated internally. With upward mobility, the range of diversity within the caste increases, and insofar as society begins to differentiate interactionally between various levels of the caste, elaboration in caste ranking will decline and caste solidarity will be weakened. At the integrated stage, political solidarity is maximal, yet the very success of the community in fulfilling its aspirations accelerates internal differentiation and the formation of distinct class segments within the group.

Differentiation within the caste community fundamentally affects the elaboration of caste ranking. The traditional correspondence between economic position and ritual status loses significance, for within each community there is an increasingly wide range of occupations and economic positions. The demands of deference to new economic status erode the hierarchy of ritual purity. With the decline in the elaboration of caste ranking and the increasing differentiation within each caste, the political culture of the caste is affected accordingly. As economic interests within the community are differentiated, and as the political culture of the caste becomes increasingly fragmented, so the political identity of the individual will reflect crosscutting vertical and horizontal ties and a plurality of commitments, associations, and interests. Individual participation replaces the solidary participation of the caste community. In the process of political development, as the structures of society change under the impact of social mobilization, the old clusters of social, economic, and psychological commitments erode and break, to paraphrase Karl Deutsch, and the individual becomes available for new patterns of socialization and behavior.[1] The loosened moorings of caste and tradition, while freeing the individual for associations along class lines, also renders him available to the flux of ambivalence and apathy. The differentiated political culture is characterized by the diffusion of political support.

In the process of economic and occupational differentiation, the caste community is divided horizontally into class segments. Among all class segments within the caste community, the period of integration produces an overarching sense of shared historical experience. In terms of participation, particularly at the primary level, the class segment is the unit of greatest importance. Marriage, for example, is almost wholly confined to the class segment of the caste. Thus, within the larger endogamy of the caste, each class segment tends toward endogamy. The class segments, unlike the earlier subcastes, remain open, and within the caste, there is a high degree of upward mobility.

With a high degree of differentiation between the caste and other communities, each class segment within the caste will be bound to the other in an "interdependence of fate." [2] With the decline of such differentiation, however, as other communities begin to distinguish interactionally between the class segments of the caste, the solidarity of the caste is broken. Caste, as a primordial tie, persists in the midst of change, retaining its traditional endogamy as the basic primary unit beyond the family. Class divisions assume increasing importance, however, and as class becomes more behaviorally decisive, the bounds of caste are crossed, linking comparable class segments across caste lines on the basis of common interests and associations.

[1] Karl Deutsch, "Social Mobilization and Political Development," *American Political Science Review*, LV (September, 1961), 494.

[2] Kurt Lewin, *Resolving Social Conflicts* (New York, 1948), pp. 163–166, 183–185.

STAGES OF POLITICAL DEVELOPMENT

The Nadar Mahajana Sangam had been the agent of community socialization, the vehicle by which the Nadars were drawn as participants into the political system. The very process of politicization within the caste, however, diffused political support within the system. While there has been a developmental sequence in structural change within the community as a whole, from the parochial to the differentiated, each successive stage, in its ideal type, was characterized by a particular situational configuration in time. The parochial culture was seen in the traditionally Nadar-dominant regions of southeastern Tinnevelly and Kanyakumari districts in the early nineteenth century; the integrated, in nineteenth and early twentieth century Ramnad, where the Nadars were a threatened minority; and the differentiated culture today in the urban areas of Madurai and Madras City, where the community is but one of a large number of castes, each internally differentiated in occupation and economic status. These successive stages were combined, one with the other, over time. The development of the integrated culture in Ramnad did not displace the parochial culture in Tinnevelly. Both coexisted and were joined by the urban, differentiated culture by the 1950's. The succession of developmental stages did not, however, leave the structural integrity of the previous levels unaffected. The social and economic changes which have produced the differentiated culture, most clearly evident in the highly urbanized situation, impinge with increasing severity upon the less developed regions of Ramnad and Tinnevelly. As the Nadar community in these areas becomes increasingly differentiated occupationally and economically, the political culture will be affected accordingly. The threshold of the differentiated political culture is expanding.

In Tinnevelly today, the political culture remains essentially parochial. The political arena is *within* the Nadar community, and the factions, baring elements of the traditional client groups, aggregate support on the basis of a grab bag of interests and ties termed "personality." The integrated culture of central Ramnad is rapidly beginning to break down under the impact of occupational and economic differentiation within the Nadar community. In certain regions, where continuing caste antagonisms have sustained internal unity among the Nadars, as in Mudukullatur taluq, political life is characterized by caste opposition. In Madurai and Madras City, differentiation within the community has diffused political support, and political behavior is subjected to a variety of cross pressures. Political life reflects more of a class than a caste orientation. Differentiation within the community is most clearly evident in Madras, but with various degrees of development, it is to be found in each of the four areas. With the continuing impact of social mobilization and economic change, each will increasingly take on the character of the differentiated political culture.

TINNEVELLY

The Nadars of Tinnevelly District are concentrated in the southern taluqs, particularly Srivaikuntam, Tiruchendur, and Nanguneri, and in these regions they are the predominant caste. Politics takes place not so much between castes as within the Nadar community itself. Although the work of the missionaries among the Nadars favorably disposed the community to European rule in the nineteenth and early twentieth centuries, the pro-British Justice party found no support among the Nadars of Tinnevelly. Here the Vellalas, traditional oppressors of the Nadars in Tinnevelly, were the principal supporters of the Justice party and provided leadership for the party's highest echelons. Further, the Nadars were not united. Before 1935, few Nadars in Tinnevelly met the property qualification for voting. The Tinnevelly Nadars were, as a community, politically uninvolved, and in the areas of the highest Nadar concentration, where they were for the most part desperately poor and uneducated, political consciousness was minimal. There were among the educated Nadars, however, a few politically conscious families that extended their support to the Congress. S. T. Adityan, for example, became a devoted Congressman after hearing Gandhi speak at Tiruchendur in 1920.[3]

[3] Interview, S. T. Adityan.

Among the educated Nadars of Tinnevelly, both Christian and Hindu, there was a quickening interest in politics as Gandhi sought to mobilize the masses behind the Independence movement. The church, whose interests were inextricably tied to British rule, found itself the unwilling but helpless agent of political mobilization. The schools and colleges, operated by the church in Tinnevelly, were the vehicles of political literacy. In the classrooms, the students read Locke and Laski, and in the hostels, they talked of Gandhi, Nehru, and *swaraj*.

It was not until the mid-1930's that political consciousness and activism began to take shape among the Nadars as a community. At this time, the village of Arumuganeri, half way between Tuticorin and Tiruchendur, became the political vortex of southeastern Tinnevelly District. One of the first Nadars of this village to become politically involved was K. T. Kosalram. In 1933, at the age of nineteen, he was jailed in a Congress satyagraha against toddy shops. Four years later, Kosalram was elected president of the Tiruchendur Taluq Congress Committee, and in that same year, 1937, he led a temple-entry satyagraha in the district.[4] Kosalram's lieutenant was his young nephew, M. S. Selvaraj, also of Arumuganeri. The traditional leadership of the village, however, lay with Raja Palavasamuthu, heir to the Nadan authority of the region and later president of the Dakshina Mara Nadar Sangam. Kosalram, Selvaraj, and the Congress activists of Arumuganeri were deeply stirred by the Quit-India movement of 1942, and in August of that year, Raja Palavasamuthu agreed to join them in addressing a public meeting in Arumuganeri for the advocacy of salt satyagraha. Five hundred people of the village offered satyagraha, but Raja Palavasmuthu refused to participate. The satyagraha spread rapidly and soon turned toward violence in the burning of a railway station. Implicated in the attack, Kosalram was arrested. Violence continued to grow, and on September 21 an armed mob attacked a salt factory near Arumuganeri, killing the superintendent. At this point, the police, numbering several hundred, surrounded Arumuganeri and rounded up a thousand people. Two hundred were arrested in Tiruchendur taluq, fifty from

[4] Interview, K. T. Kosalram.

Arumuganeri alone. Two Arumuganeri Nadars were arrested for the murder of the salt superintendent. Sentenced to hang, they were released upon Independence in 1947. During the entire movement, Raja Palavasamuthu remained aloof, earning the enmity of the Nadar Congressmen.[5]

The Quit-India movement of 1942 brought K. T. Kosalram to prominence in Tinnevelly District, and in 1946 he was elected to the Madras Legislative Assembly from Tuticorin constituency, which included the whole of Tiruchendur taluq as well as Srivaikuntam. In that year, Kosalram was also elected president of the Tinnevelly District Congress Committee.[6]

S. T. Adityan of Kayamoli was a member of the Tamil Nad Congress Committee (T.N.C.C.) and served as a member of the constituent assembly in New Delhi from 1945 to 1947. Adityan favored the Rajagopalachari faction of the Congress, and in the 1950 election for the presidency of the T.N.C.C., he voted against Kamaraj. Soon thereafter Adityan left the Congress to join the Praja party (later the Praja Socialists) and to contest the 1952 elections.* S. T. originally proposed to stand for the Srivaikuntam parliamentary seat, but when the Congress put up the Nadar Christian businessman, A. V. Thomas, Adityan decided to withdraw rather than oppose his friend. Instead, he contested the Tiruchendur assembly seat, and in the election, he defeated the Congress candidate, his cousin. Five of the six candidates for the seat were Nadars, of whom one (receiving the smallest number of votes) was the grandson of the leader of the Tinnevelly schism, Rabbi Sattampillai. (For Tiruchendur parliamentary and assembly constituencies, see Tables 1 and 2.) In the Sattangulam constituency of western Tiruchendur taluq, K. T. Kosalram successfully contested the seat against two Independent Nadars and one Muslim. (For Sattangulam Assembly Constituency, see Table 3.) Another Congress Nadar, T. Ganapathy, was elected from the Nanguneri taluq. No other Nadar candidates were successful in the 1952 elections in Tinnevelly District, but there were scattered Nadar candidates in

[5] Interview, M. S. Selvaraj.
[6] Interview. Hereafter in this chapter an asterisk will indicate that information has been obtained in interviews, with the principal or with other participants or observers.

TABLE 1

TIRUCHENDUR PARLIAMENTARY CONSTITUENCY *

Year	Candidate	Caste	Party	Vote
1952	A. V. Thomas	Nadar	Congress	107,338
	M. M. Subramaniam	†	Socialist	64,916
1957	T. Ganapathy	Nadar	Congress	Uncontested
1962	T. T. Krishnamachari	Brahmin	Congress	Uncontested

Source: Tables 1–5 are based on the Madras elections reports: Madras, *Returns Showing the Results of the General Elections in Madras State: 1951–1952* (Madras: Government Press, 1953); Madras, *General Election in Madras State: 1957* (Madras: Government Press, 1960); Madras, *Report on General Elections: 1962* (Madras: Government Press, 1963).

* The parliamentary constituency embraces four assembly constituencies: Tiruchendur and Sattangulam in Tiruchendur taluq, and Nanguneri and Radhapuram in Nanguneri taluq. In 1952, the parliamentary constituency also included Tuticorin constituency and was listed as "Srivaikuntam" parliamentary constituency.

† Caste undetermined.

TABLE 2

TIRUCHENDUR ASSEMBLY CONSTITUENCY

Year	Candidate	Caste	Party	Vote
1952 *	S. T. Adityan	Nadar	Praja	25,030
	Subramania Adityan	Nadar	Congress	21,224
	G. E. Muthu	Nadar	Ind.	4,791
	Annal Jebaaith	†	Ind.	3,886
	N. Velunarayanan	Nadar	Ind.	1,834
	Eber Kulasekararaj	Nadar	Ind.	1,370
1957	M. S. Selvaraj	Nadar	Congress	30,106
	M. R. Meganathan	Nadar	Ind.‡	15,529
	O. Ponswami	Nadar	Ind.	955
	Sigamani	Nadar	Ind.	750
1962	M. S. Selvaraj	Nadar	Congress	39,944
	S. B. Adityan	Nadar	We Tamils	27,994
	N. K. K. Maraikayar	Muslim	Ind.	569
	B. Gnanaraj	Nadar	Ind.	361

* This was a double-member constituency, with an additional list for the election of a Harijan to a reserved seat.

† Caste undetermined.

‡ Supported by S. B. Adityan.

various constituencies, as, for example, in Tuticorin, where a Nadar contested for the Communist Party.

In 1955, Kosalram was unseated from the Legislative Assembly because of irregularities in his election in 1952. The case against him involved the publication of a defamatory pamphlet against one of his opponents in violation of election law. In the by-election held to fill Kosalram's seat, M. S. Selvaraj—Kosalram's lieutenant —stood as the Congress candidate for the Sattangulam seat. S. T.'s brother, S. B. Adityan, who had been elected to the Madras upper

TABLE 3

SATTANGULAM ASSEMBLY CONSTITUENCY

Year	Candidate	Caste	Party	Vote
1952	K. T. Kosalram	Nadar	Congress	12,498
	Meganathan	Nadar	Ind.	9,615
	Jeyaraj Nadar	Nadar	Ind.	8,071
	Mohamed Hussain	Muslim	Ind.	4,c78
1955 *	M. S. Selvaraj	Nadar	Congress	20,381
	S. B. Adityan	Nadar	Ind.	19,913
	Natarajan	Nadar	PSP	1,226
	Ahmed Sayeed	Muslim	Ind.	462
	D. G. Chelaswamy	Nadar	Ind.	339
1957	S. B. Adityan	Nadar	Ind.	33,636
	S. Kandasamy	Nadar	Congress	22,429
	M. Arunachalam	Nadar	Ind.	1,115
	A. P. V. Athimuthu	Paraiyan	Ind.	1,083
1962	K. T. Kosalyram	Nadar	Congress	43,428
	A. P. Raja Singh	Nadar	We Tamils	17,351
	K. S. Vallikutti	Nadar	Swatantra	2,698

* By-election.

house, the Legislative Council, in 1952, ran against him as an Independent. Raja Palavasamuthu supported Adityan, and the two, turning to their traditional family connections, tried to mobilize the old client-group ties between the Nadan landowners and the dependent climbers. The former power of the Nadars had been eroded as larger numbers of the poorer classes acquired small plots of land for garden cultivation, and as new economic opportunities enabled the climbers to leave their trees for labor in other pursuits. The Nadan power in the palmyra forests of Tiruchendur had by no means disappeared, however, and the old families still had a strong economic hold over the climbers.

Raja Palavasmuthu also used the modern association, the Dakshina Mara Nadar Sangam, to enhance Adityan's prestige. During the campaign, the Dakshina Mara Nadar Sangam held a conference in Sattangulam and invited both S. B. and S. T. Adityan to speak. The conference was opened with a procession led by an elephant— Adityan's election symbol.* Of the five candidates for the seat, four were Nadars. Selvaraj won by a margin of less than 400 votes out of a total of more than 42,000 cast. Adityan, wealthy publisher of the *Dina Thanthi,* the Tamil daily with the largest circulation, pledged to run again in the constituency and to win. He had his chance two years later.

In the 1957 elections, M. S. Selvaraj stood for the Congress in Tiruchendur assembly constituency, winning over three Nadar opponents. In Sattangulam, S. B. Adityan contested the assembly seat as an Independent against two Nadars and a Paraiyan. Adityan won the election by more than 10,000 votes over his Congress opponent. A. V. Thomas won a seat for Congress from Nanguneri taluq, and filling the parliamentary seat which Thomas had held, T. Ganapathy was returned without a contest. A Congress Nadar also won in Tuticorin. In the 1957 elections, K. T. Kosalram, president of the Tinnevelly Congress Committee and the Congress boss of the district, successfully contested the Legislative Council seat for the southern districts. S. T. Adityan was also returned to the Council as an Independent.

In the 1962 elections in Tinnevelly District, fifteen Nadars contested in eight of the district's seventeen constituencies, and five were returned to the Assembly—all Congressmen. In Tuticorin, the Congress party estimates place the number of Nadars at roughly 50 percent of the constituency's voters, with 20 percent fishermen and 12 percent Vellalas.[7] In the election, the Congress Nadar incumbent was returned with 43.9 percent of the vote. His

[7] Estimates of relative community strength in each constituency are based on figures provided in an interview with K. T. Kosalram.

Dravida Munnetra Kazhagam (D.M.K.) Nadar opponent received 27.9 percent, and the Communist Nadar, 14.8 percent. The fourth candidate, a Swatantra Brahmin, received 13.4 percent of the vote. Most Nadars in Tuticorin supported the Congress candidate, and although the D.M.K. drew most heavily upon Maravar support in the constituency, the D.M.K. district secretary residing in Tuticorin is a Nadar, and the party's candidate was a Nadar. The D.M.K. in the elections succeeded in attracting a number of middle-class Nadars, such as clerks, as well as laborers and students.[8]

While there is a tendency for each party to select its candidate from the numerically dominant caste of the constituency, there have been many cases when a minority community candidate has been selected—particularly if the predominance of a single caste is not clear. In Srivaikuntam, the Nadars form the largest single community, numbering some 34 percent of the voting population; Harijans are 27 percent; Maravars, 13; and Vellalas, 7 percent. The Congress candidate in 1962 was a Vellala, and although an Independent Nadar contested, most Nadar votes went to Congress. The Nadar received only 4.3 percent of the votes cast. Nadar support in Alagulam constituency of Sankaranakovil taluq also went to a non-Nadar. The Congress candidate, S. Chellapandian, a Maravar, captured a major portion of the Nadar vote, despite the fact that a Nadar D.M.K. candidate contested the seat.[9] The pattern was repeated in Nanguneri where the Congress candidate was a Reddiar. Although the constituency is heavily Nadar, the only Nadar in the running, a "We Tamils" candidate supported by S. B. Adityan received less than 5 percent of the votes.

In two Nadar-dominant constituencies in Nanguneri and Ambasamudram taluqs, Nadar Congressmen were returned to the Assembly with substantial majorities. In Sattangulam constituency of Tiruchendur taluq, K. T. Kosalram stood as the Congress candidate for the assembly seat in opposition to two other Nadars, a "We Tamils" candidate and a Swatantra man. Kosalram received nearly 70 percent of the vote and the overwhelming support of the Nadar community. The "We Tamils" candidate gained the

[8] Interview, Sivaswami Nadar, Tinnevelly District D.M.K. secretary.
[9] Interview, S. Chellapandian.

support of those Nadars loyal to Adityan, but his strength was derived mainly from non-Nadars, primarily Muslims and Maravars who polarized in opposition to the Nadar-dominant Congress in the taluq. The pattern of voting revealed his support to be almost wholly in the larger towns, particularly Udankudi, with a substantial Muslim population. Without organization in the villages, he concentrated his efforts on the cities and on village influentials, caste leaders and landowners who commanded local bodies of votes.[10]

Kosalram had a reservoir of support in Sattankulam and campaigned only three days in the constituency. He devoted himself instead to Selvaraj's campaign in Tiruchendur constituency. Here the Nadars number 40 percent of the voters and are almost entirely rural. The Harijans constituted 15 percent of the vote; the Muslims, 12 percent; the Vellalas, 5 percent; and the Brahmins, 3 percent. Selvaraj's major opponent was S. B. Adityan. There was also an Independent Muslim candidate and a Christian Nadar. Selvaraj won with 58.0 percent of the nearly 69,000 votes cast. Adityan received 40.6 percent. The Muslim got only 0.8 percent, and the Nadar Christian, 0.6 percent. As in Sattangulam, there was a tendency for castes to polarize around one of the two major Nadar candidates. Although Adityan was able to draw support from many Nadar landowners, such as Raja Palavasamuthu, tapping the traditional loyalties and ties with the Nadans and the vestiges of their client groups, his support was based, by his own admission, largely on the urban non-Nadar community. The D.M.K. urged its followers in Tiruchendur to support Adityan, and Mohammed Ismail, leader of the Muslim League, pledged his support for Adityan.[11]

Adityan, residing in Madras, had had almost no contact with Tiruchendur and in standing for the assembly seat had hoped to rely on the "personal touch" of his brother, S. T., who had a wide following in the region. S. T. Adityan was seriously ill, however, throughout the period of the campaign, and S. B. had to rely on election agents. Money was lavished on both sides, but Adityan

[10] Interview, A. P. Raja Singh.
[11] *Malai Murasu* (Tirunelveli), February 4, 1962; February 8, 1962.

had the greater sources to draw upon.[12] In the course of the campaign, Selvaraj visited each village, asking the people why they would want to vote for an Adityan, one of the Nadans who in years past had held the people in virtual slavery. Selvaraj played heavily on his own humble background as a school teacher in Arumuganeri and sought to associate himself with another "man of the people," Kamaraj. Selvaraj traveled with huge pictures of Kamaraj, which proclaimed, "Strengthen Kamaraj: vote for Selvaraj." Adityan was portrayed as a traitor to the Nadars because of his opposition to Kamaraj. Adityan, in reflecting on the election, was convinced that he was defeated, not by Selvaraj, but by Kamaraj—for, he said, the people voted for Kamaraj Nadar, not for the Congress party. The vote for Adityan was determined in part by the same factor, for the Muslims and Maravars supporting him did so in opposition to the Nadar community.*

Although Kosalram stood for the Sattangulam assembly seat, he had originally planned to contest the Tiruchendur parliamentary seat which had been held by T. Ganapathy. As the seat was con-

---

[12] "Money politics" is an important aspect of Indian political life. Increasingly in many constituencies the payment of money to voters by all candidates has been accepted as normal and expected. The extent to which such payment has affected political behavior has not been systematically studied—but it is clear that a man cannot "buy" his election by bribing the voters. A candidate spending a disproportionate amount frequently loses. It is no guarantee of victory.

Vote-buying is less prevalent in the cities than villages, but even in Madurai in certain wards and among certain classes (the Harijans particularly), candidates will enclose a few rupees in the election propaganda. In Virudhunagar city council elections, money has been one of the main lubricants of political life, as voters have come to expect, and demand, increasingly larger payments from each candidate. Many politicians will speak openly of "the price of a vote," but there is no definite pattern of voter response. There seems, however, to be four forms of reaction. Some voters will accept money from no candidate. Others will accept payment from all candidates and feel bound to none. Some barter their vote to the highest bidder, negotiating with each candidate to see who will pay the most. Once the bargain is struck, they feel bound to support the candidate. There are others who will accept money only from the candidate to whom they are already committed.

"Money politics" may also be functional to the democratic system, insofar as it impresses the people with the importance of a single vote and its power. Money may serve to draw a non-participant to the polls, very much as the gifts of the American political machines politicized the new immigrants to the United States. As the individual becomes increasingly involved politically, payment declines in importance. Interviews.

sidered "safe" for Congress, however, it was decided that T. T. Krishnamachari, the former finance minister and an all-India political figure, would stand, since a cabinet appointment awaited him in New Delhi and a quiet campaign was desired. So that he might run unopposed, a few minor candidates were persuaded to step down. The Swatantra party candidate was not so easily convinced, but in the end, T. T. K. was elected without opposition.

In Tiruchendur taluq, all major candidates for the assembly seats from the two constituencies until 1967 have been Nadars. The Congress party under the leadership of Kamaraj has retained the allegiance of most Nadars. The growing strength of the D.M.K., however, has affected Congress popularity among Nadar youth, and within the Congress in Tiruchendur, "groupism" has split the Nadars into two opposing political factions, reflecting the division at the district level. In 1960, K. T. Kosalram, aspiring to become a major figure in the state Congress, sought to contest the presidential elections of the Tamil Nad Congress Committee at the Arcot meeting, but he was persuaded by Kamaraj to withdraw. Kosalram, then president of the Tinnevelly District Congress Committee, stepped down under pressure and extended his support to S. Chellapandian, a Maravar, who was favored by a majority of the committee to become the new district president. Chellapandian contested a seat for the assembly in 1962, strongly supported by a number of prominent Nadars. Upon his victory and subsequent election as speaker of the assembly, Chellapandian resigned as president of the district committee, and Tirunalavel Pillai, a Vellala from Sankaranakovil, with Kosalram in silent opposition, was elected unanimously.

In that same year, 1962, at the meeting of the Tamil Nad Congress Committee, Kosalram spoke against the continued presidency of Kirshnaswami Naidu, who had held the T.N.C.C. presidency for several years. He proposed Selvaraj for the office and forced a vote. Selvaraj was defeated 23 to 112, a severe setback for Kosalram. The election was taken by many as a challenge to Kamaraj, and this belief was compounded the following year when Kosalram supported Swaminathan, a Maravar from Ramnad District, for the chief ministership in opposition to Bhaktavatsalem, who was backed by Kamaraj. In 1964, Kosalram marshaled his forces in Tinnevelly District for a showdown over control of the district committee. Backing another Vellala in opposition to the committee's incumbent president, Kosalram sought to wrest control from the Chellapandian group. Tirunalavel Pillai, Chellapandian's man, was reelected 113 to 91. What was taken by many to be a reenactment of traditional Maravar-Nadar opposition had no caste base whatsoever, for many of Chellapandian's supporters were Nadars. Of the Nadar members of the Legislative Assembly (M.L.A.'s) from Tinnevelly District, only Selvaraj was solidly behind Kosalram. Indeed, one of the Nadar M.L.A.'s from Nanguneri who supported Chellapandian commanded increasing support among Nadars in Tiruchendur.*

Kosalram, although he lost control of the district organization, retained his hold over the Tiruchendur Taluq Congress Committee. Opposition to Kosalram among Nadars in Tiruchendur was growing, however, and accusations of "bossism" and corruption were leveled against both him and T. Tangavel Nadar of Arumuganeri, who was the Kosalram-backed president of the taluq Congress committee. The most serious charge in consequence brought against Kosalram was that he had challenged Kamaraj, and it was alleged that Kamaraj was supporting Chellapandian against Kosalram. In order to divert opposition in the 1963 taluq Congress Committee elections, Kosalram put up a Christian of the fisherman caste for the committee presidency. On the day of the election, Kosalram lined up a majority, but large anti-Kosalram groups had assembled and in mounting agitation cried fraud. The polling officer, a Chellanpandian supporter, left immediately for Tinnevelly to inform the district committee of the situation. Stating that rioting was incipient, the committee announced the Tiruchendur elections postponed and superseded the Kosalram-controlled taluq committee by the appointment of four conveners—all anti-Kosalram Nadars—to administer the Tiruchendur Taluq Congress Committee. The old committee, under the presidency of Tangavel Nadar, refused to recognize the legitimacy of the conveners and, by unilateral declaration, continued to function.*

One of the conveners, "Seerkatchi" Narayanam, who had unsuccessfully sought a Congress ticket in the 1962 elections, now tried to take over the leadership of the Congress organization in Tiruchendur. Narayanam continued to play up Kosalram's "opposition" to Kamaraj and widely publicized the proceedings brought against Kosalram for conspiracy to obtain a license for the import of two rotary presses under false pretenses. Chellapandian pronounced Kosalram's political death, and Narayanam in Tiruchendur began to make plans for the next taluq Congress committee elections. Although many Nadars had lost confidence in Kosalram, he still commanded a loyal following among the Tiruchendur Nadars who had not forgotten his sacrifice during the Independence movement and his efforts for the benefit of Tiruchendur while he was in the Assembly. Factionalism in Tiruchendur had gotten out of hand, and in May, 1965, Kamaraj toured the taluq with Kosalram in an effort to smooth over the split and to convince the people that groupism in the Congress was nonexistent.

At about this same time, to revive the prospect of his political fortunes, S. B. Adityan began to push the idea of a federation of regional caste parties. In Tiruchendur, he encouraged T. Ganapathy to found a Nadar caste party. Ganapathy, elected to Parliament in 1957, had been denied a Congress ticket in the 1962 elections and was particularly bitter against the Congress party and Kamaraj. Ganapathy said that Kamaraj had not given due recognition to the Nadars and made no secret of his own ambitions and of his frustration at the hand of Congress.[13] With financial support from Adityan, Ganapathy issued invitations to a meeting for the organization of the party on August 1, 1965—the same day as the Nadar Mahajana Sangam's annual conference. Ganapathy was elected president of the new party, the Nellai Kumari Nadar Nala Urimai party. The party would seek support from the Dakshina Nadars alone, those from Kanyakumari and Tinnevelly districts, and it would seek to gain benefits for the economically backward and depressed community of tappers.[14]

The caste party would contest the elections only in the constit-

13 Interview, T. Ganapathy.
14 Letter to the writer from T. Granapathy.

uencies of Kanyakumari and Tinnevelly where the Nadar community was numerically dominant; at the state level, the Nadar party would ally with other regional caste parties. According to Adityan's calculation, the caste alliance of a Tamilnad United Front, following the lines of the Malay alliance, could gain an actual majority of seats in the Assembly. The allied parties would represent the Vanniars of North and South Arcot, the Gounders of Coimbatore, the Mukkulators (Maravars, Kallars, and Agamudiars) of Ramnad, and the Nadars of Tinnevelly and Kanyakumari.[15] Adityan's assumption that the caste parties would capture the vote in the areas of their caste dominance seemed to ignore the tendency of the dominant caste to split factionally. The Vanniars are divided among themselves, and a large portion support the D.M.K.[16] The Maravars in Ramnad are by no means united, and in Tinnevelly District, "groupism" among the Nadars is rampant. The formation of Ganapathy's Nadar party caused little excitement in Tinnevelly, where it was viewed generally as a party of a handful of rejected claimants for Congress tickets who were incapable of gaining a following. Indeed, Ganapathy's support among Nadars in his own panchayat union, in Nanguneri taluq, was so small that he was unable to win the chairmanship in the elections in 1965.* Why should we have a Nadar party in Tiruchendur, reflected one Nadar, when we are all Nadars anyway?

As the 1967 elections approached, S. B. Adityan merged his "We Tamils" party with the Dravida Munnetra Kazhagam, and following his lead, Ganapathy dissolved the virtually still-born Nadar caste party into the D.M.K. Adityan's move, however, only added momentum to the rapidly growing D.M.K. in Tinnevelly District.[17] The sweep of the elections which brought the D.M.K. to

[15] Interview, S. B. Adityan. For a discussion of the Vanniars in Tamil politics, see Lloyd I. and Susanne H. Rudolph, "The Political Role of India's Caste Associations," *Pacific Affairs*, XXXIII (March, 1960). The developments in Vanniar politics and the emergence of the Mukkulator alliance are discussed by Lloyd I. Rudolph in "The Modernity of Tradition: The Democratic Incarnation of Caste in India," *American Political Science Review*, LIX (December, 1965.)

[16] It was suggested that Kamaraj himself is behind the Vanniar caste party, hoping to cut into D.M.K. support by appealing to caste sentiments.

[17] In 1957 the D.M.K. had 700 branches in Tinnevelly District. By 1962, there were 1,573, and in 1965, at the time of the language riots, 3,200 branches. In

power in Tamilnad extended deep into Tinnevelly. In the south- eastern portion of the district, three constituencies remained with the Congress. In Nanguneri, T. Ganapathy, standing for the D.M.K., was defeated by the sitting Nadar Congress member, and in Sattangulam, S. T. Adityan (S. B.'s brother) lost to the Con- gress candidate. In Radhapuram, Soundrapandian Nadar won over his D.M.K. rival by a narrow margin. Elsewhere, however, the former secessionist party was victorious. In Tiruchendur constit- uency, the Adityan-supported D.M.K. candidate, a man of the fisherman caste, defeated the Nadar running on the Congress ticket. In Tuticorin, Sivaswami Nadar, the district secretary of the D.M.K., defeated Punnuswamy Nadar, the Congress incumbent. S. B. Adityan, for the D.M.K. in Srivaikuntam, won with nearly double the votes of his Congress Nadar opponent. In the organiza- tion of the new government, S. B. Adityan, unanimous candidate of the D.M.K., was selected as speaker of the Legislative As- sembly. The D.M.K. victories in the assembly contests were ac- companied by the success of its United Front ally, the Swatantra party, in the parliamentary election in Tiruchendur. By a margin of less than 500 votes, Dr. M. Santhosham, a Nadar Christian leader of the Swatantra party in Madras, defeated the Congress candidate, K. T. Kosalram.

The Nadars of southeastern Tinnevelly are today, as they were in the traditional society of 150 years ago, divided among them- selves. The distinctions of subcaste are largely gone, and while the Nadan families still retain some aura of aristocracy and authority, the lines which separated them from the rest of the community have blurred as those once dependent upon them have gained in- creased economic and social freedom and independence. Vestiges of the traditional client groups remain in Tiruchendur, as land- owners try to recruit their tenants and climbers to support them politically. The command relationships of the past, however, have given way increasingly to gifts of money and promises of eco- nomic betterment and village improvement. The Congress, as the party of Kamaraj and government benefits, had drawn—at least until 1967—the overwhelming support of the Nadars of Tinne-

Tiruchendur taluq alone, from 1962 until 1965, the D.M.K. had grown from 23 to 120 branches. Interview.

velly, but the lines which divided the factions of the district were not distinct at the grass roots. For most, it was a question of "personality," the Indian catch-all which describes the qualities of a leader, and also embraces the resources he commands and the benefits he can bestow. In Tiruchendur taluq, the Kosalram-Chellapandian factionalism, for example, manifested itself without coherent pattern, as local disputes took on the reflective character of the larger Congress factional opposition. Each side in the local dispute—over the construction of a new well for the village, for example—would align with one or the other of the Congress factions. As one group sided with Kosalram, the other would automatically align with the opposition; secure as the dominant caste and without challenge from other communities, the Nadars of southeastern Tinnevelly never felt the impetus to unity which drew the Ramnad Nadars into a homogeneous and politically solidary community. The political arena was within the Nadar community.

RAMNAD

While in Tinnevelly political conflict was between Nadar factions, in Ramnad the Nadars united politically as a solidary bloc in opposition to the dominant Maravar community: in political life, caste was set against caste. The Nadars in Ramnad, as we have seen, were an urban minority of merchants and traders. Confronted by a majority of communities hostile to them, the Nadars formed and developed a closely knit organization, the *uravinmurai*, for their protection and advancement. During the 1920's and early 1930's, the Nadars were solidly for the non-Brahmin Justice party, and after Independence the solidarity of the community was largely retained in support for Congress. In certain areas, however, particularly the larger urban centers, the threat of the other castes to the Nadars had declined; with diffused political support and occupational and economic differentiation, the political solidarity of the community was lost.

By the 1952 elections, most Nadars had shifted their support from the old Justice party group to the Congress. In

500 votes over his Congress opponent, also a Nadar. In the constituencies of central Ramnad, where the Maravars held a position of
undisputed dominance, the Nadars were solidly aligned with the
Congress in opposition to the Maravars' Forward Bloc party. The
political juxtaposition of the Nadars and Maravars in central
Ramnad is seen most clearly in Mudukulattur taluq where caste
antagonisms were nourished by deep roots and periodic confrontations.

During the 1920's and 1930's, the Nadars of Mudukulattur, in
which the town of Kamudi is situated, solidly supported the Justice
party in opposition to the Maravar leader, Muthuramalinga
Thevar, who controlled the Congress in the taluq. With Independence, Muthuramalinga left the Congress to form the Forward
Bloc, a Maravar caste party. The Nadars, as a community, transferred their support to the new ruling party. Muthuramalinga exploited the memory of caste hatred and politically nourished the
Forward Bloc on continuing antagonism. In the face of hostility
by the dominant Maravar community, the Nadars retained a cohesive organization. With minimal differentiation among themselves
in Kamudi, and clearly differentiated from the Maravars, the
Nadars were united politically for strength and survival.

In Mudukulattur, the Maravars are the overwhelmingly predominant caste. The community is made up almost entirely of small
landowners and agricultural laborers. The taluq is one of the most
backward economically in Ramnad District, and the arid soil yields
poor and uncertain crops. The Maravars, once proud warriors, are
today largely uneducated and backward. They have seen the merchant Nadar community, upon whom they look with contempt,
rise above them in wealth and power. The Harijans, once their
agricultural menials, have begun to advance through education and
government benefits, and the Maravars' control over them has de-

clined year by year. The Nadars of Mudukulattur are concentrated in the town of Kamudi, where they form a prosperous and advanced mercantile community. As wholesale traders and money-lenders, the Nadars have succeeded in gaining extensive economic power over the rural areas, incurring the bitterness and jealousy of the depressed Maravars.

Confronted by the hostility of the numerous Maravar community and the urban Muslim traders, with whom they were in competition,[18] the Kamudi Nadars formed a closely knit community. Because of the especially precarious position of the Nadars in Kamudi, the *uravinmurai* there was one of the strongest in Ramnad, and in Kamudi alone of the major trading towns, it has retained its control over the community to the present day. The Nadars' difficulties began in 1885, with the anti-Nadar combination led by Vellaisami Thevar. The next major confrontation was in 1897, with the famed Kamudi temple entry and the subsequent court case. Then in 1918, the Maravars attacked Kamudi with the intention of sacking the Nadar section of the town.

Although the Raja of Ramnad and W. P. A. Soundrapandian had succeeded in ending the punitive tax imposed on the town after the 1918 rioting for the maintenance of the special police force, relations between the two castes remained tense, and in 1924, at a small village owned by the Kamudi Nadar *uravinmurai*, there was a fight between Nadars and the Maravar farm laborers. Major conflict arose in 1936 during elections to the Legislative Assembly. The Nadars of Kamudi were Justice party supporters, and the *uravinmurai* directed all Nadars to oppose the Congress candidate, Muthuramalinga Thevar. The Justice candidate was the Raja of Ramnad. Both candidates were Maravars. In Mudukulattur taluq, most Maravars owed allegiance to Muthuramalinga, as they had to his father and to his grandfather, Vellaisami Thevar. The Nadars solidly aligned in support of the Raja of Ramnad in opposition to the dominance of Muthuramalinga.

During the 1936 election, Muthuramalinga called upon all

[18] Relations between the Nadars and the Muslims within the town were almost as tense as between the urban Nadars and the rural Maravars. The two conflicts, in fact, reinforced each other, as the Muslims sided with the Maravars against the Nadar community in times of conflict. Interviews.

Maravars to cease working in the fields of the Nadars and to boycott the Nadar merchants of Kamudi. The Maravars opened a shop
of their own, which failed after three years. Muthuramalinga's
threats against the Nadars grew, and on the threshold of violence,
the Nadars filed a security case against Muthuramalinga, which
would require him to place a certain amount of money, as bond, to
guarantee good behavior. Muthuramalinga refused to place security, and he was jailed for two and one-half years.

His bitterness against the Nadars grew in intensity when he felt
that he had been betrayed by his fellow Congressman, Kamaraj.
As a member of the anti-Rajagopalachari faction within the Congress, Muthuramalinga actively supported Kamaraj for the
T.N.C.C. presidency in 1940 and again in 1946. Kamaraj never
rewarded Muthuramalinga, for, according to some, Kamaraj feared
that his Maravar colleague might gain ascendancy over him.
Vengeful against Kamaraj, Muthuramalinga left the Congress in
1948 and founded the Tamilnad Forward Bloc, taking the name of
the party of Subhas Chandra Bose, the Indian nationalist who organized the Indian National Army against the British during the war.
When Muthuramalinga organized the Forward Bloc as his personal
caste party, the Raja of Ramnad shifted his support to the Congress, but Muthuramalinga's new party still commanded the support of the majority in central Ramnad.[19]

While in most other areas of Ramnad and Madurai districts,
caste antagonisms were declining as economic and occupational
differentiation within each community increased, in Mudukulattur,
the polarization of castes retained its traditional form. The Nadars'
need for unity in the face of opposition persisted. In other towns,
the cohesive organization of the *uravinmurai* began to decline, but
in Kamudi, the Nadar *uravinmurai* held its tight control over the
people.[20] The *uravinmurai* sought in the face of continued Maravar hostility to maintain community solidarity. No Nadar was permitted to contest against another in the panchayat elections. The

[19] Obituary for Muthuramalinga Thevar, The *Hindu*, October 30, 1963; and
interview.
[20] After 1947, the form of the *uravinmurai* was changed with its incorporation
as a voluntary society. The twelve trustees retained their power but much of the
work was delegated through a system of committees.

uravinmurai would decide which candidate to back for the Assembly or Parliament. After Independence, the *uravinmurai* gave its wholehearted support to the Congress, marshaling the vote of the Kamudi Nadars for whichever Maravar candidate the Raja of Ramnad would put up to face the Forward Bloc.[21]

In Mudukulattur, the breakdown of the voters by caste placed the Maravars as the largest single community, with 28,000 voters. Pallars numbered 22,000; Nadars, 14,000; Konars, 12,000; Naickers, 8,000; and Muslims, 8,000. The Maravar vote, on the basis of subcaste divisions or by intimidation, went mostly for the Forward Bloc. The Konars supported the Forward Bloc, as did the Muslims for the most part. The Harijan Pallars, dependent on the Maravars and terrorized by Muthuramalinga's bands of rowdies, voted for the Forward Bloc out of fear of reprisal. The Naickers supported Congress, as did the Nadars, to the last man.[22]

In 1952, Muthuramalinga defeated the Congress Maravar candidate 37,011 to 13,546. (For Mudukulattur Assembly Constituency, see Table 4.) Another Maravar got less than 4,000 votes, and a Nadar Christian, running as an Independent, received less than 2,000. In the 1952 election, in order to demonstrate his power, Muthuramalinga successfully contested both the assembly seat and the parliamentary seat for Aruppukottai constituency. He took his seat in Parliament.[23] (For Aruppukottai Parliamentary Constituency, see Table 5.)

In 1957, Muthuramalinga again contested both assembly and parliamentary seats. During the election, he denounced Kamaraj repeatedly and said that a Congress victory would bring the Nadars greater power for the destruction of the Maravars. He called for a boycott of Nadar merchants and declared that if Congress were elected in Mudukulattur there would be a third world war. As one of the greatest and most powerful Tamil speakers of

---

[21] Conversations with the elders of the Kamudi *uravinmurai*.

[22] Figures are fundamentally agreed upon by both Sasivarna Thevar (interview) and Rm. T. S. Soundrapandian, a Nadar Congress leader from Kamudi (interview).

[23] In 1952, Muthuramalinga campaigned against Kamaraj's election to Parliament and announced that if Kamaraj were elected, he would become a *sanyasi*. After the elections, Kamaraj sent him an ochre robe.

the century, Muthuramalinga could hold even the Nadars in a trance with his words. In the 1957 elections, the Forward Bloc repeated its 1952 victory. Muthuramalinga won the parliamentary seat, and in Mudukulattur constituency, both Muthuramalinga and the Forward Bloc Harijan candidate for the reserved seat won by a margin of more than 20,000 votes.

In the elections a few Harijans voted for the Congress, and in the by-election for the assembly seat, won by Sasivarna Thevar of the Forward Bloc, there was a degree of organized Harijan support for

TABLE 4

MUDUKULATTUR ASSEMBLY CONSTITUENCY

Year	Candidate	Caste	Party	Vote
1952	Muthuramalinga Thevar	Maravar	Forward Bloc	37,011
	Shanmuga Sundaran	Maravar	Congress	13,546
	Ganapathi Servai	Maravar	Praja	3,471
	Chandra Paul	Nadar	Ind.	1,880
1957 *	Muthuramalinga Thevar	Maravar	Forward Bloc	53,333
	A. Perumal	Harijan	Forward Bloc	53,571
	Chinniah Servai	Maravar	Congress	32,767
	A. Krishnan	†	Congress	27,013
1957 ‡	Sasivarna Thevar	Maravar	Forward Bloc	56,657
	Bhaskaran Servai	Maravar	Congress	32,875
	Chandra Paul	Nadar	Ind.	5,097
1962	Sasivarna Thevar	Maravar	Forward Bloc	37,162
	Kasinatha Dorai	Maravar	Congress	34,217
	P. Karuppiah	Konar	Ind.	3,908

* Double-member constituency.
† Caste undetermined.
‡ By-election.

the Congress. V. M. S. Velsami, a Nadar of a village about five miles from Kamudi, sought to advance his political fortunes in Mudukulattur by winning the Harijan community to the Congress. He spoke against Muthuramalinga and the Maravars' exploitation of the Harijans, and many Harijans slipped through Muthuramalinga's grasp into the Congress fold.* Bitterness grew between the Maravar and Harijan communities in the two months following the by-election, and in an effort to ease the situation, the

TABLE 5

ARUPPUKOTTAI PARLIAMENTARY CONSTITUENCY *

Year	Candidate	Caste	Party	Vote
1952	Muthuramalinga Thevar	Maravar	Forward Bloc	90,512
	M. G. Mohideen	†	Congress	70,724
	R. Ramanatham Chettiar	Chettiar	Ind.	19,575
	A. Nellippa Pillai	Vellala	Ind.	15,703
	Sasivarna Thevar	Maravar	Ind.	4,224
1957 ‡	Muthuramalinga Thevar	Maravar	Forward Bloc	206,999
	R. S. Arumugam	†	Congress	167,676
	S. S. Natarajan	†	Congress	150,087
	A. Velu	†	Forward Bloc	133,996
	V. V. Ramasamy	Nadar	Ind.	80,227
	M. Ramadoss	†	C.P.I.	51,155
	K. S. Krishnan	†	Ind.	37,886
	A. Srinivasan	Brahmin	C.P.I.	28,293
1962	Muthuramalinga Thevar	Maravar	Forward Bloc	175,772
	Arumugasami	Nadar	Congress	155,919
	Lakshmanasubba Rajulu	Naidu	Ind.	8,148
1964 **	R. Kasinatha Dorai	Maravar	Congress	138,358
	K. Velanudha Nair	Nair	Forward Bloc	131,281
	Lakshmanasubba Rajulu	Naidu	Ind.	9,348
	S. S. Karuppasamy	Maravar	Ind.	3,952

* The parliamentary constituency in 1962 included the following assembly constituencies in central Ramnad: Tiruchli, Mudukulattur, Aruppukottai, Sattur, and Sivakasi. In 1957, the demarcation was slightly different, with the inclusion of Srivilliputtur, with the constituency known under that name.
† Caste undetermined.
‡ Double-member constituency for reserved Harijan seat.
** By-election on the death of Muthuramalinga Thevar.

collector of Ramnad convened a peace conference on September 10. At the meeting, attended by Muthuramalinga and the Maravar leaders of the taluq, Emanual, a Harijan Christian leader, made a derogatory remark about the Maravar leader. Following the meeting, Muthuramalinga said to his men, "What can I do when even the Harijans have no respect." The following day at Paramagudi, Emanual was murdered, precipitating ten days of rioting between the Harijans and the Maravars.* Muthuramalinga and eleven other Maravars were arrested on charges of criminal conspiracy in the murder. Muthuramalinga was charged with abetment by insti-

gating the other accused to murder the Harijan. Muthuramalinga
was acquitted; three of the accused were sentenced to hang.[24]
Four Harijans were also arrested for murder and were defended by
Dharmaraj Santhosham, a prominent Christian Nadar attorney of
Madurai. Dharmaraj took the case at P. R. Muthusami's request, in
order to put an end to talk that Dharmaraj, as a friend of
Muthuramalinga, was implicated in the rioting.[25] Another Nadar,
K. T. K. Tangamani, the Communist Member of Parliament from
Madurai, suffered because of his association with Muthuramalinga.
Mudukulattur was one of the most backward and undeveloped
taluqs of Ramnad District. Road and communication facilities were
minimal, and it was widely believed that Muthuramalinga kept it
that way in order to keep the people in ignorance and subservience.
K. T. K. Tangamani, however, testified that the region was ne-
glected by the government because the people there did not return
Congressmen to the Assembly.[26] After the riots, Tangamani went
to Mudukulattur to see for himself what had happened, and near
Kamudi his car was attacked by Nadars who accused him of be-
traying the Nadar community. Tangamani defended Muthuramalinga as a great but mistaken man. Tangamani did not
deny, however, that Muthuramalinga had exploited caste feelings
and that he had roused the Maravars against the Nadars.[27]

After the rioting, Muthuramalinga accused the Nadars of fo-
menting the trouble, of backing the Harijans with money and
guns. The Nadars, he said, had used their wealth to induce the
Harijans to attack the Maravars.[28] The extent of Nadar involvement in the rioting is not fully known, but the police investigations
surely whitewashed the situation in denying any connection or
support on the part of the Nadars for the Harijans.

Although in failing health, Muthuramalinga Thevar again con-
tested the Parliamentary seat for Aruppukottai and defeated the
Congress candidate by 20,000 votes. In Mudukulattur, however,
Sasivarna Thevar, the Forward Bloc candidate, won by less than

24 The *Hindu*, January 8, 1959.
25 Interview, Dharmaraj Santhosham.
26 The *Hindu*, October 6, 1957.
27 Interview, K. T. K. Tangamani.
28 *Mahajanam*, October 31, 1957.

3,000 votes over the Congress Maravar candidate, Kasinatha Dorai, the brother of the Raja of Ramnad. The Harijan vote was lost to the Forward Bloc, and the power of Muthuramalinga was waning rapidly, as the government guaranteed protection to the threatened minorities of the taluq. Illness prevented Muthuramalinga from taking his seat in Parliament, and on October 29, 1963, at the age of fifty-five he died.[29] A bachelor, he left no heir to the traditional power of the family. Although Sasivarna Thevar took over the leadership of the party, its future was erased with the death of its founder. The Forward Bloc persuaded a Nair, who was vice president of the Swatantra party in Madurai, to contest the parliamentary by-election for the Forward Bloc, ostensibly to show that the Forward Bloc was not a Maravar caste party. The Nair won a majority in three taluqs, Mudukulattur, Aruppukottai, and Tiruchili, but lost in the more heavily populated Sattur and Sivakasi taluqs, where the Nadars, Naidus, and Reddiars were numerous. The Congress candidate, Kasinatha Dorai, won the seat by a margin of about 7,000 votes. Muthuramalinga's most ardent followers had remained loyal to the Forward Bloc, but the position of the party among the Maravars was broken as many Maravars cast their votes for Congress.

In the years immediately after the death of Muthuramalinga, the communal tensions and antagonisms which had polarized the Nadar and Maravar communities politically began to decline. The Raja of Ramnad [30] had urged the Maravars to emulate the Nadars' success, not to decry it in jealousy.

The 1967 elections reactivated to some extent the old bitterness and rivalry as Maravars gravitated to the Swatantra party and Nadars to the Congress. The monolithic unity of the two communities in opposition to the other had been broken, however. Younger Nadars, sympathetic with the D.M.K., expressed dissatisfaction with their Congress elders by supporting the Swatantra candidate. Many Maravars, free from the grasp of Muthuramalinga, supported the Congress.

[29] The *Hindu*, October 30, 1963.

[30] The Raja died in 1967 soon after his defeat by the D.M.K. in the general elections.

The United Front opposition carried the day in both assembly and parliamentary constituencies. The defeated Congress candidate for the parliamentary seat was P. Ayya Nadar of Sivakasi, and in the Sattur assembly constituency, S. Ramaswami Naidu, who had resigned from the Congress for a Swatantra ticket, defeated P. Krishnaswami Naidu, president of the Tamil Nad Congress Committee. Ramaswami Naidu, in contesting the election, turned his guns on Kamaraj and extended his full support to P. Srinivasan, the twenty-six-year-old student leader of the 1965 language agitations who, as the D.M.K. candidate in Virudhunagar, sought to defeat Kamaraj for the assembly seat. The electorate of Virudhunagar numbered about 83,000, of whom some 22,000 were Nadars. The Naidus were of about the same number but were deeply divided among themselves between Congress and the D.M.K. In addition to Kamaraj and Srinivasan (a Naidu), two minor candidates, one of whom was a Nadar, also contested the seat. The Nadar "establishment" of Virudhunagar officially supported Kamaraj, while many of the older Justice generation, led by V. V. Ramasami, actively supported the D.M.K. The sympathy of Nadar youth for the D.M.K. further eroded the solidarity of the Nadar community for the Congress. In the final count, Kamaraj, president of the Congress party, was defeated.

MADURAI AND MADRAS

In the cities, the locus of economic change and social mobilization, no single caste predominates and most castes are broadly differentiated occupationally, representing a wide range of economic pursuits. In Madurai, the largest city of the southern districts of Tamilnad, though their numbers are relatively small in comparison with the population of the city as a whole, the Nadars are a major mercantile community, primarily of traders and shopkeepers who migrated from the Six Towns of Ramnad in the early twentieth century. In more recent years, Nadar Christians from Tinnevelly have migrated to the city for employment in schools and government service. From the poorer villages of Ramnad, increasing numbers of Nadars have left the lands and the palmyras to work in the cotton mills and factories of Madurai.

Economically, the community has a virtual monopoly over the city's food-grains and commodities trade, hardware, and general bazaar shops. The Tamilnad Food-grains Merchants Association, with 113 members, and the Madurai Rice and Oil Mill Owners Association, with 66 members, are largely Nadar organizations, and Nadars play a leading role in the Ramnad-Madurai Chamber of Commerce, which is made up of members of all communities. Gangaram Durairaj, one of the general-secretaries of the Nadar Mahajana Sangam, is the secretary of the chamber and has provided forceful leadership for the Madurai merchant community.

The Nadar community of Hindu merchants and traders in Madurai is concentrated in two wards, East Masi Street and South Gate, from which Nadars have been elected to the municipal council. Only two of the thirty-six councilors are Nadars, however, because Nadar numbers are small. The East Masi Street ward is the Nadar bazaar section of the city and, though once predominantly Naidu, is today 60 to 65 percent Nadar in population. Gangaram Durairaj was elected from the East Masi Street ward to the council, opposed by a D.M.K. candidate, a prominent Nadar businessman. The Nadar vote was split, as within the ward there is a large amount of D.M.K. sentiment. In the 1964 municipal election, in fact, the D.M.K. candidate was a Naidu who successfully drew a number of Nadar votes. The Nadar Congress candidate was elected, nevertheless.* In the wards around the Madurai Mills, the Nadar factory-workers, along with their Maravar fellow workers, have extended their support to the Communists rather than to Congress, despite the continuing charisma of Kamaraj, and the young Nadar students have been drawn with their fellows to the image of Tamil nationalism in the D.M.K.

In the two assembly constituencies of Madurai City, the Nadars have little influence in terms of numbers. No single community commands sufficient numbers to dominate a constituency. In Madurai East, the Saurashtra weaver community is the largest; in Madurai Central, the Brahmins command the preeminent position. In the assembly elections in these two constituencies, only one Nadar has contested as a major candidate, Dharmaraj Santhosham in 1952. He ran as an Independent, with general support from the opposition parties. The Congress Saurashtra candidate, with sizeable Nadar support, won the election. While no other Nadars contested the assembly elections, with the majority of Nadars in Madurai supporting the Congress party, the Communist party candidate for the parliamentary constituency in each election, 1952, 1957, and 1962, was a Nadar, K. T. K. Tangamani of Tirumangulam. In 1952, Tangamani lost by nearly 100,000 votes to his Congress opponent. In 1957, he was elected to Parliament in a close race with the same Saurashtra Congressman who had defeated Santhosham in 1952. Sasivarna Thevar, the Forward Bloc candidate supported by Muthuramalinga, also contested the seat. The Congress candidate was a greatly respected Gandhian, but he lacked a real following. "He was a *good* man, a Gandhian," said Tangamani, "but not an effective leader. The people voted for me because they wanted an effective representative in Parliament." [31]

One assembly constituency, Madurai East, heavily Saurashtra, supported the Congress, but in Madurai Central, middle-class Brahmins and Nadar merchants and traders, as well as the millworkers, cast their votes for K. T. K. Tangamani. A Nadar Congressman who voted for Tangamani in 1957 said that the Nadars' support for Tangamani was not so much because of caste as because he was clearly the better candidate. Nadars who had voted against Tangamani in 1952 supported him in 1957. Although Tangamani served ably in Parliament, he was defeated in the 1962 elections. The middle-class support he had gained in Madurai Central left him for the Congress candidate, Subbaraman. Many of the Nadars who had voted for Tangamani in 1957 returned to the Congress, partly because Congress offered a stronger and more attractive candidate than in 1957, but also because of Tangamani's association with Muthuramalinga in the 1957 Mudukulattur rioting.*

The 1967 elections brought Tangamani's virtual eclipse politically. As the candidate for the right faction of the Communist party, K. T. K. secured only a little more than 9,000 votes in the new Madurai West constituency; the Congressman gained some 23,000

[31] Interview, K. T. K. Tangamani.

votes; and the Left Communist, nearly 47,000 votes. The Left Communists also gained the seat from Madurai East, and in Madurai Central, the Congress was routed by the D.M.K. In the Madurai parliamentary constituency, R. Ramamurthy, leader of the Left Communists in Tamilnad, defeated his Congress opponent by a margin of more than 100,000 votes. The Left Communist and D.M.K. cut across the caste spectrum in their appeal to the voters, and they drew from the lower and middle classes of all communities, including the Nadars. In 1967, as in earlier elections, however, the greater number of the Nadar community stood with the Congress party.

Within the Congress party organization in Madurai, the Nadars have played an increasingly important role. A number of Nadars serve as members of the Madurai (Urban) District Congress Committee, and a Nadar is one of the committee's two secretaries. One of the four members of the Tamil Nad Congress Committee from Madurai town is also a Nadar. P. R. Muthusami, for years leader of the Nadar Mahajana Sangam and one of the most active Nadars in Congress politics, has never sought political office. Gangaram Durairaj, however, has expressed interest in a Congress ticket. He served as deputy leader of the municipal council, and through his business and political associations he has extensive ties. Many Nadars believe, however, that his position in the Sangam might go against him in political life, as he might be too closely associated with the Nadar community.

The Nadars of Madurai, while generally supporting Congress, are by no means politically united. The elaboration of caste ranking in Madurai, as in all major urban areas, is minimal. Most castes are broadly differentiated, and various levels within each caste are distinguished interactionally. There is a relatively high degree of occupational and economic differentiation within the Nadar community of the city. A dispersion of political support has accompanied this differentiation, as Nadar factory-workers support the Communist party, middle-class clerks and students support the D.M.K., and a few disgruntled businessmen support the Swatantra. In Madras City, however, the process of occupational and economic differentiation is even more evident than in Madurai.

The first Nadars came to Madras from Tinnevelly between eighty and a hundred years ago. The Nadar migration from Ramnad to Madras City began only after the turn of the century, and it was not until 1914, for example, that the first Virudhunagar Nadars were drawn to Madras with their mercantile skills, and many of the poor among them sought employment from the Chetti merchants of Washermanpet, an area of the city which at that time was open and was the leading terminal on the rail line to the north. Soon the Nadars had established their own shops, and Washermanpet rapidly became a Nadar settlement. Washermanpet offered sufficient "spreading room" for the drying of grains and dhal, and the area soon became the wholesale grain and grocery center of the city.* The heaviest Nadar migration into Madras City began in 1940, as large numbers of Nadars from Malaya and Burma returned to Tamilnad in the face of the Japanese invasions of Southeast Asia. These returning Nadars were, for the most part, advanced in wealth and education, and as traders in hardware, grains, and groceries, they strengthened the Nadars' hold over the trading economy of Madras City. Many were government servants who had been employed by the railways in Malaya, and others were professionals, physicians and lawyers, such as S. B. Adityan.

In the early pattern of Nadar migration into Madras City, the community settled into pockets of their traditional association. Tinnevelly Nadars lived and remained apart from those of Ramnad, and as in the southern districts, brides were not exchanged between the two groups. As in Madurai, separate *uravinmurai* were established among the Ramnad Nadars, and, supported by *mahimai* funds, three Nadar schools were built.* The pattern of migration into Madras also tended to separate Hindu from Christian. The majority of Nadar Christians settled in Vepery, an almost wholly Christian neighborhood. Here their associations with Hindu Nadars were minimal, as there was little opportunity for contact. On the other hand, the concentration of Nadar Christians in Vepery was sufficient to permit them to remain aloof from Christians of other communities. Although in more recent years, contact between Christians of different castes has increased and relations have greatly improved, there are still in Vepery several predomi-

nantly (if not exclusively) Nadar churches. After the Second
World War, and with an accelerating increase in subsequent years,
poorer Nadars from Tinnevelly and Ramnad have come to
Madras, seeking employment as coolie laborers, shop assistants, or
factory-workers, usually after employment had been arranged by
some relative or friend already in Madras; and their movement has
been into the areas of Mylapore and Washermanpet, the traditional
Nadar settlements of the city. At the same time that economically
depressed elements of the community began to migrate to Madras,
many of the more well-to-do Nadars were moving into new residential sections of the city, with increased contact and association
with other caste communities.

The Nadars are spread today throughout the city and are highly
differentiated, with a range that would include tappers, coolie
laborers, government clerks, small shopkeepers, physicians, lawyers, teachers, and wealthy businessmen with trading interests all
over the world. The differences within the caste have become increasingly more significant than the differences between the individuals of different castes sharing similar social and economic backgrounds. The decline in the barriers of ritual purity in the cities has
released the individual to form new interests and associations,
cutting across the lines of caste and dispersing political support.

Although in no constituency of Madras City are Nadars sufficiently concentrated to dominate local politics, the Washermanpet
constituency has the highest percentage of Nadars—approximately
20 percent of the voting population, mostly merchants and
laborers. Both the Harijans and Naickers, who are mainly economically depressed coolie laborers, have larger numbers, with 25 and
35 percent respectively, and Chetties number about 10 percent. In
the 1952 elections, a Communist Vellala won by a substantial plurality over his Vellala Congress opponent and the twelve other
candidates. In 1957, M. Mayandi Nadar, the Congress candidate,
defeated the incumbent by just over 500 votes. By 1962, the Communist vote had slipped to only 14.7 percent, and the D.M.K. had
risen to 35.4 percent of the vote to challenge Mayandi. The
D.M.K. candidate was a man of the fisherman community, which is
concentrated along the coast and has only 5 to 6 percent of the

constituency population. In the elections, many of the poorer
voters received monetary gifts of up to ten rupees from candidates,
and Kamaraj campaigned in the constituency for Mayandi. Congress defeated the D.M.K. by only some 1,500 votes. Most Nadars
in Washermanpet supported the Congress, but a considerable
number voted for the D.M.K., despite the fact that the Congress
candidate was a Nadar. Nadar support for the D.M.K. came
mostly from the younger members of the community, although
several prominent Nadar businessmen supported the party.*
D.M.K. support continued to grow in Washermanpet, among the
Nadars as well as among other communities, and in 1967, the same
D.M.K. candidate defeated Mayandi Nadar.

In the immediate wake of the elections, a large group of teen-age
urchins waged a stone-throwing "Nadar-go-home" campaign in
the Barber's Bridge area, where the Nadar timber merchants are
concentrated. Similar outbreaks occurred elsewhere, largely as a
result of the frustration over rising food prices, which was one of
the major ingredients of the D.M.K. victory. Nadar wholesalers
and merchants—widely believed to have fattened themselves
through profiteering and political favor during the reign of
Kamaraj—provided an easy scapegoat and were taunted over the
defeat of their leader at the hands of a student.[32]

Despite the rise of anti-Nadar feeling, the Nadars of Madras
City have no political unity. Their political support is as dispersed
as their economic positions and occupations are differentiated.
They are to be found in all parties.[33] The only Nadar other than

[32] Personal communication from George E. Stoner, Jr.

[33] The range and diversity of political support among the Nadar community is
dramatically revealed in a most unusual family. In the nineteenth century, O.
Ramasami Nadar migrated from a village in eastern Ramnad to Malaya. With
little money, he built a small toddy trade into an *akbari* contract which gave him a
monopoly in Singapore. He then went into textiles and real estate, building his
fortune into one of the largest in Malaya. Ramasami Nadar had three daughters,
and in Malaya at that time were the only three barristers in the Hindu Nadar
community. These three men, upon completing their studies in London, had come
to Malaya to practice law, and each married one of Ramasami's daughters.
   S. B. Adityan was one of these barristers. Upon his return to Madras, he
founded the *Dina Thanthi* paper and began to build a financial empire. Before the
1957 elections, Adityan founded the "We Tamils" party, a pro-Western conservative party of Tamil nationalism, advocating the formation of a separate Tamil

Mayandi to serve in the Assembly from Madras City is A. V. P. Asithambi, who, as the D.M.K. candidate, was returned in 1957 to the Assembly from the Muslim-dominant Thousand Lights constituency. In 1967, he defeated the sitting Congressman from Egmore constituency. In the 1964 municipal elections for the ten seats of Washermanpet, six Nadars contested and all lost. Of the six, one was a Congressman, one an Independent, and four were D.M.K. In the city corporation, there are now two Nadar councilors, one D.M.K., and one Congress. In November, 1965, the D.M.K. Nadar in the council, Minor Moses, a Christian, was elected mayor of Madras. As the D.M.K. candidate, he was elected by the municipal councilors without opposition.[34]

The D.M.K. in Madras has drawn considerable support from younger Nadars throughout the city and from government servants and middle-class clerks. The Swatantra has also drawn support from the Nadar community. Dr. M. Santhosham, a Nadar Christian physician and brother of the Madurai advocate Dharmaraj Santhosham, has been the chairman of the Madras City Swathantra party and was elected to Parliament in 1967 from Tiruchendur. The conservative Swathantra party has gained support from upper-class Nadar professionals and some wealthy businessmen, but the Congress is, for most Nadars of Madras, the most popular party.*

state that would embrace not only Madras but the Tamil-dominated portions of Ceylon and Malaya.

The second of the barristers was K. T. K. Tangamani, who, upon returning to Tamilnad, became involved in trade unionism and rose in the Tamilnad Communist party to a position of influence and leadership. In 1957, he was elected to Parliament as a Communist candidate from Madurai.

The third barrister, S. Chellasamy, was from one of the most aristocratic Nadan families of Kanyakumari. In Madras he rapidly became one of the most successful and wealthy barristers of the city, serving as president of the Madras Bar Association for three terms. In 1957, Chellasamy unsuccessfully contested the parliamentary seat for Kanyakumari under the name of his own party, the Peoples' Progressive party.

[34] The *Hindu*, November 30, 1965; *The Mail*, November 30, 1965. The D.M.K. has held control of the Madras municipality since 1959, and following a rule dating back to the Justice party days, the office of mayor has rotated on a communal basis. In 1965, it was time for a Christian to serve as the city's mayor, and Moses, one of the three Christians in the council (two were D.M.K.) was selected. The system of communal rotation is briefly discussed in Robert L. Hardgrave Jr., *The Dravidian Movement* (Bombay, 1965), p. 63.

CASTE AND NADAR POLITICS

The Nadars have been united politically only when they believed themselves threatened and have sought solidarity for survival and advancement. In Mudukulattur, their unity was marshaled, not for a Nadar candidate, a man of their own caste, but for a Maravar Congressman in opposition to a Maravar of the Forward Bloc. Political struggle has rarely been conducted with each caste supporting its own caste man. Generally within particular constituencies the major struggle takes place within the numerically dominant caste—the Maravars in Mudukulattur or the Nadars in Tiruchendur—and the candidates seek support from minority communities to buttress their strength within their own community. In constituencies where there is no dominant caste, a candidate of a community only marginally represented may be selected. Few politicians in India can afford to court a single caste, for in most constituencies no single community so predominates as to command a majority alone. Had Mayandi Nadar in Washermanpet or Asithambi in Thousand Lights or Egmore appealed to "caste interest," they could never have won, for the Nadar tradesmen of the area hardly command sufficient numbers to secure a majority among themselves.

Though the candidate may seek to gain the support of a caste by appealing to its particular interests in a given situation, he must do so without alienating other communities. Of the twelve Nadar members of the Madras Legislative Assembly in 1962, not one had been active in the Nadar Mahajana Sangam, although all support its activities. Kamaraj, for example, has never had any association with the Sangam and goes to great lengths to identify himself with the broader community. The appellation of "caste man" would severely limit the political horizon of an aspirant office-seeker.

Caste has not ceased to be an important factor in determining political behavior, for even in the cities, Madurai and Madras, it is a significant consideration. Many Nadars will be drawn to the Congress because of Kamaraj; others may be inclined to vote for an opposition candidate because he belongs to the Nadar community.

Caste, however, in the differentiated culture is only one of a multiplicity of variables which affect the individual voter's decision, and it is by no means the most salient. The role of caste in Indian politics is changing, but as it has operated, it suggests the broader process by which an atomized and divided community gains consciousness and unity, entering the political system as a major actor. The very success of the Nadars, however, has led to an increasing differentiation occupationally and economically which has manifested itself in a concomitant diffusion of political support. Although they have one of the largest and most active caste associations in India, the Nadars are not united politically. For some purposes and in some areas, there remains a congruence between economic interest and caste within certain levels of the community, such as among the tappers in Tinnevelly or among the Nadar traders in Ramnad. That it was possible at one time, or even today in certain constituencies, to speak of "the Nadar vote" only underlines the situational and temporal character of caste as an actor in politics, for there had never really been, nor is there now, a partisan Nadar interest.

The structural changes of differentiation, most advanced in Madras, are being felt throughout the Nadar community. The parochial political culture of Tiruchendur is rapidly giving way to the differentiated, as political behavior becomes increasingly less determined by the traditional command relationships of the old client groups. In Ramnad, the solidary, integrated culture is beginning to break down as the community becomes more differentiated and mutual caste hostilities decline. The process toward differentiation is perhaps least evident in the region of Mudukulattur, but even here, the election of the Congress Maravar in 1964, supported by the Nadars of Kamudi, has opened the door to a diffusion of political support—evidenced already in the attraction of Kamudi Nadar youths to the D.M.K.

Chapter VIII

POLITICAL SENTIMENT: FIVE NADARS

LIFE HISTORIES

In their struggle to rise from the limbo of social degradation in which the missionaries found them one hundred and fifty years ago, the Nadars have come to share a sense of common history, but they no longer share a common fate. The rise of the Nadars has been essentially a widening of the socio-economic spectrum within the caste. As the community has differentiated in occupation and economic position, an ever-widening gap has separated the new professionals, the businessmen and traders, the clerks, and the factory workers from the climbers. The Nadars as a group are monolithic neither in behavior nor sentiment. The political culture of the community is heterogeneous, but its variety is the product of the historical experience of the caste in concrete situations. A political culture, as Lucian Pye has said, "is the product of both the collective history of a political system and the life histories of the individuals who currently make up the system. . . ." [1]

The life histories of five Nadars, based on intensive interviews, give depth to the political culture of the community, its richness and diversity. Each of the individuals, drawn from variant situations and backgrounds within the Nadar community, represents a distinct type, but the threads which run through each of their lives are intricately tied together, forming the pattern of Nadar history and political culture. Their lives and sentiments, set against the backdrop of the community's struggle to rise and to uplift itself, reflect common themes in the Nadars' social and political history. The life of each man becomes a slice of the biography of a caste in change. [2]

---

[1] Lucian Pye, "Introduction: Political Culture and Political Development," in Lucian Pye and Sidney Verba (eds.), *Political Culture and Political Development* (Princeton, 1965), p. 8.

[2] Each of the names has been changed to protect the individual's anonymity, as have certain details of occupation and associational life. The Tiruchendur village likewise remains anonymous.

These men were drawn from four structurally different situations, ranging from the more "traditional" to the more "modern," from the parochial to the differentiated. Rajamani is a young climber from a village near Tiruchendur. His body has not yet been twisted by the arduous occupation he has inherited from his forefathers, and he dreams of the better life which will surely come. Muthusami is a Kamudi cotton merchant, a man almost wholly concerned with business and little bothered by the happenings beyond the town. Ganesan is a highly successful Madurai businessman. Deeply involved in the Justice party and the Self-Respect movement in his youth, he is today a disaffected activist, drawn toward both the D.M.K. and the Swatantra but loyal to neither. Rajendran is a Madurai mill-worker, a man of relatively low political literacy, but a class-conscious supporter of the Communist Party of India. Doraisami is a respected Madras physician, a man to whom all Nadars look with pride. His house, his dress, the manner with which he carries himself, all suggest the substantial, upper-middle-class state of "arrival."

NADANKUDI: P. RAJAMANI

The village of "Nadankudi" lies eight miles southwest of Tiruchendur in the country of the palmyra forests. Although only a dirt road connects the village with Tiruchendur, daily bus service has operated since 1957, and electricity came to the village in 1963. A school has been established under missionary auspices, and a number of the village children continue on at the Bishop Asriah

---

The life histories are based on intensive depth interviews, which utilized an interview schedule patterned after that used by Robert E. Lane in *Political Ideology*. In addition, each individual was administered a modified thematic apperception test (TAT), designed specifically to tap the latent reservoir of sentiments toward the political world. Where an individual often has no opinions or attitudes with regard to a specified political object, the TAT stimulates a projection of the individual's orientation to the political world around him, revealing his unconscious feelings and emotions. The picture stimulus may also elicit data regarding the latent and manifest content of the picture, revealing—where direct questions might otherwise fail—specific knowledge about things political. Thus the TAT may be used as a tool in the analysis of both the cognitive and affective aspects of the political personality—the two elements constituting what we have called *sentiment*.

High School a few miles away. Four Nadankudi youths are in college. There are about 250 families in the village, nearly all of whom are Nadars, including the 15 Christian families. Although one-fourth of the villagers hold small plots for intensive garden cultivation, most of the land is owned by a handful of prominent, old Nadan families. The main source of income is from jaggery, and most of the villagers are palmyra climbers.

Until 1965, there was no formally constituted panchayat in Nadankudi. Soundrapandian, the major landowner of the village, ran things very much as he pleased. "The ignorant and uneducated and those dependent on me economically will always follow my advice on how to vote," Soundrapandian says. "No one in the village will oppose me."

Like his father and his grandfather before him, Rajamani is a palmyra climber. Although he was the first of his family to receive education (to the fifth class), Rajamani has continued the traditional occupation of his caste. His father, crippled in a fall, is unable to work, and the twenty-seven-year-old Rajamani supports the family. Sharing the yield of the trees with the landowner during the six-month climbing season, Rajamani is able to make only five hundred rupees annually, and his work during the rest of the year as a field laborer for one and a half rupees per day is irregular. In his many days without work, Rajamani dreams of going to Madurai or Madras for employment—perhaps as a bus driver for some big company. Perhaps, even in Nadankudi, if he had financial assistance, he could open a cooperative store to market the jaggery produced in the village. Unlike his father, Rajamani is restless in Nadankudi and unhappy as a climber, yet he is optimistic. He believes firmly that he can and will come up in life, as many Nadars have done before him. He has been to Tiruchendur many times and even to Tinnevelly. He has seen a more exciting world beyond the village through the Tamil films, and through the pages of the sensationalist *Dina Thanthi* and popular magazines, Rajamani has acquired a taste for the city life he has never experienced.

The films, newspapers, and radio have broken the isolation of Nadankudi. Politically literate, Rajamani admired Kennedy and has heard the name of Johnson. He speaks of Sastri and Indira Gandhi, but his evaluation of the government of India is in terms of what it has done for the palmyra climber. "A government is supposed to do good to the people. It must always work for the uplift of the poor," Rajamani says, "but it has not done anything for the palmyra climber. Government has never affected my life." While the words *democracy*, *socialism*, and *communism* mean nothing to Rajamani, *freedom* is something he understands: "Freedom from ignorance and poverty is the real freedom." Someday a government will be formed which will bring that freedom to the people.

Nadars are the overwhelmingly dominant caste of the region. Because of little contact with other castes, Rajamani's knowledge of traditional rank is virtually nonexistent. Ranking is *within* the Nadar community. He distinguishes between the landowners and the traders, who are rich and very high, and the climbers, who are low and depressed. We are all of the same mother, the goddess Bhadrakali, Rajamani asserts, and these differences between rich and poor have come only in modern times. Rajamani knows nothing of Kshatriyas or of the stories about the Nadars being kings. He has heard that the Dakshina Mara Nadar Sangam helps students, but Rajamani contends that it has done nothing for the climbers. He has never heard of the Nadar Mahajana Sangam.

Rajamani's father had no political interest, and deferred always to the will and bidding of the Soundrapandian family. The young Rajamani has grown impatient with the older generation. "The young people always want the uplift of the poor, but the older people are crooked." They will vote as they are paid. The people should cast their vote, Rajamani says, to elect someone who will help the poor and also to remove those who have not done anything after they have been elected. While Rajamani believes the political party system is good for India, each party, he says, promises the people everything and does nothing. In 1957 Rajamani voted for the non-Congress candidate, S. B. Adityan, because "in his election campaign he had promised to start a factory in Udankudi which would give employment to thousands, but he did not keep his word after he was elected." In 1962,

Rajamani voted for Congress. He feels that this is the best party, and for him its most distinctive quality is surely that Kamaraj is president—"a great honor for the Nadar community."

Rajamani says that he takes an interest in elections because he wants to elect a good representative. He attends political meetings whenever he has an opportunity, as in 1964, when Kamaraj and the chief minister, Bhaktavatsalem, spoke in the village. In 1965, Rajamani contested the panchayat elections "because I felt that if I am elected, I can do good to my village and people. If I had been elected I could have approached the government directly. . . . But two rich candidates opposed me. The palmyra climbers wanted to have a representative from their class on the Panchayat Union and they set me as their candidate. But the two others spent as much as 10,000 rupees and got support. I was defeated by a margin of seventeen votes. So I feel that only rich candidates can win in the elections."

Rajamani talks frequently with friends about politics and village affairs. He will speak with Soundrapandian about matters which concern him, and he often takes his cue from the landowner, whom he admires as a politician who cares for the people's uplift. All politicians are not like this, Rajamani says. "People contest in the election because they want to help the poor, but after their success in elections, they use their power for their own benefit."

KAMUDI: M. MUTHUSAMI

M. Muthusami is a cotton merchant, and, with subsidiary income from some paddy fields and from a betel-leaf wholesale business, his income is approximately 3,000 rupees annually. Muthusami's grandfather had been a poor peddler, going from village to village with his wares on the back of a bullock. Muthusami's father began the cotton trade, but his income was barely enough to keep the family together. As a young man, Muthusami was employed as a shop assistant in Madurai, but soon he was able to return to Kamudi, and with 100 rupees, he began his own business. Muthusami today counts himself a successful merchant. Says the fifty-four-year-old Muthusami, "I have bought some lands; I have built a house; and I have married off my three daughters. I did all these things out of my own profits." Muthusami is deeply involved in the affairs of the town. He is president of the cooperative bank and the dairy, as well as a trustee of the *uravinmurai.*

The long years of conflict between the Nadar and Maravar communities in Kamudi gave the town an acute consciousness of caste. Nadars have won the right to enter the old Siva temple, which in 1897 was the subject of a great court case. Although the temple has fallen into neglect, since the Nadars prefer to use their own Bhadrakali temple, it is a constant reminder of the deep antagonisms of the past. Until his death in 1963, the Maravar leader, Muthuramalinga Thevar, kept the wounds of bitterness open, adding the salt of vindictive oratory. After his death, his party, the Forward Bloc, was defeated by the Congress candidate, a Maravar supported by the Nadar community. The old feelings between the Nadar and Maravar communities were beginning to decline.

"Things are beginning to change," Muthusami says, and "these changes are for the good." In his business, most of his dealings are with the Maravar agriculturalists of the surrounding region, and he counts many as his friends. He feels, however, that other caste men are jealous of the Nadars' success. It is not caste which determines whether a man will come up or not: "It is all God's will if one caste is coming up and another is going down." His own success, Muthusami says, is because of hard work and honesty. The Nadars as a caste have come up because of unity and hard work and because of the caste association, the Nadar Mahajana Sangam. The *uravinmurai* is important in the Nadars' coming up—but other castes, like the Pallans, are now beginning to come up with government help. Muthusami believes that it is ridiculous to try to rank castes, for each claims superiority to the other. The Nadars are supposed to be descendants of the Pandya kings, but who can say?

Muthusami will mingle with the men of all castes, except the low Pallans and Paraiyans, and will invite them into his home. Once they would not come, he says, but times are changing and now they will. Caste rigidities are relaxing. In his grandfather's time, the

Nadars were very orthodox. They wore the sacred thread and the Brahmin tuft and invited Brahmin priests to celebrate marriages. Those days are gone. Brahmin priests are no longer used for ceremonies, but, he says, "during the dedication of my new house, I invited Brahmin priests. It was to purify the pollution caused by the entrance of other caste men during the construction of the house."

Muthusami studied up to the seventh standard in the Kshatriya High School, established by the Nadar *uravinmurai* in Kamudi, but he has never been greatly interested in education or in the world beyond Kamudi. Business and community affairs are all-consuming, and without any shop assistants, he has little leisure for reading or films. "I gather all my news mostly through talking with people in the shop," and he says that if he does not hear what is happening beyond Kamudi, it makes little difference. Muthusami is a "local," but despite his admitted unconcern with national and international affairs, he is aware of the major events outside the town, and the faces of world leaders, such as Lyndon Johnson, are familiar to him. He expresses no understanding of *democracy*, and his concern for the government, whether in Madras or New Delhi, is in terms of whether it facilitates or hinders commerce in Ramnad District.

Muthusami's father never bothered much about politics. Like all the Kamudi Nadars, "he simply supported the British government." In school, Muthusami recalls, they celebrated the birthday of George V, the English king, and in the loft of the *uravinmurai* library of Kamudi, portraits of the royal family, together with the Union Jack which once flew in the village, are carefully preserved. "Our family," says Muthusami, "has always supported the ruling party, be it the British or the Congress. . . . I change my views according to the policy of the ruling party. As a merchant I am obliged to go along with the ruling party."

In Kamudi, the candidates do not give money to the voters. "The people vote in belief that it will help the progress of the nation," Muthusami says. He supports the Congress, the party officially backed by the Nadar *uravinmurai* of the town. "This party works for the poor. They give free education and midday meals. They gave good roads and all. Kamaraj is the leader of the party—but he has never helped Nadars." Nearly all the Nadars of Kamudi vote for the Congress, but "the Maravars vote for the Forward Bloc. . . . This is the party of Muthuramalinga Thevar. Only his caste men vote for this party." Muthusami attends all the Congress meetings held in Kamudi, and if there is a procession, he will join it. During the elections, he urged his friends to vote for the Congress.

Muthusami believes that most political leaders care about what the people think. They are motivated to run for office so that they can help the poor, but then he adds ruefully, "We cannot fully trust the politician, for he could have said and promised so many things during the election." All politicians should be selfless and honest, Muthusami says. "Kamaraj is such a politician."

MADURAI: M. GANESAN

M. Ganesan is one of the leading wholesale jaggery merchants of Madurai. He has branches in both Tuticorin and Madras, where he also has interests in groundnut oil. He serves on the board of directors of three major industries in Madras State and has been an active member of the Ramnad-Madurai Chamber of Commerce and the South India Chamber of Commerce, of which he has been president. A past president of the Madurai Rotary Club, Ganesan is also involved in several local civic associations and is an active member of the Nadar Mahajana Sangam.

Ganesan, now forty-nine, grew up in Madurai. About 1910, Ganesan's father came to Madurai from Virudhunagar to open a branch outlet of the family's wholesale jaggery business. Ganesan's father established the family business on East Masi Street in the central portion of the city, and the year before Ganesan was born, in 1915, his father built a fine three-story house in the Brahmin quarter, the *agraharam*, just west of East Masi Street. They were the first non-Brahmins to live in the neighborhood, and the event scandalized those of high caste. Soon other wealthy Nadars moved in, and today more than half of the residents of the *agraharam* are Nadars; only one Brahmin family remains.

His father was a secretary of the Nadar Mahajana Sangam for

two years and was an ardent supporter of the pro-British Justice party, which ruled Madras during the 1920's. From the age of eight or ten, Ganesan recalls, he would go with his father to conferences of the Sangam, the Justice party, or the non-Brahmin Self-Respect movement. "Some people went to festivals—we went to conferences." After completing his studies at a Roman Catholic high school in Madurai, Ganesan entered the American College in the city, but he was soon caught up in active work for the Self-Respect movement to the neglect of his studies. After one year, he was forced to drop out. "My friends said that I could then devote full time to Self-Respect." Each day after classes, Ganesan would stop by the Self-Respect office, situated among the Nadar shops on East Masi Street, and there would read the literature and talk with the people. "On weekends, I would go with some of my fellow students and other Self-Respect workers to villages—really to the *cheri*, where the untouchables live. There we would take food together and violate caste prohibitions. Once I went to a wedding in my barber's family. When it came time to eat, I sat down with everyone else. Everybody was quite astir, but I refused to get up until I had been served. Many Nadars came with us on these occasions, but people from many other communities came as well."

Ganesan soon sealed his bond to the Justice party in marriage to the niece of V. V. Ramasami, the Nadar Justice leader of Virudhunagar. The wedding, a grand Self-Respect ceremony conducted without Brahmin priests, was attended by the founder of the Self-Respect movement, E. V. Ramaswamy Naicker himself. "The Self-Respect movement has had a great influence among the Nadars," says Ganesan. "In the last part of the nineteenth century, many Nadars took to wearing the scared thread and some even refused meat. They sought the services of the Brahmin priest. With the Justice party, the Nadars threw this off, and we are no longer servile to the Brahmins."

Ganesan feels a strong hostility to the caste system. From his early youth he recalls how the Brahmins of the *agraharam* where they lived looked down on their family. He is deeply sensitive both to the depressed position once held by the Nadars and to their progress in rising above it.

Ganesan, as was his father, is a member of the Nadar Mahajana

Sangam. He is a member of the Virudhunagar *uravinmurai* in Madurai and pays *mahimai*, to both the *uravinmurai* in Madurai and the one in Virudhunagar itself. In his work for the *uravinmurai* and for the Sangam, Ganesan has taken particular interest in education and has served on the board of Nadar schools. The Nadar Mahajana Sangam has been a major force in the community's rise, Ganesan believes, but today people only care for business and some do not want to pay *mahimai*. While supporting the Sangam, Ganesan is ambivalent about the caste association. He is fearful that such associations perpetuate caste and promote caste antagonisms. Teluq conferences, with their processions and fanfare, only serve to arouse caste bitterness, he says. Ganesan particularly opposes any connection between the Sangam and politics. "The secretaries mix up politics with the Sangam. . . . They claim there is no politics in the Sangam, but they do all to help the Congress."

Ganesan resists ranking castes, but he believes that each caste has special characteristics. The Chettiars, for example, are very industrious in business and are hospitable. With his business connections, Ganesan counts among his closest friends a large number of Chettiars, including the industrialist, T. Tyagaraja Chettiar. Despite his years as a Self-Respector, Ganesan bears no antipathy to the Brahmin. "They have been tamed now. They are terrible masters, but very good servants. I've always said we should use them. They're very adaptable and can go into anything." On the Maravars, Ganesan argues that they are not the enemies of the Nadar community. "We are really brothers. Probably the ill-feeling came because we were so close. Both Maravars and Nadars claim to be the Pandya kings, and also many customs are the same. Probably at one time, we were of the same sect—but the Maravars never went to climbing trees." Ganesan does bear antagonism toward the Vellalas. "The Saiva Vellalas of Tinnevelly are very powerful. My father told me when I was young that they were the greatest enemies of the Nadars. They cannot be trusted. They lie and cheat. They were the ministers and advisors of the kings and used their position to gain power. They had many lands in Tinnevelly and suppressed the Nadars."

From his youth, Ganesan has been socially and politically concerned. He reads voraciously. Each day, he reads two English dailies, the *Hindu* and the *Indian Express,* in addition to four Tamil papers and a variety of magazines. He listens regularly to the evening news broadcast and attends "serious films of social content." Politically literate, Ganesan is also politically involved. During his youth, in addition to his work for the Self-Respect movement, he participated in rallies and demonstrations, such as the 1938 anti-Hindi agitations, and he had a brief flirtation with communism.

After the decline of the Justice party, Ganesan supported E. V. Ramaswamy's Dravida Kazhagam, but with the formation of the Dravida Munnetra Kazhagam (D.M.K.) in 1949, he went with the new party. Ganesan greatly admired E. V. R., but he opposed his autocratic control of the party. He felt also that it was necessary to actually contest the elections against the Congress. Today Ganesan is still strongly sympathetic to the D.M.K., but he has come to support C. Rajagopalachari's free-enterprise Swatantra party because, as a businessman, he finds himself in agreement with the Swatantra position. "The government interferes too much in business in every way, with licenses, contracts, and so forth," Ganesan says. He opposes many of the government welfare schemes as well. "The government should not work to *help* the people, but to guide them. The people must help themselves."

Ganesan regularly attends political meetings in Madurai, like those, for example, at which the Communist leader, Dange, has spoken. Ganesan has worked actively for the election of V. V. Ramasami, and has made financial contributions to political campaigns. In the elections in 1952, 1957, and 1962, Ganesan voted for the Communist candidate, K. T. K. Tangamani, not because he is a Nadar, but because he is "a good man" and a responsive political leader. In 1952 and 1962, Ganesan cared little for the candidates for the assembly seats and did not vote. As a disaffected activist, Ganesan is perhaps like the man he described in response to a picture of a voter at the polls: "He has more interest in the campaign than in voting. He has no firm conviction in the parties or the candidates."

"I've always been anti-Congress," Ganesan says, although most

Nadars support the Congress party. The Nadar community is attracted to Kamaraj, but Ganesan expresses no love for the admired Nadar leader. "Kamaraj is all for the party. He cares nothing for Tamilnad, his community—or even his mother. He has remained silent so many times. . . . Kamaraj, however, does nothing for himself, and that's important. He does not use his position for personal gain."

Politicians are of all kinds, says Ganesan. Some care about the needs of the people and are responsive to their wishes. Others are not interested in serving the country; they serve only themselves. "A politician may say one thing, make big promises, and then he won't even give his address." As a man may run for political office because of varied motivations, so the people vote for a particular candidate for many reasons. Caste, Ganesan says, is still an important factor. Often people are paid; in the villages, the poorer people have come to expect money. "In Virudhunagar, everybody expects it, and everybody gets it. The police just look the other way."

MADURAI: K. RAJENDRAN

The Madura Mills, one of the largest cotton texile mills in the world, is situated about one mile northwest of the great Meenakshi temple in the city of Madurai. Established in 1892, the British-owned mill employs some 12,000 laborers, the largest number of whom are Kallars and Maravars. The neighborhood around the mill is populated largely by factory workers, and while there are separate houses and huts in the area, residential compounds are characteristic. Built either around a court or in long barracks-like units, the compounds are divided into tiny apartments, usually having no more than one small dark room. A single bathroom and water pump serve all the families of the unit.

K. Rajendran, a Nadar employee of the Madura Mills, lives in such a slum compound only two blocks from the mill entrance. On his street are several other Nadars employed at the mill, but most of his neighbors are Kallars and Maravars. Rajendran was born in a village near Arruppukottai in Ramnad District forty-two years ago. His grandparents had once owned a large tract of land in the village, but in disputes with other villagers, his grandfather had sold off the lands to meet court expenses. Rajendran's father soon squandered what little was left, and the family left the village.

Rajendran was the son of his father's second wife. In leaving the village, the family went to stay with her brother in Madurai. Rajendran's uncle and grandfather were both employed in a dyeing factory owned by a wealthy Saurashtra family. They succeeded in securing employment for Rajendran's mother in the factory, but the father remained idle. In 1939, at the age of sixteen, Rajendran quarreled with his uncle and left home to join the army. He went to Calcutta and Bombay and was stationed in Iran for a few months. Educated only to the third standard, Rajendran was, nevertheless, quick to learn and he rapidly acquired a knowledge of Hindi. His military career was cut short by illness and he returned to Madurai, where he immediately found employment at the Madura Mills. He began as a sorter, but gradually began to work up to a better position in the carding section of the mill.

When he was twenty-two, Rajendran married, and from his salary of 80 rupees was able to save a portion each month. His wage today is 190 rupees per month, and through his wife's frugality, they are able to put 10 rupees each month into their Post Office Savings Account. Rajendran feels that he is getting old and will not be able to work in the mills much longer. He has saved 6,000 rupees, and with the 3,000 rupees paid to him by the mill at the end of his service, he wants to move to, and to purchase some lands in, the village where his elder daughter lives, now married to a young Nadar agriculturalist from a village in Ramnad. The younger daughter is studying in the eighth standard of a Christian school.

Rajendran is a Hindu and, with his wife, goes to the Murugan temple once a month. His brother-in-law is a Christian and has exerted an influence over Rajendran and has encouraged him to attend church occasionally. Most of Rajendran's fellow workers are neither Christians nor Nadars. In the mill, Rajendran says, "caste doesn't count. . . . I mingle with people of all castes. We eat together during the lunch and even share food." Rajendran's oldest friend is of the washerman caste. "Only when I went to his house for the first time to eat did I realize that he was a *dhobi*. I felt reluctant, but I ate anyway. Later I invited him to my own house." Rajendran has a number of Maravar friends and has invited them for meals at his home. Of the Maravars, Rajendran says that "if you trust them, they are very good friends, but if they feel that you have lost your trust in them, they will cut off your head." Rajendran feels a strong identity with the depressed classes, but only antipathy toward the higher castes. The Vellalas, he says, never allow others to come up; the Chettiars care only for their own caste and family; the Brahmins pretend to be so high, but are of easy virtue. The Nadars are the most forward caste. They are Kshatriyas. Some castes, however, look down on the Nadars. "They will call us Nadar to our face, but when our backs are turned, they will say, 'He's just a Shanan.' "

In the old days, the Nadars were divided among the climbers, the agriculturalists, and the businessmen. These professions were bestowed by the goddess Bhadrakali, according to Rajendran, and the climbers were the lowest. They were dirty and undisciplined. Today the Nadars are divided between the rich and the poor. "Only the rich Nadars have come up; the poor have stayed the same."

Rajendran occasionally goes to the films, and frequently visits the reading room near his house to look over the *Dina Thanthi* or *Dinamani*. On Sunday evening, Rajendran listens to the news broadcast over the radio in the community hall and is particularly interested in following "the war news—about the bombings of Vietnam." He does not follow the news of most national or international events with great interest, however, and rarely discusses them.

With rising prices, the times seem harder every year. "The English were just," says Rajendran, recalling the days before Independence. "In those days, the British officers in our mill were very kind. The scales and power were evenly distributed. . . . Before Independence, we were not given freedom of speech, but there was no need to talk: everything was given. Now we talk much about everything, but it has no meaning." Rajendran's knowledge of the government is minimal. To him the major activity of the national

government in New Delhi is "receiving aid from other countries."
India has democratic government, with elected representatives—
but only the rich are able to reach the assembly, and they have no
understanding of the feelings of the poor. India is supposed to be a
socialist country, but socialism means equality, and there is no
equality in India. "The government works only to help the rich."
The factory workers, the peasants, and the poor should join
together to run the government, Rajendran says, and all should live
equally. Rajendran's friends are almost entirely employees of the
Madura Mills, and with them, he has tried to secure better conditions and higher wages, as in 1937, when they went on strike for
three months. "We are all one group," he says.

Rajendran is a Communist, or at least he has given his support to
the Communist party for the past fourteen years. During the Independence struggle, he says, "we all supported the Congress—but
now I have changed my views." The Congress makes good plans,
but "the ministers never execute them. They block them. All of the
ministers have ten mills each. Even Sastri has mills. The rich people
vote for the Congress and ask that their money be used to buy the
votes of the poor." Rajendran believes the Communist party is the
best, as it works for the poor. The capitalists are always trying to
suppress the party. Rajendran has voted for the Communist candidates in all elections, except in 1957, when he voted for the Congress assembly candidate on the basis of "personality." He believes
that some Nadars will support the Communists, but most, being
businessmen and merchants, "will naturally vote for the Congress."
The young people of all castes will vote for the D.M.K. Rajendran
attends all of the Communist rallies in Madurai and has participated
in the election campaigns. In the 1964 municipal election, he can-
vassed votes door-to-door for the Communist candidate, a union
leader who successfully ran in the mill-area ward. In the General
Elections, Rajendran campaigned for K. T. K. Tangamani, and on
one occasion met Tangamani. "Leaders like Tangamani care what
the people think. . . ." Most politicians seek office because of
greed. "They want to win the election so they can earn easy
money. They want a name in public life. See all the ministers who
have become rich and are having mills!"

MADRAS: P. DORAISAMI

P. Doraisami is one of the most respected physicians in India. A heart specialist, he maintains a private practice in Madras in addition to his position as a professor at the Madras Medical College. Doraisami was born in 1920 in Burma, where his father held a position of prominence in the Railway Service. Doraisami's family came originally from a small merchant town in central Ramnad. In the middle of the nineteenth century, drought conditions in Ramnad became so acute that Doraisami's great-grandfather left for Burma in hope of better business opportunities. He did well in petty trade, as did his son. Soon after Doraisami's father was born, the child was sent back to India for his education. Completing high school in Madurai, the young man returned to Burma to enter the Railway Service. At the death of his wife in 1928 he returned with his young son to India and their ancestral town to set up a business.

Doraisami's father, widely traveled and with a command of English, soon became a town leader and president of the panchayat. Although he had worked actively in organizing the Nadar *sangam* in Rangoon, he took little interest in the local *uravinmurai* and found himself in almost perpetual conflict with its trustees. When he refused to comply with its demands, he was excommunicated and finally moved to Madurai. By this time, 1946, Doraisami was serving in the army. He had completed his bachelor's degree at American College in Madurai and his medical studies in Madras. After serving as an army doctor for three years, Doraisami in 1949 went to the United Kingdom where for two years he pursued advanced medical studies at the College of Surgeons in London. In his profession, Doraisami has won renown among his colleagues, and among the Nadar community he is looked to as an example of the caste's success and progress.

Doraisami is active in both Indian and international professional societies. He serves on several government committees and acts as consultant in special cases in Bombay, Delhi, or Calcutta. His professional activities have taken him frequently to England, and in 1958 on a ten-week tour of medical facilities in the United States.

From his medical practice, Doraisami derives a substantial income, and this is supplemented by income from lands through his wife's family. Doraisami speaks flawless Tamil and English and commands a working knowledge of Hindi, Telugu, and Malayalam. His wife knows only Tamil. Their five children are all in school. The eldest daughter, now in college, plans to study medicine. Three other girls are in the convent school, and the only son is studying in a prestigious private school in Madras.

"We are not a very religious family," Doraisami says. "My father was anti-religious, although we kept a puja-room in Burma. When we returned to Tamilnad, he was greatly influenced by E. V. Ramaswamy's Self-Respect movement." Doraisami and his wife were married in a Self-Respect ceremony, with V. V. Ramasami attending. Speaking of his own attitudes, Doraisami says, "I have had a lot of Christian influence in my life. I went to Christian schools and have been to church. Even my prayers are Christian in form. When I was in American College I felt that I should become a Christian, but I got over it. I think now that it is possible to be a Hindu and a Christian as well."

Most of Doraisami's friends are from other caste communities. "City life, professional contacts, and patients, together with one's own outlook," he says, "contribute to this." Among his personal friends are prominent political leaders and diplomats. There are no other Nadars living in the new addition where Doraisami makes his home. Doraisami considers himself "tolerant" of others and would invite a man of any caste, even the lowest, into his home. "It all depends on whether he is educated and has good habits. I would certainly take food from anyone if he is reasonably clean. That's all that matters."

Doraisami believes that being a Nadar has neither helped him nor hurt him in his career. In his youth, however, he often felt discriminated against because of his caste. "In the 1930's, the Meenakshi temple was not open to us. I entered the temple one day with some of my college friends, and some of the people there caught me, suspecting that I was a Nadar. They questioned me, and I had to deny my community. I felt very bad about this." During the past forty years, the Nadars have made great progress. They were socially depressed and felt threatened by the Maravars who surrounded them. To bring unity and strength to the community, they organized the *uravinmurai*. "I used to think that the *uravinmurai* was primitive in its rigid rules and so on, but I've come to see it now as the real base of the Nadars' rise."

Doraisami, like his father before him, is a life member of the Nadar Mahajana Sangam, and he feels that the Sangam has played an instrumental role in the community's advancement. The Sangam has not only settled disputes within the Nadar community, but has tried to foster better relations with other castes. Doraisami believes that the disputes which plagued and threatened the Nadars in the past are rapidly declining. Caste has caused problems, but it has not always been a bad thing. "It has helped the growth of community socialism, where each felt bound to look after his own people." Although in rural areas, caste can still play this role, in the cities, caste must be replaced by a "broader-based socialism."

Doraisami is politically knowledgeable and follows the news with great interest. He reads the *Hindu* each morning and listens to the radio news occasionally. Although most of his reading is in professional journals, he reads the newspaper thoroughly with particular concern for international and national events. When he is visiting his wife's village, twelve miles from Madurai, he will send a messenger into the city each day to pick up the paper. His interest in cinema is for its family entertainment value.

Doraisami's father was an ardent follower of the Self-Respect movement, and as a Justice party supporter, gave his full support to British rule. When Doraisami was twelve years of age, he heard the Congress leader Satyamurthi speak in Madurai. He was greatly attracted to the powerful orator and soon became convinced that the English were exploiting India. When he was in high school, Doraisami, with difficulty, secured permission from his father to attend a taluq Congress conference. "My father thought this was a youthful enthusiasm," Doraisami says, but from then on, he attended all the Congress public meetings. He never participated in the Independence movement as such, but gave his full support as a youth to Congress. The Congress greatly stirred the imagination of youth in those days, he says, and he still supports the Congress today, although "I feel that I am a progressive . . . , more toward the left within the Congress."

The Congress, Doraisami believes, best represents the interests of the people as a whole. "They have a program. Other parties are vague; they cannot be pinpointed. . . ."

Doraisami found that while he was in the United Kingdom he was eligible to vote there and in 1952 he cast his vote for Labour. In 1957 and 1962, he voted for Congress. He does not believe, however, that it is possible to say that the Nadars as a caste supported the Congress. "Nadars are split now, with the majority with the Congress and some supporting the D.M.K.—particularly the younger people and some of the educated who find nothing to enthuse them in the Congress. Politically the Nadars are not united, but the same can be said of other communities as well. There is no real party orientation for communities—except perhaps in some rural areas like Kamudi. . . . In the cities, there is more of a class orientation."

Although Doraisami follows politics with interest—for example, the 1962 election fight between the Congress and the D.M.K. in Madras City—he does not participate in political affairs. He has not in recent years attended any political meetings, and he has never campaigned for any candidate. He does not try to use personal influence among his friends or associates in favor of the candidate he supports. Doraisami does feel, however, that if there is an issue of concern, the citizen should approach party leaders or government officials about it.

Doraisami believes that most politicians take the views of the people seriously. Many will go all around the town, seeing people, talking about their problems. While there may be some who are only self-interested, the politician who comes up with real public support will always care about the wants and needs of the people. If a politician is only interested in advancing himself or is corrupt, the people will find out and he will be defeated at the polls. The politician must listen to the people, for "there is an awareness of the power of the vote—even among the village people."

The people still have a faith in Congress because of its achievements and its leaders—Gandhi and Nehru. If a man has no particular leanings, he will vote for Congress. Satyamurthi used to say that you should vote for the Congress candidate, any candidate, even if he were a donkey. Now there is a tendency to vote for the person. If an important man stands outside the Congress, he will get the votes.

In rural areas they are influenced by caste considerations. In the cities, caste is not so important. In the cities, there is a bulk of organized labor who vote a certain way. The poorest slum dweller votes in one way. These people share the same economic position and don't care what the candidate's caste is. They are more concerned about party; it is more a class orientation.

The importance of democracy for Doraisami is that the people can always bring a change in government in a peaceful way. "The government should reflect the considered wishes of the people who can discriminate about the social needs. It is not just counting heads," he says. "At our stage of development in a country like India, I am not in favor of adult suffrage which equates the vote of an illiterate laborer with an educated individual." Doraisami believes in socialism, which he describes as "the system providing equality of opportunity to everyone irrespective of their status by birth." Doraisami believes that the government must take the lead in securing the social advancement of the people. He envisages an ideal government as "almost invisible—but powerful." "It would silently maintain peace, order, and progress. It would not be obtrusive. The real power would be the real representatives of the people—where intellectual and cultural interests will be fairly represented."

THEMES IN THE POLITICAL CULTURE OF THE NADARS

From the diversity of political sentiment to be found within the Nadar community, certain dominant themes emerge to provide texture to the pattern of Nadar political culture.

There is among the Nadars a sense of community, a self-awareness, a recognition that whatever divisions may exist within the caste—between the Nadars of Tinnevelly and those of Ramnad, between Christian and Hindu, climber and landowner, rich and poor—there is an overarching bond which unites all Nadars. The barriers of geography and subcaste which once divided the community are gone. We are all the sons of Bhadrakali, says the young Nadankudi climber, Rajamani. In the struggle to overcome social disabilities, the Nadars have come to share a consciousness of their history as a caste. This is not the history of the sons of Bhadrakali or of the Tamil Kshatriyas: it is the history of a caste in change.

While proud of their own caste and its achievements, the Nadars have a generally strong bias against the caste *system*. In Tiruchendur, where the Nadars are heavily dominant and have little contact with other castes, these feelings are less pronounced, but in Ramnad and Madurai, stronghold of the Justice party and the Self-Respect movement, there is a deep sentiment against caste. This is revealed most clearly in Ganesan's activities as a youth worker for the Self-Respect movement in the 1930's and in his ambivalence today about the role of the Nadar Mahajana Sangam.

Regardless of an individual's estimation of his own position, as with the mill-worker Rajendran, there is a general feeling among the Nadars that the caste as a whole has "come up." The Nadars' sense of having advanced in all fields, particularly in business, education, and in political life, has given to the "newly-arrived" a stance of self-confidence and to those still depressed a hope for change. The Nadars have come down out of the trees: each year there are fewer Nadars willing to continue their traditional occupation as toddy-tappers. Rajamani dreams of becoming a bus driver. An aged climber in a village near Kamudi has striven to provide his two sons with education and an alternative to the palmyra. Today one is a teacher, the other a police constable. The average Nadar firmly believes that through frugality and hard work, he can, like the many before him, come up in life—from a shop assistant to a wealthy businessman, from a village school teacher to an important government official. He might even become chief minister of Madras or president of the Congress party of India. Kamaraj did.

The changes which have brought the Nadars as a caste up in life have also differentiated them economically and occupationally. Many of Ganesan's friends are Chettiar businessmen who share his own interests and sentiments. Rajendran associates with his fellow workers at the mill, most of whom are Maravars and Kallars. Doraisami, the Madras physician, with friends from his own profession and cultural-economic level, finds few from among his own caste. Though all continue to affirm caste endogamy, the urban Nadars reach across the barriers of caste to form new associations on the basis of common interest rather than common ancestry.

The differentiation of classes within the caste has brought a diffusion of political support. The vast majority of Nadars, however, support the Congress party. Many are attracted by Kamaraj, a man of their own caste. Others—businessmen and traders, such as Muthusami—find it in their interest to support whatever party is in power. Many also are committed to the Congress ideology of socialism and the casteless society. If the greater number of Nadars support the Congress, the community is by no means monolithic. In Virudhunagar and in other pockets of Ramnad and Madurai districts, there is a carry-over of strong Self-Respect support which has manifested itself in sympathy for the D.M.K. Nadar students and government clerks also are drawn to the party of Tamil nationalism. Factory workers, like Rajendran, support the Communist party, and some wealthy Nadar businessmen and professionals back the Swatantra.

There is an undercurrent within the political culture of the Nadars, as in Indian society generally, of a degree of political alienation, of a low sense of political efficacy. Whether in Tiruchendur or Madurai, Nadars speak about the self-interest of politicians, of corruption and vote-buying. There is a strong feeling among many that, with the notable exception of Kamaraj, political leaders care little for the peoples' needs, and that they cannot be trusted once in office. The politician, in the eyes of Rajamani, is corrupted by power. Rajendran believes that the politician seeks riches and the ownership of mills. Ganesan, fascinated by political life, is sympathetic with the D.M.K., attracted to the Swatantra, yet votes for the Communist parliamentary candidate and casts no vote for the assembly seat.

The disaffection to be found among many Nadars is the partial product of frustration in the widening gap between aspiration and achievement. As a result of the communications revolution, those Nadars in a depressed condition today are highly sensitive to their position, all the more so because of the success and progress of their caste brothers. While, in fact, their actual condition may have improved considerably over the period of the past generation, their heightened consciousness of poverty has given them the impression of economic retrogression. Among the Nadars, this has most often taken the form of a nostalgia for the British past. In Madurai, the owner of a small grocery shop laments the passing of the good old days of British rule. "In my early days, I remember how we worked against the British. Now I realize how good things were then. The rain never failed. The crops had a good yield. But now there is little rain, and the crop yield is poor and the prices are high."

The Nadars have had a turbulent and colorful history, and the political culture of the community reflects the impact of accelerating change. Their efforts to rise above their depressed condition assumed uniquely dramatic form in the confrontations between the caste and its antagonists, but the changes experienced by the Nadar community are by no means unique. The Nadars' rise encapsulates the processes of change, differentiation, and mobility now being experienced, in greater or lesser degree, by caste communities throughout India.

Chapter IX

THE NADARS: AN OVERVIEW

The Nadars, in one hundred and fifty years of change, have moved from the lower rungs of the ritual hierarchy to a position of status and power. They have increasingly abandoned their traditional occupation of toddy-tapping, and as they have risen in education and wealth, the community has differentiated occupationally and economically. In their efforts to seek social status commensurate with their rising economic position, the caste turned to Sanskritization, creating a new myth of Kshatriya status, seeking the service of Brahmin purohits, and adopting a more Brahminical life-style. Their pretensions ended in ridicule and failure. The Nadars then turned from the emulation of "twice-born" cultural models to the pursuit of secular economic and political goals in the creation of the Nadar Mahajana Sangam, the caste association which became the agent of community integration and mobilization. The Sangam gave organizational strength to the new consciousness of the caste. As the voice of the community, in articulating its interests and formulating its demands, the caste association was the vehicle by which the Nadars entered the political system. The efforts of the Sangam for the uplift of the community increased internal differentiation, and with the concomitant decline in salient differentiation between comparable cultural and economic levels of the Nadar community and other castes, the solidarity of the community was affected accordingly. The diffusion of political support followed economic differentiation, and the Sangam, in order to retain its role as representative of the Nadar community, dropped its partisan role in Madras politics to pursue its interests through the indirect means characteristic of an interest group rather than the direct ones of a political association.

At the beginning of the nineteenth century, the Nadars—or the Shanars, as they were then known—were almost entirely engaged in the cultivation and climbing of the palmyra, and the community was heavily concentrated in the "palmyra forest" of the south-eastern portion of Madras in Tiruchendur taluq of Tinnevelly District. In this region, which was their traditional home, the lands were owned by the aristocratic Nadans, "lords of the soil," who constituted among themselves an endogamous subcaste. In constant conflict over the land, each Nadan commanded a client group of dependent climbers. As a Nadan succeeded in acquiring a greater number of men, he would encroach upon the lands of his neighbor or challenge his right to the estate through litigation. Thus, each village in this predominantly Nadar area was divided into opposing factions. The community was divided between the Nadans and the climbers. Since the almost total lack of roads and communications facilities precluded the horizontal extension of caste ties over a wide area, the Nadars were also divided geographically. There was no consciousness of a Nadar community, no sense of unity.

After the introduction of British rule, the missionaries found a rich field among the Nadars, and by the 1840's, a "mass movement" had brought a large portion of the community in Tinnevelly into the church. Through the organization of the mission, the Nadar converts found the strength of unity and, through educational opportunities, began slowly to advance.

During the same period, in the early nineteenth century, new economic opportunities and the development of transportation facilities had led to the migration of Nadar traders from south-eastern Tinnevelly up into the towns of Ramnad and Madurai, where they settled as merchants. Here, as a small and threatened minority, the Nadars joined together in each town in tightly knit traditional bodies called *uravinmurai*. Gradually acquiring wealth and power as traders and moneylenders, the Nadar community in Ramnad found an increasing gap between its low traditional social status and its rising economic position. In an effort to achieve a social status commensurate with their new economic position, the Nadars began to adopt the attributes of the higher castes in the process of Sanskritization. They advanced claims to high Kshatriya status, asserting superiority second only to the Brahmin, and created a whole new mythology of their origins and antiquity as the original rulers of the southern districts. With these pretensions, the Nadars, in a series of confrontations with the higher castes, sought interactional recognition for their claims though entrance into the temples forbidden to them. These efforts culminated in the late nineteenth century in the Sivakasi riots, in which 5,000 anti-Nadars attacked the Nadar trading town of Sivakasi, and in the Kamudi temple-entry case, which went to the Privy Council in London and was decided against the Nadars.

In their growing wealth, the Nadar trading community of Ramnad tried to disassociate themselves from their tree-climbing brethren in Tinnevelly, some saying that there were, in fact, no connections between the two groups. Among the Nadars of Ramnad, through their organization in the face of the hostility of other castes and through their increasing confrontations with them, a self-consciousness as a community rapidly emerged, with a deep historical memory and an inspiration for the future. As Sanskritization became increasingly irrelevant, the Nadars turned to secular goals. In 1910, these Nadar traders, seeking the uplift of the community and an association which would bring all Nadars together, even those from Tinnevelly, organized the Nadar Mahajana Sangam. The caste association soon became the largest and most active in all Tamilnad. With touring agents, the Sangam went into the villages to organize the Nadars; panchayats were established for settling disputes within the community and between the Nadars and other communities; aid was provided through a co-operative bank for the stimulation of business and industry; and schools and colleges were founded by the Sangam, with scholarships available to worthy Nadar students. In the early years, the Sangam successfully petitioned the Madras census to have its name changed for official purposes from *Shanar*, which was associated with pollution and the palmyra, to *Nadar*, "lord of the land." The Sangam also sought benefits for the poor climbers of Tinnevelly, but the association remained for the most part essentially an organization of the northern Nadar trading community of Ramnad and Madurai.

The Nadars sought the protection of the British raj, and the association pledged its loyalty to the king and its support to the Justice party, which governed Madras Presidency under dyarchy during the 1920's. Throughout the 1920's and into the late 1930's, the Nadars of Ramnad were united behind the Justice party in opposition to the Congress. In Kamudi in the early 1930's, a young Congress worker, Kamaraj Nadar, was stoned by the community as a traitor to his caste. While the organization of the Ramnad Nadars mobilized a solidary support for the Justice party, the Nadars of Tinnevelly remained largely divided among themselves. Their support, however, went mainly to the Congress, for in Tinnevelly, the Vellala community, whom the Nadars saw as oppressors, dominated the Justice party.

In 1937, C. Rajagopalachari was elected as Congress chief minister of Madras, and in that year opened the temples to all castes. Nadars were impressed by the action which enabled them for the first time to enter the temples, but they were perhaps more impressed by the changing political mood of the times. The days of the British were now numbered, and soon it would be the Congress government to whom the Nadar businessmen must apply for licenses and to whom they must pay taxes. In 1940, K. Kamaraj, a Nadar from the merchant town of Virudhunagar, was elected president of the Tamil Nad Congress Committee. He had come up in the ranks of the Congress totally without Nadar support. "Congress was his caste," the people said. The success of Kamaraj and his prominence within the party could only give luster to the Congress in the eyes of the Nadars. As his stature rose within the community, his prestige accruing to the caste, a dissident group within the Nadar Mahajana Sangam voiced its opposition to the association's continued support for the British government. Forming the National Nadar Association in 1940 to win support for the Congress from the Nadar community, the dissidents, at the height of the Quit-India movement in 1942, succeeded in gaining control of the Sangam. By Independence in 1947, the overwhelming majority of Nadars supported the Congress, the new ruling party, and the caste association aligned itself with the Congress, although it remained officially nonpolitical.

During this entire period, two groups within the Nadar community were developing along separate, although parallel, patterns. The Nadar Christians of Tinnevelly were responding to educational opportunities and, as advocates, physicians, and teachers, were migrating to the north, to Madurai, and as far as Madras City. The Nadar trading community of Ramnad, through its expanding hold over wholesale trade, was rapidly rising in wealth. The traditional correspondence between economic position and social status lost its significance, for within the Nadar community, there was an increasingly wide range of occupations and economic positions—from the toddy-tapper to the trader, the businessman, and the professional. The demands of deference to new economic status in the urban areas of change were beginning to erode the hierarchy of ritual purity, and with increasing differentiation within the Nadar community, a dispersion of political support followed. In the cities, where no single community commanded a predominant role and where most communities were broadly differentiated internally, the political identity of the individual reflected crosscutting vertical and horizontal ties and a plurality of commitments, associations, and interests. The differences within the Nadar community in occupation and economic position had increasingly become more significant for many purposes than the differences between the Nadars and members of other communities at comparable levels, and this found expression in political behavior. Although most Nadars continue to support the Congress, increasing numbers within the community can be found in the ranks of the D.M.K., the Communist, or Swatantra parties. This dispersion of political support mirrors the heterogeneity of the community's political culture and the variety of its behavior and sentiment.

REFERENCE MATTER

Appendix I

POPULATION OF THE SOUTHERN DISTRICTS

In the 1921 census, the last year in which fairly complete caste tables were provided, the Nadars were numbered as the largest single community in Tinnevelly District, with 13.59 percent of the population; in Ramnad, they were 6.53 percent; and in Madurai, 2.22 percent. In addition to this, perhaps as many as half the native Christians were Nadars, and in Tinnevelly those returned as Indian Christians were 10.10 percent of the population. The Maravars were the second largest community of the southern districts, the Pallars third, and the Vellalas fourth. (See Tables A–C.)

TABLE A

PRINCIPAL CASTES OF THE SOUTHERN DISTRICTS

Caste	Percent of District Population		
	Tinnevelly	Ramnad	Madurai
Agamudaiyan	0.9	5.55	3.10
Brahmin	2.76	2.07	1.59
Chetti	0.91	2.95	2.11
Idaiyan	5.35	7.14	2.70
Indian Christian	10.10	4.93	3.19
Kallar	0.66	2.63	9.30
Kamma	2.99	3.06	0.99
Kammalar	4.65	3.17	4.39
Labbai Muslim	2.65	3.65	2.78
Maravar	12.19	8.52	2.77
Nadar	13.59	6.53	2.22
Pallan	10.31	9.16	6.94
Paraiyan	4.19	3.75	5.27
Vellala	7.64	5.99	11.81

Source: Tables A–C are based on India, Census Commissioner, *Census of India, 1921*, Vol. XIII: *Madras*, Pt. II: *Imperial and Provincial Tables* (Madras: Government Press, 1922), pp. 118–123.

TABLE B

HINDU NADAR POPULATION IN THE TAMIL DISTRICTS, 1921

District	Nadar Percent of Total Population
Madras City	1.80
Chingleput	1.64
North Arcot	0.74
Salem	2.36
Coimbatore	3.28
South Arcot	0.57
Tiruchirapalli	0.62
Madurai	2.22
Ramnad	6.53
Tinnevelly	13.59
Nilgiris	—
Pudukottai	0.63
Tamilnad (total)	3.09

The Nadars in Tinnevelly and Rammad form a significant portion of the district population. It is within these two districts that the greatest number of Nadars is located. Nearly 40 percent of the community resides within Tinnevelly District, and the larger portion of this within the southeastern talups of Tiruchender, Nanguneri, and Srivaikuntam. Another 17 percent of the community resides in Ramnad.

TABLE C

PERCENTAGES OF THE NADAR CASTE RESIDING IN THE TAMIL DISTRICTS OF THE MADRAS PRESIDENCY

District	Percentage	District	Percentage
Madras City	1.45	Tiruchirapalli	1.82
Chingleput	3.75	Madurai	6.81
North Arcot	2.33	Ramnad	17.17
Salem	7.63	Tinnevelly	37.46
Coimbatore	11.13	Tanjore	5.73
South Arcot	2.03	Pudukottai	0.41

Among the taluqs which became the Kanyakumari District of Madras State, the 1911 census of Travancore listed the Nadar community as the largest, with 29.00 percent of the population. Vellalas were next with 5.66 percent, then Paraiyans, 5 percent. The

Brahmins numbered only 1.67 percent of the population.[1] In actual
numbers, those returning themselves as Nadars in the 1921 Census
totaled 655,252 for Madras and 200,838 for Travancore [2]—a total
population of 856,090. On this base figure, only an educated guess
can place the additional Nadars returned for the census as Indian
Christians. In southern Travancore, there were 261,112 native
Christians; in Tinnevelly, 192,110; Ramnad, 85,039; Madurai,
64,116. It is estimated that approximately two-thirds of the Christians of Kanyakumari are Nadars, and perhaps as many as 50 percent in Tinnevelly. The number is considerably smaller in Ramnad
and Madurai, where converts were drawn primarily from the Harijan communities. In these terms, the number of Nadar Christians
would probably fall somewhere between 200,000 and 275,000.
The total number of Nadars in 1921 would then be in the neighborhood of just over a million. Taking the percentage of Nadars in
the combined populations of the Tamil portions of Madras Presidency and the southern districts of Travancore at approximately
five, the present population of Nadars would be, with a normal
pattern of growth, about 1,650,000, plus or minus 100,000.[3] The
imprecision of such estimates of projected population is obvious,
but without current caste statistics, it at least brings the population
of the Nadar community into a fairly limited range—one considerably lower than the four million claimed by the Nadar Mahajana
Sangam as the population of the caste.[4]

The missionary Joseph Mullens in 1854 estimated the population
of the Nadars, including only Tinnevelly and southern Travancore, to be "upwards of half a million."[5] The greatest concen-

[1] *Census of Travancore, 1911*, Pt. III: *Provincial Tables*, pp. 152–161.
[2] *Census of India, 1921*, Vol. XXV: *Travancore*, Pt. II: *Imperial Tables*, pp.
46–47.
[3] All census figures for the "Nadar" community include the numerically small
caste of Gramanis, a toddy-tapping community in the northern districts, which is
distinct from the Nadars.
[4] The Sangam estimated Nadar population at 15 lakhs (1,500,000) in 1910 at the
First Conference, Porayar, Tanjore District. *Report* (Madurai: Nadar Mahajana
Sangam, 1910), Tamil. In a letter to the Ministry of Education, Government of
India, June 25, 1955, it was set at 30 lakhs, and in the *56th Annual Report*, 1965, the
Sangam estimated the total number of Nadars at 40 lakhs. These figures range
approximately twice what the census statistics suggest.
[5] Joseph Mullens, *Missions in South India* (London, 1854), pp. 94–95.

tration then, as now, was in Kanyakumari and in the southeastern portions of Tinnevelly District. Here the Nadars are the dominant caste and form an actual majority of the population in certain regions reaching as high as 80 to 90 percent. Stuart, in the *Tinnevelly Manual*, gave the percentage of Nadars in Tinnevelly District in 1879 at 18. Tinnevelly included at that time the taluqs of Srivilliputtur and Sattur, the latter containing the Nadar merchant community of Sivakasi. The heaviest concentration of Nadars was in Nanguneri taluq, with 34 percent and Tenkarai with 40.75 percent. The old taluq of Tenkarai included the present divisions of Srivaikuntam and Tiruchendur, and of the two, the far greater number of Nadars resided in Tiruchendur.[6]

North of the Tambraparni River into northern Tinnevelly, Ramnad, and southern Madurai districts, the Nadars are spread more thinly. A few families, employed in the traditional occupation of toddy-tapping, might be found in each village, but their numbers are few in the rural areas. In these regions, the Nadars are concentrated as merchants in trading towns, such as Sivakasi, Sattur, Virudhunagar, Aruppukottai, and Madurai. In recent years, Nadar merchants have migrated even further north to Coimbatore, Tanjore, and, in large numbers, to Madras City.

[6] The percentage of Nadars in taluqs of Tinnevelly District were as follows: Tenkarai, 40.75; Nanguneri, 32.4; Ambasamudram, 15; Tenkasi, 20; Tinnevelly, 8.5; Ottapidaram (Koilpatti), 12; Sankaranayinarkovil, 7.5; Srivilliputtur, 8.75; Sattur, 14. J. A. Stuart, *Manual of the Tinnevelly District* (Madras, 1879), p. 164.

Appendix II

THE MYTH OF NADAR ORIGIN

There are a number of variations on the legend of the Nadars' origin. In an account in one of the 1961 Madras Census village surveys, it is Lord Brahma rather than Indra who fathers the seven sons. This version of the legend also adds that the traditional occupation of toddy-tapping was ordained by the goddess Kali, who granted them the implements of their profession.[1] Another version is offered by a villager from the area of Kamudi. He says the father was a *rishi*, or saint, who on seeing the virgins seduced them. Pate, in the Tinnevelly gazetteer, says that the sons of the seven maids were "formed from the eye-sight of the god Narayana."[2]

In addition to the published versions of the legend in the 1961 census and in Pate, it was related by Dr. A. Devasugnayom of Madras and in interviews with village tappers in Tiruchendur and Kamudi areas and with a Nadar factory worker in Madurai. The factory worker gave a different version of the Nadars' origin. "We are all sons of Bhadrakali," he said. "She had seven sons, each one taking a different profession and hence there are seven different kinds of Nadars." He knew about only four. "The first son took a scissors, and the deity said you will be a barber, and henceforward he was shaving the Nadar community only. The second son climbed the palmyra tree, and the deity said you will be a climber. The third son took the scales, and the deity said you will be a merchant. The fourth son took the plough, and the deity said you will become a farmer."

A completely different story of the Nadar origin is related by the Reverend Samuel Mateer from his knowledge of Travancore. The Nadars, following the legend, are descended from Adi, the daughter of a Paraiyan woman, who taught them to climb the palmyra and prepared a medicine which would protect them from

[1] *Census of India, 1961*, Vol. IX: Madras, Pt. VI: Village Survey Monographs, No. 19, *Kuttuthal Azhamkulam*, pp. 6–7.

[2] H. R. Pate, *Madras District Gazetteers: Tinnevelly* (Madras, 1917), p. 129.

falling from the trees. (The squirrels also ate some of this and enjoyed a similar immunity.) Uppei, daughter of Adi, took the form of Mariamman upon her death, and the younger sister, Valli, became the wife of Subramania, the second son of Siva.[3]

Although a few Nadars are able to relate the legend, nearly all know of the prohibition of touching the basket. There is, however, a great dispute over exactly what kind of basket cannot be touched. Some say it is a bamboo basket; others, a twig basket of the type used by scavengers.

[3] Samuel Mateer, "The Pariah Caste in Travancore," *Journal of the Royal Asiatic Society*, New Series, XVI (1884), 181.

Appendix III

CHRONOLOGY OF NADAR
CASTE HISTORIES

1871 H. Martyn Winfred. *Shandrar Marapu* (Shandrar Customs).

1874 S. Winfred. *Shandrar Kula Marapu Kattala* (Safeguarding the Customs of the Shandrar Community).

1880 Samuel Sargunar. *Dravida Kshatriyas.*

1883 P. David Nadar. *The Tinnevelly Shanars, or a Notice under this heading that appeared in the Madras Times on the 16th of June, 1883, reprinted with notes.*

1883 Ponnoosamy Nadar. *Pandiya Kula Vilakkam* (An Account of the Race of the Pandyan Kings).

1883 Samuel Sargunar. *Bishop Caldwell and the Tinnevelly Shanars.*

1889 K. Shanmuga Gramani. *Shandrarakiya Surya Chandra Vamsa Paramparai* (The History of the Genealogy of the Sun and Moon Dynasties Who Were Shandrars).

1889 Y. Gnanamuthoo Nadar. *Shanars are Kshatriyas, Being a Reply to the Objectionable Statements Made by Chenthinatha Iyer regarding the Shanars.*

1892 *Nallor Kalambakam* (Poem of the Good People).

1892 K. Shanmuga Gramani. *Pallihal Vayappu.*

1900 Manikka Kavairayar (ed.). *Sivakasi Prabanatham* (In Praise of Sivakasi).

1901 J. S. Cornelius Nadar. *Amarar Puranam, Being the Antiquities of the Gods of India, as described in the Sacred Writings of the Hindus, treated Historically.*

1901 S. B. Nayaga Natar, alias P. V. Pandion. *A Short Account of the Cantras or Tamil Xatras.** [1]

1902 K. Kannayira Nadar. *Tamil Kshattriya Kula Vilakkam Vinavilai* (Catechism of the Tamil Kshatriya Community).

[1] Asterisk denotes works unavailable to the writer, but referred to in contemporary sources.

1910 Dr. A. C. Asirvatanadar and T. T. Thomas Nadar. *Shandrar Ethnography.**

1910 T. Vijaya Doraiswamy Gramani. *Arya Kshatriyakula Vilakkam* (A Treatise on the Arya Kshatriya Community).

1911 P. V. Pandion. *Chantror Sangam.*

1911 P. V. Pandion. *A Memorial from Nabbi P. V. Pandion, on Behalf of the Nadar Community, to J. C. Malony, Esq., I.C.S., Superintendent of Census Operations, Madras, 1911.*

1911 A. N. Sattampillai-Aiya. *The Chantro-Memorial, a petition of the Chantra (Nadar) Community praying the Government authorities to admit this treatise as a review of the incorrect statements about their caste, misspelt "Shanar," found in the Ethnography, Census Reports, Manuals, Gazetteers and other reference works published under Government orders. Prepared at the request of the Community by Rabbi A. N. Chattampillai-Aiya.*

1914 Sattainatha Kavirayar. *Shandrar Puranam* (Myth of the Shandrars).

1918 B. J. M. Kulasekhara-Raj. *Nadar Kula Varalaru, A Brief Account of the Nadar Race, being an address by Rabbi B. J. M. Kulasekhara-Raj (son of Rabbi A. N. Chattampillai-Aiya, Prakasapuram, Nazareth, Tinnevelly Dt.) concerning the Origin, History, Names, Titles, Subdivisions, Clans (ancient and modern), Occupation, Religion, Manners and Customs, Social Position, Characteristics, Present Status, etc. of the Chantras or Mara-Nadars, the original Lords of the Tamil Country, delivered on 6th June, 1918, at the Fourth Conference of the Nadars, held at the Victoria-Edward Hall, Madura.*

1922 T. Vijaya Doraiswamy Gramani. *Namathu Kula Toril Yaathu?* (What Is Our Community Occupation?).

1923 T. Vijaya Doraiswamy Gramani. *Kshatriya.*

1924 Pupathi Chinnalakshmana Raja. *Shanar Kshatriya?*

1926 T. Vijaya Doraiswamy Gramani. *Namathu Kula Toril* (Our Community Occupation).

1927 T. Vijava Doraiswamy Gramani. *Nadar Ennung Sol Araychi, Arasa Kulattai Kurittu Eruthiya Orpirapandam* (Research on the Word Nadar, a Manual Relating to the Kingly Community).

1927 S. A. Virasami Nayadu. *Nadar Kulatilaha Nattrimil Kalanjiyam* (Anthology in Chaste Tamil of Nadar Leaders).

1931 T. Masillamani Nadar. *Pandiya Desa Aditta Vamsa Sarittiram* (History of the Adityan Family of the Pandiya Country).

1937 Ramalinga Kurukkal and V. A. Kumaraiya Nadar. *Nadar Mannarum Nayakka Mannarum* (The Nadar Kings and the Nayak Kings).

n.d. A. M. S. Shenbahakkutti Nadar. *Sivakasi Tala Puranam* (The Legend of Sivakasi).

n.d. Shanmuga Gramani. *Shandrar Kula Purvottiram* (The Antiquity of the Shandrar Community).*

n.d. Chenthembera Nadar. *Shandrar Kula Theepam* (Light of the Shandrar Community).*

n.d. Marthanda Nadar. *Prabanasatham* (Essay).*

n.d. *Shandrar Maru* (Shandrar Petition).*

n.d. *Nadar Shanmuga Varalaru* (History of the Nadar Community).*

n.d. *Shandrar Kummi* (Song of the Shandrars).*

GLOSSARY

Agamudaiyar—Tamil caste of the southern districts

agraharam—Brahmin quarter

Aiya or Aiyar—Sir, or priestly title

akbari—distillation

ambalakaran—headman

Ambattan—Tamil barber caste

ammankovil (or *ammankoil*)—a goddess temple

bania—moneylending caste of North India

Bhadrakali—demonic goddess, consort of Siva

Brahma—supreme deity

Brahmin—highest priestly class

Chandra—moon god

Chera—early Tamil kingdom

cheri—untouchable quarter of village

Chetti—Tamil merchant caste

Chola—early Tamil kingdom

dakshina—southern

desia—national

devastanam—temple

Dewan—prime minister

dwija—"twice-born"

Ezhava—tapping caste of Kerala

Ganesa—elephant-headed son of Siva

gosha—female seclusion

Gounder—Tamil agricultural caste

Grammani—tapping caste of northern Tamilnad

gurukkal—temple priest

Harijan—untouchables, "children of god"

Inamdar—holder of rent-free land

Indra—Vedic god

Kali (or Kaliamman)—demonic goddess, consort of Siva

kalla—false or spurious

Kallar—Tamil caste of the southern districts

Kamma—Telugu caste of Andhra

kaval—village watch system

Konar—Idaivan, or Tamil shepherd caste

Kshatriya—warrior class

kula—community

kuttam—clan or sept among Nadars

Lakshmi—goddess of prosperity

mahajana—great people

mahimai—Nadar common fund payments

Manadu—the land of southeastern Tinnevelly

Maravar—warrior caste of the Tamil southern districts

Mariamman—smallpox goddess

Mopla—Muslims of Malabar

Mudaliar—high Vellala subcaste

Mukkulators—the three allied castes, Maravar, Kallar, and Agamudiar

munsif—village police authority

muppan—title for headman

muraikarar—member of Nadar community council

Murugan—second son of Siva

Nadan—title of Nadar gentry

nadu—country

Naicker—Telugu caste of Tamilnad

Nair—warrior caste of Kerala

Nambudiri—Brahmin subcaste of Kerala

nandavanam—bathing place

Nayaks—Telugu rulers of the southern Tamil districts

Nawab—title of distinction conferred upon Muslims in India

ooliam—corvée service

palayakar—local governor under the Nayak dynasty

palayam—country or district

Pallan—untouchable Tamil caste

Pallava—early Tamil kingdom

panaiyeri—climber

Pandya—early Tamil kingdom with capital in Madurai

Paraiyan—untouchable Tamil caste

pettai—fortified enclosure

Pillai—Vellala title

pucca—complete, ripe, "very good"

pujari—attendant priest

pulukka—cow dung

purohit—chief priest

Rajput—warrior caste of northern India

Rama—hero of the epic Ramayana

Rao Bahadur—title of distinction conferred by the British

Reddi—Telugu caste of Andhra

sabha—council or committee

sangam—association or academy

sanyasi—wandering religious mendicant

saru—toddy

Sassnas—edicts

Saurashtra—weaving caste, originally from Gujarat, resident in Madurai

Siva—destroyer and creator, third deity of the Hindu triad

Smritis—a class of religious literature, including especially lawbooks

Subramania—second son of Siva

Sudra—lowest of the four classes of Hindu society

Surya—sun god

swaraj—self-rule

teris—sandy stretches of Tiruchendur

Thevar—Maravar title

Tiyan—tapping caste of Kerala

udai—thorny scrub bush used for firewood

Upanayanam—ritual of the sacred thread

uravinmurai—local Nadar community organization

Vaisya—the third, mercantile class of Hindu society

Vannan—Tamil washerman caste

Vanniyar—agricultural caste of northern Tamilnad

Vellala—upper Sudra caste of Tamilnad

vidyasala—school

Vishnu—a principal Hindu deity

zilla—district

BIBLIOGRAPHY

PUBLIC DOCUMENTS

Great Britain. *Parliamentary Papers*, 1859, Session II, XXV, No. 158, 353. East India (Travancore), "Copies of the Official Papers Sent from India Touching the Recent Disturbances of Travancore." India Office, August 5, 1859. J. W. Kaye, Secretary in the Political and Secret Departments, Ordered, by the House of Commons to be Printed, August 6, 1859.

India. Census Commissioner. *Report on the Census of Madras Presidency, 1871*. Madras: Government Press, 1874.

———. *Census of India, 1881: Madras*. Vol. I. Madras: Government Press, 1883.

———. *Census of India, 1891*. Vol. XIII: *Madras. Report*. Madras: Government Press, 1893.

———. *Census of India, 1891*. Vol. XV: *Madras*. Madras: Government Press, 1892.

———. *Census of India, 1901*. Vol. XV: *Madras*. Pt. I: *Report*. Madras: Government Press, 1902.

———. *Census of India, 1911*. Vol. XII: *Madras*. Pt. I: *Report*. Madras: Government Press, 1912.

———. *Census of India, 1921*. Vol. XII: *Madras*. Pt. II: *Imperial and Provincial Tables*. Madras: Government Press, 1922.

———. *Census of India, 1961*. Vol. IX: *Madras*. Pt. II-A: *General Population Tables*. Madras: Government Press, 1963.

———. *Census of India, 1961*. Vol. IX: *Madras*. Pt. VI: Village Survey Monographs, No. 8, *Kootumangulam*. Madras: Government Press, 1964.

———. *Census of India, 1961*. Vol. IX: *Madras*. Pt. VI: Village Survey Monographs, No. 10, *Pudukulam*. Madras: Government Press, 1964.

———. *Census of India, 1961*. Vol. IX: *Madras*. Pt. VI: Village Survey Monographs, No. 14, *Visavanoor*. Madras: Government Press, 1965.

———. *Census of India, 1961*. Vol. IX: *Madras*. Pt. VI: Village Survey Monographs, No. 19, *Kuttuthal Azhamkulam*. Madras: Government Press, 1965.

———. *Census of Travancore, 1911*. Pt. III: *Provincial Tables*. Trivandrum: Government Press, 1912.

———. *Census of India, 1921*. Vol. XXV: *Travancore*. Pt. II: *Imperial Tables*. Trivandrum: Government Press, 1922.

————. *Census of Travancore, 1931.* Pt. I: *Report.* Trivandrum: Government Press, 1932.

Madras. *Disturbances in Madura and Tinnevelly.* Judicial, 1899 (Confidential), G.O., etc., Nos. 2017, 2018, December 12, 1899, from M. Hammick, I.C.S., Special Commissioner in Madura and Tinnevelly, to the Chief Secretary to the Government, August 15, 1899. Madras: Government Press, 1899.

————. *Madras Legislative Council Proceedings.*

————. *Madras Legislative Assembly—Who's Who, 1962.* Madras: Government Press, 1962.

————. *Manual of the Administration of the Madras Presidency.* 3 vols. Madras: Government Press, 1885.

————. *Return Showing the Results of the General Elections in Madras State: 1951–52.* Madras: Government Press, 1953.

————. *General Election in Madras State: 1957.* Madras: Government Press, 1960.

————. *Report on General Elections: 1962.* Madras: Government Press, 1963.

Tinnevelly District. *Selections from the Records of Tinnevelly Collectorate, Madras Presidency, on the Subject of Palmyra Plantations, Jungle Conservacy and Tree Inams from 1843.* Tinnevelly: Collectorate Press, 1900.

Travancore. Census Commissioner. *Report of the Census of Travancore, 1891.* Madras: Addison & Co., 1894.

TAMIL SOURCES

Chettiar, S. M. L. Lakshmanan. *Tirunelveli Mavattam.* Madras: Pari Nilaiyam, 1963.

Dakshina Mara Nadar Sangam. *Annual Reports,* 1951–1964.

Gramani, K. Shanmuga. *Pallihal Vayappu.* Madras, 1892.

————. *Shandrarakiya Surya Chandra Vamsa Paramparai Saritaram: Traditions of the Solar and Lunar Races, and the Claims of the Shanar Caste to Kshatriya Origins on These Grounds.* Madras, 1889.

Gramani, T. Vijaya Doraisamy. *Arya Kshatriyakula Vilakkam* (Treatise on the Arya Kshatriya Community). Madras: Progressive Press, 1910.

————. *Kshatriya.* Madras: Kshatriya Mittran Press, 1923.

————. *Nadar Ennung Sol Araychi, Arasa Kulattai Kurittu Eruthiya Orpirapandam: Research on the Word Nadar, a Manual Relating to the Kingly Community.* Madras: Kshatriya Mittran Press, 1927.

————. *Namathu Kula Toril* (Our Community Occupation). Madras: Kshatriya Mittran Press, 1926.

————. *Namathu Kula Toril Yaathu?* (What Is Our Community Oc-
cupation?) Madras: Kshatriya Mittran Press, 1922.
Hindu Nadar Mahajana Sabha. *Second Annual Report.* Rangoon, 1919.
Kavairayar, Manikka (ed.). *Sivakasi Prabanatham* (In Praise of Sivakasi).
Madras, 1900.
Kavirayar, A. Sattainatha. *Shandrar Puranam* (Myth of the Shandrars).
Poraiyar: N. Vadivel Nadar, 1914.
Kshatriya Mitran (monthly).
Kulasekhara-Raj, B. J. M. *Nadar Kula Varalaru, A Brief Account of
the Nadar Race.* Palamcottah: Darling Printing Press, 1918.
Kurukkal, Ramalinga and V. A. Kumaraiya Nadar. *Nadar Mannarum
Nayakka Mannarum* (The Nadar Kings and the Nayak Kings).
Virudhunagar: Satchithanandam Press, 1937.
Iyer, S. Chenthinatha. *Shan Kshatriya Pirasanda Marutam* (Shanar-
Kshatriya Storm), *Shanars not Kshatriyas.* Palamcottah: Subramania
Pillai, 1883.
Mahajanam (bi-weekly, Madurai).
Malai Murasu (daily, Tirunelveli).
Nadar, A. M. S. Shenbahakkutti. *Sivakasi Tala Puranam* (The Legend
of Sivakasi). Madras: Sri Nilaiya Press, n.d.
Nadar, J. S. Cornelius. *Amarar Puranam, Being the Antiquities of the
Gods of India, as described in the Sacred Writings of the Hindus,
treated Historically.* Salem: A. Ramasami Mudaliar, 1901.
Nadar, K. Kannayira. *Tamil Kshattriya Kula Vilakkam Vinavilai* (Cat-
echism of the Tamil Kshatriya Community). Madras: Chinnaiya
Nadar Press, 1902.
Nadar Kula Mitran (monthly).
Nadar Mahajana Sangam. *Annual Reports* and *Circulars,* 1910–1965.
Nadar, Ponnoosamy. *Pandiya Kula Vilakkam* (Account of the Race of
the Pandyan Kings). Madras, 1883.
Nadar, S. A. Siralinga. "Our People," *Kshatriya Mitran,* VI (1925–
1926).
Nadar, T. Masillamani. *Pandiya Desa Aditta Vamsa Sarittiram* (His-
tory of the Adityan Family of the Pandya Country). Madurai:
Nadar Press, 1931.
Nadar, Y. Gnanamuthoo. *Shanars are Kshatriyas, being a Reply to the
Objectionable Statements Made by Chenthinatha Iyer Regarding
the Shanars.* Madras: V. N. Jubilee Press, 1889.
Namasivayam, M. *Kamaraj Varalaru.* Madurai: Parathi Puttaha Nalai-
yam, 1963.
Navanithakiruttinan, A. K. *Muthalamaichar Kamarajar* (Chief Minis-
ter Kamaraj). Tirunelveli: South India Saiva Siddhanta Society, 1957.
Nayadu, S. A. Virasami. *Nadar Kulatilaha Nattrimil Kalanjiyam* (An-
thology in Chaste Tamil of Nadar Leaders). Sivakasi, 1927.

Pandion, P. V. *Chantror Sangam.* Madras: Diamond Press, 1911.

Raja, Pupathi Chinnalakshmana. *Shanar Kshatriya?* Salem: Srinivasa Press, 1924.

Sargunar, Samuel. *Bishop Caldwell and the Tinnevelly Shanars.* Palamcottah: Subramania Pillai, 1883.

————. *Dravida Kshatriyas.* n.p., 1880.

Sattampillai-Aiya, A. N. *The Chantro-Memorial.* Madras: Golden Stream Press, 1911.

Winfred, H. Martyn. *Shandrar Marapu* (Shandrar Customs). Madras, 1871.

Winfred, S. *Shandrar Kula Marapu Kattala* (Safeguarding the Customs of the Shandrar Community). Madras: Pastor &.Co., 1874.

BOOKS, PAMPHLETS, AND REPORTS

Abbs, John. *Twenty-Two Years' Missionary Experience in Travancore.* London: John Snow & Co., 1870.

Agur, C. M. *Church History of Travancore.* Madras: S.P.G. Press, 1901.

Aiya, V. Nagam. *The Travancore State Manual.* 3 vols. Trivandrum: Government Press, 1906.

Appasamy, Paul. *Centenary History of the C.M.S. in Tinnevelly.* Palamcottah: Palamcottah Printing Press, 1923.

————. *Legal Aspects of Social Reform.* Madras: Christian Literature Society for India, 1929.

Ayyar, Rao Sahib V. S. Padmanabha. *A Short Account of the Tinnevelly District.* Palamcottah: Palamcottah Printing Press, 1933.

Bailey, F. G. *Caste and the Economic Frontier.* Manchester: University Press, 1957.

————. *Tribe, Caste, and Nation.* Manchester: University Press, 1960.

Baliga, B. S. *Madras District Gazetteers: Madurai.* Madras: Government Press, 1960.

Barth, Fredrik. *The Political Leadership of the Swat Pathans.* London: University of London, 1959.

Beals, Alan R. *Gopalpur: A South Indian Village.* New York: Holt, Rinehart and Winston, 1963.

Bhattacharya, J. N. *Hindu Castes and Sects.* Calcutta: Thacker, Spink & Co., 1896.

Bower, H. *Essay on Hindu Caste.* Calcutta: Calcutta Tract and Book Society, 1851.

Buchanan, Francis. *A Journey from Madras through the Countries of Mysore, Canara, and Malabar.* London: Bulmer & Co., 1807.

Caldwell, Robert. *A Comparative Grammar of the Dravidian*. London: Turner & Co., 1875.

———. *Lectures on the Tinnevelly Mission*. London: Bell & Daldy, 1857.

———. *Mission of Edeyenkoody: Report 1845*. "Missions to the Heathen," No. 10. London: Society for the Propagation of the Gospel, 1847.

———. *A Political and General History of Tinnevelly, in the Presidency of Madras, from the Earliest Period to Its Cession to the English Government in A.D. 1801*. Madras: Government Press, 1881.

———. *Records of the Early History of the Tinnevelly Mission*. Madras: Higginbotham & Co., 1881.

———. *Tinnevelly and the Tinnevelly Mission*. Madras: Foster Press, 1869.

———. *The Tinnevelly Shanars: A Sketch of Their Religion, and Their Moral Condition and Characteristics, as a Caste*. Madras: Christian Knowledge Society Press, 1849.

———. *The Tinnevelly Shanars: A Sketch of Their Religion, and Their Moral Condition and Characteristics, as a Caste*. "Missions to the Heathen," No. 23. London: Society for Promoting Christian Knowledge, 1850.

Chandler, John. *Seventy-five Years in the Madura Mission*. Madras: American Madura Mission, 1909.

Chitty, S. C. *The Ceylon Gazetteer*. Ceylon: Cotta Church Mission Press, 1834.

Church Missionary Society. *Proceedings of the Church Missionary Society*. Annual Series. London: C.M.S., 1820–1920.

Cotton, G. E. L. *The Tinnevelly Mission*. n.p., 1864.

Coube, Steven. *Au Pays des Castes*. Paris: Victor Retauz, 1901.

Cox, John. *Travancore: Its Present Ruin Shown and the Remedy Sought*. Nagercoil: London Missionary Press, 1857.

Dakshina Mara Nadar Sangam. *Memorandum Submitted to His Excellency the President, Republic of India, New Delhi, on Behalf of the Palmyra Sweet Juice Tappers by Dakshina Mara Nadar Sangam, Tirunelveli. In pursuance of a resolution passed February 18, 1950*. Tirunelveli: D.M.N.S., 1950.

———. *Memorial to Pandit Jawaharlal Nehru*. Tirunelveli: D.M.N.S., 1949.

Day, E. H. *Mission Heroes: Bishop Caldwell of Tinnevelly*. London: S.P.C.K. Press [c. 1896].

Dumont, Louis. *Une Sous-Casts de l'Inde du Sud: Organization Sociale et Religion des Pramalai Kallar*. Paris: Mouton, 1957.

Ferguson, William. *The Palmyra Palm.* Colombo: Observer Press, 1850.

Francis, W. *Madras District Gazetteers: Madura.* Madras: Government Press, 1909.

———. *Madras District Gazetteers: South Arcot.* Madras: Government Press, 1906.

"Gandhite." *Kamaraj—the Shrewd, 1903–1940.* Madras: Renaissance Publishers, 1961.

Hardgrave, Robert L., Jr. *The Dravidian Movement.* Bombay: Popular Prakashan, 1965.

Harrison, Selig. *India, the Most Dangerous Decades.* Princeton: Princeton University Press, 1960.

Hodgeson, John. *Report on the Province of Tinnevelly* (1807). Tinnevelly: District Press, 1914.

Hough, James. *History of Christianity in India from the Commencement of the Christian Era.* 5 vols. London: R. B. Seeley and W. Burnside, 1839–1860.

Hutton, J. H. *Caste in India.* Cambridge: University Press, 1946.

Inquiries Made by the Bishop of Madras, Regarding the Removal of Caste Prejudices and Practices, in the Native Church of South India. Madras: Christian Knowledge Society Press, 1868.

Iyengar, S. Sundaraja. *Land Tenures in the Madras Presidency.* Madras: Commercial Press, 1922.

Iyer, L. K. Anatha Krishna. *Lectures on Ethnography.* Calcutta: University of Calcutta, 1925.

Kearns, J. F. *Kalyan'a Shat-anku or the Marriage Ceremonies of the Hindus of South India.* Madras: Higginbotham & Co., 1868.

Kitts, L. T. *Caste in Courts.* Rajkot, 1912.

Krishnaswami, S. Y. *Rural Problems in Madras.* Madras: Government Press, 1947.

Kumar, Dharma. *Land and Caste in South India: Agricultural Labour in Madras Presidency in the Nineteenth Century.* Cambridge: University Press, 1965.

Lane, Robert E. *Political Ideology.* New York: Free Press, 1962.

Lewin, Kurt. *Resolving Social Conflicts.* New York: Harper, 1948.

London Missionary Society. *Annual Report of the Travancore District Committee (L.M.S.) for the Year 1859.* Nagercoil: London Mission Press, 1860.

———. *Annual Report of the Travancore District Committee (L.M.S.) for the Year 1859.* Nagercoil: London Mission Press, 1860.

Mackenzie, G. T. *Christianity in Travancore.* Trivandrum: Government Press, 1901.

Marriott, McKim. *Caste Ranking and Community Structure in Five*

Regions of India and Pakistan. Deccan College Monograph Series, No. 23. Poona: Deccan College, 1960.

————. *Village India.* Chicago: University of Chicago Press, 1955.

Mateer, Samuel. *The Land of Charity: An Account of Travancore and Its Devil Worship.* New York: Dodd and Mead, 1870.

————. *Native Life in Travancore.* London: W. H. Allen, 1883.

Mayer, Adrian C. *Caste and Kinship in Central India.* London: Routledge & Kegan Paul, 1960.

Memorandum Submitted to the Honourable the Premier and the Honourable Minister for Prohibition by and on Behalf of the Public of Tirunelveli District. In Pursuance of the Resolution Passed at the Conference of the Tappers and Palmyra Owners of the Tirunelveli District held at Tiruchendur on 18/12/1948.

Molony, J. C. *A Book of South India.* London: Methuen & Co., 1926.

Mulla, Dinshah Fardunji. *Jurisdiction of Courts in Matters Relating to the Rights and Powers of Castes.* Bombay: Caxton, 1901.

Mullens, Joseph. *A Brief Review of Ten Years' Missionary Labour in India between 1852 and 1861.* London: James Nisbet & Co., 1863.

————. *Missions in South India.* London: W. H. Dalton, 1854.

Nadar, M. S. Shanmuga. *The Sack of Sivakasi and Other Atrocities in Tinnevelly District.* Madras: Addison & Co., 1899.

Nadar, P. David. *The Tinnevelly Shanars, or a Notice under this heading that appeared in the Madras Times on the 16th of June, 1883, reprinted with notes.* Palamcottah: S. Subramania Pillai at Chinthamani Press, 1883.

Nadar Mahajana Sangam. *Rules and Regulations of the Nadar Mahajana Sangam, Madura.* Madurai: N.M.S., 1919.

————. *To His Excellency the Governor of Fort St. George in Council. The Humble Memorial Presented by the Nadar Mahajana Sangam, Madura.* Madurai: N.M.S., 1921.

Narasimhan, V. K. *Kamaraj: a Study.* Bombay: Manaktalas, 1967.

Nelson, J. H. N. *The Madura Country Manual.* Madras: Government Press, 1868.

Nesamony, A. *Inside Travancore Tamil Nad.* Madras: Thompson & Co., 1948.

Niehbur, H. Richard. *The Social Sources of Denominationalism.* New York: Henry Holt, 1929.

Oliver, George. *Anthropologie des Tamouls du Sud de l'Inde.* Paris: Ecole Française d'Extrême-Orient, 1961.

Pandion, P. V. *A Memorial, on Behalf of the Nadar Community to J. C. Molony, Esq., I.C.S., Superintendent of Census Operations, Madras, 1911.* Trichinopoly: Southern Star Press, 1910.

Pascoe, C. F. *Two Hundred Years of the S.P.G.: An Historical Ac-*

count of the Society for the Propagation of the Gospel in Foreign Parts, *1701–1900*. London: S.P.G., 1901.

Pate, H. R. *Madras District Gazetteers: Tinnevelly*. Madras: Government Press, 1917.

Paul, S. *Caste in the Tinnevelly Church*. Madras: S.P.C.K. Press, 1893.

Pettitt, George. *The Tinnevelly Mission of the Church Missionary Society*. London: Seeleys, 1851.

Playne, Somerset. *Southern India: Its History, People, Commerce, and Industrial Resources*. London: Foreign and Colonial Compiling and Publishing Co., 1914–1915.

Ponniah, J. S. *et al. The Christian Community of Madura, Ramnad and Tinnevelly*. Research Studies in the Economic and Social Environment of the Indian Church. Madurai: American College, 1938.

Pye, Lucian W., and Sidney Verba (eds.). *Political Culture and Political Development*. Princeton: Princeton University Press, 1965.

Raghavaiyangar, S. Srinivasa. *Memorandum on the Progress of the Madras Presidency during the Last Forty Years of British Administration*. Madras: Government Press, 1893.

Raju, A. Sarada. *Economic Conditions in the Madras Presidency, 1800–1850*. Madras: University of Madras, 1941.

Ransom, C. W. *A City in Transition: Studies in the Social Life of Madras*. Madras: Christian Literature Society for India, 1938.

Rao, Raja Rama. *Ramnad Manual*. Madras: Government Press, 1889.

Report of the Madras Church Conference, February 24, 1876. Madras: Athenaeum and Darly News Office, 1876.

Report of the Madras Diocesan Committee of the S.P.G., 1877–78. Madras: Madras Diocesan Committee, 1878.

Rhenius, C. T. E. *Memoir of the Rev. C. T. E. Rhenius, Comprising Extracts from His Journal and Correspondence, by His Son*. London: James Nisbet & Co., 1841.

Richards, F. J. *Madras District Gazetteers: Salem*. Madras: Government Press, 1918.

Risley, Herbert. *The People of India*. London: Thacker, Spink & Co., 1915.

Robinson, William (ed.). *Ringeltaube, the Rishi: Letters and Journals*. Sheffield: Sheffield Independent Press, 1902.

Rudolph, Lloyd I., and Susanne H. *The Modernity of Tradition: Political Development in India*. Chicago: University of Chicago Press, 1967.

Sastri, K. A. N. *A History of South India*. Oxford: University Press, 1958.

Sattampillai, A. N., alias S. A. Nayaga Nadan. *A Brief Sketch of the*

Hindu Christian Dogma. Palamcottah: Shunmuga Vilasam Press, 1890.

Sharrock, J. A. *Bishop Caldwell, a Memoir.* Calcutta: Whitaway Press, 1896.

———. *Indian Problems: Caste.* Ramnad: S.P.G. Press, 1894.

———. *South Indian Missions.* London: S.P.G., 1910.

Sherring, M. A. *The History of Protestant Missions in India, from Their Commencement in 1706 to 1881.* London: The Religious Tract Society, 1884.

Slater, Gilbert. *Some South Indian Villages.* Madras: Oxford University Press, 1918.

Smith, Donald E. *India as a Secular State.* Princeton: Princeton University Press, 1963.

Srinivas, M. N. *Caste in Modern India and Other Essays.* Bombay: Asia Publishing House, 1962.

———. *India's Villages.* Calcutta: West Bengal Government Press, 1955.

———. *Religion and Society among the Coorgs of South India.* Oxford: University Press, 1952.

———. *Social Change in Modern India.* Berkeley: University of California Press, 1966.

Stuart, J. A. *A Manual of the Tinnevelly District.* Madras: Government Press, 1879.

Subrahmanyam, M. V. *A Study of Emigration in Relation to the Life of the Tinnevelly Church.* Research Series in the Economic and Social Environment of the Indian Church. Guntur: U.L.C.M. Press, 1938.

Sundkler, Bengt G. M. *Bantu Prophets in South Africa.* London: Lutterworth Press, 1948.

Thurston, Edgar. *Castes and Tribes of Southern India.* 7 vols. Madras: Government Press, 1909.

Tucker, Sarah. *South Indian Sketches.* London: James Nisbet & Co., 1848.

Weiner, Myron. *The Politics of Scarcity.* Chicago: University of Chicago Press, 1962.

Wyatt, J. L. (ed.). *Reminiscences of Bishop Caldwell.* Madras: Addison, 1894.

Venkataswami, T. *A Manual of the Tanjore District.* Madras: Government Press, 1883.

ARTICLES AND PERIODICALS

Baylis, F. "The South Travancore Tamil Missions," in *Proceedings of the South India Mission Conference, 1858.* Madras: S.P.C.K. Press, 1858.

Béteille, André. "A Note on the Referents of Caste," *Archives Européennes de Sociologie,* V (1964), 130–134.

Brookes, E. H. "Tribes of South India: Maravars and Kallars," *Madras Review,* V (November, 1899).

Brotherton, T. "Sketch of a Mission in Tinnevelly," *Mission Field,* XIII (June, 1868).

Caldwell, Robert. "Fifth Annual Letter to the Bishop of Madras, dated 1882," *India Churchman* (Calcutta), New Series, III (February 3, 1883).

———. "Native Education in Tinnevelly," *Mission Field,* V (September, 1860).

———. "Observations on the Kudumi," *Indian Antiquary* (1875).

———. "On Demonolatry in Southern India" (dated 1886), *Journal of the Anthropological Society of Bombay,* I (1901).

———. "Ten Years in Tinnevelly: a Missionary's Review," *Mission Field,* XVII (October, 1872).

Chetti, P. T. "The Non-Brahmin Manifesto," in T. Varadarajulu Naidu (ed.), *The Justice Movement: 1917.* Madras: Justice Printing Works, 1932.

Church Missionary Intelligencer (London).

Church Missionary Record (London).

Deutsch, Karl. "Social Mobilization and Political Development," *American Political Science Review,* LV (September, 1961).

Gough, Kathleen. "Criteria of Caste Ranking in South India," *Man in India,* XXXIX (1959).

Hardgrave, Robert L., Jr. "Caste and the Kerala Elections," *Economic Weekly,* April 17, 1965.

———. "Caste, Class, and Politics in Kerala," *Political Science Review* (University of Rajasthan), III (May, 1964).

———. "Caste in Kerala: a Preface to the Elections," *Economic Weekly,* November 21, 1964.

———. "The DMK and the Politics of Tamil Nationalism," *Pacific Affairs,* XXXVII (Winter, 1964–1965).

Harrison, Selig. "Caste and the Andhra Communists," *American Political Science Review,* L (June, 1956).

Hindu (Daily, Madras).

Huxtable, H. C. "The Mission of Sawyerpuram," *Mission Field*, I (September, 1856).

India (Weekly, London).

Indian Churchman (Calcutta).

Indian Church Quarterly Review.

Indian Express (Madurai).

Lukas, J. Anthony. "Political Python of India," *New York Times Magazine*, February 20, 1966.

Madras Diocesan Record.

Madras Mail (Madras).

Mani, L. S. "A Golden Age," in *Sri K. Kamaraj 60th Birthday Commemoration Volume.* Madras: Sri Kamaraj 60th Birthday Commemoration Committee, 1962.

Margöschis, Arthur. "Christianity and Caste," *Indian Church Quarterly Review*, VI (October, 1893).

――――. "Tinnevelly: Being an Account of the District, the People, and the Missions," *Mission Field*, XLII (October, 1897).

Marriott, McKim. "Interactional and Attributional Theories of Caste Ranking," *Man in India*, XXX (April–June, 1959).

――――. "Little Communities in an Indigenous Civilization," in *Village India.* Chicago: University of Chicago Press, 1955.

――――. "Social Structure and Change in a U. P. Village," in M. N. Strinivas (ed.), *India's Villages.* Calcutta: West Bengal Government Press, 1955.

Mateer, Samuel. "The Pariah Caste in Travancore," *Journal of the Royal Asiatic Society*, New Series, XVI (1884).

Meadows, R. R. "Our Home in the Wilderness: Recollections of North Tinnevelly," *Church Missionary Gleaner* (London), VI (April, 1879).

Miller, Eric J. "Caste and Territory in Malabar," *American Anthropologist*, LVI (June, 1954).

Mission Field (London).

Missionary Herald (Boston), "The Anti-Shanar Riots," XCVIII (1902).

――――. "Remarks on the Province of Tinnevelly," XXI (1825).

Missionary Magazine and Chronicle (London).

Moodaliar, A. Raja Bahadur. "The Manners and Customs of Some of the Castes of the Madras Presidency," *Madras Review*, VI (February, 1900).

Narasimhan, V. K. "Kamaraj—the Party President," *Forum Service* (London), No. 710 (May 2, 1964).

Neale, Walter C. "Reciprocity and Redistribution in the Indian Village: Sequel to Some Notable Discussions," in Karl Polyani (ed.), *Trade and Market in the Early Empires*. Glencoe: Free Press, 1957.

Pettitt, George. "The Tinnevelly Mission," *Madras Quarterly Missionary Journal*, New Series, II (October, 1851).

Ponniah, J. S. "Human Geography of the Ramnad District," *Journal of the Madras Geographical Association*, VII (1932–1933).

Pope, G. U. "Missions of the Church in Tinnevelly," Pt. IV, *The Colonial Church Chronicle*, III (June, 1850).

Rudolph, Lloyd I. "The Modernity of Tradition: The Democratic Incarnation of Caste in India," *American Political Science Review*, LIX December, 1965).

———. "Urban Life and Populist Radicalism: Dravidian Politics in Madras," *Journal of Asian Studies*, XX (May, 1961).

Rudolph, Lloyd I., and Susanne H. "The Political Role of India's Caste Associations," *Pacific Affairs*, XXXIII (March, 1960).

———. "Barristers and Brahmins in India: Legal Cultures and Social Change," *Comparative Studies in Society and History*, VIII (October, 1965).

Sharrock, J. A. "Caste and Christianity," *Indian Church Quarterly Review*, VI (January, 1893)

———. "Caste and Christianity," *Indian Church Quarterly Review*, VII (January, 1894).

———. "Caste and Christianity—II," *Indian Church Quarterly Review*, VII (April, 1894).

Singer, Milton. "The Social Organization of Indian Civilization," *Diogenes*, XLV (Spring, 1964).

Somasundaram, N. "V. V. R., a Versatile Genius," in *V. V. Ramasami Paaraattu Malar*. Virudhunagar: V. H. N. Senthikumara Nadar College Old Boys' Assn., 1964.

Srinivas, M. N. "Profile of a Southern State—Mysore," *Economic Weekly*, July 21, 1956.

Thangarajan, P. "History of the College," in *V. V. Ramasami Paaraattu Malar*. Virudhunagar: V. H. N. Senthikumara Nadar College Old Boys' Assn., 1964.

Thapar, Romesh. "Caste and the Future: the Problem," *Seminar*, No. 70 (June, 1965).

Yeshwant, T. T. "Rural Migration—A Case Study in Four Ramnathapuram Villages," *Agricultural Situation in India* (September, 1962).

COURT CASES

Additional Sessions Court, Tinnevelly. C. C. No. 39 of 1899 (F. D. P. Oldfield, presiding). Citation incomplete.

Kamudi Looting Case. Records of the Preliminary Enquiry in Connection with the Kamudi Looting Case, First Batch, Pt. I., R. O. No. XX of 1918. On the file of the Special 1st Class Magistrate of Ramnad at Madura. Order of Commitment.

Mariappa Nadan v. *Valthilinga Mudaliar.* 1913 Madras Weekly Notes 247.

S. A. Muthu Nadar et al. v. *K. Hussain Rowther et al.* In the High Court of Judicature at Madras. Appeal, No. 570 of 1950. November 19, 1954.

Gnanadoraisami Nadar et al. v. *S. P. Sivasubramania Nadar et al.* In the Court of the Subordinate Judge, Tinnevelly. Original Suit No. 13 of 1942. Judgment.

Sankaralinga Nadan et al. v. *Rajeswara Dorai et al.* On Appeal from the High Court of Judicature at Madras. Privy Council. Reported in Indian Law Reports 31 Madras 236 (1908) and in 35 Indian Appeals 176 (1908).

Sankaralinga Nadan et al., v. *Rajeswara Dorai et al.* In the High Court of Judicature at Madras, February 14, 1902. Appeal No. 11 of 1900 and Appeal No. 77 of 1900.

Kattalai Michael Pillai v. *J. M. Barthe.* All India Reports 1917 Madras 431.

Plessy v. *Ferguson.* 163 U. S. 537 (1896).

Rajah M. Bhaskara Sethupathi v. *Irulappan Nadan.* In the Subordinate Judge's Court of Madura (East), February 6, 1899. Record of Proceedings.

Rajah M. Bhaskara Sethupathi v. *Irulappan Nadan.* In the Subordinate Court of Madura East, 20 July 1899. T. Varada Rao, Subordinate Judge. Original Suit No. 33 of 1899. Judgment.

Thirugnanapal, alias Vaikunta Nadan v. *Ponnammai Nadathi and 88 Others.* In the Court of the Subordinate Judge of Tuticorin. Original Suit No. 48 of 1911; Appeal No. 185 of 1913, High Court of Judicature, Madras; Privy Council, Appeal No. 106 of 1918; Judgment of the Lords of the Judicial Committee of the Privy Council, delivered, June 8, 1920.

UNPUBLISHED MATERIAL

Bailey, F. G. "Caste and Politics in India." (Mimeographed.)

Dakshina Mara Nadar Sangam. Correspondence and files. Tirunelveli.

Dakshina Mara Nadar Sangam. "Special Features of the Nadar Community." Manuscript.

Devapackiam, Mary. "The History of the Early Christian Settlements in Tinnevelly District." Unpublished Master's dissertation, Department of Tamil, University of Madras, 1963.

Devasugnayom, Dr. A. "The Nattatti Nadars." Manuscript. Madras, June, 1965.

Elliott, Carolyn. "Caste and Faction in Andhra Pradesh." Unpublished Ph.D. dissertation, Department of Government, Harvard University, 1967.

Irschick, Eugene F. "Politics and Social Conflict in South India: The Non-Brahmin Movement and Tamil Separatism, 1916 to 1929." Unpublished Ph.D. dissertation, Department of History, University of Chicago, 1964.

Jayaraj, E. M. "The Nadars." Manuscript.

London Missionary Society. Manuscript Collections. London.

Madras State Palmgur Co-Operative Federation. "A Note on Palmgur and Palm Products Industries in Madras State." Manuscript.

Nadar, A. V. Arunagiri. Diary in Tamil. Manuscript. Dated Sivakasi, 1899.

Nadar Mahajana Sangam. "Memorandum to the Simon Commission." Manuscript.

Nadar Mahajana Sangam. Correspondence and files. Madurai.

Raj, Hilda. "Persistence of Caste in South India—An Analytical Study of the Hindu and Christian Nadars." Unpublished Ph.D. dissertation, Department of Sociology, American University, 1958.

Sangammal, Smt. Prepared statement, Sivakasi, July, 1965.

Society for the Propagation of the Gospel. Manuscript Collections. London.

Swamidoss, Raj Kumar. "The Nadars." Manuscript. New Delhi, October, 1964.

Tangasami, L. S. "The Nadars." Manuscript. Tirunelveli.

Turnbull, Thomas. "Statistical and Geographical Memoir, Maravar or Ramnad, the Isle of Ramiseram and Tondiaman's Country, surveyed in 1814." Fort St. George, Surveyor General's Office, 1817. Manuscript. India Office Library, London.

Western, F. J. "The Early History of the Tinnevelly Church" [c. 1950]. (Mimeographed.)

OTHER SOURCES

Personal interviews conducted in the field with approximately one hundred Nadars.

INDEX

Adityan, S. B., 233; business career, 149, 235n; campaigns for Assembly, 209, 210-211, 213-214, 242; political leadership, 212, 213, 219; encouragement of caste parties, 217-218; forms "We Tamils" 218, 235-236n; becomes Assembly speaker, 219

Adityan, S. T., 149; N.M.S. leadership, 191; political leadership, 206, 207, 211, 213; political career and elected offices, 208, 209, 211, 219

Adityan, Subramania, 208, 209

Adityan family, 30, 149

Agamudiars, 218

Agestheswaram, relations between Nadars and Nadans, 56, 62

Agriculture, 18, 150, 244; Nadar, 53-54, 125, 135, 252; trade in, 95; Sivakasi, 185

Alagappa Nadan, 51

Alagulam constituency, 212

Amada, Nadar legend about, 79-80n

Ambalakaran, 101, 103; defined, 100

Ambasamudram (taluq), 34; Nadars, 33, 96, 21

Ambattans (barber caste): caste rank, 3-4, 23; Nadars not allowed to use, 24; relationship to Nadar barbers, 34

American Madura Mission, 80

Anglican Church: missionary efforts, 43-51; acceptance of caste, 92-93. See also Missionaries; specific missionary societies

Annadurai, C. N., forms D.M.K., 195-196

Arcot Districts, 218

Arumanayagum. See Sattampillai

Arumugam Nadar, 194

Arumuganeri (village): Nadars, 132; Nadans, leadership, 167, 207; salt satyagraha riot, 207

Arunachalam of Kumbakonam, *Tala Villasam*, cited, 25

Aruppukottai (town), Ramnad District: Nadar traders settle in, 97, 98; in *1814*, 98; *uravinmurai*, 102,

Madurai branch of, 105; branch *pettai* in Madurai, 104; Nadar school, 106; conflict between Nadars and Maravars, 109; growth, 130; Maravars, 183

Aruppukottai Assembly and Parliamentary Constituency, elections, 224-225, 226, 227-228

Aruppukottai Nadar Education Association, 85n

Aryans, 7, 179; Nadar "descent" from, 79, 86-87, 126

Asithambi, A. V. P., election, 236, 237

Ayya Nadar, E., 116

Ayya Nadar, P., 190, 229; business success, 150-151

Ayya Nadar Janakiamal College, founded, 146

Backward Classes Commission, listing of Nadars for, 141-145, 169

Bailey, F. G.: quoted, 6, 9, 11; cited, 6

Balaguruswami Nadar, V., quoted, 158

Barbers, Nadar, functions and rank, 34-35, 100, 101, 172. See also Ambattans

Beals, Alan, quoted, 5

Besant, Annie, 180

Bhadrakali (Mariamman, Kaliamman), as Nadar deity, 19, 38, 242, 252. See also Priests

Bhaktavatsalem, M. (candidate), 215, 243

Boag, G. T., as census superintendent, 134-136, 191, 193

Bose, Subhas Chandra, 183, 223

Brahmins, 155; rank, 3, 6, 7-8, 22; number, 22; opposition to Christianity, 50; Nambudiri, signs of respect to, 57, 59; honor Tamil rulers, 86-87; attend Nadar school, 106n; customs and symbols of caste rank, 107, 108, 112-113; sue Nadars for entering temple, 109;

Brahmins (*continued*)
role in Sivakasi riot, 115, 119;
pujaris, rights, 122; preside at
N.M.S. conferences, 174; political
power, 174, 175, 213, 230, 231; political movement against, 175, 180;
use of caste system, 179; relations
with Nadars, 246, 247, 248, 252.
See also Priests
Breast cloth: Nadars forbidden, 22,
57; controversy over, 59-70;
church-state conflict over, 61-69
British rule: effect on caste system,
10-11, 78-79; comes to southern
districts, 16; effect on Nadars, 42,
49, 87; religious toleration,
[Queen's proclamation on] 64-65,
67-68; Nadars support, 87, 180,
184-185, 188, 195, 206, 245, 261,
264 (*See also* Nadar Mahajana
Sangam); improvement of transportation facilities, 95-97 (*see also*
Railroad); responsiveness to
Nadars, 135-136, 181; Justice party
supports, 175; Nadar Congressmen
call for end of, 191, 192 (*see also*
Congress party; Independence
movement). *See also* India; Madras
(state)
Burma, Nadars from, 233

Caemmerer, A. F.: as head of Nazareth mission during schism, 72-
75; quoted, 74, 75
Cail (Kayal, city), 14
Caldwell, Robert, missionary and
Bishop of Tinnevelly: quoted, 15,
18, 19, 20, 21-22, 28, 37, 38, 48, 49,
50, 51, 52, 64, 95n, 200; theory of
Nadar origin, 20-21, 81; cited, 30;
analysis of Nadars in *Tinnevelly
Shanars*, quoted, 39, 40-41, 46-47,
54, 73, cited, 74, 81; establishes
mission in Tinnevelly, 41, 46, 47-
48; attacked for *Tinnevelly Shanars*, 73-75; later attacks on, 82-84
Calini, Father, quoted, 43
Carnactic territory: southern districts in, 15, 16, 28; ceded to British, 16
Caste: relation to Indian political
culture, 1-2, 202-204, 237-238; per-

sistence in modern times, 1, 199-
200; system attributes, 2-11; subdivisions, 2, 219 (*see also* Subcastes); associations, 8, formation
of, 10, function, 199-201, 203, 248;
Victoria's proclamation on protection of, 64-65; histories, function,
78-79, 90, 94, 123; and schools, 106;
Nadar attitudes toward, 119, 179-
180, 259 (*see also* Self-Respect
movement); in cities, 154, 171, 229,
232, 234; parties, 217-218. *See also*
Kshatriya status; Missionaries; Ritual purity hierarchy
Caste relations, Nadar: in parochial
society, 42; with Harijans, 58, 92,
178-179; antagonisms caused by
Nadar advancement, 113, 114, 119,
154, 171, 172, 182, 183, 244, 264;
N.M.S. efforts to improve, 154-
162; in integrated society, 154-155,
248; in differentiated society, 154-
155, 171-172, 251-252, 255, 257-
258, 260, 266; with other tapper
castes, 178. *See also* Ritual purity
hierarchy; specific castes
Census of India: 1891: cited, 35-36,
109, quoted on Nadars' caste position, 133; *1911:* cited, 109, listing
of Nadars in, 133, 135; *1921:*
Nadars name changed from *Shanar*
in, 133-136, 181, discontinues traditional caste occupation listing, 135-
136; *1961:* quoted and cited, 159
Ceylon, 74n, 236n; Nadars as emigrants from, 20-21, 86; Chola invasions, 21; plantations opened, 52-
53; Nadar migrant workers, 52-53,
168; Nadar association, 132
Chandra, Nadar "descent" from, 85,
89
Chantror, name for Nadars, 135
Character, Nadar: 39-40, 125, 127-
128, 147-148, 154
Chelaswamy, D. G., 210
Chellapandian, S., political career,
212, 215, 216, 217, 220
Chellasamy, S., biographical note,
236n
Chelmsford, Lord (viceroy of India,
1918), 173. *See also* Montagu,
Edwin

Chenthinatha Iyer, S., *Shanars Not Kshatriyas*, 83, attacked, 83-84

Chera dynasty, 12, 14; Nadar claim to descent from, 33, 85, 126

Chetties, Chettiars (merchant caste), 131; Nadars claim to be, 106; relations with Nadars, 171, 246, 252, 260; Madras City, 233, 234

Chidambara Nadar, P. C., unites N.M.S., 194

Chidambaram (town), South Arcot District, Nadars in, 124

Chingleput District, Gramanis, 169

Chitty, S. C., *Ceylon Gazeteer*, cited, 35

Chola kingdom: dynasty, 12, 14, Nadar "descent" from, 126, 134; Nadar origins in, 20, 21, 33

Christianagram (village), Tinnevelly District, 45

Christian Nadars, 134n, 213; Nattatti, 33, 168; recognition of *kuttam*, 36; conversion, 43-51, 58; temporal advantages, 47-54, 57, 59, 61, 67, 142, 148; aspirations to higher caste status, 49, 59, 71-72, 78, 85, 94 (*see also* Breast cloth); education, 51-52, 145, 170, 265-266 (*see also* Education; Schools, mission); unity and village political structure, 54-55, 59, 69-70, 99; numerical dominance in churches, 55-56, 83; relations with other castes, 57 (*See* Breast cloth); relations with Hindu Nadars, 69-70, 90-91, 170-171, 233; caste sensitivity and Tinnevelly schism over, 72-78, 79, 82-83; strong caste feelings, 79, 90-94; spared in Sivaskasi, 117; professionals and government servants, 142, 152, 229, 266; government benefits, 143-145; in N.M.S., 164; loyalty to British, 174, 185; relations with Christians of other castes, 233-234

Church Missionary Society (C.M.S.), in Tinnevelley District, 45, 46, 47, 76, 145

Cities: Nadar caste relations in, 154, 171-172, 229, 251-252, 255, 257-258, 260, 266; caste and politics, 237-238, Nadar, 257, 258. *See also*

Political culture, differentiated

Civil Disabilities Act. *See* Removal of Civil Disabilities Act

Climbers. *See* Ezhavas; Gramanis; Palmyra climbers; Tiyars; Toddy-tappers

Coconut palm, 18; tappers, 20, 35, 169. *See also* Ezhavas; Gramanis

Coffee: plantations, 52; sale by Nadars, 147, 149-150

Coimbatore District: Nadars, 106-107, 124; caste parties for, 218

Colleges: Nadar, 132, founded by N.M.S., 146-147; mission, 145, 207, effect on Nadars, 171

Communications facilities: effect on caste, 1, 8-10; effect on Nadars, 31-32, 128, 263

Communist party: Nadar support, 199, 230, 231-232, 240, 253, 260; Nadar candidates, 210, 212 (*see also* Tangamani)

Community consciousness, Nadar: lack of in parochial culture, 42, 128 (*see also*) Tinnevelly District); emergence of, 70, 78 (*see also* Christian Nadars); relation to Nadar advance, 128, 162; in integrated culture, 128-129 (*see also* Merchants; Ramnad District); effect of confrontations on, 129, 244; effect of caste associations on, 132, 154-157, 159, 161, 167-168, 177-178, 256, 262; between northern and southern Nadars, 169-170, 178; decline in, 171-172, 260; effect of political involvement on, 182, 183; effect of Kamaraj on, 190; present-day, 258-259; historical review of, 263-264

Congress party, 180; first ministry (Madras, *1937-1939*), 138, 188-190, 191, 195, 265; Kamaraj's career in, 153. (*See* Kamaraj); passes resolution for noncooperation, 174; agitation for Independence, 169, 194, 195, 207-208; boycotts British commission, 182; Maravars support, 183, 221, 223, 224-225, 228; Nadar support, 184-190, 195, 197, 199, 250, 260, 265, 266, in Tinnevelly District, 184-185, 206, 219-

Congress party (*continued*)
220, 243, in Ramnad, 220, 221, 224, 225, 228, 229, 237, 245-246, in Madurai City, 230, 231, 232, in Madras City 234-235, 236, 256-257; swarajist wing, 186, 190; Nadar opposition to, 186, 195-196, 249, 253, 257, 265, 266 (*see also* Justice party); social (caste) legislation, 188-190, 193, 194, 265; Nadars take control of N.M.S., 191-195; factions, 208, 215-217, 220, 223; Nadar candidates, in Tinnevelly, 208-220 *passim*, in Ramnad, 222, 224-229 *passim*, Madurai City, 230, Madras City, 236; Kosalram's control of Tinnevelly District, 211, 215-217, 220; loses to D.M.K., 218-219, 229, 232; Muthuramalinga's leadership against, 221, 223, 224-225; Madurai organization, Nadars in, 232. *See also* Tamil Nad Congress Committee

Cooperatives, Nadar: societies, 146; *See also* Nadar Bank; industries, 151; stores, 241

Cornelius Nadar, J. S., *Amarar Puranam*, cited, 85

Cornish, W. R., quoted, 78, 79

Corvée labor. *See* Taxation

Cotton: cultivation, 18; Nadar trade in, 97, 98, 150, 243, *uravinmurai*, 104; textile mills, Nadar factory-workers, 230, 250-251

Cotton G. E. L., Bishop of Calcutta, quoted, 55, 79

Courts: Nadars forbidden entry to, 22; Nadar, 101-102; cases on Nadar social disabilities, 81n, 109-110, 118, 120-128, 142, 155, 189, 222, 244, establishing D.M.N.S., 166, by Nadars against Muthuramalinga, 223

Cox, John, 63

Cullen, General W.: in breast-cloth controversy, 61-63, 66-67, 69; quoted, 64; cited, 66; as British resident of Travancore, 68, 69

Dakshina Mara Nadar Sangam (D.M.N.S.), 207, 242; lobbies for climbers, 138-140; concern with

Nadars' backward class status, 142, 144; origin and organization, 164-166; lack of communal services, 167; conferences, 167, 211; support of British, 184; political use of, 211, 217

Dakshina Mara Nadu Nadars Sabha, 165-166

David, A., 71-72; quoted, 71-72

De Nobili, Robert, 91

Deutsch, Karl, cited, 204

Devasugnayom, Dr. A., quoted, 168

Dina Thanthi (Nadar Tamil daily), 149, 211, 235n, 241, 252

Distilleries. *See* Jaggery

D.M.K. *See* Dravida Munnetra Kazhagam

Doraisami Nadar, V. S. K.: quoted, 143; biographical information, 152

Doraisamy Gramani, T. V.: *Research on the Word Nadar*, quoted and cited, 84-85; founds *Kshatriya Mitran*, 85

Dravida Kazhagam, 195, 249

Dravida Munnetra Kazhagam (D.M.K.), 197, 199; formed, 196; supported by Nadars, youth, 212, 228, 229, 230, 232, 234-235, 238, 240, 249, 253, 257, 266, Maravars, 212; Nadar candidates, 212, 236; political leadership, 213, 215; election victories (*1967*), 218-219, 229, 232, 235

Dravidian: culture and language, 10; Nadars as, 86-87, 89

Dress: as caste status mark, 4; Nadar: pre-missionary, 38, 46, 57, 59; Christian women, 60-62 (*see also* Breast cloth); Nadar, Sanskritized, 107-109, 112, including sacred thread and brahmin tuft, 108, 120, 121, 170, 179, 245

Drew W. H., quoted, 57

Dwijas, 7; defined, 108

East India Company, 16, 95, 98

Economic position of Nadars: early nineteenth century, 23-24, 38-42, 262-264; effect of missionaries on, 49, 51, 52, 55-59; benefit from opening of plantations, 52-53; increase in land ownership, 53-54;

differentiation within caste, 127, 128, 130-131n, 141-143, 154, 171, 172, 199, 260, 262, 266, effect on political culture, 205, 206, 262, within cities, 232-240 *passim*; improvement, 147-148, 255, 256, 259, effect on social position, 78, 90, 119, 127, 239, 262, 263
Economic system: of caste, 1, 4, 5-6, 7; relation of prosperity to rank, 1, 6-7, 9, 10, 203; effect of British rule on, 10, 52-53, 95-96; role of palmyra, 95, 138-140; of Six Towns, 105; Nadar response to changes in, 119; village, 263
Edeyengoody (Idaiyangudi), Nadars and Caldwell's mission at, 41, 46
Education: effect on caste solidarity, 1; illiteracy of Nadars, 40-41, 142; Nadars in, 51, 142, 152, 171, 266; effect on toddy-tapping production, 53; Nadar advancement through, 90, 127, 151-152, 262, 265-266; relation to caste feeling, 93, 128, 170, 171; N.M.S. efforts to improve, 132, 140-147, 178, 264; government concessions to Nadars for, 141-145; effect on Nadar politics, 207; of typical Nadars, 241, 245, 247, 251, 254-255. *See also* Colleges; Schools
Eetchan Shanars, 35
Emanuel (Harijan leader), murder of, 226-227
Ezhavas (tapper caste), relation to Nadars, 20, 81n, 178

Factory workers, Nadar, 230, 234, 250, 251, support Communist party, 231, 232, 253, 260; Maravar and Kallar, 250, 251-252
Fireworks industry, 150
Forward Bloc party. *See* Tamilnad Forward Bloc party

Ganagasabai Nadar, 164
Ganapathy, T.: political offices and campaigns, 208, 209, 211, 214, 217, 219; Nadar party of, 217-218
Gandhi, Mohandas Karamchand, 150, 190; and Harijans, 23, 188; efforts for Independence, 174,

187, 191; Nadar support of, 184, 206, 207
Ganesan, S.: biographical information on, 151-152; quoted, 172
Gangaram Durairaj, V. P. R.: identified, 194; leadership, 230, 232
Gnanamuthoo Nadar, Y., 83; *Shanars are Kshatriyas*, quoted, 84
Gnanamuthu, Alexander, quoted, 140
Gough, Kathleen, quoted, 5
Gounders, of Coimbatore, 218
Government of India Act (Reforms Act; *1919*), 174, 175, 181-182
Government servants; civil service: Nadars, 142, 152, 180-181, 233; Christian Nadar, 229; Nadar clerks, 239
Gramani Kulam, 169
Gramani Kula Mahajana Sangam, 169
Gramanis (toddy-tapping caste): relation to Nadars, 85, 169, 178; as backward class, 143, 144

Hammick, M., report on Sivaskasi riot, quoted and cited, 118
Harijans (Untouchables): rank, 3, 6, 7-8, 214n; named by Gandhi, 23; right to temple entry, 153 (*see* Temple entry); Soundra pandivans work for, 178-179, represented by N.M.S., 161; support Congress, 187; political strength, 212, 213; advancement, 221; Ramnad Maravar control of, 221-222, political, 224, 225-228; rioting between Maravars and, 226-227
Hindu, 249, 256; review of Sivakasi riot, 118, quoted, 119
Hindu Church of Lord Jesus, 75-78, 79, 89-90
Hindu Nadar Mahajana Sabha, Rangoon, 132
Hindu Nadars: religion, 22, 36-38, 255; unity, organization, 54, 99 (*see also* Community consciousness; Ramnad, Six Town Nadars; Nadar Mahajana Sangam); adopt breast cloth, 62-63; social aspirations, 67, 78, 119, 127 (*see also* Kshatriya status; Sanskritization;

Hindu Nadars (*continued*)
Temple entry); influence of missions, 70; educational concessions to, 143; relations with Christian Nadars, 170-171 (*see also* Christian Nadars); support British, 185 (*see also* British rule); *See also* Merchants; Nadans
Home Rule movement, 174, 175, 180
Hough, James (C.M.S. missionary), quoted, 45
Huxtable, H.C., 71; quoted, 72

Independence Movement, Nadars in, 191, 192, 194, 207, 217, 257. *See also* Quit-India movement
Indhia Kshatriyakula Nadar Mahajana Sangam (Ceylon), 132
India, quoted, 119
India, government of (British raj): accedes to Nadar wishes on caste name, 135-136, 169, (*see also* Census; Backward Classes Commission); dyarchy system started, 173 (*see also* Madras Legislative Council); caretaker government (*1939*), 191
India, Republic of: prohibition, 138-140; General Elections, N.M.S. interest in, 196-197; Nadar attitudes toward, 242, 245, 249, 252-253, 258
Indian Express, 249
Indian National Congress, *see* Congress Party
Industry, Nadar, 150-151
Irulappan Nadan, in Kamudi case, 81n
Irwin, Lord, governor-general of India, 182
Ismail, Mohammed, 213

Jaggery, 241; production process, 24, 26; arrack made from, 26, 131n; cakes, 26, as medium of exchange, 95; increased price and demand, 52, 130n, 140; traders, 130-131n; for distilleries and sugar factories, 246; production, effect of campaign and prohibition against hard toddy on, 137-140

Jayaraj Nadar, biographical information on, 148
Justice party (South Indian Liberal Federation), 240, 259; formation and rule, 174-175, 264; wins Nadar support, 176-180, 184, 188, 195, 196, 220, 221, 222, 247, 256, 265; and Self-Respect movement, 179, 180; Nadars opposed to, 184-186, 206 (*see also* Congress party); Vellalas support, 185, 265; decline, 187, 188, 189, 249; Vellala leadership, 188; leadership of N.M.S. challenged, 191-195; present influence in N.M.S., 198

Kalla Shanars (Pulukkas; Servais; Nadar subcaste), 168; identified, 34, 169; resistance to Christianity, 48, 50; in modern times, 169
Kallars, 115, 218, 250
Kalugumalai (village), Tinnevelly District, riot over Nadar procession, 111, 113
Kalyana-Shanars, 3ı
Karmaraj Nadar, K.: Congress leadership, 147, 208, 214, 215-217, 218n, 219, 235; biographical information on, 152-154, 186; effect on Nadars, 154, 162, 190, 195, 230, 237, 243, 259, 260, 265; political career, 186-188, 197, 259, 265; Muthuramalinga against, 223, 224; defeat, 229, 235; relation to N.M.S., 237; as Nadar politician, 246, 250, 265
Kamudi (town), Ramnad District: Court case on Nadar entry of Meenakshi Sundareswara (Siva) temple, 81n, 118, 120-128, 155, 189, 222, 244, 264; Nadar merchants settle, 97; described (*1814*), 98; *uravinmurai*, 103-104, 222, 223-224, 245; *kuttams*, 103; Nadar school, 106, 245; Nadar merchants relations with other castes, 120, 121; Nadar-Maravar riots and punitive tax (*1918*), 155-157, 178, 222; Maravars, 183; Maravar-Nadar social and political conflicts, 221, 222-223, 244, 246; Nadar political alignments, 238, 245-246; life history of typical mer-

chant from, 240, 243-246, 260; Nadar caste consciousness, 244

Kanyakumari District: political history, 12, 14, 17; geography, 18; palmyra season, 25n; Nadars, 56; breast-cloth controversy, 59-70; Nadar College founded, 147; Nadar association, 165 (*see* Dakshina Mara Nadar Sangam); lack of *uravinmurai*, unity, 167; Nadar political culture, 205; politics, 217, 218

Karukku-pattayars (Karukkumattaiyans; Karukkupattaiyans; Manattans; Mara Nadars), 32-33, 36

Kasinatha Dorai, R., candidacies, 225, 226, 228

Kattaboma Nayaka, 16, 33

Kaval system. *See* Villages

Kearns, Rev. J. F., 74-75, 78; quoted, 40, 49

Kerala, 17, 18, 178

Kodikkal (Nadar subcaste) 34

Konars (caste), 161, 224

Konga-Shanars, 35

Korkai (Kolkhoi city), Tinnevelly District, 12

Kosalram, K. T.: identified, 170; quoted, 171; political activities and leadership, 207-217, 219

Krishnamachari, T. T., election, 209, 214-215

Krishnaswami Naidu, P., 215, 229

Kshatriya Mahajana Sangam, 130

Kshatriya Mitran, 85

Kshatriya status: defined, 7; rising castes aspire to, 8; Nadars claim through descent, 80-90 *passim*, 94, 106-110, 113, 123, 252, 262, 263; courts disallow, 125-129; attributes, Nadars adopt, 108 (*see* Dress; Sanskritization); Nadars seek government recognition of, 133-136; right to temple entry, 122, Nadar attempt to claim, 264 (*see* Temple entry

Kudu Nadars. *See*-Mel-natars

Kulasekararaj, Eber, 208, 209

Kulasehara-Raj, B. J. M.; quoted, 74n; identified, 77

Kumbakonan (town), Nadars admitted to temple, 124

Kuttam (Nadan village): Nadans, 30, 41, 44; opposition to Christianity, 51

Kuttams, 36-37, 103

Landowners: power, 9; Vellala, 28, 56; control over Nadars, 28, 57, 159; Nadar, 53, 58, 127, 141 (*see also* Nadans); Nair, 56, 57, 64

Lawyers, Nadar, 142, 152, 171, 235-236n

Legislative Assembly. *See Madras* (state)

Litho printing, Sivakasi, 150-151

London Missionary Society, 45, in Travancore, 47, effect on Nadars, 55-59, and breast-cloth controversy, 59-70. *See also* Ringeltaube

Madras (city), 131; Nadars migrate to, 130, 233-234, 266; Nadars in, 148, 154, 170; *Dina Thanthi*, 149; Nadar political culture and power, 205, 206, 232, 234, 238; Nadar elected officials, 236

Madras (State; Madras Presidency; Tamilnad): political history, 12-17; geography, 17-19; British governor, 118, 173; High Court of Judicature, decision on Kamudi case, 126-127; British government of, 63; response to breast-cloth controversy, 63, 68, 69 (*see also* Trevelyan); relation to Travancore government, 68; actions in Sivakasi riot, 114, 115, 117-118, 119; first Congress ministry (1937-1939), 138, 191, 265, prohibition laws, 138-140, social legislation, 188-190; Assembly, 208, 215; Parliament, Muthuramalinga's elections to, 224-225, 227-228, Kamaraj's election, 224n; use of "Shanars," 143 (*see also* Backward Classes Commission)

Madras Legislative Assembly, 197; Tinnevelly Nadars elected to, 208-220 *passim*, 237; control of, 218-219; Ramad elections to, 222-223, 224-225, 229

Madras Legislative Council (upper
house, Madras legislature), 197;
Nadar elected to, 210, 211
Madras Legislative Council (under
dyarchy): lack of Nadars in, 131;
started, 173; Gandhi, Congress
boycott, 174; Nadar representation on, 175-177, 181; Nadars inability to elect member to, 176,
182-183; Congress position on,
186, 187; Kamaraj elected to, 187-
188
Madras Bar Association, 236n
Madras Mail: quoted, 117, 126, 137;
coverage of Sivakasi riot, 119
Madurai (city), 150; Pandyan rule
from, 14, 15, 87; Nadars, 46, 141,
170, migrate to, 104-105, 130, 266,
branch *uravinmurai* in, 104-105,
233, *pettais* in, 104, 166; N.M.S.
headquarters in, 131-132, 163-164;
Nadar college founded at, 146-147;
uravinmurai of, 147n; Council,
Nadars on, 181, 230; politics, 197,
214n, 230-232; Nadar political
strength and culture, 205, 206,
230-232, 237-238; mills and factories, 230, 250-251; Brahmins, 230,
231, 246, 247, 248; Maravars and
other castes, political behavior,
230-232, 250; life history of typical
Nadars in, 246-253; Meenakshi
temple, 250, Nadar entry case, 109
110, opened, 189
Madura Mills, 250, 251, 252, 253
Madurai District: political history,
12, 16; Nadar origins in, 20; Nadars,
35, 162; "Kshatriyas," 109; marauders in Sivakasi riots, 115; Subordinate Judge, decision on Kamudi
case, 126; relation between Christian and Hindu Nadars, 170; elections for Legislative Council, 176;
Board, 177, 181; political alignments, 183-184. *See also* Ramnad,
Six Town Nadars
Madurai (Urban) District Congress
Committee, Nadars on, 232
Madurai Rice and Oil Mill Owners
Association, 230
Mahajanam (newspaper), 164;
quoted, 196

Mahimai, 172, 178, 248; defined, 99;
council controlling, 99, 100 (*see
also Uravinmurai*); uses of, 105-
106, 112, 145, 158, 165, 192; disputes over, 158
Malaya, 236n; Nadars emigrate to,
52, 168; Nadar association, 132-
133; Nadars leave, 233; Ramasami
Nadar's success in, 235n
Manattans, Mara Nadars. *See* Karukku-pattayars
Marameris. *See* Palmyra climbers
Maravar Mahajana Sabha, 157
Maravars (caste): poligars and *kaval* system, 15-16, 159; caste rank
compared with Nadars, 23, 123,
126; animosity toward Nadars, 23,
155, 220, 248, economic and social
causes, 98-99, 109-113, 119, 221,
222 political effects, 184, 214, 220-
228; land ownership, 28; Nadars
migrate into region of, 96-99;
hired by Nadars, 108; hostilities
between Nadars and, 110, 114-
119, 155-157, 160-161, 221-223;
leaders, 120, 183-184, 221, 222,
228 (*see also* Muthuramalinga
Thevar; Vellasami Thevar); boycott Nadars, 121; effect of Kamudi
case on, 125-26; represented by
N.M.S., 161; emulation of Nadars,
162; political alignment, 183-184,
187, 212, 213, 214, 218, 228 (*see
also* Tamilnad Forward Bloc);
candidates, 215, 216, Nadar support of, 237; voting strength, 224;
present-day Nadar attitudes toward, 244, 248, 252, 256, 260; laborers, 250, 252
Margöschis, Arthur, quoted, 47, 73,
94
Marriage: forbidden between castes,
2; forbidden to Hindu Nadar
widows, 22, 107, 170, 179; between
Nadans and other Nadars, 31, 36;
between Nadar and Ambattan
barbers, 34; within and between
Nadar *kuttams*, 36, 37; Hindu
laws on, 77; between Christian and
Hindu Nadars, 91; banns, use of
caste title, 93, 94; between Nadar
merchants and climbers, 106, 170;

Sanskritization of Nadar, 108, 179-180, 245; among Nattattis and other Nadars, 168; between Nadars and Gramanis, 169; Self-Respect, 179-180, 245, 247, 255; in integrated castes, 204; between Tinnevelly and Ramnad Nadars, 233

Marriott, McKim: cited, 3; quoted, 6-7

Match industry, 150-151, 185

Mayandi Nadar, M., election campaigns, 234-235, 237

Mayer, Adrian, quoted, 2

Mead, Charles: quoted, 56, 58, 61; stand on breast-cloth controversy, 60, 61. *See also* South Travancore Mission

Megnanapuram (village), Tinnevelly District, 45.

Mel-natars (Kudu Nadars; Menattans; Nadar subcaste), identified, 33

Merchants and traders, Nadar, 24, 53, 54, 124, 135; social aspirations, 58, 78, 169-170 (*see also* Hindu Nadars); itinerant traders, 95-97, 165, 243, *pettais*, 97, 99, 104, migration of, 97 263 (*see also* Ramnad, Six Town Nadars), migrate from, 104-105, relation to Nadar merchants, 106, wealth from demand for jaggery, 130-131n; illiteracy, 100; attempt to disassociate from climbers, 106, 124, 126, 133, 135-136, 140 230; wealth and power, 125, 127, 222 (*see also* Economic position of Nadars); dominance in N.M.S., 132, 184; reputation, 147-148, 154; individual successes as, 148-151; political behavior, 174, 194-195, 245, 260; in Madurai, 229, 230, 231; in Madras, 233, 235; typical life histories, 243-250; history of, summarized, 263-266. *See also* Ramnad Six Town Nadars.

Miller, Eric J., quoted, 9, 10-11

Missionaries: view of Nadars, 37-41, 43, 46, 57-58, 61; build villages, divide fields, 45-46; success with Nadars, 48-50, 195, 263; temporal aid, 49-50; effect on Nadar social and economic status, 54-59, 171, 263, 265-266 (*see also* Christian Nadars); Nadans oppose, 50-51; political authority, 54-55, 63; mission organization, 55; relation to government, 61-69 *passim*, reaction against, 72, 75, 76-77; attempts to deal with caste recognition rites, 92-94; educational efforts, 145 (*see* Colleges; Schools); Nadar merchants hostility toward, 170; political effect, 185, 206, 207

Molony, J. C. (census superintendent), quoted, 109, 133

Moneylenders, Nadar, 33, 97, 98, 113, 119, 125, 222, 263

Montagu, Edwin, 173;-Chelmsford reforms, 173-175

Moses, Minor, elected mayor, 236

M.S.P. family, 149, 196. *See also* Nadar; Rajah; Senthikumara

Mudalur (village), Tinnevelly District: founded, 44; political structure, 54; mission, 76

Mudukulattur (taluq), Ramnad District; Nadar political behavior, 206, 223-224, 237, 238; culture and caste antagonisms, 221-228; Harijan-Maravar riots, 226-227, 231. *See also* Kamudi

Mudukulattur Assembly Constituency, elections, 224-225, 227-228

Munro, Col., 59

Muraikarars, defined, 100, 103

Muslims, 111, 186, 236; invasion of South India, 14; traders' rivalry with Nadars, 96, 114, 222; Nadars "become," 117; candidates, 208, 209, 213; political behavior, 213, 214, 224

Muthuramalinga Thevar, 231; as Maravar political boss, 183-184, 221, 222-228, 244, 246. *See also* Forward Bloc

Muthusami Nadar, P. R.; quoted, 147; success, 148; split with N.M.S., 191; speech to National Nadar Conference, 192; given control of N.M.S., 194; as N.M.S. general-secretary, 197, 198-199; leadership, 227, 232

Nadan (title): used by Christian Nadars, 93, 94; used by Ramnad merchants, 106
Nadans (Nadar landowners): origins, 20; land ownership, 28-29, 30-31, 53, 56, 241, 263; relationship with climbers, 28-32, 36, 41, 42, 210-211, 214, 219; hereditary tax collectors, 29; social and economic rank, 29-31; factionalism, 30-31, effect on Nadar development; 202, 203, 263; slaves of, 29, 34, 48; as subcaste, 33; literacy, 40-41; oppose missionaries, 44, 50-51, 72; allowed breast cloth, 62; customs, 108; political influence, 210-211, 213, 214
Nadar (title): etymology, 84; used by Ramnad traders, 106; census caste name changed to, 133-136
Nadar, M. S. P., 196
Nadar Bank, 146, 264; name changed to Tamilnad Mercantile Bank, 161
Nadar Kula Mitran, 85n; cited, 175-176
Nadar Mahajana Sangam (N.M.S.), 217, 230; objectives, 129, 131, 163, 262, quoted, 131, 132, 162, 163; founded, 130-132, 262; conferences, 131-132, 158, 162-163, 173, 193, 194, 196-199 *passim*, 248; membership, 131, 162-163, 164, 178, 184, 200, 247; support of British, 131, 134, 173-175, 176, 181, 191; educational efforts, 132, (*see* Education); mercantile orientation, 132, 140, 147, 151, 184; gets official caste name changed, 133-136, 143-145; memorial on census, quoted, 134-135; anti-toddy campaign, 136-138; work for climbers, 138-144; position on Nadars as backward class, 140-143; efforts to improve Nadar relations with other castes, 154, 157, 158-162, 264; work for Nadar solidarity, 157-158, 170, 172, 177-178 (*see also Uravinmurai*); touring agents, 157-158, 159, 164, 264; panchayat system, 158 (*see also* Panchayats); interest in casteless society, 161-162; recognition, 162, 167-168; or-

ganization, 162-163, 194; newspaper, 164; quoted, 196; recognition of Servais, 169; conference presidents, 174-175; work to have Nadars in Legislative Council, government, 175-177, 181-183; Soundrapandian's influence and position in, 177-178; involvement in politics, 177, 184, 185, 191, 195-199, 201, 237, 248, 265; memorandum to Simon Commission, quoted, 182, 183; politics divides, 185, 191-195; position on Nadar temple entry, 188, 189; Muthusami's role in, 191, 194, 197-199; reunified under Congress leadership, 194, 198, 199; Hinduism of, 198, 248; role and history summarized, 200-201, 205, 264; Nadar attitudes toward, 244, 248, 256, 259
Nadar Parpalana Sangam, 133
Nadars' National Association. *See* National Nadars' Association
Naddikals (Nadars of Sivakasi), 97-98
Nagercoil (town), Travancore District: mission, 63 (*see* South Travancore Mission); riots between Sudras and Nadars, 65-66
Naickers (caste): 23; land ownership, 28; animosity toward Nadar merchants, 98-99; voting strength and alignment, 187, 224; laborers, 234
Naidu, G. T., 197
Naidus (caste), 106n, 228, 230
Nairs (caste): dominance over Nadar tenants, 56-59 *passim*, 64; attack Nadars over breast-cloth issue, 60-66; anger against missionaries, 63-64
Nanguneri (taluq), Tinnevelly District, 18; Nadars, 33, 143, 169; missionaries, 46; emigration, 52; Nadar political behavior, 206, 212, 218, 219; Nadar candidates, 208, 211, 212
Narayanam, "Seerkatchi," 216-217
National Nadars Association (Nadars' National Association), 191-195, 265; conferences, 191-193, 194

Nattatti (village), Tinnevelly District, 33, 168
Nattattis, as Nadar subcaste, 33, 34, 168
Nayaks (Telugu rulers), 14-16, 29, 87-88
Nazareth (town), Tinnevelly District: Nadars, 44, 132; mission, schism caused by Sattampillai, 72-77, 79, 82, 89
Nehru, Jawaharlal, quoted, 154
Nellai Kumari Nadar Nala Urimai party, 217-218
Nellaimaikkarars (Nadans), 33
Newspapers and journals: caste, 10; Nadar, 85, 211; reaction to Sivakasi riot, 118-119; N.M.S., 164, 196; effect on rural Nadars, 241; read by Nadars, 249, 252, 256
Non-Cooperation movement, 181, 186; N.M.S. against, 137, 174, 191; Nadar support, 184

Occupation, traditional, effect on caste rank, 3-4, 5, 133
Occupations, Nadar: traditional, 23, 24, 144, 252, merchants attempt to disassociate from, 106 (see Merchants); listing dropped from census, 133, 135-136; subcastes, 33, 35 and n; differentiation in, 52-53, 124-125, 199, 252, 259, 260, 262, 266, social effect, 171, effect on political culture, 205, 206, 232, 234, 235, 238, 239, 262; of Christian Nadars, 142, 265-266; urban, 230. See also specific occupations
Origin of Nadars, 19-21, 32-35 passim, 56; myth of, 19-20, 32; Nadar histories and mythologies on, 78-90, 94

Palamcottah, Tinnevelly District, 16, 83; Nadars converted at, 44; missionary work at, 45; failure of seminary, 92; college, 145
Palayakars. See Poligars
Palaiyampatti (town), Ramnad District: Nadar traders settle in, 97, 98; uravinmurai, 100-103; pettai in

Madurai, 104; Nadar traders migrate from, 105; conflict between Nadars and Maravars, 109
Pallans (Pallars; untouchable caste): social status, 22, 23, 92, 126, 133, 244; slaves of Nadans, 29; support Maravars, 114, 115, 224. See also Harijans
Palmyra (palm): distribution, 18; Jaffna, 20; as basis of Nadar economy, 24, 95; location and cultivation, 24-28 (see also Tiruchendur); products, 24, 25-26, 28 (see also Jaggery; Toddy); myths, 25, 85, 86; ownership of, 27, 28-29, 30-31 (see also Nadans); production, lack of climbers for, 53; Nadar "history" on, 87; as symbol, 106, 140; industry, prohibition restrictions on, 138-140
Palmyra climbers (Panaiyeris; Nadar toddy-tappers): ritual impurity, 3, 22-23, 24, 122, 126 (see also Ritual purity hierarchy); origins, 20-21, and subcaste names, 32-36 passim; economic status, 24-25, 27-28, 31, 39-41, 57, 130n, 140-142, 210-211, 219, 252, 259; life and work, 24, 26-28, 240, 241-243, 259; conversion to Christianity, 48, reasons for, 48-50, 51; decline in number of, 52-54, 140, 259, 262; seasonal migration, 57; N.M.S. discourages hard-toddy production by, 137-138; sangams lobby for, 138-140; effect of prohibition on, 139-140; as backward class, 140-145; social and economic position among Nadars, 170, 171 (see Merchants; Nadans); votes solicited, 217-218; parochial social and political culture, 239
Panan Shanar (Pannematte Chanars), 35
Panchayats (committee of caste elders), 5, 103, 158, 241; function, 30, 155-156, 161, 264; elections, 223
Panchayat Union, 160, 243
Pandarams (Gurukkals; Aiyars; Nadar subcaste), 35, 112

Pandion, Rabbi P. V. (alias S. V. Nayaka Natar): identified, 77; *A Memorial* (caste history), quoted, 88, claim of Nadar origins, 89; *A Short Account of the Cantras*, 89; petitions for N.M.S. on Nadar caste name, 133

Pandyans: rule and fall, 12, 14, 15, 29, 87-88; Nadars in land of, 20, 33, 34; legends about palmyra, 25n; Nadar supposed descent from, 33, 35, 87-88, 89, 106, 182; kings, Nadan and Nadar alleged descent from, 80, 85, 134, 244-248, myths on, 88, disallowed, 126; Maravar alleged descent from, 248

Paraiyans (untouchable caste): status, 22, 23, 126, 133, 244; slaves, 29, 57; caste disabilities in Nadar villages, 92; pastors, status, 93; candidates, 210, 211. *See also* Harijans

Paramagudi (taluq): Nadar conflicts with other castes, 160-161; riots, 226

Paranjothy, G., quoted, 51

Pate, H. R., *Tinnevelly Gazeteer*: cited, 29n, 32, 33, 34; quoted, 52, 53-54, 90, 127-128

Patro, Sir A. P. D., 175

Peoples' Progressive party, 236n

Pettais: established by Nadar traders, 97, 99, 104; *mahimai* funds for, 99; Dakshina Mara Nadar, 165-166

Pettitt, George, quoted, 39, 49-50

Physicians, Nadar, 142, 152, 171; life history of typical, 254-258

Pillai, Vellala title, 22; used by Nadars, 106-107

Plantation estates, opening of, 10, 52-53

Poligars (palayakars), 15-16; Wars, 16, 87; Nadars under, 29, 41; duties, 96

Political culture: Nadar Christian village, 54-55, 263; factors affecting, 202; parochial, 202, 240, 241-243, Nadar (Tinnevelly), 42, 205, 206, 212, 219, 220, 238, 263; integrated, 202-203, 204, Nadar (Ramnad), 183-188, 205-206, 220-229,

237, 238; differentiated, 202, 203-204, 229-236, Nadar (Madurai and Madras City), 205, 206, 237-238, 257, 266; interaction between types, 205-206

Politics: relation to caste, 1-2, 182, 184-185, 212, 219-220, 237-238; Nadar strength, 129, 176, 178, 181, 183; Nadar successes in, 152-154 (*see also* Kamaraj); N.M.S. involvement in, 175-178, 180-184, 191-199, 201, 262, 265; involvement of Nadars in, 177, 181, 201, 203, 205-206, 207, 262; alignment of Nadars, 182-190, 237-238, 264-266; effect of Nadar inter-caste antagonisms on, 183-184, 206, 220-228, 237; Nadar attitudes, 194-195, 239-240; 242-243, 245-246, 247, 249-250, 253, 256-258, 260-261, 264-265, 266; candidates, 196-197, 208-236 *passim;* role of caste association in, 199, 200-201, 203, 237; "money," 214n, 219, 235, 242, 243, 245, 250, 260. *See also* British rule; specific parties

Pollution. *See* Ritual purity hierarchy

Ponnusami Nadar, V., 124, 131, 173

Ponnusamy Nadar, W. P. A., 173

Pope, G. U., quoted, 31

Pope, Henry, becomes missionary at Nazareth, 76; quoted, 76

Poraiyar (town), District: presidents of N.M.S., 130, 164; first N.M.S. conference in, 131

Poraiyar family, admitted to temple, 124 refuses to handle toddy, 138

Praja party (Praja Socialists), 208

Presidency College, Calcutta, 180

Priests: Nadar, 35, 112; for Mariamman temples, 38, 103-105 *passim*, 112; Brahmin (*purohits*), used by Nadars, 108, 113, 179-180, 245, 262

Privy Council, rules on Kamudi case, 120, 126, 264

Professionals, Nadar: Christian, 152, 266; social position, 171, 239, 254-255, 260, 266; Madras City, 233; political alignment, 236, 239, 255-258, 260

Prohibition Act, 144; effect on Nadars, 138-140, 169
Pulukkas. *See* Kalla Shanars
Punnuswamy Nadar, 219
Purohits. See Priests
Pye, Lucian, quoted, 239

Quit-India movement, 194, 207, 208, 265

Radhapuram constituency, elections, 219
Railroad: effect of, 104-105, 150; Nadar employees, 233
Rajagopalachari, C., 187; Congress ministry of, 138, 188, 265; legislation against caste disabilities, 188, 189, 265; Nadar division on, 191-193; presides at Nadars' National Association conference, 194; Swatantra party, 199, 249; Congress faction, 208, 223
Rajah, M. S. P., 196, 198; biographical information on, 149-150
Rajan, P. T., 176
Raja Palavasamuthu: in D.M.N.S., 144, 167; biographical information on, 167; political leadership, 207, 208, 210-211, 213
Rama, Lord, Nadar interpretation of, 38, 85
Ramamurthy, R., election, 232
Ramasami Nadar, O.: biographical note, famous sons-in-law, 235-236n
Ramasami Nadar, V. V., 247, 249, 255; biographical information on, 180; political career and Nadar leadership, 187-188, 195, 196, 197, 198, 221, 229; offices in N.M.S., 193, 194; address to N.M.S. conference, quoted, 193
Ramasamy, M. S., 198-199
Ramaswami Aiyar, Sir C. P., 174, 193
Ramaswami Naidu, S., election, 229
Ramaswamy Naicker, E. V.: starts Self-Respect movement, 179-180, 247; influence, 184, 199, 255; founding and control of Dravida Kazhagam, 195, 196, 249

Ramnad, rajas, zamindari of. *See* Sethupathi
Ramnad (taluq), *sangam* conference, 164
Ramnad District, 45, 109; political history, 12-17; geography, 17-18; Nadars, 21, 24, 36, 143, 162; palmyra tax, 138; effect of prohibition on climbers in, 139; tensions between Nadars and other castes, 154-157, 159-161 (*see also* Maravars); relations between Christian and Hindu Nadars, 170-171; Legislative Council elections (*1920*), 176; Nadar and Maravar political alignments, 183-184, 185, 195-197, 220-229, 264-265; Board, 187, Soundrapandian's presidency of, 177, 178-179, Nadars on, 181; Nadar political culture, 205-206 (*see also* Political culture); caste parties for, 218; political strength of Nadars, 221, 224; Nadars migrate to Madras City, 233, 234; history summarized, 263-266
Ramnad, Six Town Nadars (merchants of northern Tinnevelly, Ramnad and Madurai districts): identified, 97; traders start, 97-98; wealth, 97, 98, 107, 141-142 arouses higher castes, 98-99, 113, 114, widens gap in Nadar social and economic positions, 106, 107, 108, 109, 125, 127; community organization, 99-105, 128-129; emigrants from, 104-105, 167, 229; effect of railroads on, 105; community welfare programs, 105-106; Sanskritization and higher caste pretensions, 106-110, 125, reaction to, 109, 110, 112-114, 120, 121, 129, 155; need for larger organization, 130; influence in N.M.S., 132, 163, 164, 184; attitudes toward climbers, Christian Nadars, 140, 170-171; start schools, 145; political position, 176-177, 180, 183-184, 185-186; rivalries between towns, 185; history summarized, 263-264. *See also* Merchants
Ramnad-Madurai Chamber of Commerce, 230, 246

Rangoon, Nadar *sangam* in, 132, 254
Rattinasami Nadar, Rao Bahadur T.:
political ambitions, 130-131;
founds N.M.S., 131, 164; nominated to Legislative Council, 176
Rayappan (Indian pastor), 43-44
Reddiars (caste), 23, 98-99, 187, 212,
228
Removal of Civil Disabilities Act
(*1938*), 142, 189
Rhenius, Rev. Charles T. E.; quoted,
23-24, 39, 92, 93; missionary work,
92
Richards, F. J., *Salem Gazetteer*,
cited, 35
Ringeltaube, Rev. William T.:
quoted, 24, 35, 38-39; missionary
work, 45
Ritual purity hierarchy: polluting
occupations, 3-4; Nadars traditional rank (as half-polluting
caste), 3-4, 22-23, 48-49, 58, 71-72,
106, 113, 122-126, 133, 159, 262;
attributional rank distinctions, 3-4,
57, 59, of Dwijas, 7, 108; group
and individual mobility and interaction, 3, 4-12, 78, 203-204, 233;
erosion in urban areas, 4, effect
on Nadars, 154, 171, 260, 266; relation to economic status, 6-7, 171,
172, 203; structure, 21-23; Nadar
social disabilities under, 22, 24, 55,
56-57, 71, 142, 159 (*see also* Breast
cloth; Courts; Temple entry); Nadar caste attributes, 22, 133; Nadar
sensitivity on position in, 58, 71-
72, 74-76, 82-83, 91-94; preserved
by missionaries, 91-94; *See also*
Caste
Roman Catholics: Jesuit missionaries
and Nadar converts, 43, 47, 111;
acceptance of caste system, 91
Rudolph, Lloyd I. and Susanne H.:
quoted, 1, 201; cited, 200

Sachiapuram mission, 170
St. John's College, 145
Salem District, 106
Salt, 95. See also Satyagrahas
Sangams, founding of, 130-133; or-
ganized under N.M.S., 158; con-
ferences, 164

Sankarankovil (taluq): Nadars, 33;
politics, 212
Sanskritization: defined, 7; and varna
status, 7-8; vegetarianism, as characteristic of, 7, practiced by
Nadars, 22, 108, 109, 112, 247; of
Sudras, 8; purpose, 10, of Nadars,
90; by Vellalas, 23; customs and
symbolic dress of, Nadar adoption
of, 107-109, 112-113, 179 (*see also*
Dress; Ramnad Six Town Nadars);
role in converting Christian
women, 170; Nadars abandon, 179-
180, 245 (*see also* Self-Respect
movement); summary of Nadar
attempt, 262, 263-264
Santhosham, Dharmaraj, 227, 231,
236
Santhosham, Dr. M., 219, 236
Sargunar, Samuel: *Dravida Kshatriyas*, 80, 81, *Bishop Caldwell and
the Tinnevelly Shanars*, 82-83,
quoted, 81-82; imprisoned for
Chenthinathanukku Cheruppadi,
83-84
Sasivarna Thevar, 225, 227, 228, 231
Sattampillai, Rabbi (Arumanayagum), 208; causes Tinnevelly
schism, 72-76; pamphlet on Nadars,
74-75, 78; founds Hindu Church
of Lord Jesus, 76-77; efforts in
Kamudi temple-entry case, 123
Sattangulam assembly constituency,
elections, 208, 210-214 *passim*, 219
Sattankudi (town), Madurai District:
Nadar traders settle in, 97; *uravinmurai*, 102-103; Nadar leadership of Six Towns, 130
Sattur (taluq), 17; riot over Nadar
procession, 110; elections, 228
Sattur assembly constituency: Kamaraj elected from, 187-188; elections (*1967*), 229
Satyagrahas: Vaikom, 153, 186; salt,
187, 207-208
Satyamurthi, S., 256; Kamaraj pro-
tege of, 153, 186-187; political po-
sition, 186, 258
Satyanathan (catechist), 43-44
Saurashtra weavers, 230, 231
Sawyer (European merchant), 44, 45
Sawyerpuram (village and mission),

Tinnevelly District; founded, 45; schism, 71-72; seminary, 72; church, 92, 93

Schools: mission, 45, 55, 70, 145, 207, 240-241, Hindu Nadars attend, 51, 70; Nadar teachers, 51-52, destroyed, 61, 66, effect on Nadars, 152, 171; Nadar, 125, 132, 158, 163, 178, established in Six Towns, 105-106, Christian Nadars staff, 171, opened to Harijans, 179, in Madras City, 233; town, 146; village, 160

Scott (Tinnevelly collector and district magistrate), 116, 117, 119; quoted, 115

Self-Respect movement, 191, 195, 221, 240, 247; Nadars support, 179-180, 184, 255, 260; marriages, 179-180, 245, 247, 255; leads Nadars to de-Sanskritize, 180, 189, 247, 259; relation to politics, 179, 185; and N.M.S., 194, 198, 199

Selvaraj, M. S.: political leadership, 207, 216; campaigns for Legislative Assembly, 209, 210-211, 213-214

Senthikumara Nadar, Rao Bahadur M. S. P.: helps found college, 146, 149; biographical information on, 149; political positions and Nadar leadership, 188, 195, 196

Senthikumara Nadar College, 146

Servais. See Kalla Shanars

Sethupathi, M. Bhaskara, Raja, Zamindar, of Ramnad: suit against Nadars for temple entry, 81n, 118, 120-128; involvement in Sivakasi riot, 118-119, 125; quoted, 119

Sethupathi, R. Shanmuga Rajeswara, Raja of Ramnad: quoted, 157, 162; presides over N.M.S. conference, 157, 174-175; helps repeal Kamudi punitive tax, 178, 222; political candidacies and leadership, 184, 228, Nadars support, 222, 224; death, 228n

Shanar: as name for Nadar caste, 19, 20; dispute over etymology of, 80-82, 85; derogatory usage, 84, 134, 135; Nadar merchants refuse to be called, 106, 124, 126; N.M.S. gets government to stop using, 133-136, 143-145, 181; used by climbers, 143

Shandrar (Ceylon caste), 20

Shanmuga Gramani, K., *Traditions of the Solar and Lunar Races,* 86

Shanmuga Nadar, A., business success, 150

Shanmugam Chettiar, Sir R. K., Dewan of Cochin, 175

Sharrock, J. A.: cited, 72-73, 92-93; quoted, 90, 93, 127; efforts to form casteless society, 93-94

Shenbagakutti Nadar, P., 112, 116

Shencottah (taluq), Travancore District, 17; Maravars attack Nadars in, 117

Shopkeepers, Nadar, 53, 130n, 137, 147-148, 171, 243-246

Simon Commission, 182-183

Sivagnanam Gramani, M. P.: identified, 169; opens National Nadar Conference, 192

Sivagunga (*palayam* or zamindari), 16

Sivakasi (taluq), 228

Sivakasi (town), Ramnad District, 130; Nadar traders settle, 97-98; described (*1821*), 97-98, 112; *mahimai* levy, 99; *pettais* of, 99, 104; *uravinmurai,* 102, 104, 105, 112; decline, 105, 150, 185; Kshatriya Vidyasala High School, 106, 145; population, 111-112; Nadar-Maravar riot of *1899,* 111-119, 156, 157, 190, 264, Vellalas in, 115; Sanskritization of Nadars, 112-113, 170; Viswanadhaswamy temple, 113-114, 190; Christians, Muslims, in, 117; Nadar college, 146; trade and industries, 150-151, 185; Nadars, break with Justice party, N.M.S., 185, 187-188

Sivasami Iyer, Sir P. S., 174

Sivaswami Nadar, election, 219

Sivism, 37-38. See also Bhadrakali

Slaves: of Nadans, 29, 34, 48; Nadar descendants, 34; agricultural, 39 abolition of, 63, 67

Social uplift movements of Nadars: missionaries aid to, 55-70; breastcloth controversy as, 59-70; in Tinnevelly, 71-72; role of Nadar caste histories, 78-90, 94; by Hindu

Social movements of Nadars: (*cont.*)
Nadars, 105-109, 127-129 (*see also*
Kshatriya status; Sanskritization);
through *sangams*, 130-133 (*see also*
Nadar Mahajana Sangam); history
summarized, 262-266

Society for Diffusing the Philosophy
of the Four Vedas (Salem Street
Society), 50n

Society for the Promotion of Christian Knowledge (S.P.C.K.), missionary efforts in Tinnevelly, 43,
45, 46, 47

Society for the Propagation of the
Gospel in Foreign Parts (S.P.G.):
Tinnevelly missions, 46, 47; Tinnevelly schism, 72-78, 82. *See also*
Caldwell

Soundrapandian Nadar, election
(*1967*), 219

Soundrapandian Nadar, W. P. A.
(*1893-1953*): quoted, 157; gets repeal of Kamudi tax, 157, 178, 222;
family, 176-177; work as first
Nadar in Legislative Council, 176-
178, 181; N.M.S. offices and influence, 177-178, 184, 191, 194, 195;
seeks Nadar support of Justice
party and Self-Respect movement,
177, 179-180, 184, 185, 191, 195;
aids Harijans, 178-179; supports
D.M.K., 196

South Indian Liberal Federation. *See*
Justice party

South Indian Peoples' Association,
"Non-Brahmin Manifesto," 175

South Travancore Mission, Nagercoil: Nadar converts, 56, 57; supports Nadars in breast-cloth controversy, 60, 61, 63, 65, 67, 69;
political pamphlets, 63, 69

Srinivas, M. N.: cited, 1; quoted, 1,
7, 10

Srinivasa Iyengar, S., 174

Srinivasan, P., defeats Kamaraj, 229

Srivaikuntam (taluq), Tinnevelley
District, 18; Nadars, 33; missionaries, 46; emigration from, 52;
. Nadar politics, 206, 219; election
of Nadars, 208, 212 (*see also* Tuticorin constituency); communities
in, 212

Srivilliputtur (taluq), 17; Nadar attempts to enter temple at, 110;
Kamaraj wins in, 197

Subbaraman, election, 231

Subcastes: nature of, 2; Nadar, 29-
36, 41, 128, *kuttams*, 36-37, disappearance of, 168-169, 219, unity
between; 178; in types of political
cultures, 202, 203, 204

Subramaniam, M. M., 209

Sububrayan, P., 146

Sudras: defined, 7; Sanskritization,
8; relation of Nadars to, 22; Travancore, anger at Christian Nadars,
60, 61, 64-66, 67; caste relations
with Nadars, 92 (*see also* Maravars; Vellalas); right to temple
entry, 122; Nadars judged below,
126

Sugar refineries, 52, 130n

Sundaram (David; Nadar catechist),
44-45

Sundaran, Shanmuga, 225

Sun Paper Mills, 149

Suter, T. H., quoted, 54-55

S. Vellaisami Nadar College, founded
by N.M.S., 146-147

Swamiadian (catechist), 74-75

Swaminathan (Maravar candidate),
215

Swatantra party: Rajagopalachari
founds, 199; candidates, 212, 215,
219, 228, 236; Maravars join, 228;
Nadar support, 232, 236, 240, 249,
260, 266

Symonds, W. A., quoted, 53

Tambraparni River, 18

Tamil Arasu party, 169

Tamil: kings, 15, 23, Nadar "descent" from, 81, 85, 87, Dravidian
origin of, 86; language, 12, derivation of *Shanar* from, 80-82; literature, ignores Nadars, 21, alleged
rewriting of, 88

Tamil Lexicon, 81

Tamil nationalism, 196, 235-236n. *See
also* Dravida Munnetra Kazhagam

Tamilnad. See Madras (state)

Tamil Nad Congress Committee
(T.N.C.C.), 192, 208; Kamaraj

president of, 153, 190, 233; Kamaraj elected to, 187; power struggle in, 215-216; Nadars in, 232

Tamilnad Food-grains Merchants Association, 230

Tamilnad Forward Bloc (Maravar caste party), 244, 246; formed, 221, 223; Nadar opposition to, 221, 224, 237; election campaigns, 224-228; Harijans break from, 225, 228

Tamil Nad Harijan Sevak Sang, 192

Tamilnad Mercantile Bank. See Nadar Bank

Tamilnad United Front, defeats Congress, 229

Tangamani, K. T. K.: political career and support, 197, 227, 231, 249, 253; biographical note on, 236n

Tangavel Nadar, T., 216

Tanjore District: mission and breast-baring controversy, 43 (see South Travancore Mission); Nadars, 34, 124

Tapper castes. See Toddy-tapping

Taxation: of palmyra, 28-29, 138; Nadan collectors, 29; of Nadars, 57, 58, 61, by corvée labor, 57, 58, 61, 62, by self-tax, 99 (see Mahimai); of jaggery production, 130n; of Kamudi for police, 156-157, 178, 222

Temple entry: forbidden Nadars, 22, 30, 71, 81, 88, 108, 123-124, 188; through western gates, 88; attempts by Nadar merchants in northern districts, 94, 124, 264 (see also Courts; Kamudi; Madurai; Sivakasi); forbidden Harijans, 126, 153, 186; Harijans, Nadars, gain right to, 142 (see Temple Entry . . . Act); effect on politics, 188-190, 265; Tiruchendur satyagraha on, 207

Temple Entry Authorization and Indemnity Act (*1939*), 142, 188, 189-190, 244, 265; Nadar appreciation of, 191, 192, 193; limitations, 193

Temples, Nadar, 102, 108, 127, 163; family (*kuttam*), 21, 36-37, 112; *ammankovil*, 38, 112; as seat of *uravinmurai*, 100, 103, 112; proces-

sions, 110-111, 112; openness, 179, 193

Tenkasi (taluq), 34, 97; Nadars, 33, 96; Maravars attack, 117

Tennan Shanar (Tennamatte Chanar), 35

Thomas, A. V., 152; business success, 148-149; elections, 208, 211

Thomas, Daniel, 139, 194

Thurston, Edgar: ethnographic work, 89; *Castes and Tribes of Southern India*, 89-90, cited, 32, 53n, 106

Timber merchants, Nadar, 235

Tinnevelly (town), Tinnevelly District, 18, 105

Tinnevelly (Tirunelveli) District: political history, 12-17; geography, 17-19; transportation facilities, 32, 95, 104-105; Nadars, 33, 39, 40, 132, 233, 234, lack of unity and community, 31-32, 99, 128, 184, 220, 263, emergence of, 70, 78, effect of missionaries on, 43-55, 90-91 (see also Christian Nadars); southeastern, Nadar economic and social status, 48-49, 52-53, 95, 139, 263, Nadar toddy-tapping in, 137-140 (see also Toddy), Nadar political culture and behavior, 174 (see also Political Culture; Tiruchendur), Nadar migrant labor, 52-53, 57, 63; Nadars wear breast cloth, 60, 63; Nadar attempts at social uplift, 71-72; schism, 72-78, 79, 82, 83; Nadar mythologies, 79-90; northern, 94ff (see also Ramnad, Six Town Nadars), riots of *1899*, 110-111, 117-120, 124, 125-126, development of Nadars in, 128, tensions between Nadars and other castes, 154-155; "Kshatriyas," 109; government, stops Nadar attacks on toddy shops, 137; Nadar association, 138, 164-168, 264; relations between Christian and Hindu Nadars, 170, 171; Legislative Council elections (*1920*), 176; Board, Nadars on, 181; political alignments by caste, 184-185, 218-219; summary of Nadar history and life in, 263-264, 265-266

Tinnevelly District Congress Committee, 208, 211, 215, 216

Tinnevelly Mission: under S.P.C.K., 45; transferred to S.P.G., 46; under Caldwell, 46-50, 82-83; caste rank preserved in, 93

Tiruchendur(taluq), Tinnevelly District: Palmyra forest (teris; Manadu), described, 18-19, Nadar origins in, 20-21, 32, 36, 56, 87; relations between climbers and Nadans, 25, 28-29, 137, 211, 240-242, 259, 263, lack of Nadar unity, 32, 41-42, 167, 263, Christian Nadars, 51-52, emigration from, 52, Nadar agriculture in, 53-54, travel through, 95n; climbers, 143 (see Palmyra climbers); missionaries, 46; mass conversions, 50 (see also Christian Nadars); imports, 96; Nadar traders migrate from, 97; Nadars, leadership, 167; Nadar temple entry, 109, 190; Adityan holdings in, 149; Nadars support Gandhi, 184; Nadar political culture and behavior, 206, 215-217, 219, 220; sayagrahas, 207; assembly seat, Nadar candidates for, 208, 209, 212-214, 215 (see also Sattangulam and Tuticorin constituencies)

Tiruchendur (town), 240

Tiruchendur assembly constituency, 209, 211

Tiruchendur parliamentary constituency, 208, 209, 214-215, 219; Nadar elected from, 236

Tiruchendur Taluq Congress Committee, 207, 216-217

Tiruchili (taluq), 228

Tirumangulam (town), Madurai District: Nadar traders settle in, 97; uravinmurai, 102, 130; Kamaraj welcomed in, 186

Tirunalavel Pillai, 215, 216

Tirunelveli. See Tinnevelly

Tiruppattur (taluq), Ramnad District sangam conference, 164

Tiyars (tapper caste), 20, 178

Toddy: hard, 26, extraction process, 26-27, Nadar abstinence from, 39-40, increased demand for, 131n, campaign and laws against, 136-140; sweet, 26, 137, production during prohibition, 138-139; shops, shop keepers, 130n, 137, satyagraha against, 207

Tapping (toddy-drawing), defined, 3, as defiling occupation, 3-4, 122, as Nadar traditional occupation, 22-23 (see also Occupations; Ritual purity hierarchy); economic importance to climbers, 24; trees and subcastes, 35; Nadar exaltation of, 82; N.M.S. attempts to disassociate caste from, 133, 135-136, campaign against, 136-138

Traders. See Merchants

Transportation facilities: lack of, effect on Nadar unity, 8-10, 32, 95-96, 128, 263; development of, 96-97, 240, 263. See also Railroad

Travancore District, southern: history and geography, 17, 56; Nadar origins in, 20; migrant Nadar climbers, 21, 53, 57, 63; Nadar subcastes, 33; Christian Nadars, 47; effect of missionaries on Nadars in, 55-70 (see also Breast cloth); slavery abolished in, 63; riots over breast-cloth controversy, 65-66; tobacco import, 98; Nadar pettais in, 99; Nadars, as backward class, 141; temples opened, 193

Travancore Hindu Nadars Association, 132

Travancore kings, 14, 29n, 56

Travancore, Maharaja of, 63, 65, 67, 68, 69, 193

Trevelyan, Sir Charles, settles breast-cloth controversy, 67-68

Trichinopoly (town), Nadars, 124

Trichinopoly (Tiruchirapalli) District, 15, 43, 106

Trivandrum, 153

Turnbull, Thomas: cited, 71, 98; quoted, 97-98, 112

Tuticorin (town), Tinnevelly District, 79; Nadars converted at, 44; church, attempt to exorcise caste in, 93; railroad built to, Nadar traders migrate to, 105; conference on palmyra, 139; uravinmurai, 167; Nadar politics, 212

Tuticorin assembly constituency (Tiruchendur taluq and Srivaikuntam), elections, 208, 210, 211-212, 219
Tyagaraja Chetti, P., 175
Tyagaraja Chettiar, T., industrialist, 248

Udankudi (village), Tinnevelly District, 45, 213, 242
Ukkarapandia Thevar, 156
Upanayanam, for Nadars, 108
Uravinmurai, 131, 220, 263; structure and operation, 99-105, 200; law, 101-103; town branches in Madurai and Madras cities, 105, 233; use of *mahimai* funds, 105-106 (see also *Mahimai;* leadership of, 130; schools founded by, 145; N.M.S. organizes, 158, 163, 178; outside Six Towns area, 167, 184; purpose and effect on Nadar community, 171-172, 184, 220, 244, 256, 263; loss of power, 172, 223; facilities opened to Harijans, 179; political control, 184, 223-224. See *also* specific towns and cities

Vadakkankulam (village), Nanguneri taluq, Jesuit parish, 43, 91-92n
Vadamalayan, Dr. P., quoted, 171-172
Vaikom satyagraha, 153, 186
Vaihunda Nadan, Tiruvarudi, 33
Vaisyas: defined, 7; Nadar, 37; Hindu status rights, 108, 122
Vannans (washermen caste): caste rank, 23, 251-252; Nadars not allowed services of, 24, 121
Vanniars (caste), 218
Vellaisami, S., 147, 148
Vellaiya Thevar, leads attack on Sivakasi, 115-116
Vellalas (Pillai; Saiva Vellalas; Sudra caste), 106n; caste rank, 22-23, 92, 126; traditional relationship with Nadars, 28, 56, 206, 248, 265; accountants for Nadars, 41, 100; opposition to Christianity, 50; Nadar claim of superiority to, 80, 82 (see *also* Kshatriya status); Christian, 90, 92; suits against Nadars on caste

rights, 109, 155; aroused by Nadar aspirations, 110-115, 252; support of Justice party, 206; effect on Nadar politics, 185, 188, 265; political strength, 212, 213; candidates, 234
Vellasami Thevar, 156, 183; identified, 120-121; leadership against Nadars, 121, 222
Velsami, V. M. S., 225
Venkataswami, *Tanjore Manual*, cited, 35
Vibuthi Sangam (Sacred Ash Society), 50
Victoria, Queen, proclamation on British rule of India (see British Rule)
Villages (mixed): caste system, 2-3, 9-10; caste relations between, 8-11, 41-42, 160-161; political structure and culture, 9-10, 202, 214n, 242-243; *kaval* system, 15-16, 29n, 159; Nadars position in, 22, 24, 127, 142, 154, 158-159; Christian Nadar, unity and structure, 54-55, 69-70, 99-100; Nadar right of procession in, 110-111; schools, 146, 160; N.M.S. aid to Nadars in, 157-161 (see *also Uravinmurai*); Nadars leave, 229-230; life and beliefs of typical Nadar, 240-243, 259, 260
Villages, Nadar: conversion, 45-50, 90; criers, 34; factionalism and disputes, 54, 99, 158, 159, 202, 263; treatment of Harijans, 92; established by Nadar traders, 97; Maravars attack (*1899*), 115, 117-118, 119; *uravinmurai* in, 172
Virudhunagar (Virudhupatti; town), Ramnad District, 117; Nadar traders settle in, 97; *uravinmurai*, 102, 104; Madurai branch, 105; Madurai *pettai*, 104; growth, 105, 130, 150; first Nadar school in, 106; school system, 145; Nadar colleges, 146, 149; Nadars' business reputation, 147; name changed, 149; dispute over Nadar *mahimai*, 158; Nadars on N.M.S. council, 163; dispute over Tinnevelly Nadars *pettai* in, 165; Nadar political strength and

Virudhunagar (*continued*)
alignment, 180, 185-186, 196, 197,
221, 229; Maravars, 183; Sivakasi
rivalry with, 185; rejects Kamaraj,
186, 188, 229; city council elections, money politics, 214n, 250;
Nadars leave, 233
Visvanatha Nayaka, 14
Vivekananda College, founded, 147
Voluntary Society for the Suppression of Caste, 94

Washermen caste. *See* Vannans

Western Ghats, 17, 97; Nadars, 33,
53, 96
We Tamils: Nadar candidates, 209,
210, 212-213; merged with D.M.K.,
218
Widows. *See* Marriage
Winfred, Rev. H. Martyn, *Shandror
Marapu, Shandror Kula Marapu
Kattala,* 80
Wyatt, Rev. J. L., quoted, 50

Zamindars, 110, 111; poligar, 16;
Nattatti, 33; Maravar, attack
Nadars, 115-118